A.6.
o.

SARAH DUCHESS O

Sarah Duchess of Marlborough

DAVID GREEN

COLLINS

St James's Place, London

1967

© David Green 1967
Printed in Great Britain
Collins Clear-Type Press
London and Glasgow

Contents

Introduction	*page*	17
I The Observant Child 1660-1685		23
II James and the Revolution 1685-1688		43
III William and Mary 1688-1702		55
IV Hail, Glorious Anna! 1702-1704		77
V Princess of Mindelheim 1705-1706		99
VI Cue for Vipers 1707-1708		116
VII Favour Declines 1709-1710		139
VIII The Great Change 1710-1712		156
IX A Sort of Pilgrimage 1712-1714		178
X No Armour 1714-1717		196
XI The Crooked Scythe 1718-1722		212
XII Provocations and Proposals 1722-1727		234
XIII The Fruitful Vine 1727-1735		255
XIV The Grandsons 1720-1740		275
XV Without Hope or Fear 1740-1744		293
Genealogical table	*between pages*	312-13
Appendices	*page*	313
Bibliography		326
References to manuscripts and printed books		330
Index		339

Illustrations

Mrs. Jennings   *facing page* 32
By courtesy of the Earl Spencer

Sarah Duchess of Marlborough   33
By courtesy of the Earl Spencer

Sarah Duchess of Marlborough   48
Photograph by the Courtauld Institute of Art by courtesy of the Earl
Spencer

Sarah Duchess of Marlborough with Lady Fitzharding   49
By courtesy of His Grace the Duke of Marlborough

John Duke of Marlborough   64
National Portrait Gallery

The Ladies Henrietta and Anne Churchill   65
By courtesy of the Earl Spencer

Queen Anne   80
By courtesy of the Earl Spencer

Prince George of Denmark   81
National Portrait Gallery

Mrs. Morley and Mrs. Freeman: the handwriting of
Queen Anne and the Duchess of Marlborough   96
By courtesy of His Grace the Duke of Marlborough

Sidney Earl of Godolphin   97
National Portrait Gallery

Sarah Duchess of Marlborough and her children   112
By courtesy of His Grace the Duke of Marlborough

Anne Countess of Sunderland   113
By courtesy of His Grace the Duke of Marlborough

Elizabeth Countess of Bridgwater   113
By courtesy of His Grace the Duke of Marlborough

ILLUSTRATIONS

Robert Harley Earl of Oxford   128
National Portrait Gallery

Lady Masham   *facing page* 129
National Portrait Gallery

Queen Anne   144
By courtesy of His Grace the Duke of Marlborough

Sarah Duchess of Marlborough: the mantilla portrait   145
By courtesy of His Grace the Duke of Marlborough

Arthur Maynwaring   164
National Portrait Gallery

Sir John Vanbrugh   165
National Portrait Gallery

Blenheim: the Grand Bridge   172

Blenheim from the north-west   172

Blenheim: the Marlborough monument   173

Marlborough House   208

Blenheim: the Column of Victory   209
Country Life

Lady Henrietta Godolphin, afterwards 2nd Duchess of
Marlborough   224
By courtesy of His Grace the Duke of Marlborough

Francis 2nd Earl of Godolphin   225
National Portrait Gallery

Mary Duchess of Montagu   256
By courtesy of His Grace the Duke of Marlborough

Diana Duchess of Bedford   257
By courtesy of His Grace the Duke of Bedford

Sarah Duchess of Marlborough (the Petworth portrait)   272
Courtauld Institute of Art (from the Petworth Collection)

Charles 6th Duke of Somerset   *facing page* 273
National Portrait Gallery

Elizabeth 3rd Duchess of Marlborough   288
By courtesy of His Grace the Duke of Marlborough

ILLUSTRATIONS

Charles Spencer 3rd Duke of Marlborough   289
  By courtesy of the Earl Spencer

Lady Anne Bateman   304
  By courtesy of the Earl Spencer

John Spencer   305
  By courtesy of the Earl Spencer

Endpapers: Blenheim: north front. Fourdrinier's engraving dated 1745, the year after the death of Sarah Duchess of Marlborough

Acknowledgements

It should be said at the outset that this book is based mainly, as any full biography of the Duchess of Marlborough must be, on the Blenheim Papers; and that without free and frequent access to them one would have been rash indeed, if not hopelessly handicapped, in attempting such a task. Although from long experience I believed I could count upon the Duke of Marlborough for this very big favour, it was none the less deeply appreciated when it was granted. It has increased a debt to Blenheim which I can never hope to begin to repay.

By concentrating on the ninety-three files labelled *Sarah Duchess of Marlborough*, in Blenheim's muniment-room, I had hoped to complete that part of the research in three months. If however I had paid closer attention to Dr Reid's *Report & Classification of the Blenheim Palace Archives* (1891) I would have realised that those ninety-three bundles were by no means all and that important papers, 'discovered in a closet' and handed to Archdeacon Coxe in 1820, had been filed in fat folders in a different place. It meant, in fact, working at Blenheim on this one subject for rather more than four months; and if I outstayed my welcome in the Estate Office, Mr W. L. Murdock and Miss K. M. Gell were kind enough not to show it; while in the Palace I had at all times nothing but kindness and help from the owner, from his secretary Mrs E. M. Sharpe, from Mr A. M. Illingworth and from all the staff.

If Blenheim was, obviously, the first port of call, Althorp was the second. 'I have been at Althorp', the Duchess tells Mrs Clayton in 1722, 'which is a fine place and there is what I call more sense in that house than in any I have yet ever seen, and I had rather have it than Blenheim if I had nothing to consider in it but myself'. I would like now to express my thanks to Althorp's owner, the Earl Spencer, for going out of his way to help me, not only with manuscripts but with answers to my many questions and for allowing me to reproduce portraits from his famous and quite astonishing collection.

While thanking owners of manuscripts in country houses I must say

11

ACKNOWLEDGEMENTS

how grateful I am to the Duke of Bedford for permission to quote from the Duchess of Marlborough's letters to her granddaughter Diana Duchess of Bedford; to the Duke of Devonshire and to his curator, Mr Tom Wragg, for information from the Devonshire Collections; and to Mr T. Cottrell-Dormer for letting me examine the manuscripts at Rousham. When I had all but despaired of tracing a rare and interesting pamphlet of 1712—*The St Albans Ghost*—Lord Rothschild was good enough to send me a copy: again my grateful thanks.

In the Manuscript Room of the British Museum, thanks to the Keeper and Assistant Keeper and their assistants, I was directed to unpublished material which threw fresh light on a hitherto misty period (1712–14) when the Marlboroughs were in exile or, as the Duchess preferred to call it, on a sort of pilgrimage. I feel particularly grateful to those who helped me in that and also in my attempts to track down unpublished Masham letters.

But how can I hope to thank at all adequately all those historians, archivists, curators, librarians and others who so kindly and so readily came to my assistance? I can but give their names and trust that they may realise how deeply I have appreciated their co-operation. At the St Albans Library Miss Muriel Wilson the librarian was extremely efficient and helpful; while Mr O. J. Weaver gave up his time to drive me to Sandridge and to Water End. Mr S. W. Shelton, the archivist at Glyn, Mills, was good enough to show me the Childs Bank records and to have them copied for me. Miss Angela Green, archivist, of the Berkshire Record Office, told me of her discovery of correspondence to do with the completion of Blenheim and the Column of Victory. Mr W. A. Speck of Newcastle University drew my attention to an important letter at Blenheim which I might otherwise have overlooked.

For reference to manuscripts in the Harrowby Trust I am grateful to the Earl of Harrowby and to Miss Pauline Adams, archivist, of the Stafford County Record Office; and for similar facilities in connection with the Gorhambury estate archives in the Hertfordshire County Record Office my thanks are due to the Earl of Verulam and to Mr Peter Walen; and also, in connection with the Panshanger Letters in the same office, to Lady Monica Salmond.

To Mr David Piper of the National Portrait Gallery and to Mr Oliver Millar of the Lord Chamberlain's Office I am much indebted for their expert guidance through the labyrinth of portraits of the Spencers and the Churchills and their many connections.

ACKNOWLEDGEMENTS

I would like to say thank you again too to Sir Owen Morshead, Mr Howard Colvin, Mr Laurence Whistler, Miss Audrey Russell, Mr Geoffrey Beard, Mr T. L. Ingram, Miss Pauline Croft and Miss Elizabeth Burton; to the Curator and staff of the National Register of Archives; to the Librarians of the London Library, the Library of the Society of Antiquaries and the Huntington Library at San Marino, California; and to Miss Jill Ross of the Oxfordshire County Libraries for her kindness and patience.

At the most trying stage of all—the collating of material and indexing of fourteen shorthand notebooks, involving more than three thousand entries—I was helped in Cornwall by my wife and son, who devoted many hours to a most tedious and exasperating task.

To the conspicuous end I have left one of my biggest debts of gratitude, that to Miss Anne Whiteman, historian and fellow of Lady Margaret Hall, who at every stage of this biography has unstintedly helped me with advice and encouragement.

It remains only to add that if, in spite of checks and counter-checks, this book still has its shortcomings, they must most certainly be blamed on the author and not on the kind and clever people who have so generously helped him.

No more must soothing musick please
  but Sighs & Sorrow fill ye plains.
A tortured mind no Sounds can ease,
  The Nymph is fled, ye Love remains.

Let Nature lye dissolved in night,
  The powerfull sun forbear to rise.
The Spacious world needs want no Light,
  'Twill flow from Lady Marlborough's eyes.

Sir Samuel Garth

Introduction

It was an age of greatness and of littleness, of grandeur and of absurdity, and to evoke it we need sound though it be no more than the notes of a turret-clock, striking today from Townsend's tower at Blenheim as it struck for the first Marlborough and his duchess. But we are not so impoverished. There are Purcell and Handel and Bach; and we have but to listen to an overture to sense the majesty of the reign of Anne, or to their dances—gavotte, bourrée, gigue—to savour the frolic nonsense of those Kit-Cat quipsters Sir Samuel Garth, Sir John Vanbrugh and the rest; or to join in the rustic junketings at the founding of Blenheim.

This is the ambience of Queen Anne's governing (she who, as Johnson said, seemed born for friendship, not for government); and to the strains it may be of a pavane on Anne's harpsichord, the same that was lent to Abigail but given to Sarah, we watch the decline of a once passionate friendship.

But need all this be enacted again? Perhaps not; and yet when crumbs fall from rich men's tables they may be worth gathering; and where the men are of Trevelyan's calibre or Churchill's and the table Blenheim's muniment-room, the answer may be yes. Without such giants as forerunners one's task would have been harder; for they having, biographically speaking, fixed Marlborough on his high pedestal for all time, have left the field that much clearer for his duchess.

As for the Duchess of Marlborough, though not, like Marlborough, determinedly enigmatic ('My actions shall speak for me'), she is more complex and more secretive than she would have us suppose. 'I am of the simple sex', she says, and 'I tumble my mind out on paper without any disguise'; and yet when she chooses she is a past-mistress of the smoke-screen and the red herring; so that sooner or later the reader comes to realise that the path through the labyrinth, along which this most candid of guides is leading him, has been deftly bounded by herself. Dr Johnson of course saw this as plainly as did Pope and Horace Walpole. To Pope she was 'by turns all womankind'; for she was favourite, politician, doctor, lawyer, architect, wife, mother, grandmother and a good deal more.

'I have been a kind of author', she said. She had indeed and to such good purpose that as one slogs through the reams she has written, at Blenheim, one finds oneself wondering whether there can be anything left to say about her which she has not already said, with merciless repetition, herself. But it is because she is such a good letter-writer (her ink, too often acid, is sometimes wine and never water), that she deserves the stage and in this book, wherever possible, she is given it. She leaves nothing to chance. She even remembers to remind posterity, 'As one is the worst judge of one's own simplicity, one is the best of one's sincerity', and adds, 'I will therefore say nothing of the first.'

From time to time, in one generation or another, she has been whitewashed and worshipped and all but canonised; though whether that says more for the whitewasher than the whitewashed it is not easy to decide. Sir Winston Churchill praises her courage, her spirit, her commonsense, qualities which set her niche higher than that of other favourites, if no higher than Queen Anne's. With those virtues too we must list her beauty and her love of Marlborough, which was tempestuous and real.

On the dark side there are the quarrels with everyone from the sister-queens Anne and Mary to her own children and grandchildren; and though at the time they meant heartbreak, they may safely be skimmed now for some insight into her turbulent mind. Her own Green Book of her children's shortcomings, though devoured with palpable horror by her own friends before breakfast (or so they told her), would today hardly rank as bedside reading. No, as a writer she is at her best in letters and on the subject of her own melancholy; though there again, like Mother Hubbard's dog, she stirs our pity only to surprise us next day in the guise of an upholsterer (and 'the best upholsterer in England'), singing a ballad while she stitches away at yards of red damask for a granddaughter's bed.

Though it pleased her to shock the world, her fascination is not in her violence but in her tragedy, in that *hamartia* or tragic flaw which ensured her downfall. For beyond the tragedy common to everyone hers would seem sometimes to approach greatness, in part because of her fall but even more perhaps because of the outrage it meant to her, because she saw herself as frank, conscientious, patriotic and well-disposed and could never for the life of her understand how or why calamity had overtaken her. Was she to be damned for disdain, banished for temperament? Savagely she strikes through the charges—'hard thoughts', 'long absence', 'resentments', 'sullen looks' —and hurls into the scale the £100,000 she claims to have saved Queen Anne in her Wardrobe. Yet even at the death of Prince George she seems to have been thinking more of her own self-justification than of the Queen.

After her fall, that disappointment should succeed disappointment seems natural enough, if only because Sarah was embittered and needed to get even with the world. For the first half of her career, she could say, she had served the nation; but in her long widowhood it was her family she slaved for; that and Marlborough's glorification, and her own self-vindication; all of them, to her mind, feverish and desperate tasks.

Time and again, in friendship, in religion, her reason was her enemy, she was so hopelessly self-reliant. Quick to suspect motive and to see what did not exist in hearts and minds, she could never believe in the intangibles of faith or of art, for to have done so would have been to betray her intelligence. She knew herself to be a rational being and if others were less so they were probably fools or knaves.

> On human actions reason though you can,
> It may be reason, but it is not man.

She could never have learned such a lesson, any more than she could have been made to realise that it might be better occasionally to be fooled than to be perpetually suspicious. It was that as much as anything that lost her the love of her daughters Henrietta and Mary. If she had fallen out with them only, we could the better believe in their 'barbarous behaviour' and 'monstrous usage', but sooner or later she quarrelled with most people till at last she found she had grown sick of humanity and of life itself.

And this being so, all might well be dreariness were it not for the presence of such frolicsome spirits as Dr Garth and the Duke of Somerset. For Sarah they were heartening and for us, even when discovered in a windowless muniment-room, they step out from their letters as warmblooded witnesses to her extraordinary charm. The gargantuan doctor, who seems from the first to have been dumbfounded by Sarah's beauty, was happy to remain so for the rest of his life. His championship was unquestioning if not glorious. Not very articulate, he is chanced on at a patient's dinner-table where, 'like one who is forst from the power of truth & the aboundance of his hart, & after he had been silant for a good while, lay down his knife & with a solom aseveration sayed the Duchess of Marlborough was the best woman in the world, the most generous & compassionate & ready to do good when any cause was rightly represented to her, & he pondered how one of so much merit ever came to be a favorit . . .'

Somerset too, at sixty-five (Sarah was then sixty-three), completely, ardently and joyfully lost head and heart. If only she could have taken life as lightly! But no; wit, unless sarcasm, was not to her taste, while hearts, as she well knew, could be desperately wicked. She would shut herself up at Windsor or at St Albans and soothe herself with books. She would do this when in umbrage with Anne; and much later she would retire to Wimbledon, to the house she had meant for the granddaughter she had loved. 'As I am quite alone at this place', she writes at eighty-one, 'I am better pleased than I have been a great while, for I see nobody, & at London one is always in dread of seeing those one wishes never to see or in expectation of seeing some few that are generally better employ'd than to come. Hopes, I think, seldom come to anything & upon the whole I think my situation is not an ill one. I cannot be disappointed when I have no hope & I fear nothing in the world but the French'.

At such times one is inclined to echo Abigail (of the dying Anne): 'This good lady deserves pity'. And yet might she not, as the richest of widows, have won even more sympathy if she had indulged in less self-pity and had done more positive good? After all, there have been women just as ill-used who have scorned to air, even to their intimates, their melancholy. And yet again who are we to sit in judgment or to decide how it was that she found no comfort in God or man? Her courage must have been the greater for it. In solemn mood she would confide to Maynwaring that when she felt devout she would choose 'a little poor church where there were none but plain husbandmen & women in straw hats'; but this mood he might shatter by saying he had noticed that 'even the most devout do still indulge themselves in their favourite inclinations' and that he doubted if Christians had the monopoly of salvation. 'I have seen several even Indians', he wrote to her, '(I don't mean negroes but those of the East Indies) that I have thought better made in all respects both as to body and mind than myself and why they should be destined to be forever miserable I could not possibly conceive . . .'

Such thoughts could be stimulating and at the same time disquieting. She took comfort in the reflection that she had an excellent brain and that sooner or later everything in heaven and earth must yield to reason, as surely as that all the walls of Blenheim must one day meet, no matter where the masons began.

There is the unlikely tale (there are so many apocryphal tales) of her being stumbled over in the dusk, a bundle of black shawls containing an old invalid, prostrate in prayer. It is next to incredible; but if we can believe as we must that a chambermaid supplanted her as Keeper of the Privy Purse, we can surely believe anything; for as Hardy remarked, 'Though a good deal is too strange to be believed, nothing is too strange to have happened.'

In old age, as a diligent seeker, she must have thought she deserved to discover truth, for she read in translation the Greek philosophers and spent many an hour copying into her commonplace-book page after page of the Old Testament. It is there that we find Job and the Proverbs, but never her greatest need of all, St Paul on charity. In fact there were lessons she rejected, and Bishop Hare's home truths on 'resentment' were among them.

If at times her life reads like a bombardment, (Lord Wolseley's 'torpedo in petticoats'), she herself, though appalled, remains resilient; outraged by what has happened, yet ready to be astonished anew at every fresh instance of inhumanity and ingratitude. What had she done to deserve such treatment, she the loyallest of servants, she the kindest of mothers and of grandmothers? Unfailingly the answer is nothing; there was nothing, she calls heaven to witness, to reproach herself with, she had always been right and had acted correctly; it was simply that for the thousandth time the world had let her down. And for this she demands sympathy and keeps on demanding it, like one who insists upon showing operation scars.

But this is not a psychological study. Often enough her own writings reveal her as unbalanced and emotional. At times she seems to border on madness; at times she seems too coldly sane. That she lived to be eighty-four was, for her day, phenomenal and in that time she lived several lives. Indeed, like her descendant Sir Winston, she came nearer than most to knowing the gamut of human experience. She knew favour and disfavour, eminence and exile, happiness and bitterness; she was wife, mother, widow, grandmother, and was forever wishing she had been a man. For years she was often in pain and she died completely disillusioned.

It has been said that Sarah belongs to history and so, for what that is worth, she does. But was she great? If toughness is greatness she was. Her courage was beyond praise. Marlborough had never hoisted a white flag and nor would she. She had never owned one. For the rest, posterity will judge for itself.

CHAPTER I

The Observant Child

1660-1685

———◆———

There was little time for childhood. For most, though not for Sarah Jennings, life was short, often very short indeed. If one survived birth and infancy one was popped into grown-up clothes and briskly sent about the business of living.

Schools? Yes there were schools, but a girl was lucky to find in her hand anything more instructive than a hornbook. For what should a woman do with learning? 'Hardly one woman in a hundred', wrote Lord Peterborough, 'can write or read', and who should mind it? It was almost something to be proud of.

'What a scholar would you have been if that had been your business!' wrote Arthur Maynwaring to Sarah Duchess of Marl-borough, many years later, 'but I am perfectly of your mind that I never yet saw a lady that was the better for her learning, and very seldom a man.'[1] And Sarah? 'I am no scholar,' she said, 'nor a wit, I thank God.'; and again, 'An ounce of mother wit is better than a pound of clargy.' [book learning].

Sarah Jennings was born on the 29th day of May, 1660* in a small house in that part of St Albans known as Holywell. Her brothers, both of them, died in infancy. Of her sisters, Frances, eight years Sarah's senior, preceded her to court as a maid of honour. The other sister, Barbara, married Edward Griffith and died at the age of 26 in 1678.

---

* Sarah Jennings was christened in the abbey or (as it is now called) cathedral of St Albans on June 17th, 1660. The baptismal register, lost for 137 years, was found in 1880.

Sarah thought nothing of pedigrees, ('I value nobody for another's merit'), but owned that her father's was reckoned a good one and that 'he had in Somersetshire, Kent and St Albans £4000 a year'.[2] The St Albans estate was at and about the village of Sandridge,* three miles north-east of the city.

The Kent estate of Agney had belonged to her mother when, as Frances Thornhurst, daughter of Sir Gifford Thornhurst, baronet, she had married Richard Jennings (then spelled Jenyns) in 1643.

It is a pity that almost every word that has come down to us of Mrs Jennings is to her detriment. In the seventeenth century it was not hard to acquire a reputation for witchcraft, and in her case it could be that it was based on nothing more sinister than, as one contemporary put it, 'knowing more than the common race of mortals'. Nevertheless it must be owned that in the newly cleaned Kneller† which hangs at Althorp, the face of old Mrs Jennings is disturbing (Plate 1). No gracious chatelaine this, but a gaunt old beldam, the huge manly nose and watchful eyes looming from the darkness, her sandy wisps thrusting from beneath a widow's coif. Next to it in the gallery hangs the Kneller of Sarah (Plate 2) which, Queen Anne told her, 'I have at last got home and am so mightely pleas'd with I would not part with it for anything.',[3] and the same which, when all was over, was returned to the sitter.‡

Ignoring the unkind contrast between mother and daughter, for we have nothing of Sarah in old age, we may unreservedly admire herself as, in her prime, she looks slantingly at us with all the confidence of her undeniable beauty, the blue satin setting off the gold of her hair, the lustrous eyes, the cherubic lips. She has her mother's

* 'I know that in old deeds that I have which belong to the Manor of Sandridge that estate came from Sir Ralph Rowlett, and that might have been in William the Conqueror's time for ought I know'.
                              Sarah to David Mallet, 4 Oct. 1744 (Spencer mss.)
† Sir Godfrey Kneller (1646–1723).
‡ In an undated letter from Campden House Anne tells Sarah: 'I was yesterday at ye picture drawers in leister feilds. There was but a few pictures of people I know but those weare very like and the work methinks looks more like flesh and bloud then Sir Godfrey Nellars. He is to draw ye Prince and if that proves well I shall be tempted to desire my deare Mrs Freeman would once more give her self ye trouble to sitt for her picture, for I would fain have one that is likly to last longer then I doubt this I have will do.' (Blen e 17)

24

high-domed forehead, but never that nose. Sarah's nose, admired by Marlborough for its straightness, is well modelled and very slightly tip-tilted. The poise of the head is enchanting, while about the whole—head, neck, shoulders, the bust half-revealed by the careful-casual folds of the bodice—there is a bloom and a radiance which, we are told, were in fact quite exceptional.

It was this startling radiance in Sarah and her sister Frances (Grammont's La Belle Jennings) which first astonished all who saw them. Well hidden at Blenheim is a *jeu d'esprit* written for Sarah when she was a maid of honour by a young friend, Mistress Loughry, then in Touraine:

Having ye curiosity to climbe up a pare of steep staires where none of my company would follow mee, I found there in a little high Terrasse an old man setting with a huge perspective [glass] which hee rested on ye wall. Hee was in a strange wild habitt, with a mighty long beard almost to his feet . . . Hee told me it was a perspective left him by an enchantress and he could if it were but rightly placed see what was done at that time in any part of ye world. I began to be half out of my witts to look too. I turn'd it wether hee wold or noe as nigh as I could guess towards England and 'twas very strange I was soe lucky it seems as just to hitt upon St Jeamses Park . . . Hee would not lett mee look for a minet but told mee with amazement that hee saw hundreds of wemen or Angels, for hee could not distinguish which of the two they were, but for his part hee was of an opinion 'twas paridice. 'twas between 6 & 7 aclock at night & there happen'd to bee a great deale of company . . . But at last, giving a great cry out of a suden, 'I see', said hee, 'a young beuty coming down ye great walk with rayes about her head like a sun, but 'tis impossible for mee to distinguish at this distance whether 'tis the lustre of her complexion or of her eyes that produces them. Shee is in a crowd that follows her wherever shee goes but there is people that never quitts her one minet. She has without doubt a witt & goodness as extraordinary as her beuty, for of these adorers ther's not one that reproches her of any kindness to one more then another. I shov'd him something rudly from his seat and taking his place I saw you standing as hee had described you. You can't imagine ye joy I had in that sight, I was like a thing transported. I shouted, hollow'd after you. I call'd you by your name a hundred times as lowd as I could hollow—'Miss Ginings! Miss Ginings!' But Miss Ginings was cruell to nothing but mee. You never as much as turned your head that way, and I was only answer'd by ye Ecoes who all found a pleasure in repeating your name after mee. I however never seast calling to you till at last I saw you turn in to St Jeamses House. Ye sun that was about your head was it seems that which gave light to all ye park for, in a minet after, all ye Company quitted it and it grew soe dark 'twas impossible for mee to see any longer.

> Yet oh her beauty shineth as the sun
> And dazzl'd Reason yields as quite undone.

It was this devastating radiance of Sarah's which, from girlhood to old age, enraptured at sight the hardbitten and the naïve, the Garths and the Somersets, the Coningsbys and the Cibbers . . . Such beauty was not long to be hidden at Holywell nor at Water End, her grandfather's gabled house beside the watersplash near Sandridge. Like Frances, she must go to court; like her to be ogled by James Duke of York and, again like her, to resist him.

Sarah, claimed Dr Hare,* was almost born in a court.[5] Long before she was a maid of honour she visited it; and so she had met Princess Anne, James's daughter by Anne Hyde, when Sarah was ten and Anne six.[6] 'The beginning of the Princess's kindness,' Sarah remembered, 'had a much earlier date than my entrance into her service. My promotion to this honour was wholly owing to impressions she had before received to my advantage; we had used to play together when she was a child, and she even then expressed a particular fondness for me. This inclination increased with our years. I was often at Court, & the Princess always distinguished me by the pleasure she took to honour me, preferably to others, with her conversation & confidence. In all her parties for amusement I was sure by her choice to be one.'[7]

The two little girls, the Princess and Miss Jennings, were intro-

* Dr Francis Hare (1671–1740), Marlborough's chaplain and afterwards Bishop of Chichester.

duced to each other by a Miss Cornwallis, who was related to Anne; not, one might guess, a momentous meeting; a princess meets dozens of little girls and soon forgets them as Anne, we are told, forgot Miss Cornwallis; but with Anne the captivation by Sarah was instantaneous, lasting and profound.

'Very early indeed in these young lives', observes Sir Winston Churchill, 'did those ties of love, kindling into passion on one side and into affection and sincere friendship on the other, grow deep and strong, as yet unheeded by the bustling world. There was a romantic, indeed perfervid element in Anne's love for Sarah to which the elder girl responded warmly several years before she realised the worldly importance of such a relationship.'[8]

Anne, lacking Sarah's vivacity, had quiet charm. Her voice was low and musical, her brown hair curled, her hands and figure were pleasing. Like her sister Mary she suffered from weak eyes which were later to cause a chronic frown. But in temperament the contrast with Sarah was even greater than in looks. Timid, she longed for friendship and assurance. Often morose and pessimistic, even sullen and cold, she turned thankfully to one radiating confidence and fire.

In her own 'character' of Queen Anne, written in old age, Sarah says she had 'a person and appearance very graceful and something of majesty in her look. She was religious without affectation and certainly meant to do everything that was just', although towards the end of her reign she was imposed upon and fell into evil hands.* To which Dr Johnson, after reading the Queen's letters published in Sarah's *Conduct*, adds, 'There is indeed [about Anne] nothing insolent or overbearing, but then there is nothing great or firm or regal, nothing that enforces obedience and respect or which does not rather invite opposition and petulance'.[9] By blood and by upbringing she had every excuse for becoming a bad queen. That she did not, that with certain reservations her reign was glorious was largely owing to the good intentions she set out with and to her

* In another paper however (Blen G-1-16) the Duchess enlarged upon this: 'The queen was extremely well breed & never made a harsh or uncivel answer to any body tell that vile woman got so much power over her [Abigail] & she allways ment well but after she grew so fond of that creature & her minesters she often spoak in her stile who tho she was not a fool she had been used to very low company & her nature was brutal'.

strength of will, repeatedly undermined though it was by ill health on the one hand and the faction of parties on the other.

Anne could not remember the face of her mother, Anne Hyde. Her father, James Duke of York, on the death of his first wife, turned Roman Catholic and married a fifteen-year-old Catholic, Mary of Modena who, up till that time, had never heard of England and so, luckily, had no notion of what it would mean to be Duchess of York.

Charles II, James's brother, restored to the throne in the year of Sarah's birth, had the wisdom to realise that his nieces Anne and her elder sister Mary, as potential queens, must be raised as protestants; and for that reason the girls were closeted at Richmond Palace and later at St James's with staunch protestants to look after them: Lady Frances Villiers and Henry Compton Bishop of London.

Anne was taught French and drawing, singing and acting (she could strum a guitar) and very little else besides etiquette and religious observance, not forgetting of course the annual day of mourning for her martyred grandfather. Into her world, narrow as a cell, came occasional rumours of plots. Frightened, she hurried to her chaplains. Who were these papists and how could she escape them? They were not altogether reassuring. According to Sarah they were 'Such Divines as could have said but little in Defence of their own Religion, or to secure her against the Pretences of Popery'.[10] Yet with the wisdom of Solomon how could they have convinced her that her only safety lay in the Church of England, when her own father, who with all his failings was kind to her, was a papist repeatedly banished from his brother's kingdom on long, rough journeys—to Brussels, to Edinburgh—when Anne herself would go with him and Sarah too?

Anne's mind, as it chanced, was of the kind that can be captivated by repetition; and once that had been grasped, all bishop and chaplains needed to do was to press home their lesson daily and leave the rest to time. It was a method which worked so well that Anne became a fervent Anglican, recoiling from Dissent on the one hand and hating everything Roman Catholic on the other.

Mary of Modena Duchess of York, Anne's very young step-mother, herself beautiful, chose her maids of honour for their looks. Of these Frances Jennings was the most startling; and it was natural enough that when she was old enough, which meant when she was twelve,* her handsome sister Sarah should follow her into the duchess's service. Both of them of course, in the court of Charles II, were much run after. Frances, spritefull as John Evelyn calls her, and flighty, was soon married to Captain Sir George Hamilton and had had six children when he was killed in action in 1676. After three years of widowhood she married a Roman Catholic, Richard Talbot who, on the accession of James II, became Duke of Tyrconnel. Judging from her scrawls at Blenheim Frances was very different from her sister, scatter-brained, ultra-feminine and sufficiently pious to found an order of nuns.

As for Sarah, she came, as she tells us, 'extream young into the court and had the luck to be liked.'[11] She found herself at first in a nest of queens or potential queens: Mary of Modena (15), Anne (8) and her sister Mary (11) who would marry Dutch William and with him reign as Queen Mary II. To Charles and James, busy with their own affairs, this feminine coterie may have had no more significance than a cage of linnets or, in a phrase of Vanbrugh's, a parcel of foolish plants. Certainly it must at times have seemed like a hothouse for exotics, with the young Duchess of York, a ravishing brunette introduced by James as 'your new playfellow', the most exotic of all.

In the Victoria & Albert Museum one may see a doll said to have been given to Anne by a lady-in-waiting. Its low-necked, full-skirted dress is what one would expect, but the high head-dress of fine lawn, its lace edging sewn on to a wire framework, is perhaps rather surprising;[12] although we find Sarah, on Anne's behalf, sending to France for 'a fine lace headdress agreed for 400 franks (£36 1s. 3d.)'[13] Sometimes these 'heads' took the form of pleated lace fans, hazardous in sedan-chairs or with candles. 'You may tell his lordship', Sarah wrote to a friend, 'that I have burnt the best head I have in writing this letter'.[14]

In play as in dress they naturally aped their elders; and so boredom, with luck, would be kept at bay with endless games of ombre, basset or whist or their childish equivalents. There was very little reading and apart from gossip not much conversation. To divert them

---

* Most authorities give twelve as her age of entry to court. In a letter at Blenheim, however, the Duchess herself says: 'I have know the court since I was thirteen years old'. (Blen G-I-16. Undated)

nothing more exciting could be thought of than to command them to act a play: John Crowne's masque *Calisto the Chaste Nymph*, performed on December 2nd, 1674, with in the caste two queens-in-embryo (Anne and Mary) and in the audience two kings (one reigning, one to be); while a rival claimant, the Duke of Monmouth, danced in the ballet. Sarah took the part of Mercury; Diana being played by the saintly Margaret Blagge. Miss Blagge, ablaze with diamonds one of which she lost, after saying her piece hurried to the wings 'where several ladies, her companions, were railing with the gallants triflingly enough till they were called to re-enter. She, under pretence of conning her next part, was retired into a corner, reading a book of devotion.'[15]

Such frolics fly to the head, yet even in that company Sarah has left it on record that she was bored. 'I think anyone that has common sense or honesty', she wrote long afterwards, 'must needs bee very weary of every thing that one meets with in courts. I have seen a good many & lived in them many years, but I protest that I was never pleased but when I was a child, & after I had been a maid of honour some time, at fourteen I wishd my self out of the court as much as I had desired to come into it before I knew what it was'.[16]

All too well she remembered the tedious company, the endless card-games by candle-light and the stuffy rooms they played in. Even so, fourteen must have been an exaggeration, for she was sixteen when she won a battle with her mother as to which of them should leave the court, and it was she who then chose to stay:

> Mrs Jennings and her daughter, Maid of Honour to the Dutchesse, have had so great a falling out that they fought; the young one complained to the Dutchesse that if her mother was not put out of St James's, where she had lodgings to sanctuary her from debt, she would run away; so Sir Alleyn Apsley was sent to bid the mother remove, who answered, with all her heart, she should never dispute the Duke and Dutchesse's commands, but with the Grace of God she would take her daughter away with her . . . So rather than part with her, the mother must stay, and all breaches are made up again.

But a month later comes the dénouement:

Mistress Sarah Jennings has got the better of her mother, who is commanded to leave the Court and her daughter in it, notwithstanding the mother's petition that she might have her girle with her, the girle saying she is a mad woman.[17]

It has the authentic ring; and further tiffs are more than hinted at in letters at Blenheim. Yet when the old lady lay dying, Sarah sat up with her at St Albans night after night, so that the Queen begged her to have a care of her own health. It was a strange relationship, realistic to the point of cynicism and, like Sarah herself, doggedly unsentimental.

Of London Marlborough was to write later, 'I looked upon it as a place habited by wolves';[18] and in that context it was no bad thing for a young person to be able to assume an air of serene detachment. 'I made it my business', declared Sarah, 'to observe things very exactly without being much observed my self'.[19] And there was plenty to observe. It did not take Sarah long to realise that life at court was a good deal less polite than she had been led to suppose. One evening she was sitting alone in a window-seat when a door opened and a girl scarcely older than herself came out sobbing and wringing her hands. What was the matter? She would say nothing except that her mother had undone her by her advice.* Mrs Jennings's advice, we may be certain, had been far more sensible, and when the testing time came, Sarah would be glad of it. In the meantime perhaps it was as well, though again perhaps not, that her companions, the queens-in-embryo and their tiny circle, were so religiously segregated. Pawns as they were, matches would of course be made for them (a princess customarily married at fifteen); but while they were waiting it was considered wise to make theirs, except for the odd cleric, a manless world; and of course heavy boredom set in. For with every saint's day observed and every card-game played there must still be interminable evenings when all the girls could think of was to play at mothers and fathers or at husbands and wives and to write more or less imbecile letters to their friends. Strange indeed were the letters written by Anne to Mistress Cornwallis, and stranger still Anne's and her sister Mary's to Frances

* The girl, a Miss Trevor, was, according to Sarah, with the connivance of her mother, betrayed by Thomas Thynne of Longleat.

Apsley and hers to them. There are writings—Swift's letters to Stella, the Brontës' Gondal sagas—which defy classification, and these are of them; and when their editor, Colonel Bathurst, calls them grotesque protestations of devotion, that seems as near the mark as we shall get. Anne's letters to Miss Cornwallis were, according to Sarah, soon censored, but that was of small consequence. Either her father or her stepmother (it is not clear which), reading an unsealed letter, was 'very much displeased at the passionate expressions with which it was filled.' On the grounds of her Roman Catholicism, though that of course would have recommended her to James, he forbade Miss Cornwallis the court and commanded Anne to cease writing to her.* Anne was expected to spend some time in tears, but no. In a fortnight, says Sarah, she seemed to have forgotten that her friend had existed. It was Sarah herself who years later coaxed Anne to grant the unfortunate woman a small pension. Anne however did remember once or twice to send a footman to suggest she stand at her window to see her drive to Hyde Park. 'What became of her afterwards', Sarah muses, 'I could never learn, but that probably she sank unregarded into a state of very low poverty and misfortunes. Thus ended a great friendship of three or four years' standing in which time Lady Anne had written, it was believed, above a thousand letters full of the most violent professions of everlasting kindness'.[20]

Both then and later Anne, in her attempts at the clandestine—letters, secret meetings and so on—was apt to be far less lucky than her sister Mary who, in pursuit of what Sarah called 'pretty Entertainments and Romantick Amusements to help the time to pass away', showed ardour and industry and was never discovered. In her effusions to Frances Apsley Mary's pen flies over the paper without a comma to show a gift for love letters which might well have been better employed. Feigned names taken from the plays in which they had both acted were but a beginning. Mary, signing herself Mary Clorine, writes to Frances as 'dear dear dear dear dear dear Aurelia', and continues,

* In her *Lives of the Queens of England* (1884) Miss Strickland makes no mention of an intercepted letter. She maintains that Sarah, finding that Miss Cornwallis was a Roman Catholic, denounced her as such to Bishop Compton, who had her dismissed.

Mrs. Jennings, mother of Sarah Duchess of
Marlborough. Kneller

Sarah Duchess of Marlborough. Kneller

I may if I can tel you how much I love you but I hope that is not douted I have given you proves anufe if not I will die to satisfie you dear dear husban if al my hares were lives I wold lose them al twenty times over to sarve or satisfie you . . . I love you with a flame more lasting then the vestals fire thou art my life my soul my al that heaven can give deaths life with you without you death to live. What can I say more to perswade you that I love you with more zeal then any lover can I love you with a love that ner was known by man I have for you excese of friandship more of love then any woman can for woman & more love then ever the constanest lover had for his mistress. You are loved more then can be exprest by your ever obedient wife vere afectionate friand humbel sarvent to kis the ground where once you go to be your dog in a string your fish in a net your bird in a cage your humbel trout.

Mary Clorine[21]

Understandably, Anne felt outclassed. 'I am not one of those', she told Frances Apsley,

who can express a great deal & therefore it may be thought I do not love so well, but whoever thinks so is much mistaken, for tho I have not may be so good a way of expressing my self as some peopel have, yet I asure you I love you as well as those that do & perhaps more then some . . . Farwell deare Semandra.

Ziphares[22]

From all of which nonsense Sarah the observant stood aside, so much so that Frances complained of finding her cold as ice; but if she had bothered to read Anne's letters she would have found phrases which might later have echoed with a familiar ring: 'Be as free with me as ever . . . I hope you will do me the justice to beleeve that I will never change . . . I am ye same I ever was & ever will be to ye last moment of my life . . .'

After their marriages, and all three married, their friendships became more ordinary and Frances, as the wife of Sir Benjamin Bathurst, settled decorously at Anne's court. But long before that, in fact when Sarah was fifteen, John Churchill, page to the Duke of York and ten years her senior, had begun his courtship.

The story of John Churchill first Duke of Marlborough has for all time been told by his descendant, Sir Winston Churchill; how he was born at Ashe House near Axminster in 1650 (one of twelve children, seven of whom died in infancy); how his family had been divided against itself by the civil wars; how his father, the gallant but impoverished Sir Winston, rewarded for his part as a royalist by an augmentation to his arms, chose as his motto *fiel pero desdichado* (faithful but unfortunate); and how Churchill himself, after a nominal education at St Paul's School (Lord Chesterfield found him 'eminently illiterate'), was appointed page to James and so entered the court circle where sooner or later he was bound to meet Sarah Jennings.

It is at this point that Sir Winston cautions his readers to 'brace themselves for what will inevitably be a painful interlude', while he deals with the affairs of Arabella Churchill (John's elder sister, born in 1649, who became James's mistress), and of John Churchill himself who for three years was the lover of Barbara Villiers, Duchess of Cleveland, herself the mistress or ex-mistress of Charles II. In Sarah's directions to Marlborough's biographers, as set out in her will, she tells them to begin after the revolution of 1688. Much that preceded it she preferred not to dwell on, and nor need we. She was particularly scornful of those she called 'the Duke of Marlborough's sister and her Train of Bastards' who with some deference had been mentioned by Thomas Lediard in his *Life of John Duke of Marlborough*, a biography she had not commissioned. 'Because they had Titles', she says, 'he seems to think that was an Honour to the Duke of Marlborough. I think it quite the contrary. For it seems to insinuate that his first Introduction was from an infamous Relation, when the whole Truth of that matter was as follows: His sister was a Maid of Honour to the first Duchess of York, Hyde. She had at least two or three Bastards by the Duke of York or others, when her Brother was whipt at St Paul's School for not reading his Book . . . Now I would fain have any Reasonable Body tell me what the Duke of Marlborough could do when a Boy at School to prevent the Infamy of his Sister, or why Mr Lediard could have any Judgment in mentioning King James's Favourite.'

It was as well that the paths of Sarah and her sister-in-law diverged. In Marlborough's biography, Sarah told David Mallet, 'I would have nothing named of her nor of any of the family she produced. I see no reason for giving any account of her husband Godfrey, nor any of the children's promotions . . . There can be nothing said that is good of any of them.'[23] True, Colonel Godfrey, whom Arabella eventually married, was of no great distinction; but no history of Marlborough could be written without mention of Arabella's son the Duke of Berwick, who fought as valiantly for France as Marlborough did for England.

As for the Cleveland affair, it was to be ignored altogether. And indeed in the biography of a hero to show blemishes at the outset— the clay foot protruding from the statue's sheet—is manifestly rash. However, in the event Mallet never wrote a line of Marlborough's history; and when at long last his biographer was found he proved to be not only his own descendant but a fighter after his own heart. 'Audacity', Sir Winston Churchill has written in another connection, 'is the only ticket'; and here too that is his watchword. Stung by the attacks on his ancestor by Macaulay, Sir Winston in battle-dress makes for the ramparts. He admits that the affair with the Duchess of Cleveland lasted three years, that Charles II expelled Churchill from court and that the Duchess gave him £5000 with which he bought an annuity; but what of that? 'How disgusting', he exclaims, 'to pretend with Lord Macaulay a filthy, sordid motive for actions prompted by those overpowering compulsions which leap flaming from the crucible of life itself! Inconstant Barbara loved her youthful soldier tenderly . . . He returned her love with the passion of youth. She was rich and could have money for the asking. He had no property but his sword and sash. But they were equals, they were kin, they lived in the same world. She was now the mother of his child'.*[24]

What has shocked posterity has not of course been the infatuation which, as Sir Winston suggests, was too predictable for comment,

---

* The child Barbara, born 16 July, 1672, was sent to the convent of the Immaculate Conception in Paris, there to become Sister Benedicta. After having a child, Charles Hamilton, by the Earl of Arran, she became prioress of the convent of St Nicholas at Pontoise.

See A. L. Rowse: *The Early Churchills*, pp. 143–4.

but the careful investment of the lover's gains, for which the receipt survives. It is an unedifying incident and one that might happily be omitted from a biography of Sarah did it not provide the key to her seemingly unreasonable reaction to Churchill's wooing. Their love letters make at Blenheim a pitiful bundle,[25] the more so for Sarah's endorsement: 'Read over in 1743 to burn them but I could not doe it'.*

John is the ardent, sighing lover, Sarah the mocking, elusive nymph. If his are *billets doux*, hers are *billets durs*. John tells her he is sick, his head aches, his heart is ready to break and death must be his ease if she will not love him. 'Had I the will, I have not the power ever to break my chains'. Yet he still fails, in the acceptable sense, to propose. 'If it were true', retorts Sarah, 'that you have that passion for me which you say you have, you would find out some way to make yourself happy—it is in your power. Therefore press me no more to see you, since it is what I cannot in honour approve of, and if I have done too much, be so just as to consider who was the cause of it.' At which her lover exclaims, 'How unjust you are! . . . Give me leave to do what I cannot help which is to adore you as long as I live . . . Could you ever love me I think . . . it would make me immortal'.

Sarah gets cross. He writes only to tease her, 'but 'tis to no purpose to imagine that I will be made ridiculous in the world when it is in your power to make me otherwise'. Finally of course, with groans at being treated like a footman, the lover toes the line. All along, we may be sure, Sarah knew what she was about and played her hand with precision. Everyone at court, including Sarah and her mother, knew about Barbara Cleveland; and now that that liaison was broken, another obstacle had arisen in the shape of Catharine Sedley (heiress of Sir Charles Sedley and later to take her turn as mistress to the Duke of York and to become Countess of Dorchester), on whose behalf Sir Winston and Lady Churchill had, according to Sarah, been making 'a disagreeable noise in the town' because they had a

---

* A second endorsement in Sarah's hand reads: 'leters from Mr Churchill before & after I was marri'd which I desire Grace Ridly may have to burn without reading them. read over in 1736. read again in 1743.' Grace Ridley, her favourite servant, was in attendance at her death in 1744.

mind to have their son marry this 'strange creature' for money. However, that came to nothing.

Sarah of course had had other proposals, one of them from the Earl of Lindsey, ever afterwards to be jestingly called her lover. Years later she was told of a coffee-house conversation, overheard by Arthur Maynwaring,* between a Mr Hopkins ('Hoppy') and Peregrine Bertie, vice-chamberlain and Lord Lindsey's brother.

Hoppy: Well, here's my Lady Duchess's health. I fancy she must have been the finest woman that ever was.

Bertie: Ay, she was mighty agreeable. My brother Lindsey was in love with her and had like to have thrown himself away upon her.

Maynwaring (to himself): God eternally damn him and sink him —He throw himself away upon her!

Bertie: Why, ay, she was no fortune.

Hoppy: What, was she not? She was worth at least £8000 when she married Lord Marl and has been since the best fortune and the best wife in Europe.[26]

Sarah was annoyed with Lediard not only for his deference to royal bastards (Marlborough, she said, was very much shocked when his children took notice of relations he was ashamed of), but also for saying that Marlborough had 'made a Considerable Figure among the Beau Mond'.[27] 'That', said Sarah, 'I interpret to be a fop. He was naturally genteel without the least affectation, and handsome as an angel tho', ever, so carelessly dress'd.'[28] The good looks of John and Sarah together were long remembered. 'Impartial judges will, I am persuaded, allow that I may without flattery mention beauty to your Grace', wrote Dr Hare to Sarah when she was sixty-six, 'who with your great Consort was beautiful to a proverb and who still retain more of it than any Lady of your age and have shewn it in a race of children that I believe no one family can equal.'[29]

History, as Sir Winston Churchill remarks, cannot proceed by silences, and history is coy about the date of Sarah's wedding. She herself, she who boasted of a good memory but could not remember dates, does not help us. All she says, and that of marriage in general,

* Arthur Maynwaring (1668–1712), M.P., auditor of imprests, member of Kit-Cat Club, writer (contributed to *Whig Examiner* and *Medley*). Lifelong admirer of the Duchess of Marlborough, he called himself her secretary (unpaid).

is: 'If it be necessary, the sooner it's got over the better. I think that where the affection is grounded upon good reason it cannot be too soon, but if one marries from Custom and for Posterity only, I think I should delay that heavy Yoke as long as I could.'[30] In her own case it seems safe to assume that affection was indeed grounded upon good reason, though if for once in her life heart overruled head, no one would blame her.

At Blenheim an undated fragment in the Duchess's hand is endorsed by her: 'My letter to my sister before I was marry'd about my Brother Griffith'. It reads:

> . . . who I am more weare of then of any thing in the world. Hee has larnt french ever since my sister deyd & thinks there is no body understands more nor prononceys it beter then him self. I am in admeration every time I see him how my poor sister could have such a passion for him. Then hee is soe ill bred & fancyes him self such a wet [wit] & makes such a noise from morning to night & that as my Mother says hee turns my head. I beleeve I had not had his company but that hee wants mony. I cannot imagin how hee will doe to live being of a humer that makes him uncapable of anything but spending. I confess I have not much concarn for him & all I desire is that hee may not spend all at St Albans without paying the interest which hee will doe if hee bee not prevented I do realy beleeve & then the poor child will bee undun.[31]

The letter, a characteristic one, is addressed to Sarah's sister Frances and refers to her brother-in-law Edward Griffith, then a widower with an infant daughter who died the following year. The child's mother, according to an inscription in St Albans Cathedral, died on March 22nd, 1678; and the wretched Griffith had learned French and paraded it 'ever since', while his young sister-in-law Sarah had to tolerate his maddening company in the same (her mother's) small house.

Yet for the date of Sarah's secret wedding (sponsored and financed, it is said, by Mary of Modena), Dr Reid gives the spring of 1678[32] and Sir Winston Churchill 'some time in the winter of 1677-78'. Added to which we have Archdeacon Coxe in 1847 observing, 'The biographers of the duke, as well as historians in general, place his marriage as late as 1681, which cannot be correct because Henrietta, the eldest daughter, was born July 20, 1681.'[33] Their first child Harriet, who did not live, was in fact born in October, 1679.

When John Churchill, writing to Sarah in April, 1678, addresses the letter to Miss Jennings, Sarah endorses: 'When this was writt I think I was married but it was not known.' From such evidence as we have it seems probable that they were married late in 1678 or early in 1679. Secret weddings were not uncommon. In 1675, the year John Churchill met Sarah Jennings, Margaret Blagge, whom we last saw reading Jeremy Taylor under cover of *Calisto*, quietly married Sidney Godolphin. It was nearly a year before John Evelyn, who regarded her as his adopted daughter and with whom she had signed a pact of 'inviolable friendship', heard of it; and in 1678 she died after giving birth to a son Francis, who would in due course marry Sarah's eldest daughter, Henrietta. A third secret wedding, that of Abigail Hill and Samuel Masham in 1707, would again, for Sarah, have momentous significance.

For the first five years of their marriage the Churchills had no home of their own. For a time, while he attended the Yorks on their journeys of exile, Churchill tried leaving his wife in his bachelor lodgings in Jermyn Street and it was there that their first child was born and died. Later Sarah stayed with her mother-in-law in Dorset, but that did not serve either. John wrote calmingly to Sarah, begging her patience, 'for she is my Mother and I hope at last she will be sensible that she is to blame in being peevish'.[34] It was the old story. 'From the beginning of the world', wrote Sarah in widowhood, 'there has not been two women that were good mothers-in-law'.[35]

And what of her own mother at St Albans? She and John Churchill seem to have liked each other well enough, but the house was small and he could not often be there; nor was it unknown for there to be 'disorder & ell humer' when mother and daughter lodged together. On the whole it seemed better to correspond. 'I was sorry I ded not see you before I came out of town', Sarah writes to her at Lady Anglesey's in Jermyn Street, 'but I never heard one word of your being there tell Munday . . . and being in waiting & to goe early the next morning to St Albans it was impossable to get time enough from the hurry I was in all that day to have found you out, except I had known derectly whare you lay & you know that is allways very uncartain. I find somebody has been deverting them selves with my shape which is not yet grown soe slender but I am sure the first thing you will say to me is good god Deare child what makes you soe monstrous big sure you must bee with child tho you dont own it. You will see by this you are to expect noe change in my person but I find my self something free-er from vapours & the waight upon my eyes that I us'd soe often to complain of sence I drank the watters, which is of much more consiquance to me . . .'[36] and so on.

It was an uncomfortable time. James and his duchess, as Roman Catholics harried by the Test Act, were in almost constant exile. When they went to Brussels or to Edinburgh the Churchills went with them, unless Sarah was pregnant (Henrietta was born on July 19th, 1681), when she stayed in England.

In 1682 Churchill, returning with James from Scotland, was shipwrecked in the *Gloucester*. They barely escaped with their lives. In December James awarded him the barony of Churchill of Aymouth in the peerage of Scotland. In the same year Frances Apsley married Sir Benjamin Bathurst, and John Sheffield (Lord Mulgrave) flirted with the Princess Anne. Anne liked him, and indeed he compared most favourably with the Elector of Hanover (later George I of England) who had approached her the previous year but returned to his country without proposing, a slight she never forgot. In the bleak nunnery Anne then lived in Mulgrave's attentions were welcome and—who knows?—had Anne been as secretive as her sister, she might have married him and had healthy heirs; but it was not to be. Discovery fell upon them like a thunderclap and sent Mulgrave mouldering in a leaky vessel to Tangier.* Though by no means the end of Mulgrave, it was the end of the courtship and the signal to Charles and James for a worthier suitor to be found quickly for their niece.

All in all it made an unpromising introduction for Prince George of Denmark, but Prince George was not easily abashed. Blond and handsome, with only a few pockmarks, he looked the part, and little more was expected of him. Anne tolerated him and later, perhaps to

---

* Miss Strickland, echoing Mrs Manley, asserts that it was Sarah who reported the Mulgrave affair to James. She sensibly adds that the leaky vessel can hardly have been deliberate on James's part, since to hazard a whole crew to be rid of one scapegrace would surely be beyond even a Medici's malevolence.

her own surprise, found she could love him. In the summer of 1683 they were married. From the outset, to everyone except Anne it was obvious that Prince George could never be more than a lay figure, but in some ways that was as well. Charles II's opinion has been quoted and misquoted ad nauseam. Sarah's version reads as follows:

> King Charles II had tried him all ways & at last thought he might make something of him & best discover of what he was made in the way of drinking, but declared upon the experiment that he could compare him to nothing but a Great Jarr or Vessel standing still & receiving unmoved & undisturbed so much liquor whenever it came to its turn.[37]

Anne, now lodged in the Cockpit in Whitehall and beginning her long and tragic series of births and miscarriages, begged for Sarah as a lady-of-the-bedchamber and was given her wish. In one of her many narratives Sarah writes, 'Lord Marl: intended that I should allways live near London & never see the court, but soon after made me lady of the bedchamber to the Princess of Denmark'.[38] In the meantime, perhaps to humour her, he built Holywell House* at St Albans where, for better for worse, they would be neighboured by Mrs Jennings, widowed since 1668 and still living in the house where Sarah had been born. The site, with its holy well and water meadows beside the Ver and at the foot of the abbey slope, was a pleasant one. True, as Marlborough was to write from Flanders, St Albans was 'not famous for seeing far', but the abbey was on the skyline, the lapping of water in one's ears and in spring perhaps even the song of the nightingale, of which Sarah was especially fond.†

Of London and court life there Sarah felt she had observed more than enough; for if the restoration had been gay (and she herself, too young to remember, had been lucky to escape the plague and the fire), Charles's reign now looked to be ending in a blood bath. 'I remember nothing that happened in King Charles's time worth mentioning', she noted, 'Only ye many executions upon that which

---

* Holywell House. 'However ordinary it may be,' wrote Sarah in 1714, 'I would not part with it for any house I have seen on my travels.'

† 'This being the season I hear the Nightengales as I lye in my bead I have wish'd them with all my hart with you, knowing you love them.' John to Sarah, 23 April, 1703. (Blen E 2).

was called Lord Russells plot & a great deal of horror to that I felt. My nature carried to an aversion to ye proceedings in ye end of that reign. I was sorry not to find that compassion in the breast of another [the Princess Anne's]. All I could prevail on my self to do was to say nothing.'[39]

In old age Sarah amused herself by dictating to her favourite granddaughter Lady Diana Spencer a history of England; but what with the gout and 'perpetual interruptions', both resented, grandmother and granddaughter never got very far. Still there it is, bound in yellowing white vellum, with many blank pages, and stored away in its box at Blenheim.[40] 'Charles the 2nd', we read on page one, 'his Restoration . . . Charles profess'd in Publick the Protestant religion but (if he was any) he was the Roman Catholick. He was thoroughly convinced that there was no such thing as Virtue or Sincerity and that everyone acted from interested principles. He had good parts but hated application to business. The Duchess of Cleveland his first mistress us'd him extreamly ill. He was too much led by his brother the Duke of York.

1681. From this time the King began to be absolute. The nation was divided by two parties, viz. Torys & Whigs. The former were for the Court & never thought the King had too much Power. The latter were the greatest ennemies to arbitrary government & to popery, consequently hated by the King. The Bishops, by their aversion to Presbyterians, threw themselves into the Tory party & were protected by the King.

1684. The King makes the people give up to him all their privileges. Jeffreys [Judge Jeffreys] in his Circuit distinguish'd himself greatly by his unheard of cruelty. Charles was become absolute, or rather the Duke of York, for he led the King.

Charles died aged 54. Some suspect he was poison'd.

CHAPTER II

James and the Revolution

1685-1688

———————◆———————

Sarah's history of England, dictated to her granddaughter, ends with three paragraphs on the brief, disastrous reign of James II:

> 1685.   James makes no Alterations as to Places, which was not surprising as those already in place were all his creatures and put in by him self in his Brother's reign. The Tory's were arriv'd to the hight of their wishes. James went publickly to Mass & declar'd publickly that his Brother had died in the Roman Catholick faith, which was a very great prejudice to K: Chas II's memory who had in his lifetime so often declar'd him self a Protestant.
>
> The King sends the Lord Cheif Justice Jeffreys to try the rebells [Monmouth's] & Maj: Gen: Kirk went with some troops to keep the people in awe. These two comited unheard of cruelties such as were never before practis'd in any country.
>
> James had now two things in view, to make him self absolute & to establish Popery.

At the time of dictation, in the reign of George II, the sixth reign she had known, Sarah tended to view former monarchs with some indulgence. James's brutality she could never forgive, but as a ruler, she reflected, he could have been worse. He was 'a good Manager for the publick without breaking any Law but what proceeded from his Weakness of having a Mind that every body should attend him in Heaven by establishing Popery here'.[1] And again, 'Hee was under a great temptation of bringing in a Religion which hee was perswaded was so meritorious a thing that it would secure him honour in this world & everlasting happynesse in the next'.[2] For a king damned by most historians as cruel, vicious and blundering, this might almost rank as a reprieve. Bishop Burnet* finds that he had 'no personal vices but of one sort',[3] which again, for a Stuart, was markedly in his favour. John Churchill James had always had faith in and in the year of his accession he made him Baron Churchill of Sandridge.

It was true that James went publicly to mass. Indeed, of all his rash acts few were rasher than, at the very outset, commissioning Wren to build, for his palace at Whitehall, a sumptuous Roman Catholic chapel. The statues and carving for it were entrusted to Grinling Gibbons and Arnold Quellin, the frescoes to Verrio; and Wren was told that, even if it meant calling in hundreds of extra workmen, the building, inside and out, must be finished by the following autumn. It was. The first service was held there on Christmas Day, 1686. 'I could not have believed', wrote John Evelyn, 'that I should ever have seen such things in the King of England's Palace'.[4] Even this however might have been stomached had not James proved a persecutor. Braced by the victory Churchill had won him over Monmouth at Sedgemoor, James sent Jeffreys on his western circuit of vengeance with such effect that wherever one looked there seemed to be, on the skyline, a corpse swinging from a gallows.

'I hope', remarks Lediard gently in his life of Marlborough, 'it will not be look'd upon as foreign to my purpose if I just hint at some of the principal Instances of His Majesty's evil & unhappy Conduct (I may say unhappy as well with regard to the Nation as Himself), as they justify the Conduct of our Hero in the most critical and difficult Scene of his whole Life'.[5] And certainly in the dilemma of divided loyalties which Churchill was soon to find himself faced with, the brutality of James would help substantially to tip the balance.

In the meantime James attacked the Church of England, beginning with Anne's Bishop Compton and Dr Sharp, who was to become Archbishop of York and her favourite churchman. After that James tackled the army or rather, set out to convert it, an attempt which had 'little Effect with the Soldiery, nor did I', says Lediard, 'ever hear that many Proselytes were gained.' It did however sting a

* Gilbert Burnet, Bishop of Salisbury (1643-1715).

parson called Johnson into publishing a pamphlet addressed to 'the English Protestants in King James's Army', and this so maddened the King that 'it gave his Majesty & his Favorites a new Opportunity of gratifying their Revenge. Johnson was immediately imprison'd & arraign'd at the King's Bench Bar before Sir Edward Herbert, who sentenc'd him to stand thrice in the Pillory, to pay a Fine of 500 Marks, and to be whip'd from Newgate to Tyburn; which latter in particular was perform'd with so great Severity & in such deplorable Manner as was of no great Service to their Cause . . . Yet all these Things were but the bare Earnests of more egregious Tyrannies and Follies. Change of Religion was now made the only Step to Preferment, and all who adher'd to their old Principles were soon discharged the Royal Service.'[6]

This last was not strictly true. Sarah and her husband were not discharged the royal service; although Churchill told the Earl of Galway, on James's accession, that 'if the King was ever prevail'd upon to alter our Religion, he would serve him no longer but withdraw from him.'[7] To which Burnet, writing of the Churchills in the reign of Anne, adds, 'He never betrayed any of the King's secrets, nor ever set the King on violent measures . . . but on the contrary gave him always moderate counsels . . . His wife is about the Princess [Anne] and has gained such an ascendant over her that there never was a more absolute favourite in a court. She is indeed become the mistress of her thoughts & affections & does with her, both in her court & in her affairs, what she pleases.'[8]

At their first childhood meeting Anne had found Sarah delightful, an impression reinforced by almost everything that had happened since. Those she had formerly confided in, Frances Apsley and her own sister Mary, had married and, for the time being, left her. They were strange, desolate times. There had been Mary's wedding day when, after a day and a half of weeping, it was all they could do to force the bride to attend the ceremony. Anne, then thirteen, was sickening for smallpox. Even so Mary, in Holland now, seemed like Anne herself to be happier in marriage than she had expected; and certainly George was in almost every way preferable to William. However, in Anne's case, as Sarah tells us, a friend was what she most coveted, someone beautiful, self-possessed and entertaining. someone to shield and love her and lead her through that thicket of vipers which, as she saw it, was the *beau monde* of James II. Flawless, radiant, utterly self-possessed, Sarah was that person. But such harmony is in immortal souls. Anne, ever a pessimist, trembled for it. With Sarah she had all happiness. She was terrified of losing it. By a lucky chance she was soon able to promote her. It happened like this.

When Anne's old 'lady governess' and First Lady-of-the-Bed-chamber, Lady Frances Villiers, died, she had been succeeded by Anne's aunt Lady Clarendon. Sarah disliked her, and so it seems did Anne for she wrote, 'My poor Countes growes more & more naucious every day'. Others speak more favourably of her, but Sarah insists she was 'a Lady whose Discourse & Manner could not possibly recommend her to so young a Mistress, for she looked like a mad Woman'. But there, as the same witness testifies, 'Her Highness's Court was throughout so oddly composed that I think it would be making my self no great Compliment if I should say her chusing to spend so much of her Time with me did no Discredit to her Taste'.

One of the old countess's more irritating habits was prayer. 'They called her a good woman', remarks Sarah, 'I suppose because like her lord she made a great rout with prayers'. It was all Church Party window-dressing to impress the Princess Anne. But there it was. No matter how obnoxious an aunt, she could hardly be dismissed for praying. On the other hand, if reasons could be found for getting rid of Mrs Jennings and Miss Cornwallis, surely it should not be beyond the wit of woman to oust Lady Clarendon. When at last the solution was hit upon, it was so brilliant and at the same time so simple and obvious, Anne wondered why she had not thought of it herself. Lord Clarendon was appointed Lord Lieutenant of Ireland, 'to which Country', runs Sarah's record, 'his Lady was to go with him. The Princess received a sensible Joy from this Event as it gave her an Opportunity of promoting me to be First Lady of her Bedchamber, with a Satisfaction to herself that was not to be concealed.'

After that, the next step was to banish any hint of inequality. 'She grew uneasy', Sarah remembers, 'to be treated by me with the Ceremony due to her Rank & with the Sound of Words which implied Superiority. It was this turn of Mind which made her one Day propose to me that whenever I should happen to be absent from her we might in all our Letters write ourselves by feigned Names such as would import nothing of Distinction of Rank between us. Morley and Freeman were the Names her Fancy hit upon; and she left me to chuse by which of them I would be called. My frank, open Temper naturally led me to pitch upon Freeman, & so the Princess took the other; & from this Time Mrs Morley and Mrs Freeman began to converse as Equals, made so by Affection & Friendship.'[9]

What could be more delightful? Yet there was a snag, a warning even in that innocent-seeming proviso 'whenever I should happen to be absent'; for Sarah, with a growing family, had often to be absent, and no matter how Anne might try to content herself with letters (and they both wrote every day), Sarah's absence was to Anne 'in appearance a sort of death'. 'Upon my word', writes Anne to Sarah, 'I cannot live without you, and tho I wish you and Mr Freeman every thing your own harts can desire, you must not think . . . that it is reasonable for you to live out of ye world as long as I am in it'.[10] For weeks, sometimes for months, Anne had to let her stay at St Albans, herself making do with her portrait ('a pleasing thing to look upon when I can't see the original') while impatiently expecting the next letter. If it failed to arrive she would again take up her own pen. 'I hope that next to Lord Churchill', she wrote, 'I may claime ye first place in your heart. I know I have a great many Rivalls, which makes me sometimes feare loosing what I so much value, but knowing that I never have nor never will do any thing to deserve it, I comfort my self that you will not do any thing that is unjust'.[11]

It was a theme to return to: '. . . and give me leave to assure you my happiness or unhappiness depends wholly on my deare Mrs Freeman, for as long as I have the second place in her heart I can never be ye last & if ever I should loos it (which Christ forbid) it would be impossible for me to be ye first tho all other things on erth concur'd to make me so'.[12] And yet again: 'I hope ye litle corner of your heart that my Lord Churchill has left empty is mine.'[13]

What John Churchill thought of all this we shall never know; but when he writes to his wife (and he hated writing) he sounds too pleased with his young family ('the little poppetts', as Anne calls them) to care. 'You cannot imagine', he tells his wife, 'how pleased I am with the children, for they having noe body but their maid, they are soe fond of me that when I am att home they will be always with me, kissing & huging me . . . Miss is polling me by the arme that she may writt to her dear mamma, soe that I will say noe more, only beg that you will love me always soe well as I love you & then we cannot be but hapy'. To which Henrietta adds shakily: 'I kise your hands, my dear mamma. Hariote.'[14]

There was no doubt about it, he was the kind of father every wise child would choose; but then again, was this wise from the parents' point of view? Was there not in such a relaxed atmosphere a danger of discipline and good management being undermined? As Sarah afterwards put it, 'I have heard it much objected of me that I waited so seldom on the queen [Anne] and was so little about her, and because this is so contrary to the practice of all Favourites I shall give a particular account of it. Soon after my marriage, when our affairs were so narrow that a good deal of frugality was necessary, Lord Marlborough, though his inclination lay enough that way, yet by reason of indulgent gentleness that is natural to him he could not manage matters so as was convenient for our circumstances. This obliged me to enter into the management of my family. I likewise thought I owed a great deal of care to the education of my children'.[15] And indeed, as Burnet testified, 'She stayed much at home and looked very carefully after the education of her children.' It sounds sensible in the extreme. Time alone would show how the children responded.

In the family bible[16] at Holywell Sarah wrote the names of her six children (omitting the first, Harriet) and of their godparents. From this we know that the godmothers for Henrietta (born 19th July, 1681) were Arabella (Mrs Godfrey) and Mrs Jennings; that Anne's (born 27th February, 1684) were Lady Sunderland and the princess after whom she had been christened; and that the heir Jack (born 12th January, 1686. He became Lord Blandford) had as his godfathers Lord Tyrconnel (Sarah's brother-in-law) and Sidney Earl of Godolphin. The godparents of the remaining three children—Elizabeth (born 15th March, 1687), Mary (born 15th July, 1689) and Charles who was born on the 19th August, 1690 and died in infancy—included two of Anne's ladies-of-the-bedchamber, Lady Fretchville and Lady Fitzharding.*

---

* Lady Fitzharding's brother, the Earl of Jersey, married to a Roman Catholic, became a favourite of King William's, and their sister Elizabeth, later Lady Orkney, his mistress. Another sister married William's Dutch favourite Lord Portland.

ah, Duchess
e Marlborough.

Sir Godfrey Kneller.

Sarah Duchess of Marlborough. Described in her will as 'my own
Picture drawn by Sir Godfrey Kneller, which is only a Head', and
bequeathed to her favourite servant Grace Ridley

Sarah Duchess of Marlborough at cards with Lady Fitzharding. Kneller

Though it was a small circle, soon to widen enormously, for the time being all of Sarah's close friends were there. The Prince and Princess of Denmark, Lady Sunderland, Lady Fitzharding, all these were intimates; but to Anne and the Churchills the time was approaching when no name would have more significance than that of Sidney Godolphin. Anne affectionately nicknamed him Mr Montgomery; and with him and the Freemans to protect her she, perhaps for the first time, felt safe.* Lord Chamberlain to Queen Mary of Modena, widower of Margaret Blagge (she died in 1678) and godfather to the Churchill heir, Godolphin (Pope's Patritio) had a great deal more to him than his looks, or Kneller's versions of them, would have us believe (p. 97). 'Physiognomists would hardly discover by consulting the aspect of this lord', wrote Swift, 'that his predominant passions were love and play, that he could some-times scratch out a song in praise of his mistress, with a pencil and a card, or that he had tears at his command like a woman, to be used either in an intrigue of gallantry or politics. His alliance with the Marlborough family & his passion for the duchess were the cards which dragged him into a party [the Whigs] whose principles he naturally disliked & whose leaders he personally hated as they did him.'[17] That of course was a biassed view. Godolphin was not Sarah's lover but her admirer, as she was his. Looking back she all but worshipped his memory. His was 'the most disinterested and honest service that ever was, I believe, performed by man'; and at his death she wrote in her bible: 'the best man that ever lived'.

Godolphin, a short, grave Cornishman, disfigured as were so many people then by smallpox, was indeed devoted to the Churchills, as he was devoted too to Anne and to James's exiled queen to whom, says Swift, he continued to send 'little presents of those things which are agreeable to ladies, for which he always asked King William's leave.'[18]

---

* 'The unreasonableness, impertinence & Brutalety that one sees in all sorts of people every day makes me more & more sensible of ye great blessing God Almighty has given me in three such freinds as your dear self, Mr Freeman & Mr Montgomery, a hapynesse I beleeve no body in my Sphere ever enjoy'd before & which I will allways value as I ought but never can express ye true sense I have of it tho to my last moment I shall make it my endeavour.' Anne to Sarah (undated). (Blen E 18.)

In the Estense Gallery at Modena and now disintegrating from the ravages of woodworm there hangs, in carved limewood, an elaborate vanitas.[19] From the skull in the middle is suspended a medallion bearing the self-portrait of the carver, Grinling Gibbons, and near it, among festoons of flowers, fruit and shells, a score lies open at that verse of James Shirley's, here set to music, which runs:

> The glories of our blood and state
> Are shadows, not substantial things;
> There is no armour against fate;
> Death lays his icy hand on kings.
> Sceptre and crown must tumble down
> And in the dust be equal made
> With the poor crooked scythe and spade.

Of the provenance of the panel nothing is known; yet what more likely than that it was one of those presents so thoughtfully sent by Godolphin to Queen Mary? But that is looking ahead. At the time Godolphin stood as godfather to Jack Churchill, James was still on the throne and, according to Burnet, 'saying every day that he was king and would be obeyed . . . He had both priests and flatterers about him that were still pushing him forward. All men grew melancholy with this sad prospect'.[20] One harsh measure succeeded another until, with the Declaration of Indulgence, it seemed clear that James was bent on disaster. Archbishop Sancroft and six bold bishops refused to read it in public and were sent to the Tower. While their trial was pending Mary of Modena gave birth to a son;* but there were more bonfires and bellringings later for the release of the bishops.

While the Queen had been pregnant, Mary in Holland had by letter closely questioned her sister Anne as to symptoms. 'There was a current report', says Lediard, 'that whilst the Queen either was or pretended to be with Child, the Princess Anne being one Day at Her Majesty's Toilet too inquisitive about that Matter, She received a severe Check from the Imperious Queen (or, as some say, She threw Her Glove at Her Royal Highness's Face), upon which She retir'd from Court.'[21] Whether or not the warmingpan in which the child was said to have been smuggled into the royal bedchamber was a

* James Francis Edward Stuart (the Old Pretender), born June 10, 1688.

figment of Mary's mind or another's (it was soon discarded), her correspondence with Anne gives an impression of conscience opposed by self-interest and of conscience coming off a poor second. They wanted to believe it and so, by a process well known to modern commerce, they did believe it. 'I shall never now be satisfied', Anne wrote to her sister, 'whether the child be true or false. Maybe 'tis our brother . . . Where one believes it, a thousand do not. For my part, unless they do give a very plain demonstration . . . I shall ever be of the number of unbelievers'.[22]

Few births can have been more public, for James had invited many witnesses and many came, but most of them were Roman Catholics. Anne stayed at Bath; Churchill sent excuses; Sarah's sister Frances was there but Sarah was not. The most she could testify to was the pregnancy, and even in that she seemed full of doubt. She had been, she said, 'an eye-witness of all that proceeding for about seven months and I must say there was great cause given for jealousies. If it was a true child it was certainly very ill order'd, but if it was not I don't see how it could bee better'.[23] Ambiguity was in the air; but one might have thought that Sarah and Anne as mothers would appreciate that were every mother expected to prove her child her own, the judgment of Solomon would be called for every day.

James's time was running out and nothing, nor anyone except himself, could now save him from exile. On the day of the bishops' acquittal the invitation, signed by the Bishop of London and others, had gone to William in Holland. In Whitehall there were as always rumours, but Mary of Modena, nursing her babe, simply could not believe that her friend and stepdaughter, the other Mary, would come over with William to seize the crown. 'That I will never believe', she wrote to her, 'for I know you to be so good that I don't believe you could have such a thought against the worst of fathers, much less perform it against the best, that has always been kind to you & I believe has always loved you better than all the rest of his children. Besides, if you knew anything of this horrid design, I am sure you could never writ so many kind letters & so full of indifferent subjects as you have done of late both to the King and to me. You have too much sincerity'.[24] But Mary's will had become William's and William saw himself as the saviour of Europe.

And so 'a great king with strong armies and mighty fleets fell all

at once, and his whole strength, like a spider's web, was so irrecoverably broken with a touch that he was never able to retrieve what for want both of judgment and heart he threw up in a day'.[25] On November 5th, 1688, with the Protestant wind behind him, William landed near Torbay.

The desertion of James by Churchill rankled in Sarah's mind for the rest of her life. It was not of course that she doubted him, but she hated the thought that posterity might do so. Even in her will she inserts a note 'for the history' that Churchill left James 'with great regret at a time when 'twas with hazard to himself, and if he had been like the patriots of the present times he might have been all that an ambitious man could hope for by assisting King James to settle popery in England.'[26]

At Blenheim one can still see the King's warrant for Churchill's command at Salisbury in 1688, beginning, 'Right Trusty and Well-beloved We Greet you well . . .' and it gives one pause. Yet remembering all the hangings and whippings and hopeless mismanagement, what better did James deserve? The defection of his daughter Anne is said to have cut him to the heart. It was nothing to him that her weak husband—'Est-il possible?' as he called him—had gone over to the enemy; it might be an advantage; but Anne he loved and her going grieved him. In Anne's flight from London Sarah played a leading part. In her *Conduct* she remembers:

> Upon the landing of the Prince of Orange the King went down to Salisbury to his Army and the Prince of Denmark with him; but the News quickly came from thence that the Prince of Denmark had left the King and was gone over to the Prince of Orange, and that the King was coming back to London. This put the Princess into a great Fright. She sent for me, told me her Distress and declared that rather than see her Father she would jump out at the Window. This was her very Expression.
>
> A little before, a Note had been left with me to inform me where I might find the Bishop of London (who in that critical Time absconded) if her Royal Highness should have occasion for a Friend. The Princess, on this Alarm, immediately sent me to the Bishop. I acquainted him with her Resolution to leave the Court and to put herself under his Care. It was hereupon

agreed that he should come about Midnight to the Neighbour-
hood of the Cockpit and convey the Princess to some Place
where she might be safe.

The Princess went to Bed at her usual Time to prevent
Suspicion. I came to her soon after; and by the back Stairs which
went down from her Closet Her Royal Highness, Lady Fitzharding and I, with one Servant, walked to the Coach, where we
found the Bishop and the Earl of Dorset. They conducted us
that Night to the Bishop's House in the City and the next Day
to my Lord Dorset's at Copt-Hall. From thence we went to the
Earl of Northampton's and from thence to Nottingham, where
the Country gathered about the Princess; nor did she think
herself safe till she saw that she was surrounded by the Prince of
Orange's Friends.

As this Flight of the Princess to Nottingham has by some
been ignorantly not to say maliciously imputed to my Policy
and premeditated Contrivance, I thought it necessary to give
this short but exact Relation of it. It was a Thing sudden and
unconcerted; nor had I any Share in it farther than obeying my
Mistress's Orders in the Particulars I have mentioned; though
indeed I had Reason enough on my own Account to get out of
the Way, Lord Churchill having likewise at that time left the
King and gone over to the other Party. Quickly after this the
King fled into France.

It is a careful account, bettered only perhaps by Pepys who fills in
the detail: that Sir Benjamin Bathurst 'heard a sudden outcry of
women and . . . found it to be a universal cry among the ladies that
some[one] or other had carried away the Princess . . . Upon Mrs
Danvers going into her Highness's chamber to call her & receiving noe answer to her call, she opened the bed and found the
Princess gone & the bed cold, with all her yesterday's cloaths even to
her stockings & shoes left behind . . .'[27] The Bishop had had the
gumption to bring with him his sturdy gardener, George London,
so that one way and another the women were well protected and
the only loss (in the mud) was one of Anne's shoes.

Professor Walcott, commenting on 'the superbly timed defection
of Marlborough' adds, 'The defection of his wife was possibly just

as decisive. She was responsible for persuading the Princess Anne to forsake her father and . . . contemporaries considered her desertion the final blow that led James to abandon his kingdom.'[28] As for Sarah's contention that the flight was unpremeditated, a contemporary critic of her *Conduct*, called it downright affectation. One wonders too what she thought when she read in Lediard:

> About six Weeks before the Princess left Whitehall She had order'd a private Staircase to be made, under Pretence of a more commodious Passage to the Lady Churchill's Lodgings, but in Reality that she might make her Escape that Way when Her Person or Liberty was in Danger. The Night before Her Royal Highness withdrew, the Lord Chamberlain [Godolphin] had Orders to apprehend the Ladies Churchill and Berkeley [Fitzharding]; but the Princess desiring him to defer executing those Orders till she had spoken to the Queen, the Lord Chamberlain did so accordingly.

At Nottingham Colley Cibber was called in to help wait at table:

> The post assigned me was to observe what the Lady Churchill might call for. Being so near the table, you may naturally ask me what I might have heard to have passed in conversation at it; which I should certainly tell you had I attended to above two words that were uttered there, and those were "Some wine and water". These I remember came distinguished and observed to my ear because they came from the fair guest whom I took such pleasure to wait on. Except at that single sound all my senses were collected into my eyes, which during the whole entertainment wanted no better amusement than stealing now and then the delight of gazing on the fair object so near me. If so clear an emanation of beauty, such a commanding aspect of grace, struck me into a regard that had something softer than the most profound respect in it, I cannot see why I may not without offence remember it; such beauty, like the sun, must sometimes lose its power to choose and shine into equal warmth the peasant and the courtier . . .[29]

CHAPTER III

William and Mary

1688-1702

———◆———

'I know not how it happens', wrote Arthur Maynwaring to the Duchess of Marlborough in 1709, 'that from the beginning of the world to this day it was hardly ever known that any one was called to govern a kingdom, either as principal or deputy, that was extremely fit for the office.'[1]

To the nation and to the world James II had appeared manifestly unfit to govern, but when William landed from Holland the English thought him, at first sight at least, little better. Grotesquely ugly and with a chronic asthmatic cough which hindered conversation, he hated talking and, adds Burnet who knew him well, business of all sorts. He had been, says the bishop, much neglected in his education and had moreover 'a very ungraceful manner of laughing, which he seldom did unless he thought he had outwitted somebody, which pleased him beyond measure'. His favourite pursuit was war and after that, hunting. 'The depression [*sic*] of France was the governing passion of his whole life. He had no vice but of one sort in which he was very cautious and secret. He had a way that was affable & obliging to the Dutch but he could not bring himself to comply enough with the temper of the English, his coldness & slowness being very contrary to the genius of the nation.'[2]

Sarah was from the first poorly impressed by King William's friends. He was 'not very nice in the Company hee keept, for by his choice hee had for the most part men that one should think oneself very miserable to bee condemned often to bee shut up with';[3] but then, as she said, she had not expected William to stay. After saving

England from slavery he would, she supposed, return to Holland. 'But I do solemnly protest', she added, 'that if there be Truth in any Mortal, I was so very simple a Creature that I never once dreamt of his being King. Having never read, nor employed my Time in any thing but playing at Cards, and having no Ambition my self, I imagined that the Prince of Orange's sole Design was to provide for the Safety of his own Country by obliging King James to keep the Laws of ours, and that he would go back as soon as he had made us all happy. I was soon taught to know the World better. However, as I was perfectly convinced that a Roman Catholick is not to be trusted with the Liberties of England, I never once repined at the Change of the Government. I might perhaps wish it had been compass'd by some other Man, who had more Honour and Justice than he who could depose his Father-in-law and Uncle and then act the Tyrant himself; but I never once wished that the Change had not been made.

And as to giving King William the Crown for Life, at first I did not see any Necessity for such a Measure; and I thought it so unreasonable that I took a great deal of Pains (which I believe the King and Queen never forgot) to promote my Mistress's Pretensions. But I quickly found that all Endeavours of that kind would be ineffectual; that all the principal Men except the Jacobites were for the King and that the Settlement would be carried in Parliament whether the Princess [Anne] consented to it or not. So that in reality there was nothing advisable but to yield with a good grace.[4]

The gist of it was this. After James II the crown was his elder daughter Mary's and after her Anne's. Dutch William, as Mary's husband, could reign jointly with her only with her consent; and although Mary, utterly submissive, readily gave it, Anne, with every probability of her sister's having an heir, saw her own chance of reigning diminish. In the event, Mary had no child and died young, and William outlived her by only eight years; but if fate had been kinder to them they might easily have outlived Anne, who died in 1714.

If Sarah, loyal to Anne, had been disgusted by the attitude of William, who insisted on wearing a crown as Mary's equal and not, as a courtier put it, as his wife's gentleman-usher, she was equally so by the behaviour of Mary. In her *Conduct* she continues:

> On the Arrival of Queen Mary in England, the Princess of Denmark went to meet her, and there was great Appearance of Kindness between them. But this quickly wore off and a visible Coldness ensued, because Queen Mary grew weary of any Body who could not talk a great deal, and the Princess was so silent that she rarely spoke more than was necessary to answer a Question. And indeed, whatever good Qualities Queen Mary had to make her popular, it is too evident, by many Instances, that she wanted Bowels.
>
> Of this she seemed to me to give an unquestionable Proof the first Day she came to Whitehall. I was one of those who had the Honour to wait on her to her own Apartment. She ran about it, looking into every Closet and Conveniency and turning up the Quilts upon the Bed as People do when they come into an Inn, and with no other sort of Concern in her Appearance but such as they express; a Behaviour which, though at that time I was extremely caress'd by her, I thought very strange and unbecoming. For whatever Necessity there was of deposing King James, he was still her Father, who had been so lately driven from that Chamber and that Bed; and if she felt no Tenderness, I thought she should at least have looked grave or even pensively sad at so melancholy a Reverse of his Fortune. But I kept these Thoughts in my own Breast, not imparting them even to my Mistress, to whom I could say any thing with all the Freedom imaginable. And it was impossible for any Body to labour more than I did to keep the two Sisters in perfect Union and Friendship.

Queen Mary's conduct does indeed sound unfeeling until one reads in Burnet that William had commanded her to be 'so cheerful that nobody might be discouraged by her looks or be led to apprehend that she was uneasy by reason of what had been done. This made her put on a great air of gaiety when she came to Whitehall ... in which she might perhaps go too far because she was obeying directions and acting a part which was not very natural to her'.[5] In any case, to one who studied faces as closely as Sarah did, the performance was a crude one; but what extraordinary people these were! First the warming-pan myth and now a ghoulish forced gaiety to show a clear conscience . . . But one remembers that they were Stuarts and that both Mary and Anne had a strange automaton quality which made them, given their lesson, carry it out almost as though under hypnosis, unfeelingly and to the letter.

As for Sarah's contention that Mary soon tired of anyone not willing to talk, an early critic pointed out that 'no Person in the World can be so agreable to a woman who loves to talk a great deal as another who loves to talk very little'.[6] However, there was plenty of cause for dissension, and not the least Sarah's monopoly of Anne and the certainty that everything Mary said to her sister would be repeated to her favourite.

For his part in the revolution John Marlborough was now rewarded with the earldom of Marlborough.* William also confirmed his rank of lieutenant-general and gave him the task of reconstituting the army.

In May, 1689 war was declared against France and so, at the head of 8000 men, Marlborough set out for the allies' headquarters in Flanders. Sarah was left to labour, as she has said, to keep the two sisters in perfect union and friendship. Both Sarah and Anne were pregnant; Sarah of her last daughter, Mary; Anne of the Duke of Gloucester. There was a small quarrel about lodgings (always a fruitful source of bickering. Anne asked for some and was denied them), and a much bigger set-to about Anne's allowance. She had heard, she told Mary, that her friends had a mind to make her some settlement. And 'Pray', demanded the Queen, 'what friends have you but the King and me?' This of course was deliberate rudeness. 'I never saw her', says Sarah, 'express so much Resentment as she did at this Usage, and I think it must be allowed she had great Reason. For it was unjust in her Sister not to allow her a decent Provision, without an entire Dependance on the King.'[7]

When the question was raised in the Commons, 'all possible Endeavours' were used to get Sarah to dissuade Anne from pursuing it.

---

* The earls of Marlborough of a former creation had been distant connections on his mother's side of the family.

My Lady Fitzharding, who was more than any Body in the Queen's Favour, and for whom it was well known that I had a singular Affection, was the Person chiefly employed in this Undertaking. Sometimes she attacked me on the Side of my own Interest, telling me that if I would not put an End to Measures so disagreeable to the King and Queen it would certainly be the Ruin of my Lord and consequently of all our Family. When she found that this had no Effect she endeavoured to alarm my Fears for the Princess by saying that those Measures would in all Probability ruin her, for no Body but such as flattered me believed the Princess would carry her Point, and in case she did not, the King would not think himself obliged to do any thing for her. That it was perfect Madness in me to persist and I had better ten thousand times persuade the Princess to let the Thing fall and so make all easy to the King and Queen. But all this was so far from inclining me to do what was desired of me that it only made me more anxious in the Prosecution of it.[8]

Time and again when courage and spirit were called for—to fight smallpox, it might be, or William's meanness to her young mistress (who, after all, had helped him to her father's throne)—Sarah met the challenge magnificently. Anne's sister and brother-in-law were determined that her allowance should come from them as a royal favour. Sarah advised Anne to let Parliament grant it as her own right. Sarah won and Anne was voted her allowance of £50,000 a year, but the resentment of William and Mary was formidable.

Anne was not ungrateful. 'A little above a Year after the Settlement was made', Sarah's record continues, 'I was surpris'd with a Letter from her, wherein she offer'd me the yearly Pension of 1000 l. Some of her Words are these: I have had something to say to you a great while and I did not know how to go about it. I have designed ever since my Revenue was settled to desire you would accept of 1000 l. a Year. I beg you would only look upon it as an Earnest of my good Will, but never mention any thing of it to me; for I shall be ashamed to have any Notice taken of such a thing from one who deserves more then I shall be ever able to return.'[9] It was typical of Anne's gracious way of giving. A thousand pounds was more than many then earned in a lifetime;* and Sarah's own circumstances, she tells us, were not very great. She consulted Lord Godolphin who said there could be no reason in the world for refusing it. She accepted.

Disappointingly, the perfect union and friendship between Anne and her sister deteriorated. In a comic–pathetic Gilbertian way Anne saw her husband, Prince George of Denmark, as admiral, field-marshal and lord-high-everything-else; a fixation which, when Anne came to power, was to prove a nuisance. William, a professional soldier, could not tolerate amateurs in uniform and, in Ireland, snubbed the Prince by refusing to let him travel in his coach. There was but one alternative and it became known as the Prince's Design of Going to Sea. 'You will allow, I believe', Sarah comments, 'that it was very natural for the Prince to chuse a Sea Expedition rather than expose himself again to the like contemptuous Usage'. And we then have the farce of George's volunteering 'and without any Command'; at which 'the King said nothing, but immediately embraced him by Way of Adieu'.[10] Tact was called for, although the word in its present meaning was then unknown.† A desperate attempt at face-saving seems to have been made, even Sarah being appealed to, gently to dissuade the Prince from his Design. It was the sort of ludicrous situation at which only posterity may be allowed to laugh. For want of humour and sensibility Prince George had in the end to be positively forbidden by Queen Mary to go to sea. But the next blow was far more serious. Early in January, 1692, the Queen sent for her sister, again pregnant, and after chiding her about the £1000-a-year allowance, told her that Sarah must be dismissed. Anne meekly but firmly refused and the Queen lost her temper. The following day, recalls Sarah, 'the King was pleased (without assigning any Reason) to remove my Lord Marlborough from his Employments. And I think it is not to be doubted that the principal Cause of it was the Court's Dislike that any Body should have so much Interest with the Princess as I had, who would not

* To give some notion of present-day values one needs to multiply these sums by at least fifteen.

† The O.E.D. gives 1804 as the date of the first usage of 'tact' in its modern sense.

implicitly obey every Command of the King and Queen. The Disgrace of my Lord Marlborough therefore was designed as a Step towards removing me from about her.'[11]

That may have been one of the reasons, but historians have not accepted it as sufficient in itself to warrant the dismissal of Marlborough, whom William had made virtually commander-in-chief. As with outbreaks of war, so in crises of this kind, a number of things will simmer until suddenly some trifle—a rebuff, an intercepted letter, even a barrackroom guffaw—touches off an explosion. 'As a matter of fact', wrote the Marquess of Halifax in 1693, 'he [Marlborough] had been upon secret terms with the Court of St Germains, from which he obtained a written promise of pardon and to which he had succeeded in reconciling his wife's obedient tool the Princess Anne'. After mentioning Marlborough's 'ostentatious jealousy of the Dutch elements' (in particular William's Dutch favourite Hans Bentinck Earl of Portland), Halifax records that the sudden dismissal on January 10th, 1692 aroused the liveliest excitement and considerable sympathy.[12]

On the question of Marlborough's Jacobite dealings, since almost the only contemporary sources are Jacobite, we are on unsure ground; nor can we know how much he told his wife. It is now generally accepted that Marlborough, in common with Godolphin, the Duke of Shrewsbury and others, sought a pardon from James as a matter of insurance, (for after all, if one rash king could lose his throne, so could another), and that for further correspondence with the exiles the Marlboroughs found natural channels in Arabella's son and Marlborough's nephew the Duke of Berwick and in Sarah's exiled sister Frances Duchess of Tyrconnel. Sarah, ever a staunch patriot, is most unlikely to have been directly involved, and the fable concocted at the time about her disclosure of military secrets (a Jacobite invention) has long since been discounted. There remains the belief that in 1689 Marlborough secured a pardon from James on the understanding that Anne too should send a contrite letter, which she did, receiving in return, it is said, forgiveness conditional on her never wearing the crown. For the rest of Marlborough's manoeuvres with St Germains, and they were many, Sir Winston, though perhaps too charitably, dismisses them as so much political expediency and bluff.

At the end of January Anne received from someone who seemed curiously well informed an anonymous letter:

Madam, You may billive if I had not all the respect Imagenable for your Heyness I would not give you this trouble. I begg of you for your own sarke that you will have a care of what you say before Lady Fitzharding, remember shee's lord Portland & Betty Villars is sister. You may depend upon't that these two are not ignorant of what is said and done in your lodgings. Then I leave you to judge whether they make not their court att your expense that's by exposeing you & preserving the King as they call it. You know you are but an Honorable Person being in the hands of the Dutch Gards and should there be anny vilence offerd what cann wee doe for you? or indeed for our selfs. The King & Queen has been tould that there has not passed a day since lord Marleborrow's being out that you have not shed tears. If I durst I could soone convince you that his misfortune coms from your own ffamelly [household]. If it ended in his turning out he meight leave it with patience, but if resolutions hold he will be confined as soone as the Parlement is up, and if you doe not parte with his Lady of your selfe you will bee obliged to it. Would you but inquire where Lady Fitzharding was the weeke before he had his dismission you would feind that her tiers were not verry sinceare . . . Upon the whole matter he's the Lookiest Gentleman in England* who's sister governs the King and his wife the Queen & is the entire confidant of poor deluded Lady Marleborrow. If you sleight this advice I wish you may not have cause to repent it.

I am with all respect your
Heyness's unknowen dutyfull humble servant
J.H.

The postscript reads: It has been taken great notice of Lord

* Probably referring to Edward Villiers first Earl of Jersey (1656–1711), brother of Lady Fitzharding, Betty Villiers (Lady Orkney) and Lady Portland (all children of Lady Frances Villiers and cousins of Barbara Villiers Duchess of Cleveland). Lord Jersey was popular with William. Lady Jersey was a close friend of Queen Mary's.

Godolphen & Cherrey Russele's* being at lord Marleborrow's
Lodging so late ye neight he was turn'd out.[13]

There was not much Anne could do about it except to pass on the
letter to Sarah, who kept it as she kept everything. As for Lady
Fitzharding, Anne had long been suspicious of her, even jealous, but
Sarah would not listen. She preferred on the whole to suspect Lady
Fitzharding's sister Betty. 'The world said', comments Sarah, 'that
Lady Fitzharding betrayed my Lord Marlborough to King William
& Queen Mary. I had proofs that she did many things that were
wrong . . .'[14] but she was probably no worse than a trimmer with a
foot in each camp. Betty Villiers, William's mistress, was different.
'There was very good reasons to believe', runs one of Sarah's
endorsements, 'that in the time of King William's anger against
Lord Marl. Mrs Villiers did a great deal of mischief, tho' I had been
extreamly civill to her not out of any design which is allways the
reason that such wemen are courted, but I loved her sister Fitzharding
when I was but a child & living with all the intimacy imaginable
with her, that friendship introduced her sister Mrs Villiers afterwards
my lady Orkney to my lodgings where she heard us talk with
freedom, but nothing that ought to have don Lord Marlb. or me any
prejudice. There was no doubt but she joynd with every body that
were Lord Marlboroughs enemys at that time in order to remove
him from his employments . . .'[15]

Although in the role of wife-kept-in-the-dark Sarah is never
altogether convincing, this does seem to have been a puzzle she
brooded on, as she brooded on Marlborough's desertion of James.
Years later we still find her protesting utter ignorance of the reason
for Marlborough's dismissal although, she owns, she had 'often
thought it might have been compassed by the malice of the tories
who were very well with my lord Portland & he had ever a great
prejudice to my Lord Marl. And my lady Orkney, then Mrs
Villiers, was so great an enemy of mine that it was very probable
she would help forward anything of that Nature . . .'[16]

Of Lady Fitzharding Sarah says frankly, 'Tis certain I had more
fondness & inclination for her then any body I ever knew in my
life'.[17] And later, 'She had a great deal of wit but was interested.

* Admiral Edward Russell, later Earl of Orford (1653–1727).

And Queen Mary showed more inclination for her than any body. I lov'd her extremely tho' I found at last her morals were not good.'[18] The two ladies-in-waiting were often together gossiping or, as one sees in the Kneller at Blenheim (p. 49), playing interminable games of cards. Anne's jealousy, although she was ashamed of it, was not to be hidden.

'I have in another paper', remarks Sarah, 'explain'd something of the Naggs Head & Loupa, which ment Lady Fitzharding & Lady Bathurst. They were both entertaining wemen & I was often with them, but the queen [Anne] did not care for any body that I gave any time to.'[19]

Bewildering indeed is the labyrinth that winds among these nick-names and grisly the snares and pits that beset it. Lady Fitzharding (née Villiers and at one time Mrs Berkeley) sets a double problem in the form of twin nicknames: Loupa* and Mrs Hill; which last (a really monstrous red herring) has understandably led biographers to suppose that Sarah's cousin, Abigail Hill, made a much earlier appearance than she did and that Sarah made such a fuss of her that Anne became jealous. All of which of course is nonsense. Some things are more deeply hidden than others, and it is not to be wondered at that at Blenheim a slight endorsement of Sarah's (one of thousands) eluded Sir Winston's team of experts and those who have followed them. Upon an undated letter of Anne's Sarah has written: 'When the queen† thought I was too kind to Lady Fitz' and 'This letter shews that it was not unreasonable for me to speak to her upon her kindness to Mrs Masham since it appeares that she was uneasy at my kindnesse for Mrs Hill which was the name then that my Lady ffitzharding went by.'

Anne's letter begins:

'tis impossible to be better satisfyed then I am with you in every thing & I hope I have not done any thing lately that should make you think other ways. I must confess Mrs Hill has hereto-

---

* Loupa. 'Coupa' (as sometimes printed) must surely be a wrong transcription. The obvious interpretation is Lupa: a harlot. The Nag's Head was almost certainly Lady Bathurst, née Frances Apsley.

† Sarah as often as not, when writing of the past, refers to Anne as queen when, at the time in question, she was Princess of Denmark.

John Duke of Marlborough. Attributed to Closterman

The Ladies Henrietta and Anne Churchill. Kneller

fore made me more uneasy then you can emagin but seeing every day more & more how litle reason I had for my feares I should be ye unreasonablest creature in ye world if I gave way to them any longer & what is past I beg may be both pardoned & forgot for I am ashamed & angry with my self that I should have bin so troublesome to my deare lady Marleborough. I fancyed that Mrs Hill had out of Curiosity intercepted my letter* but I beleeve I am mistook . . .[20]

And again:

. . . I can't end this without beging deare Mrs Freeman to have a care of Mrs Hill for I doubt she is a Jade & tho I can't be sure she has done any thinge against you there is too much reason to beleeve she has not bin soe sincer as she ought. I am sure she hates your faithfull Mrs Morely & remember none of her famely weare ever good for any thing. That which makes me say this is becaus I see she begins to talk more freely & to be more with you then she has bin of late & knowing some yeares ago you weare quite fallen out & by degrees you weare made up till at last you weare as much bewitch'd by her as ever & knowing besides your inclination for her & her very agreeable humour I feare you may in time againe grow as fond of her as you have formerly bin. . . . I beg your pardon for saying so much on this subject & if you are angry I will never mention any thing of it more . . .[21]

Since the Villiers set were far too powerful to be ousted, Anne decided on a line of indifference. 'Lady Fitzharding', she complained to Sarah, 'has bin ye spleenatick'st out of humoure creature that ever was seen when she has bin with me but to all others she has bin very easy, but it dos not att all afflict me nor nothing can as long as my deare deare Mrs Freeman continues kind, her freindship being one of the things I valu most & which I would not loos to be empress of the world'.[22]

* Anne's letters to Sarah were so frequently intercepted that to one of them (undated) she added: 'Who's ever hands this lights in I wish they may be so good natur'd after they have reade it to lett it go by this night's post, that my deare Mrs Freeman may not have any cause to think her faithfull Morely neglected writing, for she never will fail her in any thing that lyes in her power . . .' (Blen E 17).

Had the Morley–Freeman friendship needed the cement of shared affliction there was now no want of it. In the spring of 1692, and not for the last time, a false and baseless charge of conspiracy to murder William and restore James was trumped up by one Robert Young, then in gaol, against Marlborough and others. Young was a forger (though not having lost his ears made him, said Sarah, an irreproachable witness) and the net he had prepared was a crude one. There were of course forged signatures, Marlborough's included; and there was also said to be an incriminating note hidden in a flowerpot at the Bishop of Rochester's, but it could not be found. However, Marlborough was arrested, those refusing to sign the warrant were ignored, and he was sent to the Tower, where he stayed from May 5th to June 15th. As Sarah was preparing to visit him there (and she had difficulty in getting a pass), another blow fell. On May 22nd Charles, their younger son, died. All she could do was to write; and so it is that we have that rare thing (for the rest she insisted on his burning) a love letter from Sarah, and one of such feeling as to make us wish there were more:

> Wherever you are, whilst I have life, my soul shall follow you, my ever dear Lord Marlborough, and wherever I am I should only kill the time wishing for night that I may sleep and hope the next day to hear from you.[23]

Later, with the help of a bribe, she was admitted, and in the meantime there were soothing letters from Anne:

> I hear that Lord Marlborough is sent to the Tower; and though I am certain they have nothing against him . . . yet I was struck when I was told it, for methinks it is a dismal thing to have one's friends sent to that place. I have a thousand melancholy thoughts, and cannot help fearing they should hinder you from coming to me; though how they can do that without making you a prisoner I cannot imagine . . . But let them do what they please, nothing shall ever vex me so I can have the satisfaction of seeing dear Mrs Freeman; and I swear I would live on bread & water between four walls, with her, without repining; for as long as you continue kind, nothing can ever be a real mortification to your faithful Mrs Morley, who wishes she may never

enjoy a moment's happiness, in this world or the next, if ever she proves false to you.[24]

Every day Anne sent more encouragement:

I am sorry with all my heart dear Mrs Freeman meets with so many delays; but it is a comfort they cannot keep Lord Marlborough in the Tower longer than the end of the [legal] term; and I hope, when Parliament sits, care will be taken that people may not be clapped up for nothing, or else there will be no living in quiet for anybody but insolent Dutch and sneaking mercenary Englishmen. Dear Mrs Freeman Farewel; be assured your faithful Mrs Morley can never change . . .[25]

Finding Sarah downcast she begs her, 'For God's sake have a care of your dear self and give as little way to melancholy thoughts as you can . . . I fancy ass's milk would do you good and that is what you might take morning or afternoon, as it is most convenient . . .'[26]

When Marlborough was released there was no return to favour. On the contrary, he was to remain in the wilderness for six years. William, insecure in a strange country, is believed to have been far more concerned about the strength of the Anne–Marlborough faction and the possibility there of a rival court than of any danger from the direction of St Germains. Sarah saw it differently, both then and later, and perhaps it is time to take up the thread of her tale:

I protest that the loss of my Lord Marlborough's Employments would never have broke my Rest one Minute, but the being turned out is something very disagreeable to my Temper; and I beleive it was three Weeks before my best Friends could persuade me to go to a Court which (I thought) had used my Lord Marlborough very ill. However, at last they prevailed. And I remember Lord Godolphin said that it could not be thought I made any mean Court to the King and Queen, since to attend the Princess was only paying my Duty where it was owing. I waited therefore on my Mistress to Kensington. The Consequence was such as my Friends, having no Reason to apprehend it, had never thought of.

The consequence was in fact consternation and fury; and if

Sarah's friends were surprised they must have been as naïve as they were foolish. As a matter of commonsense and common politeness, as well as of etiquette, when a courtier was disgraced his wife stayed from court; so that when Anne entered the drawing-room attended by Sarah, Mary was dumbfounded. It was the strangest thing that ever was done, she wrote to Anne the day after, and the only thing that had prevented a scene was Anne's condition. 'But now I must tell you plainly, Lady Marlborough must not continue with you . . .' It is a long letter and not in its general tone an unkind one. It ends: 'At some other Time we shall reason the Business calmly, which I shall willingly do, or any Thing else that may shew it shall never be my Fault if we do not live kindly together, nor will I ever be other by Choice but your truly loving and affectionate Sister'.[27]

Mary as Queen had a right to exact obedience, but in demanding Sarah's removal she was asking for something Anne felt it would be death to give. Sadly then but with Stuart obstinacy Anne refused, and was promptly told to remove from the Cockpit. This of course on Mary's part was malicious and also probably illegal since the place, on the Downing Street side of Whitehall, had been given to Anne by Charles II. It was Anne's turn to decide not to make a scene. Having begged Syon House of the Duke and Duchess of Somerset, she quietly withdrew there with her modest court. William, says Sarah, tried his utmost to dissuade the owner from letting Anne stay there, 'but his Grace had too much Greatness of Mind to go back from his Promise,* so there was an End of that Matter'.[28]

When, at Syon, Anne gave birth to a dead child, she sent a message to Mary, who visited her, but there was no reconciliation. Sarah's dismissal was again demanded and again denied and Anne was left trembling and as white as the sheets. After that, several snubs were devised for Anne and her husband. They were not saluted. They were no longer to have guards (Anne was robbed). Friends were forbidden to call. At St James's Church the custom of leaving the text of the sermon upon the Princess's cushion was to be discontinued . . . and so on. It was all too spiteful and petty to be bothered with; yet to Sarah it meant much and she brooded on it. Repeatedly she proposed to Anne that she herself should retire and so make things

---

* This tribute of Sarah's, in her *Conduct* (1742), to the Duke of Somerset was written long after his proposal of marriage to her in 1723.

easier; and each time, with increasing agitation, Anne implored her not to think of it:

> But I beg it again for Christ Jesus's Sake that you would never name it any more to me. For be assured, if you should ever do so cruel a Thing as to leave me, from that Moment I shall never enjoy one quiet Hour. And should you do it without asking my Consent (which if I ever give you, may I never see the Face of Heaven) I will shut myself up & never see the World more but live where I may be forgotten by human Kind.[29]

The Earl of Rochester, uncle to Anne and Mary, offered to act as go-between and was rebuffed. With Stuart pride and obstinacy on both sides the case was hopeless and would remain so until the Queen's death. The only possible link might have been Anne's sickly child the Duke of Gloucester, to whom the Queen sent rattles and other presents, but on those occasions no more notice was taken of Anne 'than if she were a Rocker'.

From Syon Anne and her household moved to Berkeley House, Piccadilly. She can never have felt the need of Sarah's company more than in this winter of 1692–3 when Mrs Jennings had a stroke and her daughter was sent for to St Albans. Although paralysed, the old lady lingered, to die the following May. Anne sent doctors and as usual wrote every day: 'I hope in Christ your Mother will do well & am sorry with all my Soul I have this occasion to serve you. I have nothing more to say but beg my dear Mrs Freeman would always be so just as to beleeve I would go round ye world upon my baire knees to do her or hers ye least service & she may be assured ye least command from her shall be obeyed with all ye hast emaginable by your faithfull Morley'.[30]

As the time dragged on, Anne became concerned for Sarah's health—

> . . . your Mother may lye as she is now a good while. I must beg once more that you would try to get a little rest or else you will never hold out; & since your own house is so neare that you may be called in a minute upon ye least accident, in my humble opinion you had better go to bed there every night & get what sleep you can. Nature cannot beare to be so harassed as you do

your deare self but will at last sink under it. For God's sake be perswaided to take some ass's milk, that will not hinder you from any thing but will cool & sweeten your blood which must needs be heated & out of order with sitting up so perpetualy. I have an ass in St James's Park & if you will make use of it send me word & I will take care you shall have it a Saturday morning. I have bin led about my chamber today & was caryed into ye garden for a litle aire . . . but 'tis impossible for your faithfull Morley to be at ease in her mind while dear Mrs Freeman is in such a tormenting condition.[31]

Anne's gout* is already severe (she is only twenty-eight), but she is unselfish enough to say, 'I swaire I could with pleasure endure 10,000 fitts of ye gout or any risk in ye world if it could be but a reliefe to my deare Mrs Freeman when she is in trouble'.[32] When Sarah asks for Dr Radcliffe's† opinion, Anne tells her he is surprised that Mrs Jennings has lasted so long. To which Anne herself adds, 'I cannot see that you have any just cause to reproch your self for any thing. I am confident you never omitted ye least title of your duty to your Mother while she was living & in her sickness you have shown your self ye best & tenderest daughter that ever was'.[33]

Anne offered a horse-drawn litter to bring Sarah and her mother to London, but it was too late. After twenty-five years of widowhood and a trying illness, Mrs Jennings had died. Her will, dated February 12th, 1692, is curious. After directions for burial 'att the Aby church att St Albans as near as I can conveniently be laid by my four first children . . . my daughter's coach to follow my hearse directly to the church gate without any further ceremony', she left everything to her 'dear and loving daughter Sarah Countess of Marlborough' and for her 'sole and separate use and benefit'. As for Marlborough, her 'dear son-in-law', she added, 'tho I love him with all my heart he shall not hereafter have any benefit concern or intermedleing with any part or parts of my estate . . . but shall be therefrom . . . fully &

---

* Gout is not common in women. Both Anne and Sarah may have suffered from it, but it seems more likely that most of the trouble in their hands, knees and elsewhere was due to some form of arthritis.

† Dr John Radcliffe (1650–1714), chosen by Anne as her principal physician in 1686. Later he fell from favour and declined to attend at her death.

wholly debarred & excluded . . . my said dear & loving daughter to be sole executrix'.[34]

When Frances Tyrconnel, exiled in France, heard of the will she was displeased and said so. Of all the many good reasons man has provided for family discord, wills and money have always come first; and in this case there may have been cause for grievance. When in the revolution of 1688 the Tyrconnels had fled to Ireland, 'We came away', Frances reminds Sarah, 'with nothing but close on ouer backs', and for years, again according to herself, they were kept on very short commons. During that time she bombarded her sister, in a huge and all but illegible scrawl, with undated screeds mainly, it would seem, about petticoats and 'father beads'. (Her spelling even for those days is wonderful). But of Sarah and her own nieces she writes from time to time quite fondly. 'I hope the little butys is well though you say nothing of them . . . I think I love mis Harriat & her Mother better then all the world put togather'. Could Sarah possibly send her half-a-dozen 'right worickshire cheses & one chestershire chise'? (At 'Cheshire' she makes three attempts and crosses them out). 'Allso a litle berill of grots or ote mele. I have been mighty happy thus for lent . . .' Cheese? Sarah scribbles on the back of the letter: 'The 3 horse shoes in newgate street over against St Martans the best chese is to bee had', and so the parcel goes off. 'Yuer magnificent parsel of cheses would make me a fraide of begeing', exclaims Frances gratefully, 'Wee will in a privat way drinke yuer helth this lent & do less penance then if wee had not shuch friends'.[35]

And then comes the will trouble, Frances 'not being so much as named in my poore Mother's will. I need not', she tells Sarah, 'believe you contributed to the making so unkind a will . . .' She sends a load of complaints and ends, 'All these things might apeare less heavey then at a time when some are starveing & others not'. To which Sarah replies testily, 'I hope I shall bee in better temper to answer then I beleive you were at the writing'. As for their mother's will, 'I have no reason to find fault with it because it was certainly intended very kind to me, tho I know nothing but debts you are excluded from. I am very far from saying or thinking you had noe reason to expect a share in what my mother left, but I ded not make my mother's will and if she had lived a thousand years I should never have named the settling her estate to her . . .'[36] And so on. Frances must have known what she was up against. She sounds warmhearted, scatterbrained, uncomplicated. This is typical of her:

> Yuer letter made me wet it more then you could have don when a writing & if you can in the least remember the reall passion & inclination I ever had for you 'tis what you will esele belive & I must again aferme that in my hole life I never ded love any thing better then yuer selfe whatever star rained for thes late yers to make all a peare rong . . .[37]

And so for Sarah it was back to Berkeley House for consoling talks with Anne. They had no need to weep over old Mrs Jennings; but in the loss of young children there was deep mutual sorrow, and in William and Mary, or so they thought, mutual tyranny and dislike. In conversation of course it was perfectly safe to refer to William as the Monster or Caliban or the Dutch Abortion. Everybody did it. But when the same epithets appeared in Anne's letters, Sarah thought it best to cross them out. 'What is blotted out', she is careful to explain, 'is something that frighted me where she expresses so much haterid to her sister but', she adds, 'if it were to bee don now I should not bee so carefull'.[38] (The endorsement is undated).

Was Mary so disagreeable? Bishop Burnet, who had known her since girlhood, did not think so. 'She seems', he wrote, 'to be a person raised & prepared by God Almighty to make the nations happy . . . All that I can possibly set against her is that she is the most reserved person alive, unto whose thoughts no creature can enter further than as she discovers them'. As a queen she was all but idolised; as a wife she loved William; her spare time was spent stitching, praying, gardening, building, or arranging porcelain, which last was her passion.

Switzer refers to 'that excellent Princess' [Mary] who 'lost no Time but was either measuring, directing or ordering her Buildings; but in Gard'ning, especially Exoticks, she was particularly skill'd'.[39] At Hampton Court, to set off Wren's new front, Charles II's Great Fountain Garden was perfected; while at Kensington the cottagey palace that had lately been Nottingham House was given the kind of box and yew troytown Dutch William liked.

'The Queen brought in the Custom or Humour as I may call it', wrote Defoe, 'of furnishing Houses with China-Ware . . . piling their China upon the tops of Cabinets, Scrutores & every Chymney-Piece, to the Tops of the Ceilings'.[40] At Kensington the Queen's Gallery alone displayed 154 pieces of porcelain and in the overmantel-sketches Grinling Gibbons made for the Queen every inch is packed with pots of all sizes, even to the cornice.[41]

It all sounds innocuous enough. Queen Mary was popular and the nation's grief real when in 1694 she caught smallpox and died. Burnet, who attended, wrote:

> We were, God knows, a sorrowful company, for we were losing her who was our chief hope & glory upon earth . . . She died on the 28th of December about one in the morning in the 33rd year of her age. During her sickness the King was in an agony that amazed us all, fainting often & breaking out into most violent lamentations. When she died his spirits sank so low that there was great reason to apprehend that he was following her. For some weeks after he was so little master of himself that he was not capable of minding business or of seeing company.[42]

While Mary lay dying Anne, herself ill, sent daily messages, on one occasion delivered by Lady Fitzharding who 'broke in, whether they would or not . . . to express in how much Concern the Princess was'.[43] Burnet records a 'reconciling message' from Mary to Anne, which Sarah denies; but while Gibbons was drafting Mary's monument (never erected), Lords Sunderland and Somers were trying to heal the breach between William and Anne. 'My lord, do what you will', said the King wearily when Somers found him alone at Kensington, 'I can think of no business.'

On Anne's side, such was Stuart resentment, there was just as little enthusiasm. As heir-presumptive she now felt strong enough to dictate her terms, which meant of course that there must be no question of Sarah's dismissal. 'Caliban', Anne warned Sarah, 'will without doubt endeavour to make us yeild rather then make one step towards it him self', but she will never part with her 'till she is fast lockt in her coffin'.[44] In the meantime Anne, again referring to William, trusts 'in Heaven we shall not be better freinds then we are now unless we chance to meet there'.[45]

When in the following September (1695) William took Namur

somebody, not Sarah, persuaded Anne to write and congratulate him. 'Nobody upon earth could have made me do it', Sarah commented later, 'but I was never the councellor upon such great occasions'.[46] Though William sent no answer it was obvious to everyone that the quarrel must end and so it did. Anne was allowed to move into St James's Palace and Sarah with her; and everyone else flocked there to pay them court.

Marlborough, however, still out of favour, became in 1696 involved in another Jacobite plot to murder William. This was no flowerpot penny-dreadful, but a full-scale conspiracy headed by Sir John Fenwick who, when arrested, accused Marlborough, Russell, Godolphin and Shrewsbury with having written treasonably to the exiled king. According to Macaulay Marlborough, under the long ordeal, remained serene and even slightly contemptuous, Godolphin uneasy but self-possessed; whereas Shrewsbury, who was probably the least to blame, crumpled, resigned and retired abroad. Godolphin too retired for the time being. Yet nothing was proved and the charge recoiled. Fenwick was executed on January 28th, 1697.

In the following October with the Treaty of Ryswick signed, England found herself no longer at war with France. William, his chief occupation gone, 'reassumed his farther Pursuit of Gard'ning, in altering & making a considerable Improvement to the Gardens [of Hampton Court] and making that great Terrass next the Thames, the noblest Work of that kind in Europe'.[47] It could have had a mellowing effect. In 1698 he at long last recalled Marlborough, reinstated him in the army and Privy Council and made him Governor to Anne's nine-year-old son the Duke of Gloucester. The child was delicate (all of Anne's children were hydrocephalic) and subject to fits of 'ague', but Marlborough's appointment was of course a mark of restored favour, and the two young heirs, Gloucester and Jack Churchill, then twelve, could now play at soldiers together. But Sarah was not overjoyed. There was a muddle over the young Duke's household: Anne was to choose whom she pleased and then, later, no she was not to, the King would do it. When Marlborough ventured to tell William 'that the Princess . . . had engaged her Promises to several Persons and that not to be able to perform those Promises would be so great a Mortification as he hoped His Majesty would not give her at a Time when any thing of

74

Trouble might do her Prejudice, she being then with Child', the King 'fell into a great Passion and said She should not be Queen before her Time'.[48]

It was sad that one so expert at war should prove crude at peace; and it was a great deal sadder that Gloucester should have Marlborough as his guardian for only two years before he died. In the glimpses we catch of him in Anne's letters he is almost always ill. 'Dr Ratcliffe . . . asures me ye child is in no manner of danger but however I can't help being afraid till he has quite lost his ague for methinks 'tis an ugly thing for such a distemper to hang so long upon one of his age . . .' And, 'tho I love him very well, I cant bragg of his beauty'.[49]

Some blamed his death on the cramming he had had from his over-zealous preceptor, Bishop Burnet, who boasted:

> I went through geography so often with him that he knew all the maps very particularly. I explained to him the forms of government in every country . . . I acquainted him with all the great revolutions that had been in the world & gave him a copious account of the Greek & Roman histories & of Plutarch's Lives. The last thing I explained to him was the Gothic constitution & the beneficiary & feudal laws. I talked of these things at different times near three hours a day . . . He was then eleven years old . . . He was the only remaining child of seventeen that the Princess had borne, some to the full time & the rest before it . . . His death was a great alarm to the whole nation. The Jacobites grew insolent upon it & said now the chief difficulty was removed out of the way of the prince of Wales's succession.[50]

The close of William's reign saw a handful of seemingly unconnected happenings, all of which were to have great influence in Sarah's life. In 1698 Henrietta, her eldest daughter, married Francis, son of Sidney Godolphin and Margaret Blagge. The following year their son Willigo was born, and Anne, Sarah's second daughter, married the Earl of Sunderland's heir, Charles Spencer. In or about the year 1700 one Abigail Hill was introduced by her cousin Sarah, Countess of Marlborough, to the Princess Anne as a bedchamberwoman; and Bishop Burnet married for the third time. On March 3rd, 1701 the Act of Settlement was passed, to exclude the Pretender from the English throne and to ensure the Protestant succession; and on September 6th Marlborough, as commander-in-chief of the English forces in Holland, signed the Grand Alliance treaty between England, Holland and Austria, at Loo, in Sarah's presence. Ten days later James II died in France and Louis XIV proclaimed the Pretender, James III King of England. In January, 1702 Robert Harley, a moderate Tory, was narrowly elected Speaker of the House of Commons; and on March 8th King William died. Sarah commented:

And now, after all I have related of the King, and after so much Dislike as I have expressed of his Character & Conduct, you will perhaps hardly believe me in what I am going to say. When the King came to die, I felt nothing of that Satisfaction which I once thought I should have had upon this Occasion. And my Lord and Lady Jersey's writing and sending perpetually to give an Account, as his Breath grew shorter and shorter, filled me with Horror. I thought I would lose the Best Employment in any Court sooner than act so odious a Part. And the King, who had given me so much Cause to hate him, in that Condition I sincerely pitied: So little is it in my Nature to retain Resentment against any Mortal (how unjust soever he may have been) in whom the Will to injure is no more.[51]

CHAPTER IV

Hail, Glorious Anna!

1702-1704

The glorious scene opens, the reign that is to see the victories of Marlborough, the capture of Gibraltar, the union with Scotland; in science the discoveries of Newton, in architecture the masterpieces of Wren and Vanbrugh and Hawksmoor, in literature the works of Swift and Defoe, of Addison, Congreve and Pope; the reign that will foster the Protestant Succession and put England herself in the foremost place in the world . . . and all this to be launched by a queen who is very nearly a cripple.

After seventeen pregnancies and numberless attacks of gout or arthritis Anne limped, with assistance, to her coronation. She was thirty-seven and had no heir. Of her four chief assets it might fairly be said that the Marlboroughs and Godolphin made three. The fourth was her Stuart will, reinforced by faith, which meant, beyond obstinacy, that when put to it she could and would force herself to accomplish the near-impossible and so, by example, inspire others to do likewise.

Sarah, though not, like Marlborough, at all times an asset, undoubtedly was so at the beginning of the reign when Anne was groping and Sarah's competence, plus Godolphin's, was worth more than a queen's ransom. And while it would be a shocking thing, as historians warn us, to see Queen Anne only as Sarah saw her, the views of an observant witness, no matter how biassed, are, in the absence of a definitive biography, not to be despised.

Sarah's opinion of Queen Anne—written, printed, incised in marble—ranges from the kindly to the savage and then, in old age, back nearly to the kindly again. When Voltaire, visiting Blenheim in the autumn of 1727, asked if he might see the Duchess's memoirs, she said, 'Wait a little, I am at present altering my account of Queen Anne's character. I have begun to love her again since the present lot have become our governors'.[1] Sarah was then drafting for the Rysbrack statue the inscription which began:

> Queen Anne had a person and appearance very graceful, something of majesty in her look. She was religious without any affectation, and certainly meant to do everything that was just. She had no ambition* . . . She was extremely well bred and treated her chief ladies and servants as if they had been her equals; and she never refused to give charity when there was the least reason for any body to ask it . . .

and so on. 'I have put these facts together', Sarah explained, 'for materials for the person who writes the inscription. They are all true, notwithstanding what she was imposed upon in doing at the end of her reign.'[2]

Bashfulness, a minor weakness of Anne's not inherited from her father, had to be overcome before her first speech, which she made 'with great weight and authority and with a softness of voice and sweetness in the pronunciation that added much life to all she spoke'.[3]

On April 23rd, 1702 Anne was crowned, and on May 4th war was declared against France. Louis XIV's proclamation of 1701, acknowledging the Pretender as king, had given 'a universal distaste to the whole English nation'.[4] It was a challenge William would have leapt at had he lived. It was bequeathed to Anne and to Marlborough, now Knight of the Garter, Captain-General and Master of the Ordnance—a trust formidable enough to daunt any soldier and any queen—to vanquish the seemingly unconquerable power of France.

On May 6th the Queen appointed Godolphin Lord Treasurer, the office most nearly approximating then to Prime Minister. Sarah, looking back from a later reign, says that Godolphin, in his attitude to Anne, was 'like Mentor in Telemachus, Her Majesty being the most ignorant and helpless creature liveing'.[5] But already she felt well entrenched for here, as Sir Winston observes, was 'a close confederacy which had been slowly and tensely wrought. Anne had

* In another version this reads: She always meant well. She had no false ambition.

insisted upon the equality of their intercourse, but this privilege was strictly limited. Mrs Morley, Mr and Mrs Freeman and Mr Montgomery—there could not be a tighter thing. They formed a group as integral and as collectively commanding as anything of which there is record in our annals.'[6] So long as she could count upon those three champions—and that surely must be forever—the Queen felt unassailable.

On May 12th Sarah was appointed Groom of the Stole and on June 19th Keeper of the Privy Purse and Mistress of the Robes; whilst her daughters, Lady Henrietta Godolphin and Lady Anne Sunderland,* joined her at court as Ladies of the Bedchamber. It seemed the ideal plan. Marlborough must be often abroad and so, with her brood all but fledged, what else could Mrs Freeman have to do all day but play cards and talk to Mrs Morley? And when the court was at Windsor, Mrs Freeman would still be at hand because Mrs Morley had made her Ranger of the park and had given her the pleasant lodge that went with it. Anne may have been surprised at how seriously Sarah took her new duties. Zestfully she hurled herself into them and after setting the privy purse in order (no more bribes, no more poundage, no more bought places), she turned to the question of the Queen's clothes.

Some women (Frances Tyrconnel for one) would have lost their heads and ordered wildly. Sarah knew better. She knew that extravagance was senseless and that nothing, not even a queen's wardrobe, could resist the cool, calmly thought out policy of rationalisation she had long since learned to apply to everything. Jewels, for example, could be hired, and doubtless with state robes there could be similar economies; for after all, with the best will in the world, what could be more vulgar and futile than to overdress a martyr to gout? 'Some people', Sarah remembered, 'to be revenged of me for not letting them cheat have said she was not fine enough for a queen, but it would have been rediculous with her person & [one] of her age to have been otherwise drest. Besides her limbs were so weakend with the Goute for many yeares that she could not indure heavy cloaths & she really had every thing that was hansome & proper for her'.[7] For state occasions of course there

* Her husband, Charles Spencer, succeeded his father as 3rd Earl of Sunderland in 1702.

would have to be velvet and ermine, but for ordinary days clothes should be ordinary and good. It is only now and again, in Anne's letters, that one seems to catch a subdued hankering for nonsense. 'I beleeved when I writt to you about my manto* for the thanksgiving day', she wrote, 'it was a hard task, but heavy clôths are soe uneasy to me that I could not help just mentioning it tho at ye same [time] I had a mind to be fine too & in order to be soe I intended to have two diamond buttens & loops upon each sleeve . . .'8

At times the Queen could be quickly humoured, at times not. With affection on both sides much can be tolerated; but Sarah had much to do and so, when too pressed for argument, she would resort to finality and put an end to difference with her 'Lord, Madam, it must be so!'† But clothes were frills. There were far more serious things to see to, among them the Queen's politics, which all too obviously needed to be taken more firmly in hand. However, the same policy applied and in the schooling of Anne there was nothing daunting or new. 'I used to pass many hours in a day with her', Sarah recalled, 'and allways endeavour to give her notions of loving her country, of justice & governing by the laws & making her self bee beloved rather then feard & I allways showed her how easy that was to doe when she had [it] so much in her power to doe good and I ever told her that nothing was so great & honourable as to govern upon the conditions that a crown was taken nor no way so certain as that to keep it as long as she lived.'9

Excellent, what could be better? 'You shall always find me', declared Anne in her first speech, 'a strict and religious observer of my word'. But then what of parties? Was Mrs Freeman, like Mr Freeman, Mr Montgomery and Mr and Mrs Morley, a true Tory? No, she was not. She was emphatically Whig. How indeed could Mrs Freeman live up to her name and be otherwise? The Whigs were for freedom—free thinking, free acting; no shackles, no popery, no wooden shoes and every man on his own merits. It was because James had mocked at all this that he had lost his crown, and woe betide his daughter if she scorned the same lesson. Ah yes, but

* The manto (*manteau*) was referred to as a new fashion in the reign of William, when it was disapproved by Lady Fitzharding as too informal to be worn on a king's birthday.

† Quoted in the 1712 pamphlet *The St Albans Ghost*.

Queen Anne. J. Riley

Prince George of Denmark. After J. Riley

the rock upon which James had foundered, everyone knew, was the Church of Rome. Anne would never make that mistake. Her rock was the true church, the Church of England, to which the very nation was bound and wedded.* Come now, what had the Whigs to say to that? What sandy foundation had they to offer instead? To one whose grandfather had been beheaded, a Whig might too easily conceal a Roundhead or a republican. And what, pray, was the Whigs' attitude to the divine right of kings?

These were awkward questions. Not of course that Sarah could not counter them, but she knew that the answers would at this stage be unacceptable. She knew too that, as in the case of the warming-pan, Anne could make herself believe or disbelieve exactly as she chose. It was vexing. Conversion might take longer than she had thought. 'I did allways endeavour', she wrote later, 'to give the queen a true notion of our two parties, having had a great deal of experience of the men on both sides and having had certain know-ledge of a great many truths and facts which her Majesty could hear from nobody else'.[10]

It was early days for knowing how obdurate Anne could be; yet to one of Sarah's tenacity, even had she known it, the more hopeless the cause, the greater the challenge must always be. She never gave up, never spared herself for an instant and was never to be deflected from what she, quite often misguidedly, thought was right. In her draft self-vindication prepared by Bishop Burnet she makes him say:

The Duchess was now continually trying all the methods & all the arguments she could think of to remove or soften those violent prepossessions the Queen still retained against those whom the Duchess thought the best part of her subjects. With this view she argued frequently with the Queen & sometimes not without a warmth natural to sincerity which yet hitherto did not appear to leave any uneasyness behind it. To the same purpose she wrote many & long letters & by some expressions in the Queen's answers one would have judged that she had now & then laid down her prejudices, but by more & more it

---

* The first clause in the Act of Settlement (3 March, 1701) runs: That whoever shall hereafter come to the possession of the Crown shall join in communion with the Church of England as by law established.

appeared that her aversion to the very name of Whig was too deep to be cur'd. The Duchess tried to introduce other names for the opposite parties but to little purpose. For tho she found as yet no alteration in the Queen towards herself on this account, yet the work she had undertaken proceeded but by very slow degrees. Something or other still retarded it and made it go very heavy.

For Anne too it was saddening. It seemed to her such a pity that, in a hitherto flawless sky (the sunshine day they had longed for in gloomier reigns) this plague-ridden cloud of politics should have to appear at all. Why, with everything in the world to talk about, from the weather to clothes, must they always have to argue politics? Yet even so the world seemed duller than ever when Sarah was absent. 'I'me sure you can never doubt of my wishing to be with you every hour in ye day', wrote Anne, 'I am now in great hast to be drest, this being my Company Day tho ye weather is soe bad I fancy no body will come. However I will be in a readiness to receive any body that will give them selves the trouble. Therefore for this time, my deare deare Mrs Freeman farewel.'[12] After the first rush for places courtiers had begun to find Anne's court almost as moribund as William's. Many left off coming.

The Queen's Privy Council, Sarah noticed, was almost solidly Tory. That would not do at all. For the Tories favoured a limited war at sea. Only from the Whigs could Marlborough count on solid support for a full-scale land war in Europe. 'My Lord Normanby (soon after Duke of Buckingham)', Sarah noted, 'the Earls of Jersey and Nottingham, Sir Edward Seymour, with many others of the High-fliers, were brought into Place; Sir Nathan Wright was continued in Possession of the Great Seal of England, and the Earl of Rochester in the Lieutenancy of Ireland. These were Men who had all a wonderful Zeal for the Church, a Sort of publick Merit that eclipsed all other in the Eyes of the Queen. And I am firmly persuaded that, notwithstanding her extraordinary Affection for me, and the entire Devotion which my Lord Marlborough and my Lord Godolphin had for many Years shewn to her Service, they would not have had so great a Share of her Favour and Confidence if they had not been reckoned in the Number of the Tories.

'For my own part the Word Church had never any Charm for me in the Mouths of those who made the most Noise with it; for I could not perceive that they gave any other distinguishing Proof of their Regard for the Thing than a frequent Use of the Word, like a Spell to enchant weak Minds.'[13] If Anne chose to call Tories the Church Party, Sarah preferred to call them Jacobites and to warn the Queen that they were after her crown, or even her life.

'I feared the loss of Mrs Morley's life as well as of her three kingdoms', Sarah remembers, 'and out of these apprehensions, too well grounded, I was perpetually telling her that the Whigs were in her true interest and the Tories out to destroy her; and when I saw she had such a partiality for those that I knew to be Jacobites, I asked one day very seriously whether she had a mind to give up her crown, for if it had been her conscience not to wear it I do solemnly protest I would never disturb her nor struggle as I did, but she told me she was not sure the Prince of Wales was her Brother and that it was not practicable for him to come here without ruin to the religion and country . . .'[14]

In a running battle of this sort, Sarah realised, even the smallest gain was not to be despised; so that when Anne proposed four new Tory peers, Sarah begged for a fifth on behalf of Whig Mr Hervey, who was surprised and never ceased to be grateful. His benefactress ought, he said, to have been born in the Golden Age, for only then could her virtues have been appreciated. He launched into verse:

> Here beauteous Nature all her strength combined
> To form ye finest body, noblest mind.
> No single virtue can we most commend,
> Whether ye Wife, ye Mother or ye Friend.

'In short', the new lord concluded, she was 'one so every way worthy of ye Favour she possesses by her incessant Vigilance and incorruptible Fidelity . . . that ye People as well as we her Friends ought to pray for ye Continuance of it for their own Sakes'.[15]

Whether Marlborough, a moderate Tory who strove to keep clear of parties, approved of his wife's proselytising for the Whigs at the risk of friction with the Queen is extremely doubtful; and that too when he must have known Sarah was being egged on by their violently Whig son-in-law Charles third Earl of Sunderland. Sunderland, whom Sir Winston calls a rasping figure, obnoxious to the Queen, was to be one of the five tyrannising lords, as Anne called them—the others were Wharton, Somers, Halifax and Orford —who, as the Junto, formed a self-appointed Whig Cabinet in which lay much power.

Queen Anne, while begging Godolphin to save her from the merciless men of both parties, believed that she could take her pick of Whigs and Tories (mostly Tories) and so rule with an ideal coalition. With this, in theory at least, Marlborough, loathing faction, showed sympathy; and the Marlborough-Godolphin ministry soon formed, which was to last eight years, was in fact a mainly Whig coalition. But the situation was complicated by two conditions which would not apply today: one, that no politician could afford to ignore the Court Party (those who supported the crown on the principle that all opposition was more or less factious and on the practical grounds that the crown was the source of patronage in church and state); and two, that England, with a total population of less than six million, was ruled by the sovereign with the help of a relatively small company drawn for the most part from a few aristocratic and landed families who between them controlled huge blocks of votes in parliament and in the counties.

What nobody could then of course be expected to realise, let alone rectify, was that the machinery of government was so primitive and antique, the wonder was that it could be made to work at all. The sovereign, no longer omnipotent but still powerful, chose or dismissed her ministers as she would. She was not bound to choose them from the party with a majority in the House of Commons; while the House of Lords had infinitely more power than it has today. There was no Prime Minister, as we know that office, although the Lord Treasurer was sometimes given that name; and the Cabinet system was only just beginning to evolve.

Yet if anyone in Anne's reign could have foreseen the twentieth-century pattern, with the ultimate power vested not in sovereign, Lords or Commons but in Prime Minister and Cabinet, with a handful of Civil Service and trades union leaders, he could scarcely have been expected to understand or to believe it. Even now, to foreigners at least, it seems a strange way of governing; and indeed, as Sir Winston remarked, it is the worst system of government in the world—except for all the other systems of government.

In writing of these times it would be as easy to overestimate the influence of Sarah as it would be to underestimate the power of Anne. Anne lacked humour, vision and intellect, her outlook was insular, but she was not shallow or commonplace and she was not, like her husband, a fool. Once her mind was made up, all the arguments in the world could not shake her; and by the same token, once her confidence had been given—to Sarah, to Marlborough—it took a vast amount of guile and disillusion to undermine it.

In the first year of Anne's reign, as in more recent times, an Englishman needed to be stouthearted. Louis XIV, brazen as Mars, had overrun the Spanish Netherlands (now Belgium) and had taken the line of fortresses there regarded by Holland as her protective barrier. Philip V, Louis' grandson, ruled in Spain, with a prospect terrifying to the whole of Europe including ourselves that the two countries, Spain and France, might be united under one crown; a horror which, it was felt, must at all costs be prevented. Marlborough's first task was to assist Holland and restore her barrier, which meant flinging the French troops back from the fortresses of the Meuse.

At the Hague Marlborough was treated like the prince he was soon to become. 'A finer work of art', says Trevelyan, 'has never been shown there. The statesmen of Europe were received at the top of the staircase by a glorious living portrait of a Milord, every inch a soldier and a courtier; said indeed to be fifty years of age but in the prime of manly beauty, with a complexion like a girl's; talking charmingly in bad French; seeming to understand all and sympathise with everyone.'[16] Already he had won the confidence of Antoine Heinsius, the Grand Pensionary of Holland, the first and by no means the least of his overseas conquests.

Yet in spite of all this and in spite of her own confidence and affection in Marlborough, Anne begged him to ask the Dutch to make her husband supreme commander of the Grand Alliance over Marlborough's head! It was solemnly proposed and with infinite tact rejected. It may have been now or later (the documents are undated) that some wag decided to compensate Prince George for his disappointment by making him Steward of Colchester. It was rather too bad. When the thing broke upon the town there were glum faces at Kensington and titters in the coffee houses. Anne wrote to Sarah:

> I can never thank my dear Mrs Freeman enough for her kindness to Mr Morley & her humble servant on all occasions, espessially for ye Consern you express for this ugly foolish thing about the Princes being Steward of Colchester. I have asked him again about it & he assures me he was never spoke to by any body nor knew nothing of it till Sir Thomas Cook came & offerd him the thing . . . I wish you would ask Lord Treasurer what I can do to putt a Stop to all this Noise that has bin made about this thing for 'tis very disagreeable & I do not doubt but my enemys will improve all things to my disadvantage.[17]

For the sake of peace Prince George was in the end allowed to call himself Lord High Admiral and was voted a huge allowance. Everyone except Anne and himself knew that it was ludicrously too much and Lord Sunderland said so, thus calling down upon himself the wrath of Sarah and the lasting enmity of Anne.

In Flanders, one might have expected that, with Prince George brushed aside, Marlborough would be given a clear field. He was granted the command and with it a squad of Dutchmen called field-deputies who made it their business to prevent engagements and forbid the commander-in-chief to fight battles, for fear of hazarding the Dutch troops. To a grave extent this recurrent nuisance was to thwart Marlborough's plans and to try his singular store of patience to the uttermost. His letters to Sarah speak very little of a triumphant general. To begin with, 'You know of all things', he reminds her, 'I doe not love writting', so much so that, with all the official mail he has to deal with, 'were it not for my Zele for her Majesty's service, I shou'd certainly desert.'[18] Yet he promises his wife, 'You shall never faile of hearing from mee every post.'[19] The labour of writing was bad enough, and when letters had been written there was the agony of waiting, no matter how pressing the message, for a favourable wind. To reach Queen Anne at Windsor the news of the victory at Blenheim took eight days.

In May Marlborough wrote to Sarah from the Hague, 'The Quiet

of my life depends onely upon your kindnes & I beg you to believe
the truth of my soull which is that you are dearer to mee then all
things in this world'.[20] In August he shows concern for her health.
'You naturally have a good constitution & if you take this illness*
in time, I hope bleeding some times & your own fisick pretty often
will give you health & a long life which I doe from my soull wish
you . . . You think your letters miscarry or that I have not time to
read them. I doe asure you that your letters are so welcome to mee
that if they should come in the time I were expecting the enemy to
charge mee I could not forbear reading them.'[21]

In spite of every disadvantage, not least the Dutch field-deputies,
Marlborough's campaign against the French on the Meuse was
successful and a thanksgiving service, attended by Anne and Sarah,
was held in the unfinished cathedral of St Paul's. On October 22nd,
1702 Anne wrote charmingly to Sarah to tell her that she had
resolved to make Marlborough a duke. Sarah was stricken. 'When
I read the letter first', she tells us, 'I let it drop out of my hand and
was for some minutes like one that had received the news of a death
of one of her dear friends . . . I was so easy for anything of that kind,
having before all that was any use, by which it is plain I have no
great taste for grandeur.'[22]

To Sarah the privileges of a dukedom were little more than a
matter of precedence ('I like as well', she said, 'to follow five hundred
as one') and the obligations were onerous. But Marlborough felt
differently and, with the encouragement of Heinsius who maintained
that the commander's prestige in Europe called for it, decided to
accept. The one serious reservation was money: how support a
dukedom without an estate? Anne, foreseeing this, made him a grant
of £5000 a year for her lifetime and in December asked Parliament
to extend that grant to benefit his heirs; but that they declined to
do.†

Privately Anne then offered 'dear Mrs Freeman & Mr Freeman'
£2000 a year out of her privy purse, 'besides the grant of the five.
This can draw no envy', she added, 'for no body need know it . . . I
beg my dear Mrs Freeman would never any way give me an answer

* Illness unspecified.

† Sir Winston Churchill estimates Marlborough's income at this time (Dec.
1702) as £60,000 a year. (Churchill, op. cit. I, 617).

to this, only comply with the desires of your poor unfortunate faithful Morley* that loves you most tenderly & is with the sincerest passion imaginable yours.'[23] Sarah declined but, as Sir Winston exclaims, 'Alas for the glitter of our story! We shall have presently to record . . . how nine years later in her bitterness she reclaimed this gift with arrears, and how the Queen paid every penny of it.'[24]

In the winter of 1702–3 Anne, who shared Marlborough's loathing for faction, found her government sharply divided over the question of Occasional Conformity, an extension of the Test Act of 1673 whereby only those taking Communion in the Church of England could qualify for state or municipal office. The Test Act had led to cynical lip-service and hypocrisy to such an extent that that professional trouble-maker Dr Sacheverell had 'hung out the bloody flag of defiance' and thundered against it. Though it bore every sign of having come from the Devil, the Occasional Conformity Bill was welcomed as a godsend by political extremists, who determined to make as much mischief with it as they could. Defoe called it playing bo-peep with God Almighty; and at first it fooled the Queen who, taking the bill at its face value, sent Prince George to the Lords to vote for it. Though rejected, it was to prove one of several political themes—The Church is in Danger! Invitations to Hanover! Jacobite Invasion!—twanged repeatedly on the one-string fiddle that was Parliament during Anne's reign; and if, for brief seasons, things seemed to be going smoothly, it was astonishing how quickly a storm could be raised simply by plucking one of those hackneyed notes.

For the Marlboroughs 1703 began tragically with the death of their son Jack, first Marquis of Blandford. He was seventeen and heir to the dukedom. Everyone had found him a delightful young man. 'Your son danced a minuet last night', Anne tells Sarah, 'which upon my word he performed very well & I do realy beleeve in time he will make a very fine dancer, therefore I hope you will encourage him in it'.[25] His godfather Godolphin, with whom he was staying at Newmarket when he died from smallpox, found him 'not only the

* This phrase, with slight variations, the Queen applied to herself after the death of her son the Duke of Gloucester in 1700. It would appear deliberately to echo the Churchill motto: Faithful but unfortunate.

best-natured & the most agreeable but the most free-thinking & reasonable creature that one can imagine for his age.'[26]

On January 2nd, 1703 young Blandford wrote to his father:

I would have answered your last letter sooner if I could have thought what to say for myself in defence of so great a fault, and I find the longer I think the less I have to say; so that I resolved to write this letter to beg my dear Papa's & Mama's pardon for what I have done, and to promise them never to do so again. I owne that I have done some of the things that my Mama complains of but she sais if she had told you them with all the agravations [exaggerations] she heard them you would have bin much more angry with me than you are, and I can't say anything to them because I don't know what they are. I would have writ to my Mama now but that by what she said to me in her letter I am afraid she never will throughly forgive me, which has greived me so much that I cannot tell how to write till I have some hopes of being freinds with my dear Mama; and I hope my Dear Papa will be so kind as to intercede for me with Mama and to be perswaded that no body can be more heartily sorry for having done amiss than, Dear Papa, your most dutyfull son

Blandford[27]

On February 9th he wrote to his mother:

I received a letter from Mr Godolphin last post and the joy I had when I found I had some hopes of being freinds with my Dear Mama is not to be express'd; but I can't think my self so happy till my Dear Mama can find some time to lett me have a letter from her and I am sure there can be no greater pleasure than [that] would be to, my Dear Mama, your most dutyfull son

Blandford

On February 20th he was dead. His death, says Burnet, went very deep in his father's heart; and as for Sarah friends feared for her reason*. Anne's offer to go to her ('ye unfortunat ought to com to ye unfortunat') was declined; nor can Godolphin's words have been of much comfort. This, he said, was 'the greatest occasion of letting the

* Inconsolable in black she is said at this time to have haunted the cloisters of Westminster Abbey.

whole world see that God Almighty has blessed you with a Christian patience and fortitude as eminent as ye reason and understanding by which you are most justly distinguished from the rest of your sex.'[28]

Marlborough, after making a new will ('If I must dye without a son') in favour of Godolphin's son Francis,* left for Holland, whence he wrote to Sarah:

I doe conjure you by all the kindness I have for you, which is as much as ever man had for woman, that you will take the best advice you can for your health & then follow exactly what shall be prescribed . . . You & I have very great reason to bless God for all wee have, soe that wee must not repine att his taking our poor Child from us but blesse & praise him for what his goodness leaves us.

He urged her to 'live soe as that one should chearfully dye when it shall be his pleasure to call for us', and ended, 'I am very sensible of my own frailtes, but if I can ever be soe happy as to be always with you & that you comfort & assiste mee in these my thoughts, I am then perswaid'd I should be as happy & contented as 'tis possible to bee in this world'.[29] Whether Sarah found consolation in his admonitions or preferred Lady Evelyn's 'Sorrow does not kill soe quick as those that feel it are apt to wish', who shall say? For a time she began to hope that she might have another son, but that too failed her.

In Flanders Marlborough was again being frustrated beyond endurance. His letters are full of troubles, from the cussedness of the Dutch to 'those little inconveniencys of the head eake which are but too naturall to mee'. Sarah, taking her cue from Anne, prescribes ass's milk. It is not a success. 'I was yesterday troubled with the head eake', he tells her, ' & this day have sickness in my stomack which I beleive is occasion'd by the ass's milk'. He will give it one more trial . . . Disaster. 'Now that I am well', he writes, 'I may acquaint you that the ass's milk had soe disorder'd mee that I did not stur out of my chamber Sunday Munday & Tuesday last, which has made me

* Francis Godolphin, married to Marlborough's eldest daughter Henrietta, was to have been made Earl of Marlborough and to have taken the family name of Churchill. Marlborough's youngest daughter Mary, then single, was left £20,000; and Sarah another £2000 a year.

take a resolution of leaving itt off. I did in my former letters desire that some more Ruborb & Licherish might bee sent mee by some Officer . . . It may bee sent by the first Yacht'. And when Sarah has leisure, will she please call at Sir Godfrey Kneller's and see 'if he has any of the Queens Pictures [portraits] by him. A good Copie will bee as good as an originall. It is for the Princess Sophia I mean the Electoris of Hannover'.[30]

The ageing Electress, a lively, personable woman next in line to the English throne and so, as can be the way with successors, frowned on by Anne, had said she would take it very kindly if someone could procure the Queen's portrait for her; and very kindly she took it. Sarah, who had been able to get her nothing better than what she herself called a very ill copy was dumbfounded by the cornucopia of bounty which cascaded in return. Sophia, vowing that she valued the portrait more than the whole universe, sent her the universe worked in tapestry, then valued at £3000, plus about £3000 in cash 'to lay out in silver table plate or sconces as I liked, to put in the room with the hangings she sent me. I ded not chuse such things as I thought uselesse & troublesome', Sarah explains, 'but I desired that the money might be laid out in plain gold plates for the table & that the Ellectors armes might bee put upon them that Posterity might see the Honour that she had don me, & this plate was given by the Duke of Marlboroughs will, at my request, after my death, to the heirs as they succeeded of his family'.*

As with Anne so with Marlborough, Sarah insists that her letters be burned. How she reacted to his complaints, to what extent she reassured him, we can only surmise from what he writes to her. Thus from Bonn:

If you had not positively desir'd that I should always burn your letters I should have been very glad to have keept your dear letter of the 9th, it was soe very kind & particularly upon the subject of our living quietly togeither, til which happy time comes I am shure I cant bee contented & then I doe flatter my self I should live with as much satisfaction as I am capable off. I wish I could recall twentie Yeares past, I doe asure you for noe other reason but that I might in probabillity have longer time &

* Only one of these gold plates now remains at Blenhein.

be the better able to convince you how trully sensible I am att this time of your kindness which is the only real comfort of my life, soe ~~that shou'd I be so unhappy as to see you return to that indifferency which has been the occation of a great deal of uneasyness, I shou'd then have noe comfort left in this life~~ & whielst you are kind, besides the many blessings it brings mee, I cant but hope wee shall yett have a Son, which are my daily prayers . . .[31]

It is easy to look back and see the victories that lay before him—and even at that time there were those who predicted that though he had lost a son, fame would be his heir[32]—but to Marlborough in 1703 it must have seemed like the end of all things, the end of his dynasty, the end of his career. There was no solution but retirement to the English countryside with a loving wife. Never child longed more impatiently for anything, he assured her, than he did for peace that he might be always with her; but of what fate had left them he must above all be able to count on her love, 'for if you doe not love mee & shou'd use mee ill I should have very little concern for anything in this world, for I believe never anybody's happiness depended soe much upon another's kindness as mine at this time does upon you'.[33] The English Malady—the spleen, the black dog of chronic depression—had him by the heart and was worrying the life out of him; and Sarah of course suffered with him. And what of Anne, she who confessed she was of a temper always to fear the worst? Unexpectedly, she now wrote Sarah one of the finest letters of her life, the letter Sir Winston calls magnificent and momentous and one which ranks her with Queen Elizabeth and the greatest sovereigns of the English line:

*Windsor, Saturday**
The thoughts that both my dear Mrs Freeman and Mr Freeman seem to have of retiring gives me no small uneasiness, and therefore I must say something on that subject. It is no wonder at all that people in your posts should be weary of the world, who are so continually troubled with all the hurry and impertinencies of it; but give me leave to say you should a little consider

---

* It is rare for Queen Anne to date a letter; nor in writing to Sarah does she include salutation or signature.

your faithful friends and poor country, which must be ruined if ever you should put your melancholy thoughts in execution. As for your poor unfortunate faithful Morley, she could not bear it; for if ever you should forsake me, I would have nothing more to do with the world but make another abdication; for what is a crown when the support of it is gone? I never will forsake your dear self, Mr Freeman, nor Mr Montgomery, but always be your constant faithful servant; and we four must never part till death mows us down with his impartial hand.[34]

With the glory of England at stake, says Sir Winston, Anne subordinated party politics to the supreme need. 'Her magnanimity and her sense of proportion expressed the genius of the English race in adversity'.[35] It remained to be seen how Marlborough and his duchess would respond. Marlborough was profoundly moved: for such a queen he would gladly lay down his life. Sarah was far less deeply impressed; indeed she seems almost to have taken Anne's gesture for weakness. 'She flattered herself', Coxe suggests, 'that little exertion was now wanting to gain a complete victory over the political prejudices of her royal mistress. She therefore teased the queen with her eulogies of the Whigs and her censures of the Tories, whom she involved in one common accusation of Jacobitism'.[36]

Marlborough too, though stubborn, was urged by his wife to change his politics, to back the Whigs who supported the war and to oust the extreme Tories who were steadily undermining him on the home front. It was high time for them to vanish and so make room for the soundly saved. When a cuckoo is in the nest it is not in its nature to be tranquil. Nothing would content Sarah until the Tory high-fliers—Seymour, Jersey and Nottingham—had been forced to fly and, in Nottingham's case, had been succeeded by Robert Harley, Speaker in the Commons and now also Secretary of State; while Henry St John became Secretary at War.

In November Marlborough returned and, with Queen and Duchess, welcomed at Windsor the Archduke Charles, the Austrian claimant to the Spanish throne. From Lady Russell we have a glimpse of Sarah in waiting after the banquet:

Now the service being done, Lady Marlborough stood ready

with her towell & bason of water. Our young King,* risen from the table, offered to take the towell from the lady. She held it fast, but he prevailed, took the napkin, diped in the water, took one of the Queens hands & washed her fingers ends & then his own, gave back the napkin to the lady & with it one of the finest diamond rings, desiring her to ware it.[37]

The winter brought its dreary crop of vexations—an attempt to deprive Marlborough of his command in favour of the Elector of Hanover (George I-to-be); a Tory effort to revive the Occasional Conformity Bill, and so on—and then, as Marlborough was leaving for Flanders and for the campaign which would lead to Blenheim, Sarah sprang a mine as devastating as it was unexpected. While bearing in mind her age, the age for pardonable tantrums, one may still think that few women would have made so much of (apparently) so little or sent a husband into battle so disheartened. Even to read his letters at this time is to feel depressed; and Sarah's of course are missing. He denies her accusation that he has been intriguing with an unnamed woman. She rejects his denial. He is utterly wretched. Her suspicion, he says, must vanish, but he can never forget that she refused to accept his word. It must forever make him miserable. 'I loved you so tenderly', he writes, 'that I proposed all the happiness imaginable in living quietly with you the remaining part of my life. I do to my great grief see that you have fixed in you so very ill an opinion of me that I must never more think of being happy . . .' And his letter ends with a curse which cannot, in Sir Winston's view, refer to anyone but Sunderland:

My heart is so full that if I do not vent this truth it will break, which is that I do from my soul curse that hour in which I gave my poor dear child to a man that has made me of all mankind the most unhappiest.[38]

Of Sunderland's share in the mischief nothing is known; nor can one with any certainty name the woman. All that need be said is that Sarah had a strange habit of keeping letters and that now and again, after centuries of burial, one—unclassified, undated—may surface to find or at least appear to find its place in the jigsaw.

* The Archduke Charles titular King of Spain; afterwards the Emperor Charles VI.

Your letter on four sides of paper', writes Lady Southwell in an undated letter to Sarah, 'I think as rediculous as your whole carriage has been to me . . . and thô in your letter you proclaim your lord an ill husband as I often heard you doe everywhere and are willing to discharge the cause of it upon any body but your self, give me leave to tell you (with the same frankness you use to me) that . . . what you call your misfortunes have proceeded wholly from your self. I should not have had a thought of giving any answer to such a letter, only to shew you I act with more sincerity by assuring you that I neither am nor ever will be Your Graces humble servant

E. C. Southwell*[39]

Edward (Swift's Ned) Southwell had married Lady Elizabeth Cromwell, 'an heiress of 2000 l a year' and daughter of the Earl of Ardglass. They had had three sons when she died in childbirth in 1709.

Nonsensical though it was, the affair had blackened his whole horizon as, on April 8th, Marlborough embarked at Harwich. To make matters still worse Sarah at the last moment handed him a paper containing the things which in the heat of argument she had forgotten to say. It was some days later that remorse overtook her, and it may have been well for England that it did. Marlborough, in his letter to her from the Hague, dated April 29th, refers to the spleen and melancholy occasioned by the Harwich paper, but on May 5th we have a more cheerful picture. 'Your dear letter of the 15th', he tells her, 'came to me but this minute . . . it is so very kind that I would in return lose a thousand lives if I had them to make you happy . . . I took yours that you wrote at Harwich out of my strong box and burnt it; and if you will give me leave, it will be a great pleasure to me to have it in my power to read this dear letter often, and that it may be found in my strong box when I am dead. I do this minute love you better than ever I did before. This letter of yours has made me so happy that I do from my soul wish we could retire and not be blamed. What you propose as to coming over I should

* The next letter in the same bundle at Blenheim is from the Duchess of Ormonde, again undated, in which she bids Sarah 'think seriously how you'd bear any bodys wishing Mr Southwell an ill husband'. (Blen E 39).

be extremely pleased with, for your letter has so transported me that I think you would be happier in being here than where you are, although I should not be able to see you often. But you will see by my last letter . . . that what you desire is impossible, for I am going up into Germany, where it would be impossible for you to follow me; but love me as you do now and no hurt can come to me. You have by this kindness preserved my quiet and I believe my life; for till I had this letter I have been very indifferent of what should become of myself. I have pressed this business of carrying an army into Germany in order to leave a good name behind me, wishing for nothing else but good success. I shall now add that of having a long life, that I may be happy with you.'[40]

It is a hazardous task to attempt to probe the minds of the dead; and in these graphs of the heart one sees strange acrobatics. 'Only Sarah Jennings', wrote the ninth Duke of Marlborough, 'could command the confidence of John Churchill . . . He was a true romantic . . . To him Sarah was a radiant and wonderful being whom he was reluctant to place in this world at all . . . He did not possess intellectual excellencies, but idolized those qualities in a woman. It was his wont to worship things; he worshipped intellect in his wife . . . Her masculine qualities made her the dearer in his eyes because they were the complement of his own nature'.[41]

The letter Marlborough prized (he will have had it by heart) is missing; but with that in his thoughts, and so new-hearted, he set out for the Danube and the greatest battle of his life.

Critics of Sarah's *Conduct* (1742) were quick to point out that although she had made room for such trifles as King William's dish of peas gobbled before Princess Anne, she had scorned to record the battle of Blenheim. But that of course, in her own self-vindication, was not her purpose; for the perpetuation of Marlborough's glory she had made other plans. So now in this present biography of the Duchess, nothing could be more needless than a chronicle of that battle, their descendant, Sir Winston Churchill, having described it superbly and for all time.

'My Lord hath joyned together the safety of Europe & the Honour of England with his own Glory', wrote Lord Methuen to Sarah, 'and trebly rendered it Eternall, since not only the wonderfull execution of so noble a designe is owing to my Lord's conduct but

opinion to; I have heard of ye Almanack you
mention, & should be very glad what it says may
com to pass, if I may be so happy when I dye
as to leave my poor Country Setled upon a lasting
foundation, I am sure nothing shall be wanting
on my part towards it; I will not say any more
now for feare my letter should not be ready against
the Duke of Marl: calls for it, but you may expect
another to morrow from your poor unfortunate
faithfull Morly, who sincerly doats on her dear
m^{rs} Freeman ——

Mrs. Freeman and Mrs. Morley: (above) Queen Anne to
Sarah; (below) Sarah to the Queen

part of
this letter was writ before all the
good impressions had made in
her when she was princesse
were worn out, for I used to
pass many hours in a day with
her, & allways endeavourd to
give her notions of loving her
country & liberty & governing
by the laws, & making her

Sidney Earl of Godolphin. After Kneller

the great designe itself hath been formed by himself alone & carried on thro difficulties thought insuperable & which would have been so to any other'.[42]

The sheer daring of it—the striding across Europe, the bluffing of the enemy, the meeting with Prince Eugene, the battle itself and then the bundling of French generals into Marlborough's coach—took and held the fancy of Marlborough's countrymen. And the last touch of romance had been added by the dusty soldier, Parke, who day after day had galloped with the news. First there was the hurried note for Sarah, pencilled by Marlborough while still in the saddle:

> I have not time to say more but to beg you will give my duty to the Queen and let her know Her Army has had a Glorious Victory. Monsr. Tallard and two other Generals are in my Coach and I am following the rest. The bearer my Aid de Camp Coll Parke will give Her an account of what has pass'd. I shal doe it in a day or two by another more att large.*

And then on to Windsor where the Queen sat in the bow-window of the long gallery overlooking the terrace.† Parke, falling at her feet, handed her the scribble which told of a victory which, in Sir Winston's phrase, opened the gateways of the modern world. Delighted, she questioned and rewarded the messenger before writing to Sarah:

> I have had the happiness of receiving my dear Mrs Freeman's, by Colonel Parke, with the good news of this glorious victory which, next to God Almighty, is wholly owing to dear Mr Freeman, on whose safety I congratulate you with all my soul.[43]

'I do not wonder you are all joy', added Mrs Burnet, 'The bishop said he could not sleep, his heart was so charged with joy. He desires your Grace would carefully lay up that little letter [Marlborough's despatch] as a relic that cannot be valued enough'.[44]

For the second time the Queen and the Duchess drove together to a St Paul's thanksgiving, 'the Queen in a rich coach with eight horses, none with her but the Duchess of Marlborough in a very

---

* The original, written in now fading pencil on the back of a bill for inn expenses, is displayed in a stateroom at Blenheim.

† There is a tradition that the Queen was at dominoes with Prince George.

plain garment, the Queen full of jewels . . . The day before was wet
& stormy but this was one of the most serene & calm days that had
been all the year.'[45]

Serenity was the keynote, for in the most unexpected though not
unprayed for way everything had begun to turn out for the best,
with Marlborough triumphant. Once again as far as the eye could
see the sky had cleared; there was nothing to hint that even there in
the coach, in that contrast of dress which could have been uninten-
tional, lay some of the ingredients of those blue-piled thunderlofts
which were one day to break upon them and speed the wreck of
their friendship, after the thanksgiving for Marlborough's victory at
Oudenarde.

In the muniment room at Blenheim there is an unsigned and
undated letter from one who declares himself too much concerned
for the recipient's beauty not to warn her of the injury she will do it
'in Case you dresse & Sett your Selfe out on the Queens birth days.
Leave ornaments to others', the note continues, 'to such as want a
Supply to their naturall beauty . . . Every ornament you putt on
takes off from your beauty. Every ornament you putt off restores
you a grace & you never are soe well as when one sees nothing in
you but your Selfe . . . Pearls look very well upon some necks that
would look very ill without them, but yours would disgrace the
finest necklace in the world . . . Lett others, then, if they please,
undoe themselves in clothes & jewells . . . and goe your Selfe in plain
Clothes with no other charme but your own beauty . . . The plain-
nesse of your Dresse won't hinder you from outshining all the
Queens in Christendom.'[46]

But these were trifles. Blenheim had shaken the world and made it
'look upon the Duke of Marlborough with a sort of amazement as
upon one destined by Providence to rescue and establish the Liberties
of Europe.'[47] 'May our generals prosper!' ran the thanksgiving
sermon, 'May our Queen live forever!' In an age of miracles when
in the same month Blenheim could be won and Gibraltar taken,
anything could happen.

CHAPTER V

Princess of Mindelheim

1705-1706

———◆———

Though crags be stormed and citadels totter, people—queens and generals, duchesses and princesses—still need to dress and eat and dose themselves with spa water or with liquorice and rhubarb.

'If I could tell how to hinder myself from writing to you every day I would', runs in her large, heavy, childish hand a typical undated, unsigned, comma-less note of Anne's to Sarah, 'that you need not be at ye trouble of writing so often to me because you say it dos you hurt but realy I cannot for all I have taken ye purging waters today for when I am from you I cannot be at ease without inquireing after you. Lady Sunderland sayes she hopes time will convince you that she is not base. If you intend to appeare on ye birth day you may be as fine as you please without gold silver point & coulourd peticotes ... Crape linen is worn with gowns & for mantoes you may weare such as you did at tunbridg ... I hope you continue both in body & mind as I left you & that you will never have any more such dismall thoughts as once you had. If my Prayers would do I am sure you should never have ye least unquiet thought but be as happy as 'tis possible for any one to be. I must desire you to send me an under peticote & a botle of ye Queen of hungarys water'.[1]

It was this tedious froth of Anne's—what she herself in others called twitell-twatell—that repelled her Groom of the Stole and now began, for long periods, to keep her from court. Since Marlborough had accepted from the Emperor Leopold, as a reward for Blenheim, the little principality of Mindelheim,* south of the Danube, Sarah

* Mindelheim. 'What is offered', Marlborough told his duchess, 'will in history

was technically entitled to call herself a princess; yet in fact it meant nothing. 'If I had been a man . . .' she was always saying. 'If I were a great man I should prefer keeping the best Company I could get with Independancy before any pleasure this world can give'.[2]

For Marlborough to ride in the whirlwind and direct the storm; for her (three times she offered to join him in Flanders and three times was refused) to stay at home and find husbands for her daughters,* or to force herself to be closeted with Anne. For though, as she wrote later, 'it was extremely tedious to be so much where there could be no manner of conversation, I knew she loved me & I suffer'd by fearing I did wrong when I was not with her. For which reason I have gone a thousand times when I had rather have been in a dungeon'.[3] And again, 'I us'd to run from the Court and shut my self up six Weeks in one of my country Hous's quit alone'.[4] But then if she failed to go to court, Anne would pursue her: '. . . Your faithfull Mrs Morley has a mind some time next week to come & inquire how they [the spa waters] agree with you a munday if it be a convenient day or els a fryday sevennight or if you had rather ye later end of this week or ye beginning of ye week after the next whatever time is easiest to you & your deare Mr Freeman do but name it & I shall fly with joy to my deare Mrs Freeman'.[5]

Without reading every one of her letters—'Great bundles of them . . . a prodigious volume', as Sarah said—it is not easy to appreciate the inexorable persistence of Anne's importunity with Sarah, both when she was princess and when she was queen. Some of the early letters, Sarah notes, were lost in the flight of 1688. There are hundreds left. There are the gracious letters of giving, when she offers a dukedom or a 'mite' (£10,000) on a daughter's marriage (Sarah accepted half); letters of condolence, fussy letters about remedies: 'The apothecarys man durst not send me the Hiera Pickra so I sent the doctor to his house but he found there was not quite one dose &

---

forever remain an honour to our family'. And so it has proved, for the princely title and rank remain in the Marlborough family today; but the principality itself was restored to Bavaria in the treaty of 1714.

* In 1703 her third daughter Elizabeth married Scroop Egerton, who became Duke of Bridgwater. In 1704 her fourth and last daughter Mary married the Marquis of Monthermer who became Duke of Montagu.

that at ye botom of a botle. He would have me take some Rubarb but that is so very naucetious to me that he could not prevail with me to take it . . .'[6] Yes there is much of that, but much more—so very much more, repeated thud upon thud in letter after letter—of what Sarah calls expressions backed with vows. These, even for the times, seem extraordinary and one wonders with how much pleasure or how much cynicism they were received.

In the earlier notes Anne contents herself with such unremarkable sayings as, 'I realy beleive one kind word from deare Mrs Freeman would save me if I weare Gasping',[7] and 'Tis not possible for any body to be so faithfully yours as I am';[8] but as time goes on the theme is developed. She implores Sarah, 'for Christ Jesus sake never think of being any where but with me as long as I am above ground',[9] and 'as I have ever had a most sincere & tender kindness for my deare Mrs Freeman soe I will preserve it to my grave & oh beleeve me you will never find in all ye search of love a hart like your poor unfortunate faithfull Morlys',[10] 'a hart soe truly soe sincerly soe intirely without reserve nor soe passionately yours'. 'I am', she insists, 'as unchangeable as fate', and 'To ye last moment of her life your faithfull Morely will ever be ye same'. No letter from Sarah means desolation; and then, when it arrives, 'Just as I had writ thus far I received your deare kind letter which I have kissd a hundred times . . . If I writt whole volumes I could never express how well I love you nor how much I long to see you'[11] . . . and so on and so on.

One such letter a year from a queen might be flattering. One, sometimes two a day became a bore and an embarrassment. Sarah, looking back, remembered Anne's letters as 'very indifferent, both in sense & spelling, unless that they were generally enlivened with a few passionate expressions, sometimes pretty enough but repeated over & over again without the mixture of anything either of diversion or instruction.'[12]

It is a little unfair perhaps that, since she insisted on their destruction, we are never, at the peak of her favour, able to judge of Sarah's letters to Anne.* 'In obedience', the Queen dutifully assures her, 'after having read & kissed your dear kind letter over & over I burnt it much against my will & I do assure you you need never be in pain about your letters for I take such care of them 'tis not possible

* Later, as favour declined, Sarah kept copies of her letters to Anne.

any accident can happen that they should be seen by any body'.[13]

What time-wasting nonsense it all was and, from Sarah's point of view, what a waste of opportunity! All she wanted to hear was that her lessons had sunk in and that Anne would support the Whigs who would support Marlborough: a subject of as little taste to the Queen as was ass's milk to Marlborough. It was high time for some extraneous stroke of fortune and sure enough, if a little late on cue, came a *deus ex machina* disguised as Lord Haversham, a mischievous Tory heartily loathed by Sarah, who in the spring of 1705 put forward in the Lords a proposal that, to ensure the Protestant succession, the Electress Sophia should be invited to live in England. This, like Occasional Conformity, was a cynical manoeuvre to trap the Queen's ministers. If they opposed it they opposed the Hanoverian succession. If they supported it they offended the Queen who had made it clear that only over her dead body should anyone of that house be allowed in England. In this she was positive and firm.

'I remember one day', recalled Sarah, 'I told the queen when she was easy with me that I thought there was nothing in the world so good for her as well as for England as to desire of her own accord to have the young Prince of Hannover & breed him as her own son, which would in the first place secure her own life against the Roman Catholicks & make the young man acquainted with the laws & customs of a country that one day (tho I hoped it was a long way off) hee would govern. To which she answerd, not being very well pleas'd, that she beleivd nobody of her age and who might have children would doe that; which was a very vain thought & I beleive proceeded more from her pride or fear of having any body here to bee courted then that she really could expect children tho she was not fourty, because she had had before seventeen dead ones'.[14]

There were of course other reasons: one the not uncommon abhorrence of harbouring a successor; two, George's (the Elector's) abortive courtship when she was princess; and three, Anne's uneasy conscience about the Pretender—'Maybe 'tis our brother . . .' On this occasion however Haversham's motion took a boomerang turn when Anne, attending incognito, heard her ex-suitor John Sheffield, Earl of Mulgrave (now Duke of Buckingham), recently ousted from his post of Lord Privy Seal, warn his fellow-peers that (to quote Sarah) it was reasonable to have one of that house [Hanover] here because the Queen might live so long as to have no understanding.[15] At this Anne was deeply offended. After seeing the motion rejected she wrote to Sarah:

I believe dear Mrs Freeman and I shall not disagree as we have formerly done, for I am sensible of the services those people have done me that you have a good opinion of and will countenance them, and am thoroughly convinced of the malice and insolence of them that you have always been speaking against.[16]

It was the moment for the Whigs to bring in their countermeasure, the Regency Bill which, in the event of Anne's leaving no direct heir, would guard the way for a successor from Hanover. Without serious opposition it was carried, but . . . There is no armour against fate; Death lays his icy hand on kings. If Anne died with a Pretender living, anything could still happen. Perhaps she would live forever. Anyway, the Regency Bill was the best they could do. In the meantime for Queen Anne in her glory it must often have seemed indeed a hollow crown:

> O wearisome condition of humanity;
> Born to one law, yet to another bound,
> Doom'd to be vaine, forbedden vanity,
> Created sick, commanded to be sound.[7]

Without comfort oneself, was it possible, she wondered, to share vicariously the happiness of others? As her reward (and the nation's) for the victory at Blenheim Anne had given Marlborough the royal estate at Woodstock, a wild place with a ruined manor house, as the site of a mansion which (so it was understood) she intended to build for him. Her Comptroller of the Works, John Vanbrugh, had already drawn plans for it and a wooden model was being constructed. It was a pleasant thought. Might there not still be hours and days for the Queen to look forward to when she and Sarah would finger brocades and even—oh happy day!—play ombre with Mr Freeman in his castle of Blenheim?

Tattered now is the document by Kneller in which he sets out his project for 'an allegorical picture which Queen Anne design'd to present to the Duke of Marlborough for Blenheim House'. His painting was to have measured twelve feet by eight and no one in it was to have been 'represented by the life' except the Queen's Majesty. Kneller had in fact completed the sketch in oils when, as he puts it, 'State Difference happening betwixt the Queen and the Duke of Marlborough', the whole scheme was abandoned. In the sketch, amidst a plethora of allegorical jumble typical of its date (1708), one sees the Queen, a portly figure, bestowing upon a kneeling figure in armour (Military Merit) a scroll upon which has been drawn the north front of Blenheim. Ceres, prominent among the goddesses, could be Sarah; but the plump female figure of Architecture, on Anne's right, is as unlike Vanbrugh as it would be possible to be. Beside her stands 'a Little Youth, the Emblem of Posterity', while at the foot of all, in the foreground, two smaller *putti* spill 'the Golden Cornucopia Shead by her Majesty's Affections'.[18]

It was a delightful idea, as was also the notion that, down the ages, a quitrent for the castle, as it was then called, should be paid by presenting the sovereign, at Windsor and on the battle-anniversary, with a silk standard emblazoned with three gilded fleurs-de-lys on a field argent;* a condition which has been and continues to be faithfully fulfilled.

On the 18th of June, 1705 the foundation-stone of Blenheim was laid. Vanbrugh of course was there, with his second-in-command Nicholas Hawksmoor, a notable architect in his own right. They and five others struck the stone with a hammer and threw down a guinea; which done, the stone—eight feet square, polished and engraved with the words: In memory of the battel of Blenheim, June 18, 1705, Anna Regina—was lowered into position beneath the site of the eastern Bow Window Room, the only room said to have met with the Duchess's approval. After which of course came toasts and junketings and a dance of old beldames. The honours had been done.

At the time of the foundation, as in Kneller's sketch, Sarah was not recognisably in the picture. 'I mortally hate all Grandeur and Architecture',[19] she said afterwards, and she hated them then. If Marlborough chose to humour the Queen and to practise both, that was their affair. She knew Anne would have 'done nothing with the

* Intended as a facsimile of the standard of the Corps du Roi (depicted in the tapestry of the battle), captured at Blenheim.

money that was better'. Sarah herself was content with Holywell and Windsor Lodge, although her ideal was 'a clean, sweet house and garden, tho' ever so small'—a description which hardly applied to Blenheim.

As for the architect, she had heard of him as a writer of comedies, she had never met him. 'At the beginning of those works', she wrote later, 'I never had spoake to him, but as soon as I knew him & saw the maddnesse of the whole Design I opposed it all that was possible for me to doe . . . I don't know that the queen had any particular favour for Sir C. Wren tho hee had been an old servant, but 'tis certain that old Craggs, who was as ill a man as ever I knew, recommended Sr John Vanbrugh to the Duke of Marl: . . . Sr John, tho hee was in the queens office of Works would not have been employed in the building if hee had not been recommended'.[20]

To suppose, however, that Duchess and architect took against one another at sight would be misleading. She found him at first, as did everyone, entertaining; for Vanbrugh was, as the jingle said, 'a most sweet-natur'd gentleman and pleasant'. Sarah laughed at his rhymes and teased him about Swift's verses on his goose-pie house in Whitehall. Perhaps if Marlborough had not found him such excellent company, Vanbrugh might have stood more chance of keeping on good terms with the Duchess; but his profession was against him, and if over Blenheim an architect had to suffer, as with Sarah every architect must, then it was as well that it was Vanbrugh (not one, as he said, to drop his spirits at every rebuff) rather than the ageing Wren.*

In 1705 Wren was still at the head of Anne's Board of Works as Surveyor, with Vanbrugh as Comptroller, an office he had held since 1702, when the Earl of Carlisle is believed to have sponsored him in reward for planning the Earl's 'top seat and garden of England' at Castle Howard.† In the year Carlisle had come into his title—1692,

* After commissioning Wren, in 1709, to build Marlborough House, the Duchess rid herself of him and directed the finishing herself. According to Vanbrugh, she was prevented by Marlborough from bringing an action against Wren, who withdrew with dignity and without open dispute.

† The Duchess maintained that Vanbrugh owed his comptrollership to Marlborough, with the understanding that he should eventually succeed Wren as Surveyor (see Chatsworth Letters 122-3). This assertion is not confirmed by other sources.

the same that saw Marlborough in the Tower—Captain Vanbrugh, as he then was, was in the Bastille, imprisoned as a spy but in tolerable comfort and busy on his first comedy *The Relapse*. His metamorphosis into architect cannot have been, as Swift gibed, without thought or lecture, but next to nothing is known of it. Genius can be a quick learner, and more especially when genius (Wren) teaches and yet a third genius (Hawksmoor) stands by to make dreams workable.

It is quite possible that James Craggs the elder,* who was a friend of Vanbrugh's, introduced him to Marlborough. At an early stage Craggs became attached to the Marlborough household where, says the Dictionary of National Biography, 'his shrewdness and administrative ability attracted the attention of the Duchess, who entrusted him with the management of her business affairs'; and indeed we shall see how thoroughly (especially when in exile in 1713–14) she relied on him.

Vanbrugh himself says that he first met Marlborough casually at the playhouse; that he later showed him the wooden model of Castle Howard, which he liked; and that he afterwards submitted a plan for Blenheim which, with amendments, was wholeheartedly approved by both Marlborough and Godolphin.

On June 9th Godolphin gave Vanbrugh a warrant which appointed him surveyor of all the works and buildings to be erected at Woodstock. In this document, which was to cause endless dispute, Marlborough was named four times, the Queen not once. At the time it was of course unthinkable to ask for the Queen's promise in writing; but later, when favour cooled, much seemed to have evaporated with it, not excluding Anne's impulsive kindness and her word.

From the outset, before a stone had been laid, Marlborough expressed delight with the Queen's present. It was fitting that the achievements of her arms should be commemorated; and as for the setting, it could not have been better. As with Vanbrugh, his fellow-romantic and fellow-visionary, he rode over it, more and more in that wild tangle appealed to them. There was Rosamund's well, the spring known to Henry II, 'that King whose Scenes of Love he [Vanbrugh] was so much pleas'd with'; there was the manor of

* James Craggs senior (1657–1721).

Woodstock, its battered walls still defiant as they were when Elizabeth I was imprisoned in its gatehouse; while between the manor and the site they had chosen for the castle lay a marsh, threaded by a rivulet, and a chasm which Vanbrugh vowed he would span with a Roman bridge. Could it be that, as marsh, stream and valley came into view, Marlborough was reminded of just such another rugged scene, but by the Danube? 'The ground bordering the Nebel, particularly between Oberglau and Blenheim', runs Coxe's description of the battle-site, 'is generally marshy and in many places impassable . . . The morass expands to a considerable breadth, and nearer Blenheim is a species of islet . . . Near the point of the islet is a stone bridge, over which runs the road from Dillingen to Donauworth'.[21]

And then the garden—how soon could it be ready? Marlborough at fifty-five thought of himself, as men did in those days, as an old man. Henry Wise was Queen Anne's head-gardener; and so Marlborough, says Defoe, pitched on him and had him consider that 'he could not expect to live till the trees were grown up and therefore he expected to have a garden as it were ready made for him. Accordingly Mr Wise transplanted thither full grown trees in baskets, which he buried in the earth, which look and thrive the same as if they had stood there thirty or forty years.'[22]

If Wise was not the perfect gardener, he certainly seemed so. Those who knew him believed that, had he worked in the garden of Eden, there would have been no Fall, for there would have been no serpent. The only snakes he tolerated were those on his coat of arms, to add point to the pun: Be ye wise as serpents and harmless as doves. His crest was a demi-lion argent holding a damask rose, the lion having in his mouth a serpent vulnerating him in the shoulder, for Wise endured much from a rheumatic shoulder and from gout. With his team at Blenheim he dug the foundations of the house and of the bridge and its causeway and planted the huge and complex 'military' garden, the long avenues and the two-thousand-acre park. 'For the Gardening & Plantations', wrote Marlborough to his wife, from Flanders, 'I am at ease, being very sure that Mr Wise will bee dilligent'.[23] And sure enough, Wise was soon able to report, 'The severall Plantacons . . . have Shot to Admiration . . . I have taken such Care of raising from Seeds Nuts & Berrys etc such Number of

Plants that I hope Your Grace will not loose time in deciding upon their disposition'.[24] It was all most heartening. There were times when even Sarah seems to have felt a glow.

'I take ye liberty to give your Grace a litle account of my jorny to Woodstock', John Howe tells Marlborough on September 20th, 1705, 'Hearing my Lady Dutchesse was there, I thought it was my duty to waite on her. I mett her Grace going to ye building whither I had leave to attend her, but am not skillful enough in architecture to pretend to give any judgment on that part. The building is about breast high above ye ground & ye gardens, which promise great beauty, very nere being finisht as farr as ye plantations, which Mr Wise says will be perfect this season so as to be gardens by this time twelve months. I had ye satisfaction besides ye honour of finding my litle compliment well receivd, to see her Grace very well pleasd with ye situation & everything belonging to Woodstock Park. I could not omitt, as I view'd it, to pray heartyly that your Grace may there enjoy, with a vigorous & quiet old age, the fruits of your past labours & services to your country'.[25]

At the beginning of the Blenheim works no fewer than a thousand men were employed there. Indeed, so great was the concentration of skilled labour, it was as well that, apart from St Paul's, then nearly finished, Anne was a modest builder. For Kensington, in this year of Blenheim's founding, she had commissioned, in warm brick and stone, a delightful orangery, which Defoe says she planned as a summer supper-house. It was to be useful in other ways too. Writing from Kensington to Sarah, about touching for the evil,* Anne tells her, 'I do that buisness now in ye Banqueting house which I like very well, that being a very cool room & ye doing of it there keeps my own house sweet & free from crouds'.[26]

It was a season of clear shining, a brief summer calm before the next political storm. Had Sarah been wiser she might have realised even at this stage that she was becoming the tool of extremists, a lever for moving the Queen in whichever direction the Junto wished her to go. This time it was the removal of the incompetent Sir Nathan Wright, the Lord Keeper, and the appointment in his place

---

* One of Sarah's duties was to see that Coggs the goldsmith kept the Queen supplied with healing gold, given to the sufferers, who on one occasion included Dr Samuel Johnson, from the evil (scrofula: a disease affecting the glands).

of the estimable Lord Cowper. Everything was in Cowper's favour except that he was a Whig and Anne still seemed to believe, as Sunderland said, that all Whigs had cloven feet. At first she said no, but after more pressure she (in Sarah's words) 'at last consented to employ him and the consequence of this was that she had not only the ablest man in England to serve her but one that she was perfectly easy & satisfied with'.[27]

So rare is high and consistent praise from the Duchess of Marlborough that a whole chapter should be reserved for her good opinion of Cowper, and his of her. 'All the time I was at Court', she says, 'and after I was removed no man could possibly behave better to me than he did, not only as a gentleman but as a friend and as if he had been my own brother'.[28] When he tried to thank her for his appointment she called for silence. Whereupon he told her, 'Madam, if I must not speak, yet you can't hinder me from thinking as long as I live'.[29]

It was ironical that such a good turn—to Cowper and to the country, to the Whigs and to Anne—should bring Sarah what she described as the Queen's first peevish letter; a letter now hard to trace among many at Blenheim of a tone that might be considered peevish. This, for example:

Kensington, Wednesday

Your poor unfortunate faithfull Morly was at her deare Mrs Freemans door today just before I came from St James's but could make no body heare & it being past two aclock I durst not venture to send round, the Prince staying dinner for me, soe was forc'd to come away without ye satisfaction of one look of my deare Mrs Freeman, which was no small mortification to her that sincerly doats on you . . . I cannot end this without repeating a request that I have often made, that is that you would leave off that formall word Majesty & lett me heare your faithfull Morly named againe that is greivd at her Soul to find my deare Mrs Freeman allways cold & grave & would give ye world to be restored to ye happyness she has formerly enjoy'd.[30]

In old age Sarah herself confessed, 'I mortally hate Madam and Your Grace which I call Bug Words',[31] and she knew perfectly well that 'Majesty' was a bug word to Queen Anne; but it had its uses.

So she persisted and gained her point and lost a great deal more. 'She not only overrated her influence in public matters with the Queen', observes Sir Winston, 'but she mistook its character. She sought to win by argument, voluble and vociferous, written and interminable, what had hitherto been the freehold property of love'.[32]

Those who, for one purpose or another, still came to court complained that the Queen was inaccessible; for her Groom of the Stole barred the door and when she was absent, the Queen would not choose to appear. There was the case of that staunch Tory James Johnston, who went to pay his respects to the Queen at Hampton Court, 'but observing the Duchess of Marlborough to look upon him with anger, he retired to his country seat & fine gardens, not far off, where he entertained himself with country recreations and the refreshment of the pleasant river'.[33]

Wherever the Queen went she was pursued by scores of importunate people with petitions, and it was one of Sarah's drearier duties to deal with them. 'I did constantly write abundance of letters in answer to petitions',[34] she remembered. The lacemakers prayed for less court-mourning, which was ruining their trade. Scotsmen and Scotswomen wanted or did not want to unite with England. Irishmen wanted back their estates. Still more persistent were those begging for pensions or for reprieves. Mrs Stephens, for example, how she haunted the place ever since her husband was sentenced to stand in the pillory. Stephens, rector of Sutton, had been found guilty of a libel on the Duke of Marlborough; but Sarah, as she often did in these cases, interceded. Three days before the battle of Ramillies Marlborough had written, 'I agree entirely with you ... I should be glad he were forgiven ... but I do not love to see my name in print; for I am persuaded that an honest man must be justified by his own actions and not by the pen of a writer, though he should be a zealous friend'.[35]

Anne's note too was typical: 'I have, upon my deare Mrs Freeman's pressing letter about Mr Stephens, ordered Mr Secretary Harley to put a stop to his standing in the pillory ... Nothing but your desire could have inclined me to it, for in my poor opinion it is not right. My reason I will tell you when I have the happiness of seeing you. Till then, my deare Mrs Freeman, farewel.'[36]

Anne may have been surprised to find Sarah, she who mocked at the Church Party, interceding for a clergyman, but in battles of that sort she was sincere and could be merciful. 'Much as I opposed the Tories', she wrote in her *Conduct*, 'I was no Enemy to the Church they talked of, so far as any thing real and excellent was meant by that Word'.

In May Marlborough's victory at Ramillies again put new heart into Queen and country as well as into Sarah and himself. 'As Blenheim saved Vienna, so Ramillies conquered the Netherlands'.* Holland was saved. Again smiles and congratulations, again bonfires and thanksgivings; and yet from Marlborough's letters we find, in spite of added rewards (the £5000 'pension' made permanent; the title to descend through the female line), that things at home were less tranquil than he had hoped.

'Hetherto', he tells Sarah, 'I really have not had time to write to my children, but when I do, bee assur'd that I shal let them know my heart & soul as to their living dutyfully & kindly with you, & let mee beg for my sake of my dear Soull that she will passe by little then faults & consider thay are very young & that thay can't do other then love you with all their hearts, for when thay consider how good a Mother you have been to them thay must bee barbariens if thay did not make a kind return'.[37] And again a month later: 'It is a very great pleasure to me to find you are satisfied with three of your children & hope in God that 392† will in time bee trewly sensible of all the great obligations she has to you'. And in July: 'It is most mortefying to see that nothing can mend 392. I beg of you to do me the justice & your self the ease to believe that whatever thay say can have no credit with me when you asure me of the contrary. I can & do greive as much as any parent can when a child is unkind. We must hope the best & bee allways carefull not to resent their Carage to such a degree as to make the town judge of who is in the right.'[38] And then, a little peevishly: 'By your saying nothing to me of your going to Woodstock I find your heart is not soe much sett on that place as I cou'd wish. Vanbrook writes me that I shall not see him in the Army, beleiving that I shal approve better of his going into Oxfordshire'.[39]

* The Spanish Netherlands, now Belgium.
† Probably their eldest daughter, Henrietta.

But Sarah had other interests, and that summer a strange thing had happened. A messenger had brought her a small packet and with it a flowery letter, full of expressions (as she called them), from Mr Brydges:*

Amsterdam   16 July 1706

Madam,

I should not have been guilty of so great a piece of confidence as to have troubled your Grace with so inconsiderable a matter as this ring . . . if I did not at ye same time hope that ye picture under it would encline your Grace to pardon my presumption to look upon it with so favourable an eye as to let it find place amongst ye rest of your jewels. It formerly belonged to ye Duke of Orleans & had ye Dauphin's picture in it, but that which makes one hope it will prove acceptable to your Grace is a picture of infinitely more value which I have put in ye room of it & which I have had drawn by one who is esteemed very eminent in this way of painting . . .[40]

She stopped reading the letter and opened the packet . . . Hm, pretty enough, the miniature of Marlborough a fair likeness, but as a ring, like its sender, far too showy. It must go back of course. She looked at it again . . . Then she showed it to Coggs the goldsmith who said yes indeed, the 'glass' covering the portrait was one vast, thin diamond. With a sigh Sarah took up her pen:

Windsor Castle   July 25, 1706

Sir,

Upon the receipt of your letter from Amsterdam and the present you sent me with it I cannot disown that I was at first very much pleased with it, beleiving the nature of it not to be so considerable as that the satisfaction I take in its buyer to be abused† upon that account, but upon a more particular examination of its nature I find it to be by much too considerable

---

* James Brydges (1673–1744), created 1st Duke of Chandos in 1719. Paymaster-General of the forces abroad from 1707 to 1712.

† Wrongly copied into Chandos letterbook? The sense is: '. . . the satisfaction I take in its buyer ran no risk of being abused'.

Sarah Duchess of Marlborough with her children. Closterman

Elizabeth Countess of
Bridgwater. Kneller

Anne Countess of
Sunderland. Kneller

for me to take & having no opportunity of sending it back I will keep it till you come home & hope you will be pleased to tell me the price of it, in order either to buy or return it.

I am with a great deal of respect, Sir,
your most obedient & most humble servant[41]

He protests. Unless she is resolved to kill him with grief he begs she will be pleased never to make further mention of it. She must bear in mind his obligations to her noble family. 'I design', he concludes, 'by ye services of my whole life to give constant proofs of ye gratitude.' As Duke of Chandos (Pope's Timon) we shall hear more of him later.

For Sarah, amid her more tedious duties, it had been a diverting if slightly embarrassing interlude, a breathing space before the next crisis: a major battle with Anne, which would mean calling out all reserves. It was nothing less than a demand that her son-in-law, Lord Sunderland, be made a Secretary of State. This was not Sarah's notion, nor Marlborough's. The move came from the five tyrannising lords of the Junto, of whom Sunderland was one; political blackmail of the kind the world even then had grown used to. For continued Whig support of the war, one of their number must have power. They threatened Godolphin, who begged Sarah to speak for him; and so Sarah, armed with argument, attacked Anne. So did Godolphin himself, and so, even more reluctantly, did Marlborough. The Queen was resentful and adamant. 'On her throne', writes Sir Winston admiringly, 'she was as tough as Marlborough in the field. She would not have Sunderland, she could not bear him. He was, she felt, a brazen freethinker and at heart a Republican'.[42] Sarah continued to hector the Queen and in August wrote:

. . . Your security and the nation's is my chief wish, and I beg of God Almighty as sincerely as I shall do for His pardon at my last hour that Mr and Mrs Morley may see their errors as to this notion before it is too late; but considering how little impression anything makes that comes from your faithful Freeman, I have troubled you too much and I beg your pardon for it.[43]

To this sour note she received no answer. Had she gone too far?

The Queen, having read Sarah's 'notion' as 'nation'* thought that she had. Godolphin intervened, but after he had patched things up, Sarah wrote again coldly, almost scathingly; yet she received from Anne a kind reply:

> . . . I hope you will not go to Woodstock without giving me one look for whatever hard thoughts you may have of me I am sure I do not deserve them, and I will not be uneasy if you come to me; for though you are never so unkind I will ever preserve a most sincere & tender passion for my dear Mrs Freeman.[44]

To which Sarah's rejoinder is again disappointing. Returning to the 'notion' for 'nation' wrangle she says she cannot for the life of her see any essential difference. Her tone is contemptuous. How very much wiser, at this time, are Marlborough's letters to his wife: 'You know that I have often disputes with you concerning the Queen', he writes from Helchin on August 9, 'and by what I have always observed, when she thinks herself in the right, she needs no advice to help her to be very firm & positive . . . I doubt but a very little time will set this of Lord Sunderland very right but . . . I have my apprehensions he will be very uneasy in it; and that when it is too late you will be of my opinion that it would have been much happier if he had been employed in any other place of profit and honour . . .'[45]

Godolphin, bludgeoned by the Junto, stonewalled by the Queen, was in despair. 'I cannot struggle against the difficulties of your Majesty's business', he told her bluntly, 'and yourself at the same time . . . I have worn out my health and almost my life in the service of the Crown . . .'[46] It was true. He now offered to retire to Newmarket, where he bred racehorses. Marlborough told him he was, like himself, 'in honour bound to undergo all the dangers & troubles that is possible to bring this war to a happy end, which I think must be after the next campaign, if we can agree to carry it on with vigour'.[47]

Anne offered a compromise but the Whigs would not hear of it. Finally she appealed to Marlborough: 'Why, for God's sake, must I who have no interest, no end, no thought but for the good of my

---

* In the version at Blenheim, in the Duchess's hand, the word appears to be 'nation'.

country, be made so miserable as to be brought into the power of one set of men? And why may I not be trusted since I mean nothing but what is equally for the good of all my subjects?'[48]

The Queen, at the climax as at the close of her reign, was in the toils of faction and of unscrupulous politicians. There was no escape. Sunderland was the last man in England she would have chosen. 'He and I should not agree long together', she wrote, 'finding by experience my humour and those that are of a warmer will often have misunderstandings between one another'.[49] Yet she, Queen of England, was compelled to have him.

By the time this pitiful thing had been accomplished, Anne, Godolphin and Marlborough had been driven to the last extremity of disgust and disillusionment. Marlborough told Sarah, 'I shall from henceforth despise all mankind and think there is no such thing as virtue'. Marlborough himself was now threatening to resign and Sarah sent the Queen his letter. To the end of her own, after referring to 'that passion & tenderness I had once for Mrs Morley' she tacked a postscript: 'I desire you would reflect whether you have never heard that the greatest misfortunes that have ever happened to any of your family had not been occasioned by having ill-advice and an obstinacy in their tempers'.[50]—a remark which she must have known would offend.

In spite of Sarah, in spite of herself and her own better judgment the Queen at last gave way. The course of the river had been forced at the cost of friendship.

There were at this time two Secretaries of State: Sir Charles Hedges and Robert Harley. On December 3rd Sunderland took the place of Hedges. Harley remained. 'And it quickly appeared', says Sarah, 'that the Difficulties raised by her Majesty against parting with Sir Charles Hedges were wholly owing to the Artifice and Management of Mr Harley . . . whose Interest and secret Transactions with the Queen were then doubtless in their Beginning'.[51]

CHAPTER VI

Cue for Vipers

1707-1708

How unfair it is and how ruinous to the fame of a politician when, after the struggles of a lifetime, the years of anonymity before the hours of glory, the rise, the fall, the years it may be in the wilderness, the memoirs, the polished self-vindication . . . all this and more may for posterity go for nothing and be totally ignored in favour of one bon mot, one sentence, a catchphrase coined in his cups perhaps by an enemy, yet one which seems conveniently to docket the man and set him forever in his nutshell.

And so it is with Robert Harley, Earl of Oxford and Mortimer. Like William III, like the Duchess of Marlborough, he has his apologists; but there are two hard phrases which no student of history can ever forget: the first, Lord Cowper's—'If any man was ever born under a necessity of being a knave, he was';[1] the second, Sarah's—'That wonderful talent Mr Harley possessed, in the supreme degree, of confounding the common sense of mankind'.[2]

Yet we are assured by kind and impartial writers that if we, with Arthur Maynwaring, damn Harley out of hand as 'the most errant tricking knave in all Britain',[3] we shall be gravely misled; and after all, if Macaulay and others could make a hero of William III, (and in recent times we have seen even less promising examples, including Judge Jeffreys), it should not be hard to say something for Harley. 'To represent him', warns Sir Keith Feiling, 'as a mere self-seeking politician would be a travesty . . . His inconsistency was rooted in something like principle. He disbelieved in the whole scheme of party but . . . his conservative purpose was sincere . . . His characteristics were caution, procrastination, improvisation and secrecy'.[4]

Unlike his friend and colleague Henry St John, Secretary at War, who was a born orator, Harley had a grotesque delivery which, in Sarah's description, makes him sound more like a dervish than Speaker of the House of Commons.

'He was a cunning and a dark man', she reflected, 'of too small abilities to do much good but with all the qualities requisite to do mischief & to bring on the ruin & destruction of a nation. This mischievous darkness of his soul was written in his countenance & plainly legible in a very odd look, disagreeable to every body at first sight, which being joined with a constant awkward motion or other agitation of his head & body betrayed a turbulent dishonesty within, even in the midst of all those familiar, jocular, bowing, smiling airs which he always affected in order to cover what could not be covered. He had long accustomed himself so much to dissemble his real intentions & to use the ambiguous & obscure way of speaking that he could hardly ever be understood when he really designed it or be believed when he never so much desired it.'[5]

At the beginning of the reign Harley, with his quips and cranks, had done his utmost to ingratiate himself with the Duchess; but though a weasel may hypnotise a rabbit, if he tries the same treatment on a tigress, one glare may send him scurrying and in this case it evidently did. With Marlborough and Godolphin he had at first more success. He admired and flattered them. They believed in him and advanced him. It was only when, rebuffed by Sarah, Harley realised that in Marlborough's absence Godolphin's moderation was too mild to resist the Junto, that he made the first cautious moves to strike out on his own. And even then there was still the formidable obstacle of Sarah, for as long as she guarded the Queen's door, so long must he be thwarted. But now Sarah was often absent; and besides that, the 'ill star' which had risen over 1707 and brought the allies disappointment at Almanza and Toulon, proved lucky for Harley and found him a go-between with the Queen, a Tory spy so nearly perfect for his purpose that even his guile could hardly have devised a better. Sarah, though she afterwards thought perhaps she had made too much of a vulgar person, never tired of writing about her poor relation, her cousin Abigail Hill, who later became Mrs

Masham and eventually Lady Masham. Bishop Burnet, looking back to her introduction, says:

> It was observed that Mr Harley, who had been for some years secretary of state, had gained great credit with the queen and began to set up for himself and to act no more under the direction of the lord treasurer. There was one of the bed-chamberwomen who being nearly related to the Duchess of Marlborough had been taken care of by her, together with her whole family (for they were fallen low) in a most particular manner. She brought her not only into that post but treated her with such a confidence that it had introduced her into a high degree of favour with the queen, which for some years was considered as an effect of the Duchess of Marlborough's credit with her. She was also nearly related to Mr Harley and they two entered into a close correspondence. She learned the arts of a court and observed the queen's temper with so much application that she got far into her heart; and she employed all her credit to establish Harley in the supreme confidence with the queen, and to alienate her affections from the Duchess of Marlborough, who studied no other method of preserving her favour but by pursuing the true interest of the queen and of the kingdom . . . This went on too little regarded. The Duchess of Marlborough seemed secure of her interest in the queen and shewed no jealousy of a favour to which herself gave the first rise.[6]

In fiction the irony of it would have been thought too crudely drawn. That the Duchess should, as she said, have taken Cinderella 'from a broom', and that Cinderella should then, once secure, turn into the wicked fairy to cast a spell upon the Queen and supplant her benefactress, seemed altogether too farfetched to be true. And indeed it was hard—a trick worthy of some malicious lord of misrule —that such a sordid situation should force itself upon Queen and Duchess and cause such an upheaval as almost to overturn the throne. As the author of *The Other Side of the Question* puts it:

> From the Intrigues of Parties, the Glitter of Courts, the Mysteries of the Cabinet, the Misunderstandings of Princes and all the Eclat of the great World, which may be called the Eminencies

of human Life, we are now to descend with your Grace to the
Flats and Marshes of Family-Affairs to a low Tale of Cousins and
their Cousins, brought to Court out of Charity, of ragged Boys
cloath'd and put to School, and good-for-nothing Fellows
preferr'd to Regiments . . .[7]

No one however has told the tale with more clarity nor with more
feeling than Sarah herself:

Mrs Masham was the Daughter of one Hill, a Merchant in the
City, by a Sister of my Father. Our Grandfather, Sir John
Jenyns, had twenty-two Children, by which Means the Estate
of the Family (which was reputed to be about 4000 l a Year)
came to be divided into small Parcels. Mrs Hill had only 500 l
to her Portion. Her Husband lived very well, as I have been
told, for many Years till turning Projector he brought Ruin
upon himself and his Family. But as this was long before I was
born, I never knew there were such People in the World, till
after the Princess Anne was married and when she lived at the
Cockpit, at which Time an Acquaintance of mine came to me
and said, She believed I did not know that I had Relations who
were in want, and she gave me an Account of them . . . [Sarah
sent ten guineas and went to see Mrs Hill] . . . She told me
that her Husband was in the same Relation to Mr Harley as
she was to me, but that he had never done any Thing for
her.*

I think Mrs Masham's Father and Mother did not live long
after this. They left four Children, two Sons and two Daughters.
The Elder Daughter (afterwards Mrs Masham) was a grown
Woman. I took her to St Albans, where she lived with me and
my Children, and I treated her with as great Kindness as if she
had been my Sister. After some Time a Bed-Chamber Woman
of the Princess of Denmark's died; and as in that Reign (after
the Princesses were grown up) Rockers, though not Gentle-
women, had been advanced to be Bed-Chamber Women, I
thought I might ask the Princess to give the vacant Place to
Mrs Hill . . . and it was granted . . . [Abigail's young sister Alice,

* According to Peter Wentworth, Harley 'promoted' Abigail's marriage to
Masham. (See Wentworth Papers, ed. Cartwright, p. 132).

later to be nicknamed by Swift the Queen of Prudes, was found the job of laundress in the Duke of Gloucester's household (in which capacity she starched Anne's 'heads'), and when he died in 1700 a pension of £200 a year. Thanks to her sister she rose meteorically to become Deputy to the Keeper of the Privy Purse, the Keeper then being Abigail].

Sarah's account continues:

The Elder Son was at my Request put by my Lord Godolphin into a Place in the Custom-House . . . His Brother (whom the Bottle-men afterwards called honest Jack Hill) was a tall Boy whom I cloathed (for he was all in Rags) and put to School at St Albans to one Mr James who had been an Usher under Dr Busby of Westminster. And whenever I went to St Albans I sent for him and was as kind to him as if he had been my own Child. After he had learnt what he could there, a Vacancy happening of Page of Honour to the Prince of Denmark, his Highness was pleased at my Request to take him. I afterwards got my Lord Marlborough to make him Groom of the Bed-chamber to the Duke of Gloucester. And though my Lord always said that Jack Hill was good for nothing, yet to oblige me he made him his Aid de Camp and afterwards gave him a Regiment. But it was his Sister's Interest that raised him to be a General and to command in that ever memorable Expedition to Quebec: I had no Share in doing him these Honours. To finish what I have to say upon his Subject: When Mr Harley thought it useful to attack the Duke of Marlborough in Parliament, this Quebec General, this honest Jack Hill, this once ragged Boy whom I cloathed, happening to be sick in Bed, was nevertheless persuaded by his Sister to get up, wrap himself in warmer Cloathes than those I had given him, to go to the House to vote against the Duke.

I may here add that even the Husband of Mrs Masham had several Obligations to me. It was at my Instance that he was first made a Page, then Equerry and afterwards Groom of the Bed-Chamber to the Prince . . .

As for Mrs Masham herself, I had so much Kindness for her and had done so much to oblige her, without having ever done any thing to offend her, that it was too long before I could bring myself to think her other than a true Friend or forbear rejoicing at any instance of Favour shewn her by the Queen. I observed indeed at length that she was grown more shy of coming to me, and more reserved than usual when she was with me; but I imputed this to her peculiar Moroseness of Temper and for some time made no other Reflection upon it.

The first Thing which led me into Enquiries about her Conduct was the being told (in the Summer of 1707) that my Cousin Hill was privately married to Mr Masham. I went to her and asked her if it were true. She owned it was and begged my Pardon for having concealed it from me. As much Reason as I had to take ill this Reserve in her Behaviour, I was willing to impute it to Bashfulness and want of Breeding rather than to any thing worse. I embraced her with my usual Tenderness and very heartily wished her Joy; and then, turning the Discourse, entered into her Concerns in as friendly a Manner as possible, contriving how to accommodate her with Lodgings by removing her Sister into some of my own.

I then enquired of her very kindly whether the Queen knew of her Marriage, and very innocently offered her my Service if she needed it to make that Matter easy. She had by this Time learnt the Art of Dissimulation pretty well and answered with an Air of Unconcernedness that the Bed-Chamber Women had already acquainted the Queen with it, hoping by this Answer to divert any farther Examination into the Matter.* But I went presently to the Queen and asked her why she had not been so kind as to tell me of my Cousin's Marriage, expostulating with her upon the Point and putting her in Mind of what she used often to say to me out of Montaigne, That it was no Breach of Promise of Secrecy to tell such a Friend any thing because it was no more than telling it to one's self. All the Answer I could obtain from her Majesty was this, I have a hundred Times bid Masham tell it you, and she would not.

* In the version at Blenheim (G-I-9) Sarah says Abigail, before answering, 'looked up to the ceiling a good while in a confused awkward manner & then said yes, the Queen taxed her with it & she believed the Bed-Chamber Women had told it her'.

The Conduct both of the Queen and of Mrs Masham convinced me that there was some Mystery in the Affair, and
thereupon I set myself to enquire as particularly as I could into
it. And in less than a Week's Time I discovered that my Cousin
was become an absolute Favourite; that the Queen herself was
present at her Marriage in Dr Arbuthnot's Lodgings, at which
Time her Majesty had called for a round Sum out of the Privy-
purse; that Mrs Masham came often to the Queen, when the
Prince was asleep, and was generally two Hours every Day in
private with her: And I likewise then discovered beyond all
Dispute Mr Harley's Correspondence and Interest at Court by
Means of this Woman.

I was struck with Astonishment at such an Instance of
Ingratitude, and should not have believed [it] if there had been
any Room left for doubting.[8]

Like one who lifts a stone and discovers a nest of vipers, Sarah
recoiled. It was the moment of cockcrow. The intrigue was
nasty, the lies were crude, the implications horrible. As a historian
she handles her material distastefully, as with gloves; yet deftly
too, for nothing—from the teeming swarms of Hills to Masham's
monstrous ingratitude—has been omitted. So much for the published
version. Other drafts have pleasing detail, as for instance that when
Abigail was at St Albans she had smallpox and was nursed by Sarah
who dosed her with ass's milk and restored her, although she
'thought she would dye'.[9]

In the matter of the secret wedding Anne, as we see, was no match
for Sarah. Her 'I have a hundred times bid Masham tell it you' was
clumsy and made Sarah the more suspicious, wondering as she did
how a bedchamber-woman came to be on such terms with the
Queen as to have had a hundred chats with her.

Odd happenings, only a little puzzling at the time, now fell into
place. There had been the occasion, for example, when Sarah went
to the Queen at Windsor, 'very privately by a secret Passage', and
was alone with her when Abigail 'unlockt the door in a loud
familiar manner and was tripping across the room with a gay air,
but upon seeing me she immediately stopped short and, acting a part
like a player, dropt a grave curtsey when she had gone a good way

without making any, and in a faint low voice cry'd, 'Did your Majesty ring, pray?'[10]

As with Harley so with his creature Abigail, the views of contemporaries are too conflicting to be of much help. Even her portrait in the National Portrait Gallery (p. 129), though exactly as one would imagine her, has a questionmark beside its catalogue-entry. According to Swift, whom she befriended, 'My lady Masham was a person of a plain sound understanding, of great truth and sincerity, without the least mixture of falsehood or disguise, of an honest boldness and courage superior to her sex, firm and disinterested in her friendship and full of love, duty and veneration for the Queen her mistress . . .'[11] According to the Earl of Dartmouth she was 'exceeding mean and vulgar in her manners, of a very unequal temper, childishly exceptious, and passionate . . . The queen had a suspicion', he adds, 'that she or her sister listened at the door all the time I was with her'.[12] In which case, why did the Queen tolerate her?

There is much unexplained, not least the secret wedding which sooner or later Sarah must have discovered. Why was she not asked? If all Anne wanted was a comforter, a soothing, useful servant, it is plain enough what balm, after Sarah, she must have found in the wench whom Godolphin, who had a nickname for everyone, called Mrs Still; even though she lacked Sarah's sparkle and was apt to be morose. To Sarah she was a monster, but to history she is of less importance as a personality than as a tool, her chief attribute— unobtrusiveness—negative, herself neither heroine nor very convincing villain. 'Abigail', says Sir Winston, 'was probably the smallest person who ever consciously attempted to decide and in fact decided the history of Europe'.[13] Her letters in an uneducated hand to Harley, full of sly nonsense about her poor Aunt Stevens's [Anne's] want of ready money [courage] give no inkling of veneration for the Queen, but on the contrary leave a sour taste and do her no service.

Of course Sarah should have ignored her and of course, being herself, she could not. 'It was so natural for me that had so much obliged her', she says, 'to resent her ill returns and to endeavour to hinder her from hurting me with the queen'.[14] How could she have sat still and shown indifference while a chambermaid was so basely supplanting her in the Queen's favour? No one could blame her, she maintained, if she expressed herself with warmth, and that she did both to the wretched Abigail and to the frightened Queen herself.

When after an interchange of notes Sarah accused Abigail to her face, she 'gravely answered that she was sure the queen, who had loved me extremely, would always be very kind to me', a reply which left Sarah speechless. 'To see a Woman whom I had raised out of the Dust put on such a superior Air, and to hear her assure me, by Way of Consolation, that the queen would be always very kind to me!* At length', she adds, 'I went on to reproach her for her Ingratitude and her secret Management with the Queen to undermine those who had so long and with so much Honour served her Majesty. To this she answered that she never spoke to the Queen about Business'.[15]

Ingratitude was, by Sarah's reckoning, the deadliest sin of all; for just as fools were often knaves, so an ungrateful person would stop at nothing. And as for discussing state business, Sarah, certain that Abigail and Anne did, took the Queen to task about it, only to be assured that her cousin 'never meddled with anything'. 'I believe others that have been in her station in former times have been tattling & very impertinent', Anne admitted, 'but she is not at all of that temper; and as for the company she keeps, it is with her as with most other people. I fancy that their lot in the world makes them move with some out of civility rather than choice; and I really believe, for one that is so much in the way of company, she has less acquaintance than anyone upon earth'.[16] It was not Abigail's fault that her other cousin was Harley, nor that his circle included Dr. Arbuthnot and Jonathan Swift. Not everyone could afford to be as fastidious as queens and duchesses.

But Sarah was not to be so easily side-tracked. Spies' reports were disquieting, her suspicion was profound. By a thousand signs it was all too obvious that Anne herself had changed, though she vowed she had not. Indeed she begged for reconciliation. Surely they might lay aside wrangling and make a fresh start? Why could they not be

---

* In another version Sarah says if she lived a thousand years she could never forget that piece of patronage from one 'that had affected such a humble way that when she met me would always offer to pin up my coat first, and must now pretend to know the Queen's mind'. (Blen G-I-8).

as they used to be? Because, said Sarah if only to herself, things had gone too far. 'It was so long before I suspected I had a secret enemy that was under trust betraying me', she wrote afterwards, 'that it was past helping before I apprehended it'.[17]

When she did apprehend it she made violent efforts by letter and by interview to oust the interloper and so, as she hoped, win back for herself the Queen's favour. In her long letter to Anne of October 29th, 1707 she refers to a recent interview when there had been no emotional scene (a thing Anne was most shy of), but long and profound silences. Sarah had stood throughout, she reminded the Queen, behind a screen, never once pulled out her handkerchief and only wept a little at parting, when Anne kissed her and Sarah 'answered as Brutus did his friend'.*[18] Yet after this, Sarah tells us, 'that vile woman' Abigail blew up the coals again to such purpose that Anne complained of Sarah to Godolphin.

Undoubtedly there were reconciliations and undoubtedly Abigail was capable of making mischief. Time and again Anne tried to heal the breach. In writing to Sarah ('Don't lett any body see this strang Scrawl') she is not ashamed to give way to emotion, although face to face she is. 'My poor hart is so tender', she writes, 'if I had begun to speak I should not have been fitt to be seen by any body . . .' Will Sarah please write too? Anne cannot trust herself to meet her just now, she would break down.[19] But Sarah is unmoved. 'This letter from the Queen', she comments, 'is extreamly kind, but 'tis plain to me that she was fearfull that I should tax her with her passion for Mrs Hill, and therefore she would not have me speak to her but write, nor shew her scrawl as she calls it which is very well writt, but she did not care that my Lord Marl: or Lord Godolphin should see this letter & she had allways allowd me to shew them any thing. As to her not being fitt to bee seen if I spoak to her, she only feared blushing if I spoak upon the subject of Mrs Hill, for when she loved

---

* *Cassius:* Have not you love enough to bear with me,
When that rash humour which my mother gave me
Makes me forgetful?
Brutus: Yes, Cassius, and from henceforth
When you are over-earnest with your Brutus
He'll think your mother chides, and leave you so.
Julius Caesar, act IV, sc. 3.

me most she was not apt to teares & it was very seldom that she expressed her greif that way either for the Duke of Gloucester or the Prince'.[20]

On the nature of a queen's private grief not many perhaps would care to act the critic. On the point of Anne's handwriting, however, it is true that this letter of hers is neatly written. On occasion emotion can make the Queen's hand tremble visibly.* Here it is the script of a composed child, with rounded letters, no blots and every i dotted, a mild hand making Sarah's endorsement look spiky and savage. 'Open your dear hart freely', begs the Queen, 'for I can have no ease till everything is sett right between us ... Your displeasure is a thing I cannot support'. But again the dry endorsement: 'This letter seems to bee very kind & tender but it shews that all the ill usage that I had afterwards proceeded from Mrs Hill & not from any fault of mine to the Queen. She loved her at this time & that was the cause of my trouble, which she observed & knew very well the occation of it, but she was ashamed of it & therefore she desires that my answer upon it might bee in writing because she never knew what to say upon that subject if she was not full prepared'.[21]

Such passages make repellent reading; yet to stack all one's sympathy with an innocent queen might not be wise. Anne had, says Sir Winston, immense powers of reserve and dissimulation;† while Sarah 'resembled in some respects the kind of woman we are familiar with in the public and social agitations of our own day. But no personal accommodation could alter the antagonism. Behind the Queen lurked Harley, the Tories and Peace. Behind Sarah stood Marlborough, the Whigs, the Grand Alliance and the War'.[22]

---

* Notably in her letter to Sarah (undated) in which she writes: '. . . to beg you would not mention that person any more who you are pleased to call ye object of my fayvour, for whatever caracter ye malittious world may give her I do asure you it will never have any worth with me, knowing she does not deserve it'. She omits three words in two lines and adds them afterwards. The hand is that of a mind in turmoil. (Blen E 19).

† 'She talks some times as if she thought her self good and keeps a clutter with religion that would make one imagine that she had really devotion & some principles ... There is nothing she will not disown, dissemble or deny if she bee but prepared for it by those that she has a passion for'. Sarah of Anne (Blen. G-I-16).

Marlborough was at first incredulous. A bedchamber-woman closeted with the Queen? Impossible! And as for political influence, no, no, that was womanish nonsense. He was soon to be disillusioned when Godolphin wrote to tell him that he was meeting with the utmost difficulty and resistance. Even so, society at large might have stayed in the dark a little longer had not Prince George given the game away when somebody remarked on the Queen's sore eyes. 'The Queen had a deflexion in her eyes as to which there happen'd some discourse in the House of Lords. Upon this the Prince said inadvertently Her Majesty would soon be free from that Malady if she did not sit up so late at Nights. This occasioned much speculation'.[23] So runs a contemporary report, to which Cunningham adds: 'About this time many things were transacted at Court in the dead of the night'.[24]

To those in the know it must have been obvious that there must soon be a crisis, and sure enough in the winter of 1707–8 there were two. Sarah, paying her Christmas visit to Anne at Kensington, learned from the page who was to announce her that Abigail had just been sent for. 'The Moment I saw her Majesty', Sarah goes on, 'I plainly perceived she was very uneasy. She stood all the while I was with her & looked as coldly upon me as if her Intention was that I should no longer doubt of my Loss of her Affections. Upon observing what Reception I had I said I was very sorry I had happened to come so unseasonably. I was making my Courtesy to go away when the Queen, with a great deal of Disorder in her Face and without speaking one Word, took me by the Hand: And when thereupon I stooped to kiss hers, she took me up with a very cold Embrace and then without one kind Word let me go. So strange a Treatment of me, after my long & faithful Services & after such repeated Assurances from her Majesty of an unalterable Affection made me think that I ought in Justice to myself, as well as in Regard to my Mistress's Interest, to write to her in the plainest & sincerest Manner possible and expostulate with her upon her Change to me & upon the new Counsels by which she seemed to be wholly governed'.[25]

In the long letter which followed, after referring to 'an Embrace that seemed to have no Satisfaction in it', Sarah issued an ultimatum. Either she was to be treated with the openness of a friend or with the reserve of a court official. After some days Anne returned a soft answer which, although in Sarah's view 'equificating', averted open strife for the time being.

In the meantime Marlborough's calming letters to his wife—surely the Queen must respond to reason?—were nevertheless full of his own weariness and despondency, a kind of fatalistic wretchedness at the futility of striving against enemies at home as well as abroad. The one glimmer of hope comes from the direction of Woodstock, where Vanbrugh and the landscape between them had clearly fired him with heroic ideas. Yet even of this he writes:

It is true what you say of Woodstock that it is very much at my heart, especially when we are in prosperity, for then my whole thoughts are of retiring with you to that place. But if everything does not go to our own desire, we must not set our hearts too much upon that place, for I see very plainly that whilst I live, if there be troubles I must have my share of them. This day makes your humble servant fifty-seven. On all accounts I could wish myself younger, but for none so much as that I might have it more in my power to make myself more agreeable to you, whom I love with all my soul.[26]

He suggests that Sarah should consult Wise about building an ice-house and should taste the fruit of every tree in the Blenheim orchard 'so that what is not good might be changed'.

But when Marlborough returned to England for the winter he found things at court even worse than he had supposed. Queen and Duchess were scarcely on speaking terms. Godolphin, steadily thwarted, yearned for retirement as Marlborough did himself. Stalemate in the war and the onerous land-tax which was paying for it reinforced the clamour of those demanding peace; while trouble at the Admiralty meant more trouble for Marlborough, whose Tory brother George shared the responsibility for its muddles with the Lord High Admiral, Prince George of Denmark.

On February 8th, 1708 the Marlboroughs and Godolphin met the Queen in an apartment adjoining the room where the lords of the council had assembled. Godolphin led by proffering his resignation, a gesture the Queen took coolly. She would give him till next day to consider; she knew many who would be glad to take his staff. Next came Sarah, 'with great duty and submission' and with reminders of

Robert Harley Earl of Oxford
and Mortimer. Kneller

Abigail Hill (Lady Masham). Artist unknown
Identity doubtful

long and faithful service, only to be told (if we are to believe James Stanhope), 'You shall consider of this till tomorrow, then if you desire it I shall advise you to go to your little house in St Albans and there stay till Blenheim House is ready for your Grace'. Lastly Marlborough, who 'lamented that he came in competition with so vile a creature as Harley' and that he too therefore must resign. To which Anne said, should he do so it would be to run his sword through her head.[27]

The Queen then withdrew alone to her council, where Harley delivered a report. 'Upon which the Duke of Somerset rose and said if her Majesty suffered that fellow (pointing to Harley) to treat affairs of the war without the advice of the General, he could not serve her; and so left the Council'.[28] He was supported by Lord Pembroke and others, but the meeting continued and the Queen refused to part with Harley until the Commons, by declining to pass the bill of supply, forced her hand. With him went Henry St John* and Sir Simon Harcourt. But Abigail, Harley's channel of communication with the Queen, remained unharmed.

For Anne's cold advice to Sarah we have only the word of Stanhope who was probably not present. Sarah had asked Anne if she might withdraw to the country until the end of the next campaign, so that she and her husband might then retire together. To this, at the interview, Anne may have made a scathing reply, though scarcely in the words quoted, which are uncharacteristic. All she probably said was, 'I shall advise you to retire to St Albans until Blenheim is ready', implying perhaps that she would prefer not to have her at Windsor.

Stanhope omits to add that Sarah had further asked (though 'much interrupted with tears') for the reversion of her court appointments for her daughters, a proviso to which, according to the Duchess, Anne had agreed.

When Marlborough returned to London to take leave of the Queen he found her more friendly and he understood that she would still be willing for his daughters, Henrietta Godolphin and Anne Sunderland, to succeed when their mother retired. To make doubly sure, however, Sarah herself cornered the Queen upon the subject, thanked her and said she had now by her goodness left them

* To be replaced, as Secretary at War, by Robert Walpole.

nothing to do but pray for her. At this Anne 'looked red and uneasy' and when pressed said she remembered no such commitment and would be glad to hear no more of it. This to Sarah was shocking; and 'what made it the more unaccountable was that the queen had so very extraordinary a memory that she hardly was ever known to forget any thing of the smallest moment . . . But thus did words, assurances & the most serious promises bind or not bind just as humour, temper or inclination worked, & honour & truth came to be no more accounted of than her new advisers would permit'.[29]

Before Marlborough left for Flanders the Queen wrote to him:

I have had a great mind to speak to you this week, but when I have met with an opportunity I have found such a tenderness coming upon me on the thought of the subject I was to speak of that I choose rather to trouble you this way with my complaints than any other. You know I have often had the misfortune of falling under the Duchess of Marlborough's displeasure, and now, after several reconciliations, she is again relapsed into her cold unkind way and . . . has taken a resolution not to come to me when I am alone, and fancies nobody will take notice of the change. She may impose upon some poor simple people, but how can she imagine she can on any that have a grain of sense? Can she think that the Duchess of Somerset and my Lady Fitzharding, who are two of the most observing, prying ladies in England, won't find out that she never comes near me nor looks on me as she used to do, that the tatling voice will not in a little time make us the jest of the town? Some people will blame her, others me, and a great many both. What a disagreeable noise she will be the occasion of making in the world besides, God knows what ill consequences it may be of. Therefore for God Almighty's sake, for the Duchess of Marlborough's, your own, and my poor sake, endeavour all you can to persuade Mrs Freeman out of this strange unreasonable resolution. I have not as yet ventured to make any answer to her letter, nor dare not, for till this violent humour be over all I can say, though never so reasonable, will but inflame her more. [30]

A more sensible, reasonable, friendly, sincere letter was surely never written. If this was deceit it showed a diabolical finesse of which no one, except her Groom of the Stole, believed Anne capable. Yet there it was, she did believe it. 'Either Mrs Morley was allways the greatest Decembler in the world', she wrote later, 'or she did not find herself touch'd in consiance after fourty years old';[31] and again: 'When she was prepared by those she had an opinion of, she could so far act a part very well as to say anything that was not true with all the ease & coldnesse imaginable & 'tis plain she never had any sense of honour in anything'.*[32]

In response to Anne's plea there will doubtless have been some gentle remonstrance with Sarah from Marlborough; but those who worship reason seem often the deafest to it; or perhaps in this case suspicion and jealousy had ousted reason, at least for a time. When Marlborough had left, Sarah wrote to the Queen to tell her that she would not be surprised nor displeased to hear that she had gone into the country, 'since by your very hard and uncommon usage of me you have convinced all sorts of people, as well as myself, that nothing would be so uneasy to you as my near attendance'.[33]

If it had been a private quarrel it would have been of small consequence, but Anne knew that sooner or later, if Sarah persisted, they must be the jest of Europe and she dreaded the consequences. 'The effects of these female jars', notes Archdeacon Coxe, 'arising from offended dignity on the one hand and disappointed ambition on the other ... produced the most sinister effects on the administration of public affairs by the perplexities into which they perpetually threw both the treasurer and general'.[34]

It was to be the supreme test of Marlborough's patience. In his letters to Sarah during this spring and summer two themes predominate: Blenheim and the 'indifferency' of his Duchess. In April he refers to her 'resolution of living with that coldness & indifferency for me which if it continues must make me the unhappiest man alive'.[35] In May he uses cypher to remind her that 39 [himself] can have no content if he must live without the esteem and love of 240 [Sarah]; and in June, 'Upon my word, when you are out of humour and are disatisfied with me I had rather dye than live. So on the contrary when you are kind I covett of all things a quiet life with

* Most of the Duchess's harsher judgments of Queen Anne were written when still smarting from 'ill usage'. In old age she toned them down.

you'.[36] When Anne complained of the Duchess of Marlborough's displeasure, Marlborough knew exactly what she meant.

As for Blenheim, Sarah is to coax the Duke of Manchester, ambassador at Genoa, to send thousands of yards of Italian velvet and damask. Marlborough himself is buying tapestry and paintings and has been 'advised by every body to have the Portico, so that I have writt to Vanbrook to have itt; and which I hope you will like for I shou'd be glad we were allways of one mind, which shall allways be endeavour'd for I am never so happy as when I think you are kind'.[37] After two years of building, Vanbrugh had changed his mind about the principal order and switched from Doric to Corinthian. Now, after nearly three, a Corinthian portico seventy feet high for the northern entrance is begged as an afterthought. Sarah would have liked it better if there had been steps to go with it, which for years there were not.

In the meantime, to Marlborough's dismay, Sarah had begged a site of the Queen at St James's, there with Wren to erect a rival to Blenheim. It would cost twice as much as the estimate, her husband warned her, and in any case she would find as a general rule that it was better to buy than to build . . . From none of which could anyone have suspected that Marlborough was about to fight his third major battle at Oudenarde.

Anne's reaction to the news of the victory—'Oh, Lord, when will all this dreadful bloodshed cease?'—was significant; and when Marlborough's account reached her, it can have given no pleasure. 'The Circumstances in this last Battle', he told her, 'I think shew the Hand of God . . . a visible Mark of the Favour of Heaven to you and your Arms'; and then, plunging further, 'Give me Leave to say that I think you are obliged in Conscience & as a good Christian to forgive & to have no more Resentments to any particular Person or Party but to make use of such as will carry on this just War with Vigour'.[38] The letter was typical and sincere; and yet how very odd it is when a christian general, the groans of the dying in his ears, tells his christian queen that she is bound in conscience to forgive her enemies!

Even so, Marlborough's invocation might have carried more weight with the Queen had his Duchess been reasoning with her on similar lines; but her approach was entirely different. She had contracted the habit of sending Anne letters she had received from others, without their permission and with her own comments. This she did in the case of Abigail when, for Anne's benefit, she compared her to Iago; and now again in the case of Marlborough: his note on Oudenarde, in which he spoke of himself as God's instrument of happiness to the Queen and nation, 'if she will please to make use of it'. This, on Sarah's part, proved a miscalculation. The last phrase offended the Queen who wrote to Marlborough for an explanation. In reply she received from Sarah another long letter in anything but a conciliatory tone [appendix i].

Yet all this was as nothing to the onslaughts the Duchess was planning with the help of him she called her secretary, Arthur Maynwaring. Maynwaring was an honest man. He was popular at the Kit-Cat Club, befriended by Vanbrugh, kept a highly reputable mistress,* sat in the Commons, wrote satire and had been made auditor of the imprests (a remunerative sinecure) by Godolphin in 1705. His health was precarious, and indeed in Kneller's Kit-Cat portrait (p. 164.) he looks at the point of death. He doted on Sarah. None of which would have amounted to much had he not been possessed of a strange, immature, schoolboyish quality of impishness, diverting at Holywell, uproarious at the Kit-Cat but, when it came to letter-writing, irresponsible in the extreme. As a secretary he is tireless. He writes draft after draft and sends them all to Sarah. 'Choose any thing you should like', he begs, 'and though I some-times press your Grace on this subject to do things that you seem averse to, I cannot help confessing that I believe in the main you certainly do what is right, for I do not think you were ever in the wrong in your life ... When I read over this morning', he continues, 'the letter for Mrs Mor: [the Queen] as I have put it together, I cannot help saying one thing pleased me in it very much, which was that tho above half of it be your Graces own writing & your very words, I am sure nobody that were to read it would guess that it were not all writ by one person, which shews that I have not imitated your style so long quite in vain'.[39]

Together they composed long, anonymous letters to Abigail [appendix ii]; and together, for Sarah to sign, they wrote outrageous letters to the Queen. Not all of them were sent, but if that written in

* The actress Mrs Oldfield.

Sarah's hand and dated July 26th, 1708 [appendix III]—between the battle of Oudenarde and the thanksgiving—reached its target, the wonder is that Anne agreed to Sarah's sharing her coach to St Paul's.

On that thanksgiving morning (August 19th) Sarah must have had mixed feelings as, in her office of Mistress of the Robes, she selected the Queen's jewels. In one account she speaks of the many hours it had cost her to do them.[40] Nothing, we can be certain, was left to chance. But this was not to be a repetition of 1704, when the Queen was 'full of jewels'. 'Her Majesty', Sarah herself tells us, 'seldom woar Jewells';[41] so why should she choose to wear them now? In the coach there was trouble; and in the portico, or even possibly in St Paul's itself, there was very nearly a public scene when Sarah, as it was said, commanded the Queen to silence. But this, Sarah insisted, was an exaggeration. Fearing that Anne was about to say something she would not have wanted onlookers to hear, Sarah had begged her in a whisper to be quiet. Whatever the truth of it, the offence was profound. Yet it was Sarah who wrote to complain of the Queen's treatment, 'when I had taken so much Pains to put your Jewels in a Way that I thought you would like, Mrs Masham could make you refuse to wear them, in so unkind a Manner; because that was a Power she had not thought fit to exercise before. I will make no Reflections upon it', she ended, 'only that I must needs observe that your Majesty chose a very wrong Day to mortify me, when you were just going to return Thanks for a Victory obtained by Lord Marlborough'.[42]

Every time Sarah wrote she made matters worse, and in this she was egged on by Maynwaring. If only Marlborough could have been there to check her! 'I cou'd wish,' he wrote mildly, from the siege of Lille, 'that Mrs Freeman would see what she so frequently obsarves that 42 [the Queen] is not capable of being chang'd by reason, so that you shou'd be quiet til the time comes in which she must change'.[43] But that was not, as none knew better than he did, Sarah's way. Reason and candour were her twin gods that everyone must yield to. The Queen might safely be left to them and to her. Anne, Sarah tells us, was at Windsor—

Through the whole Summer after Mr Harley's Dismission the Queen continued to have secret Correspondence with him. And that this might be the better managed she staid all the sultry Season, even when the Prince was panting for Breath,* in that small House she had formerly purchased at Windsor which, though as hot as an Oven, was then said to be cool, because from the Park such Persons as Mrs Masham had a Mind to bring to her Majesty could be let in privately by the Garden.[44]

Yet again, on September 9th, 1708, there seems to have been an attempted reconciliation. Anne writes to Sarah, 'According to my promise I writt this to lett my dear Mrs Freeman know if she can com to me at five aclock this afternoon I will be redy to receive you in my Gallery at ye Castle & shall think my self very happy if that meeting setts every thing right between us, there being nothing I am more desirous off then to have a thorow good understanding between deare Mrs Freeman and her poor unfortunat faithfull Morley who will tell her last moment be Soe, whether you think what I shall happen to say be reasonable or just'.[45] But red eyes and raised voices told of failure.[46] Sarah makes no mention of it. All we have are 'Heads of a conversation with Mrs Morley, Sep: the 9th, 1708', but since these include such firecrackers as 'No body countenanced & trusted by her but who is some way or other influenced by Mr Harley', 'Mr Harley never had a good reputation in the world . . . Nobody alive can either bee more odious then hee is or more contemptable to all parties', and 'Why will she not consider fairly & cooly etc',[47] it is not difficult to guess the rest or at least the tenor of it.

In the following month it became known that Prince George of Denmark† was dying. On October 26th Sarah wrote to the Queen:

Though the last time I had the honour to wait upon your Majesty your usage of me was such as was scarce possible for me to imagine or for any body to believe, yet I cannot hear of so

* Prince George was asthmatic.
† 'I think my self more obliged to him then to Mrs Morley. I remember all his justice & goodnesse to me in times past. I have a thousand things to thank him for & noe one to complain of. Hee is still the same (I beleive) to me that hee ever was & will allways bee soe unless Mrs Morley thinks fitt to give him a prejudice to me which I am sure I shall never deserve'. (Sarah to Anne, of Prince George of Denmark, 29 Oct., 1707. Blen. G-I-7).

great a misfortune and affliction to you as the condition in which the Prince is without coming to pay my duty in inquiring after your health, and to see if in any particular whatsoever my service can either be agreeable or useful to you, for which satisfaction I would do more then I will trouble your Majesty to read at this time.[48]

Taking this letter with her Sarah travelled all night to Kensington and delivered it. Next day she was received very coolly but remained and was present on October 28th when the Prince died. 'Then I knelt down to the Queen', runs her account, 'and said all that I could imagine from a faithful servant and one that she had professed so much kindness to; but she seemed not to mind me but clapt her hands together, with other marks of passion; and when I had expressed all I could think of to moderate her grief, I knelt by her without speaking for some time, and then asked her to go to St James's; upon which she answered she would stay there. I said that was impossible; what could she do in such a dismal place? and I made use of all the arguments that are common upon that head, but all in vain; she persisted that she would stay at Kensington . . . I said nobody in the world ever continued in a place where a dead husband lay, and I did not see where she could be but within a room or two of that dismal body'. At last she agreed to go and, handing Sarah her watch said, 'Don't come in to me till the hand of the watch comes to this place', and added, 'Send to Masham to come to me before I go'.*

Sarah continues: 'This I thought very shocking, but at that time I was resolved not to say the least wry word to displease her and therefore answered that I would, and went out of the room with the watch in my hand . . . but as I was sitting at the window, watching the minutes to go in, I thought it so disagreeable for me to send for Mrs Masham to go in to her before all that company that I resolved to avoid that; and when the time was come I went in and told her all things were ready, but I had not sent to Mrs Masham; that I thought

---

* 'The deportment of the Duchess of Marlborough while the Prince lay expiring was of such a nature that the Queen, then in the heights of grief, was not able to bear it, but with marks of displeasure in her countenance she ordered the Duchess to withdraw and send Mrs Masham to her'. Swift: *Prose*, v, 369.

it would make a disagreeable noise when there were bishops and
ladies of the bedchamber without that she did not care to see, and
that she might send herself to her to come to St James's at what time
she pleased.

'To this she consented and I called for her hoods, which I remember Mrs Hill* put on; and as she did it the Queen whispered with her,
I suppose some kind thing to her sister, who had not appeared
before me at Kensington; but upon the alarm of the Queen's being
to go with me to St James's, she came into the gallery with one of
her ministers, the Scotch doctor [Arbuthnot], to see her Majesty pass,
who, notwithstanding her great affection for the Prince, at the sight
of that charming lady, as her arm was upon mine, which she had
leaned upon, I found she had strength to bend down towards Mrs
Masham like a sail and in passing by went some steps more than was
necessary to be nearer her; and when that cruel touch was over, of
going by her with me, she turned about in a little passage room and
gave orders about her dogs and a strong box'.

In the coach Anne gave orders about the burial (room was to be
left in the vault for herself); and at St James's Sarah led her to the
green closet and gave her a cup of broth. That evening Sarah found
the Queen at table with Mrs Masham, who left immediately 'with
an air of insolence and anger'. The Queen took a great deal of
trouble with the funeral arrangements and showed 'bits of great
tenderness for the Prince. I remember', the Duchess concludes, 'she
wrote me once a little note at which I could not help smiling, that I
should send to my Lord Treasurer to take care that some door might
be taken down at the removing the Prince to Westminster, for fear
the dear Prince's body should be shook as he was carried out of some
room, though she had gone long jumbling journeys with him to the
Bath when he must feel it and when he was gasping for breath. I did
see the tears in her eyes two or three times after his death, upon his
subject, and I believe she fancied she loved him . . . but her nature
was very hard and she was not apt to cry.'[49]

The Queen's note, at which the Duchess could not help smiling,
ran as follows:

I scratched twice at dear Mrs Freeman's **door**, as soon as lord

* Abigail's sister, Alice Hill.

treasurer went from me, in hopes to have spoke one more word to him before he was gone; but no body hearing me, I wrote this, not caring to send what I had to say by word of mouth; which was to desire him that when he sends his orders to Kensington he would give directions there may be a great many yeomen of the guards to carry the prince's dear body that it may not be let fall, the great stairs being very steep and slippery. [50]

CHAPTER VII

Favour Declines

1709-1710

———◆———

The Queen's grief was sincere, but to one who took pleasure in the rules of etiquette there may have been some slight relief in meticulously observing them. For hours and days in the great frost of January 1709 gout kept her in bed, where she lay in a purple nightgown in a bed heavy with hangings of purple and black.

'I must desire you to bespeake a purple quilt & three couchions against I see company', she wrote to Sarah, 'but they must not be of any glossy thing; & if you please send one of your servants to ye upholsterer to know the size of ye bed that they may be made fitt. I cannot end this without beging you once more for God's sake to lett the Dear Picture you have of mine be putt into my Bedchamber for I cannot be without it any longer'.

This Sarah endorses: 'When the Queen writt this she was as much under the power of Mrs Masham as ever . . . The Picture that she mentions was the Princes which I took away because I thought she loved him & if she had been like other people 'tis terrible to see a picture while the affection is fresh upon one'.[1]

Among the royal dead perhaps only Albert the good can have been more thoroughly mourned than George the foolish. The Queen haunted the gloomy closets where he had lived and worked, closets which, Sarah remembered, 'looked only into a very ugly little close space where Mrs Masham used to dry linen . . . one was a water-closet & the other full of his tools which he worked with, and I thought nothing was more natural than to avoid seeing of papers or anything that belonged to one that one loved when they were just dead'. But 'all that time she saw everybody that Mrs Masham pleased'.[2] In another account (there are always several) Sarah says, 'It was generally thought that she only conversed there with Mrs Masham, which I my self once mentioned to her & I never saw anybody so struck, but now it appears that the great concern she shewed when those closets were mentioned was because she met the governing men there at the same time that she solemnly protested to the Duke of Marlborough & Lord Godolphin that she relied only upon them'.[3]

Sarah came to court seldom and then only for the business of her office. Princes, nay love itself might die, but petitioners persisted. Soon after Prince George's death Sarah felt it her duty to bring to Anne's notice the case of Mrs Howe, a widow with five young children and no money; for, says Sarah, she thought it would give the Queen 'an air of being greivd for the Prince to bee touch'd upon that melancholly subject', and so it proved. 'My artifice', Sarah continues, 'succeeded just as I expected, for her Majesty put on a very melancholly air as if she felt a great deal upon that subject and said yes indeed, I doe know how to pity her. I will look over a list of the lodgings att Somersett hous; & for the pention she said she would do any thing that was reasonable; but she had a hum which she allways has when she does not really care for what she does & answer'd it would bee time enough to say what she would give her when she had spoken to my Lord Treasurer.'[4]

Perhaps, thought Sarah, she might be luckier in 'the case of poor Mr Griffith, a very old servant to her & the Prince who lately died, clerk of the green cloth.* This gentleman left his family in a very ill condition and . . . recommended his children to her Majesty with the most dutyfull & moving expressions'. But the Queen said that Griffith had in his time won a great deal from Prince George at cards, which Sarah agrees he had, 'and so did a great many others very fairly . . . and it would have been a sad thing to have kept his Highness company if they had got nothing by it'.[5] Another Griffith shared with Abigail and her brother the gift of mimicry, an accomplishment Sarah detested. 'Lady Howard and Mrs Griffith have bin with me today', Anne in an undated note tells Sarah, 'The first goes

* Dr Reid states that Sarah's brother-in-law Edward Griffith became Comptroller of the Green Cloth. (Reid, op. cit. p. 31)

out of town tomorrow & says she loves ye Country mightely but yet looks very melencoly when she speakes of it. My other visiter at my request mimiked you & severall others. Lady Fretchevill* she does much ye best, but for your self she does over act you'.[6]

Friendship had made way for a time of teasing and to this Sarah was prepared to give full rein. She begged for an old harpsichord, which she almost certainly knew Anne had lent Abigail, and 'with some difficulty' Sarah was given her way.[7] It is doubtful if she played herself. She admits she 'did not love fine Musick & thought nothing so pretty as Ballads';[8]† and in this also she was encouraged by Maynwaring.

'I shall be very glad', he assures her, 'to perform a part in Ballad singing whenever your Grace has occasion for a fine voice. I saw the other day a new Ballad upon Abigal. Mrs Chetwynd had it and if I can get a copy I will try to mend the latter part of it & then I can sing it with becoming impudence, which I could not do if I made one quite myself. I am very glad your Grace can be diverted with a harpsichord & I will be sure to practise upon it against I have the honour to wait upon you in your travels. I heard you borrow one of Lady Fitzharding the other night. If you should ever have occasion again, I have one that I never use & yet would never part with because it was given me by Lord Burlington. It is a pretty one and very good but I make use of a worse because it has an uncommon quality of being very seldom out of tune'.[9]

As ballad-monger Maynwaring found a competitor in Godolphin. Neither was an Addison, but for letting off steam or venting venom their doggerel served its turn:

> Who goes to Court may see with half an eye
> Tis over run with nauseous flattery;
> Scarce one man left who will not be afraid
> To whisper Mashams an ungreatfull jade . . .[10]

But the jade too could take a hand in provocation, as when she coolly moved into Sarah's lodgings at Kensington. Sarah of course made straight for the Queen and taxed her with it. Impossible. 'Masham had none of my rooms, she was sure of it & her Majesty

---

* Lady Frescheville, a lady-in-waiting disliked by Sarah.
† See appendix IV.

was pleased to repeat it over & over & was so very positive of it that I was really ashamed & begged her pardon . . . But as I went downstairs, going by my own lodgings I could not help asking ye page of ye back stairs that carried the candle to light me if there was any use made of those rooms. He answerd ye bedchamber-woman had one part of em & Mrs Masham the other'. So back to the Queen, who remained unmoved. Next day Abigail apologised and moved out only, according to Sarah, to move back again for her lying-in. It was hardly to be wondered at that when Anne for the third time was confronted with the same grievance she lost her temper and shouted, 'Tis a lie! Tis false!'[11] And so once again Sarah was shocked. Anne would never have made such a scene in the old days, she had always seemed so well-bred. Abigail must be coarsening her. To talk with her was useless. However, one could still write.

In letter-writing as in everything else Sarah was systematic and unsparing. True, she wrote fast and tumbled her mind out on paper, but her mind was clear, she knew what she wanted to say and was indifferent as to how long it took her to say it or the recipient to make it out. A few sides of gilt-edged paper (she preferred thick paper from Paris) were nothing. When a situation grew serious it called for what she called a notum or a narrative: a recapitulation running to a dozen or more foolscap pages. In 1709 the Queen received more of Sarah's narratives than ever before, and though the field was extensive, three topics were given priority: long and faithful service, harsh usage and the shortcomings of Abigail.

Abigail was no fool and, in addition to Harley and St John, she had useful allies in Dr Arbuthnot and Swift and, on a lower plane, in the hack-writer Rivella Manley who, though apt to overreach herself, could at least be counted on for zealous support. In a crude age she relied mainly on the bludgeon where Swift would have used a sword; but she was not contemptible. She could be ingenious, and in her account of Marlborough's amours with Barbara Cleveland, whom she knew, she brings, however scurrilously, her characters and their jasmine-scented seraglio to life. She was not conscious of the ludicrous, but neither were most of her readers. Thus in her *New Atlantis*, a best-seller published in May, 1709, she credited Abigail (Hilaria) with a soul fitted for grandeur, 'a capacious repository for the confidence of royal favour'. Abigail's wit and judgment, she claimed, were of the finest and, more than that, she 'not only wore but loved the Holy awful Robe of Religion'. The long panegyric ends: 'She speaks more correct than others write'. It is to be hoped that she did.

To Mrs Manley the reign of Anne, though eventful, was not eventful enough. She therefore sat herself down, as it were, at her loom of fiction and wove melodrama, which she clearly enjoyed. Queen Anne was made to die in childbirth (Abigail adopted the princess), Marlborough of wounds, Godolphin was exiled with the Pretender, and as for Sarah (Madame de Caria), she would have been lynched by the mob had not Abigail saved her. Even as it was, her 'Superbous Palace' was stormed and looted. But the dénouement was still to come. Hilaria (Abigail) gave the Duchess sanctuary, but when the mob murmured, 'she persuaded her (tho' with much difficulty) to resign herself a Votary to Religion'; and since Sarah's status as a widow 'forbad her retirement among the Vestals', Abigail was magnanimous enough to found and endow a new order of which Sarah became Superior, 'so to atone by her perpetual attendance on & Adoration to the Mother of the Gods for the injustice she had done to Mortals'.

Maynwaring, writing to Sarah of 'that vile and nauseous book', made light of its satire. 'Tis all old incredible stuff', he told her, 'and there is one scene which I think you could hardly help laughing at, which is when 240 [Sarah] is going to be pull'd to pieces by the mob for all manner of ill done to 42 [Anne] and to England, Generous Hilaria [Abigail] sends a troop of guards to rescue her'.[12]

For Sarah it made the excuse for one of her longest letters to the Queen. From drafts at Blenheim it looks as though she at first intended a full-length review, but on consideration relegated the book to the end of her letter, in the form of an afterthought: 'I had almost forgot to tell you of a new book . . .' etc. At the beginning of her letter she asks, 'What is it that prevails with you to oppose the advice of all your old servants & councils if it be not that woman?' and suggests that if she should question the first passer-by as to what had caused so great a change in the Queen, 'he would say that the reason was because you were grown very fond of Mrs Masham & were governed by those that govern her'.[13]

Though long since warned by her husband that 'all truths are not to be spoke', Sarah had never been one for leaving things unsaid. She vaunted her candour and failed to see that no one with judgment and sensibility could have sent such letters as she did to the Queen. She 'hoped it would do good' and that Anne would no longer count it a crime for her to accuse her of 'a more than ordinary favour' for Mrs Masham. It could of course, on the contrary, do nothing but harm, and if Sarah failed to realise it, Marlborough did not.

'It has always been my Observation in Disputes', he wrote to her, 'especially in that of Kindness and Friendship, that all Reproaches, though ever so just, serve to no End but making the Breach wider. I cannot help being of Opinion that however insignificant we may be, there is a Power above that puts a Period to our Happiness or Unhappiness. If any body had told me eight Years ago that after such great Success, and after you had been a faithful Servant 27 Years that even in the Queen's Life-time we should be obliged to seek Happiness in a retired Life, I could not have believed that possible'.[14]

In May, certain of peace, he sent from the Hague for a chair of state—'I beg you will take care to have it made so as that it may serve for part of a bed when I have done with it here'[15]—but for peacemaking it was never to be needed. When the allies demanded that, should Louis XIV's grandson refuse to relinquish the throne of Spain, Louis must go to war with him, the peace preliminaries broke down: a disaster that lost us the peace Marlborough had fought for. In England, dismay and disappointment; in France, famine and fury. Soldiers reached for their arms and trudged on towards the holocaust of Malplaquet.

It was hardly the moment for chiding Marlborough for not, on his duchess's behalf, remonstrating with the Queen, yet that is what Sarah now did. Wearily, from the bloodiest of battlefields, Marlborough replied:

I do assure you upon my honour & salvation that the only reason why I did not write was that I am very sure it would have had no other effect than that of being shewn to 256 [Abigail], by which she would have had an opertunity of turning it as she pleas'd so that when I shal speake to 42 [the Queen] of their harsh Behavior to you thay would have been prepar'd . . . You are dearer to me then my whole life, for I am fonder of my

Queen Anne. Artist unknown

SARAH DAUGHTER AND HEIRESS
OF RICHARD JENNINGS OF SANDRIDGE
IN THE COUNTY OF HERTFORD ESQ:
WIFE OF JOHN CHURCHILL
DUKE OF MARLBOROUGH

Sarah Duchess of Marlborough. Kneller. The Duchess is in
mourning for her infant son

happiness then of my life, which I cannot injoye unless you are kind.[16]

At St James's, perhaps not surprisingly, the victory of Malplaquet was not mentioned. Sarah was in a whirl of pettiness not worthy of record except where some lively detail glints from her page. While she kept her offices (and Marlborough's going could not be risked by her dismissal), her duties had to be performed, and one senses the Queen's embarrassment, if not her own, while she did them. When for example the Queen of Prudes (Abigail's sister Alice) was promoted to bedchamber-woman, Sarah had most unwillingly to present her to the Queen at Windsor. She went, she tells us, and asked Abigail to announce her, whereupon 'she started back & said her Majesty was in her closset, poynting to it as if she would have me goe & as if she had not so much liberty as to scrape at the door'.[17]

That summer there was a similar scene at the presentation of Mrs Danvers's daughter who, according to Sarah, 'did not look like a human creature'. 'The Queen sent for the Dutchess from London to present Bell Danvers', reports Peter Wentworth, 'till when her Grace had not been there since the Queen was at Windsor. The town talk as if the Dutchess had thoughts of resigning the Groom of the Stole & that upon the condition Lady Sunderland should succeed her, but they say the Duke of Somersett contests the matter for his Duchess, which is what keeps the Dutchess of Marlborough from quiting . . . Her house in the Priory [St. James's] advances prodigiously, 'tis now a-covering'.[18]

It was a pity that at the founding of Marlborough House the words on the first stone, *1709 Anno Pacifico*—'neither truth nor good Latin'—had had to be altered.[19] Even so there were compensations. 'If the house be set in an equal line with her Majesty's Palace', Maynwaring told Sarah, 'it will have a view down the middle walk of her Garden . . . and being remov'd from all manner of dust & from the smoke of the houses in the Pell-mell, you will live & sleep as it were in the middle of that great Garden'.[20] Precisely so. In September, after showing the place to Vanbrugh, he wrote again:

He did really commend the inside of it very much, but I must own for the outside he found several faults there that were very obvious when he shewd them; and he has talk'd me into an opinion that he is an able Architect as to what relates to the Fabrick without; and I think you say that Blenheim is very well as to that. I believe you & he could make the best house in the world if you could agree to work together.[21]

Yes but they could not; and already Sarah had dealt him a heart-wound by demanding the destruction of Woodstock Manor. Vanbrugh bided his time against Marlborough's return, but Marlborough had other troubles and was writing to Sarah:

It is not fitt that any body but your self should know that I have just reason to be convinced that 42 [the Queen] has been made jealous of the power of 39 [himself], so that 39 is resolved not only to convince 42 but all the world that he has no ambition & at the same time be careful not to be in the power of villains nor even of 42. It is impossible to explain this in writing . . .[22]

And in the following month, to show the world that he had no ambition, he asked the Queen to make him Captain-General for life. Whoever put him up to it (the Junto?) it was a false move open, to say the least, to misinterpretation. Abigail, 'in her nauseous bufooning way', dubbed him King John.[23]

To her reply, in which she declined the favour, the Queen added:

You seem to be dissatisfied with my behaviour to the Duchess of Marlborough. I do not love complaining, but it is impossible to help saying on this occasion I believe nobody was ever so used by a friend as I have been by her ever since my coming to the Crown. I desire nothing but that she would leave off teasing & tormenting me and behave herself with the decency she ought both to her friend & Queen, and this I hope you will make her do . . . Whatever her behaviour is to me, mine shall be always as becomes me . . .[24]

And to Sarah the next day:

It is impossible for you to recover my former kindness, but I shall behave myself to you as the Duke of Marlborough's wife and as my Groom of the Stole.*[25]

* Commenting upon this in 1710 Sarah writes: 'She takes great care in the letter

Three days later Sarah sent the Queen from St Albans an immensely long letter ('as short as I could make it') in the form of a sermon. She begins by agreeing never to mention Abigail on condition that the Queen reads this 'history'—'a long & particular narrative of a series of faithful services for about 26 years past'—and ponders it before taking her Communion. Then come quotations from *The Whole Duty of Man*, e.g. The Queen should examine herself as to 'unthankfulness to those that admonish or being angry with them for it . . . Ask your own heart seriously', Sarah adds, 'whether you have ever told me of any fault but that of believing as all the world does that you have an intimacy with Mrs M: and whether those shocking things you complain I have said was any more then desiring you to love me better then her & not to take away your confydence in me'. Passing on to 'the warning before the Communion in the Common Prayer-book' she reminds the Queen of its terms and more particularly 'that we make restitution to those that we have done the least injury to' and so 'regain the friendship of those we have used ill'. Next comes Bishop Taylor on repentance; and indeed the whole letter or narrative would be most edifying were it not for the unmentionable Abigail, who somehow slides in towards the end. 'I still hope', concludes the Duchess, 'I have a better charecter in the world then Mrs Masham tells your Majesty of Inveteracy & malice . . . for I do not comprehend that one can properly bee said to have malice & inveteracy for a viper because one endeavours to hinder it from doing mischief'.[26]

Presumption on the grand scale can be stupefying, and from her failure to reply when so ordered it would seem that it had stunned the Queen. The only response, says Sarah, was a gracious smile when they met at Communion, and even that she feared was intended for Bishop Taylor rather than for herself. 'For as for friendship', she adds sadly, 'after all the most terrible vows and asseverations,

---

to tell me 'tis now impossible that her kindnesse to me can return, which is my own opinion & I need not tell you how little I desire it should. All I have don which she calls tormenting is in order that wee may bee safe & I own I have some pleasure in making her see she is in the wrong, tho I know she has not worth enough to own it or religion enough to make any body amends for any wrong, notwithstanding the clutter she keeps about her prayers & my soul'. (Blen G-I-8).

here ended even all pretences to it'.[27] But duty had been done. Both Duke and Duchess in turn had reminded the Queen of her Christian duty. They could do no more.

And now, says Sarah, their enemies' plots began to ripen. For months, 'whilst the Queen's ministers were asleep, they [Harley etc.] were frequently at court, advising in secret how to perplex those affairs of which others had the public direction'.[28] For Marlborough and Godolphin it was indeed an impossible situation and one that could not last. Early in the new year the opposition had grown bold enough for a trial of strength which, resolutely met and countered, could have led to their undoing.

The plan, crude as it sounds, was simply to sail over the head of the Captain-General by promoting Abigail's brother, Honest Jack Hill, who according to Sarah 'had never distinguished himself unless it were over a bottle',* to the head of a regiment. If successful it would show the world that the victor of Blenheim could be ignored in his own command, and at the same time it would be grossly unfair to those officers who had fought at his side and were themselves due for promotion; an injustice bound to cause disaffection and to undermine morale. The insult was deliberate, a malicious plan of which, since she supported it, one cannot entirely exempt the Queen. Sarah saw it as a contest between the Captain-General of the Allies and a chambermaid, 'a strange competition', as she told Anne, 'between one that has gaind you so many battles and one that is but just worthy to brush your combs'.[29] She was not far wrong.

At an uncomfortable interview with the Queen Marlborough protested, but all she would say was, 'You will do well to advise with your friends'. He came away, Sarah noticed, with fear in his eyes. But he was not friendless. The lords of the Junto swore that they would support him. Sunderland the extremist urged him to go to the limit with an ultimatum to the Queen—Abigail must go or he must resign—and in that he was zealously supported by Maynwaring who again and again insisted that this was the last chance and a superb one for getting rid of Carbunculata, the 'little shuffling

---

* 'Drinking & mimicking', Sarah writes, 'was his Inclenation'; but she was seemingly unaware of these habits when she got him an appointment as groom of the bedchamber to the young Duke of Gloucester, 'to run after a child from morning till night.' Disillusionment came later.

wretch' Abigail. The weak link was Godolphin. Like Marlborough he was by nature moderate; and like him, in spite of everything, he still had some tenderness for the Queen. He knew her obstinacy, none better, and remembered the lengths to which she had gone with William and Mary in her refusal to part with Sarah. To oust Abigail now, however desirable, would mean an address in the House and open scandal. It might even cost a throne. It must deeply embarrass the Queen. This could not be. And so at Windsor Lodge the last sentence of Marlborough's letter to the Queen was struck out and the ultimatum cancelled. He ended with the words: 'the malice of a bedchamberwoman'.

Marlborough absented himself from the Council meeting, but there was no repetition of the crisis of 1708; and 'by this neglect to take united action', comments Sir Winston, 'not only the Whigs but Godolphin settled their own speedy downfall'.[30] At court there was much hurrying and scurrying as Anne rallied her friends. It 'gave such a life to the Jacobit interest', says Sarah scathingly, 'that many who had never come to court in some years did now run about with very busy faces as if they thought they should soon get the government into their hands . . . Honest people', she adds, 'laughed at such proceedings or else pitied the Queens misfortune who was thus exposed to be the talk of all courts & countries for so wrong a thing as having such a fondness for a bedchamber woman'.[31]

Somers spoke for Marlborough. Godolphin was 'much distracted', Sarah detached. Marlborough, she agreed with Maynwaring, should stick to his guns and let the world see that 'he served till the war was ended only because he did not think it reasonable to let a chambermaid disappoint all he had done'.[32]

On January 20th the Queen, much shaken, told Godolphin that 'after deep consideration' she had decided not to insist upon Hill's appointment.* As Sarah read it, Abigail's fear of exposure had communicated itself to Anne, whereupon decisions had been reversed and, very temporarily, Marlborough had been restored to favour. While the glimmer lasted, the Queen 'made the greatest professions to him that were possible, and immediately, when the same lady's fears were over, she let them all fall again and returned

---

* The Queen compensated Hill with a 'pension' of £1000 a year and later made him a general, in which rank he led the disastrous expedition against Quebec.

to her former coldness . . . Tis thought', Sarah concludes, 'she will see her errors when 'tis too late as her father did before her'.[33]

For the Whigs it was a Pyrrhic triumph; for 'never', says Sir Winston, 'did the chance return of taking Abigail by the scruff and Harley by the throat'. For want of resolution they had drifted on to a course of suicide, a career in which they were to be speeded by their rash prosecution of Dr Sacheverell.

The theme of Sacheverell's sermon—'In perils among false brethren'—preached in St Paul's the previous November before the Lord Mayor of London had, not surprisingly, proved inflammable. Sarah called it 'an heap of bombast' and it was indeed a hysterical rage against dissenters and toleration which, in another place at another time, would have been brushed aside. Godolphin (Volpone in the sermon) decided to prosecute and so, with the help of Swift and Dr Atterbury, Sacheverell armed with a speech 'exquisitely contrived to move pity' was inflated from almost nothing to something which passed for a model martyr.

Sarah, not appreciating what this martyrdom might lead to, was far less interested in the defendant—'an ignorant impudent Incendiary . . . a lewd, drunken, pampered man'—than in the etiquette observed or not observed by the ladies-in-waiting who with the Queen, day after long day, attended the trial in Westminster Hall, a place still hung about with Marlborough's trophies. The whole thing —and to Sarah it was important—turned on whether the Queen's ladies should stand or sit. When on February 27th Sarah, having stood for three hours, approached the Queen, who sat incognito behind a curtain in the box Wren had designed for her, and asked if they might sit, as was usual at such prolonged affairs, she agreed at once and they did so. Later however the redhaired Duchess of Somerset arrived with Lady Hyde and they both insisted upon standing.

When, after some whispering, the rival duchess was told that they had the Queen's permission to sit, she 'started back with an air as if we had don something very impertinent' and still insisted upon standing, thus making the rest appear lacking in respect. 'It was easy to see the meaning of all this', adds Sarah, 'and that my gold key was the thing aim'd att, which design I was resolved to dissappoynt as much as I could, and for fear the Duke of Somerset should say something to the Queen or get Mrs Masham to doe it . . . I went to the Queen the next morning . . . I made my entry begging pardon for coming so early but I added that she gave some people leave to doe it & I was uneasy tell I had spoke to her alone upon what had happened the day before. She look'd angry & snap'd me up, saying she had very little time & that she expected my Lord Treasurer. I continued that I had not much to say, but finding that the Dutches of Somerset would not sett down as the rest of the ladys did & which was so known a custome, I was fearfull of doing any thing her Majesty did not like. Upon which she answerd very brutally, "I thought I should have been troubled no more with it".* "Yes, Madam", said I, "I must beg to know what you do really like in this matter, because tho' I can't think as some doe you converse with, I am sure I will never come in the way of doing any thing you don't like, & being to goe to the tryall in a few hours, I desire once more to know if you would bee better pleas'd that wee should not sett down". "If I had not liked it", answerd her Majesty, "why should you think I would have ordered it as I did yesterday?" '34

For the rest of the trial everyone sat except Lady Hyde and the Duchess of Somerset, the latter, Sarah noticed, mightily out of countenance. On March 21st the trial ended with a nominal sentence against Sacheverell, who set out upon a triumphal progress through the country, scattering blessings and kisses to devotees and putting new heart into the Church party.

Sarah brooded on the Somersets. He of course, as the Queen had once said, was a fool and a liar. She, the Percy heiress who had married for the third time at fifteen, pretended to be friendly; as who would not, when Sarah had had her appointed? But now all was clear. She aimed to be Groom of the Stole and her husband abetted her. Very well, Sarah accepted the challenge. All the same her tactics were odd for, says Sarah, 'she never was quite so kind as after she had taken the resolution to supplant me, for then she not only came to dinner & made meetings for play oftener than before, but I remember she took it into her head still to kiss me at parting, which was

---

* In another draft the Duchess writes, 'If any body had heard it I could not possibly have waited on her to the tryall, but we were alone & I was resolved to keep my temper till my Lord Marl: came home'. (Blen G-1-8).

quite new. However', she adds magnanimously, 'I took it all in good part'.[35]

The Queen's anger smouldered. Sarah, herself resilient, could not think that recent events had left deep resentment, yet rumour persisted. Even Abigail, they said (and this was cheering), was finding her mistress unmanageable. At last somebody, a Mrs Darcy, told Sarah that the Queen had been told that she often spoke of her in company disrespectfully.* It was the kind of thing Dr Hare meant when he later charged her with 'ill-grounded suspicions, violent passions and a boundless liberty of expressing resentments . . . in the most public manner and before servants';[36] the kind of indiscretion Sarah would never admit. Mrs Darcy advised her to have it out with the Queen at once and this she decided to do. Easter was approaching. What better time for heart-searching and for candour between friends? She sought an appointment. But now it was Anne's turn to be elusive. She put her off and suggested that what she had to say might better be put in writing. Sarah answered no, that would be difficult if not impossible. She must clear herself with the Queen before receiving her Easter Communion; but there would be nothing to cause dispute or even to oblige Anne to answer. Anne retreated to Kensington and there, on Maundy Thursday as dusk was falling, Sarah ran her to earth.

In her account of this last and most devastating interview with the Queen, in her small, dark closet at Kensington, Sarah as a writer is at her best:

> The Page who went in to acquaint the Queen that I was come to wait upon her staid longer than usual; long enough, it is to be supposed, to give Time to deliberate whether the Favour of Admission should be granted, and to settle the Measures of Behaviour if I were admitted. But at last he came out and told me I might go in.
>
> As I was entering, the Queen said she was just going to write to me. And when I began to speak she interrupted me four or

* In one of several drafts at Blenheim the Duchess says she had been 'informed by a friend, a reasonable woman of a very good charecter, that very false & malicious stories had been told Her Majesty of me, & some instances were named of vile inventions that had never entered into my thoughts'. (Blen G-1-8).

five Times with these repeated Words, Whatever you have to say you may put it in writing. I said her Majesty never did so hard a Thing to any as to refuse to hear them speak, and assured her that I was not going to trouble her upon the Subject which I knew to be so ungrateful to her, but that I could not possibly rest till I had cleared myself from some particular Calumnies with which I had been loaded.

I then went on to speak (though the Queen turned away her Face from me) and to represent my hard Case; that there were those about her Majesty who had made her believe that I had said Things of her which I was no more capable of saying than of killing my own Children; and that I seldom named her Majesty in Company, and never without Respect, and the like. The Queen said, without doubt there were many lies told.

I then begged, in order to make this Trouble the shorter, and my own Innocence the plainer, that I might know the Particulars of which I had been accused. Because if I were guilty that would quickly appear; and if I were Innocent this Method only would clear me. The Queen replied that she would give me no Answer, laying hold on a Word in my Letter, that what I had to say in my own Vindication would have no Consequence in obliging her Majesty to answer etc., which surely did not at all imply that I did not desire to know the particular Things laid to my Charge, without which it was impossible for me to clear myself. This I assured her Majesty was all I desired, and that I did not ask the Names of the Authors or Relators of those Calumnies, saying all that I could think reasonable to inforce my just Request. But the Queen repeated again and again the Words she had used, without ever receding.

I desired to explain some Things which I had heard her Majesty had taken amiss of me, and then with a fresh Flood of Tears and a Concern sufficient to move Compassion even where all Love was absent, I begged to know what other Particulars she had heard of me, that I might not be denied all Power of justifying myself. But still the only Return was, you desired no Answer and you shall have none.

I then begged to know if her Majesty would tell me some other Time?—You desired no Answer and you shall have none.

I then appealed to her Majesty again, if she did not herself know that I had often despised Interest in Comparison of serving her faithfully and doing right? And whether she did not know me to be of a Temper uncapable of disowning any thing which I knew to be true?—You desired no Answer and you shall have none.

This Usage was so severe, and these Words so often repeated were so shocking (being an utter Denial of common Justice to one who had been a most faithful Servant and now asked nothing more) that I could not conquer myself but said the most disrespectful Thing I ever spoke to the Queen in my Life, and yet what such an Occasion and such Circumstances might well excuse, if not justify, and that was that I was confident her Majesty would suffer for such an Instance of Inhumanity. The Queen answer'd, that will be to myself.

Thus ended this remarkable Conversation, the last I ever had with her Majesty. I shall make no Comment upon it. The Queen always meant well, how much soever she might be blinded or misguided.[37]

The interview, as recounted here by Sarah and printed in her *Conduct* of 1742, runs to 611 words. It lasted, she tells us, an hour; in which time two people in ordinary converse would speak about 7000 words. Allowing 2000 words for the two further topics mentioned by the Duchess in other versions, we are still left with at least 4000 words unaccounted for; and one cannot help wondering whether, among those missing sentences, lay the key to two problems: (i) What exactly Sarah had heard she was accused of; (ii) Why, with icy and indeed savage deliberation, the Queen persisted in denying her an answer.

Without that key the reader of the Duchess's *Conduct* must not be blamed for forming his own conclusions, which may not (as Anne once predicted) be favourable either to Queen or Duchess. If a fair verdict is to be given, the jury must have the facts, and when facts are withheld by an eye-witness (there were but two people present) it must consider circumstantial evidence. What was it that the Queen's mind was fixed on throughout the interview? Sarah begged her to say it. 'False stories', Sarah knew, 'had been made of me to her, several of which she [Mrs Darcy] repeated to me and said she was sure the Queen had been told of them. These were some of them nothing else but what we properly call Grub Street stories . . .'[38]

But there must have been something more. We know that to be accused by the Duchess of an unworthy and unbecoming friendship with Abigail was the one thing which, understandably, embarrassed the Queen. More than once and with vehemence she had so accused her and (or at least Anne probably feared so when she turned away her face) might too easily bring the same charge again. There had been tense and stormy interviews of which we know little. This was to be the last. The Queen's mind was at breaking point and there was that in it which froze her heart with fear and fury. No matter if nothing was then said of what she dreaded (though it may have been said);* the recollection of what Sarah had written, of what she had said before or of what they said she had said, would to Anne's predecessors have cried aloud for Tower Hill and the block. The most Anne could do was to slay her with silence and that she did, not pleasurably (she had once loved her) but without quarter and with bitter contempt.

---

* In her version of this last interview set out in dialogue form Sarah writes, 'I should have said, when I began to speak . . . when she saw I went on to tell her the thing, she turned her face from me as if she feared blushing upon something I might say to her'. (Blen. G-1-8).

CHAPTER VIII

The Great Change

1710-1712

'I shall make no comment upon it', says Sarah, closing her account of her last interview with Queen Anne; but she thought about it constantly and fretfully—why had the Queen been so brutal?—and kept writing about it; and each time she re-told the story she told just a little more.

From one version we find, for example, that the Queen's 'That will be to myself' (the perfect ending) was not in fact the last sentence Sarah heard her speak. But then of all the women in history, only Sarah perhaps would have dared, after such a dismissal, to return to the Queen's door:

> After I had come out from the Queen & sat me down in the long gallery to wipe my eyes before I came within sight of any body, I went back again to the closet & scratched at the door which, when the Queen had open'd, I told her that I had been thinking whilst I sat there that if when her Majesty came to the Castle at Windsor, where I had heard she was soon expected, it would not be easier to her to see me in public as I was now afraid it would not, I would take care to avoid being at the Lodge at the same time, to prevent any unseasonable clamour or stories that might be occasioned by my being so near her without waiting upon her. To this she readily answered that I might come to her to the Castle & that she should not be uneasy at it, by which I conclude that she had been made to promise that she would not enter into any conversation with me in private for fear she

should not be able to answer what I had to say, when at the same time she showed so much willingness to see me in public.[1]

In yet another draft at Blenheim there are minor variations and one substantial addition:

> Then I gave her the whole account of what had passed last summer between the Duke of Somerset & me, upon his making as if hee had a mind to doe me good offices to her, & in that relation I shewed all his falsenesse to me, for some things just before made it appear very plain that hee had been working to doe me all the mischief hee could & I am confydent I was not mistaken in beleiving hee had made an ill use of the conversation I had with him att Windsor, upon the Queen's subject, tho' I had asured him in it that no body living wished her more happynesse then I did, but that I knew she could not change to me & desired him not to mention me to her . . . which hee promised very solemnly, but hee brook that I am pritty sure, for I observed all the time I talkd to the Queen upon that matter she had a more then ordinary attention but answered not a word.

In the summer of 1709 the Dukes of Somerset and of Shrewsbury, before yielding to the blandishments of Harley, had both sounded the Duchess of Marlborough to make sure that there was no chance of a reconciliation between herself and the Queen. Somerset,* as things turned out, was to be fooled by Harley's promises of power; but Shrewsbury, playing a more subtle game, would be more successful. 'When he returned to England with his Roman Duchess', writes Sarah of Shrewsbury, 'he had a mind to come into the Ministry', and so of course it was important to back the winning side. The King of Hearts,† as he was called, then treated Sarah 'like a devinity'; but she was not to be hoodwinked. Though he had, as

---

* Of the Duke of Somerset Sarah has much to say, none of it favourable until after 1723, when he proposed marriage. e.g. 'Capricious & uncertain, lying & vain, fawning & insolent and, to avoid many words, as worthless as hee is disagreeable'; 'He was disgusted at the Duke of Marlborough & Lord Godolphin, tho' hee himself knew not why'; 'He was of no more use than my footman'. Sarah suspected him and his duchess of libelling her to Queen Anne.

† Or alternatively, Polyphemus, on account of a flaw in one eye.

she owns, 'a sort of an appearance of wisdom', he was covetous and, taken all in all, one of the falsest men living. It took him only a short time to discover where favour lay and to decide that if Abigail ordered it the Queen would, as he expressed it, stand on her head.

But it is upon Shrewsbury's Roman duchess that Sarah makes her sharpest comments. She was, she insists, a courtesan who, after chasing him from country to country, married him and pretended to turn Protestant. In England she had no inkling of behaviour and was soon the jest of the town, chucking her duke beneath the chin in public and, upon finding Anne thoughtful, flying to her with the cry, 'Oh my Queen, you must not think always of the poor Prince!'[3]

'The Duke of Shrewsbury', Sarah remembers, 'took all occasions of making great professions to me . . . but at the same time his wife blamed me for my ill behaviour to the Queen in all companys & the Duke of Somerset did the same but greived at it because they [sic] lovd me . . . It was impossible', she adds, 'for any body to bee such an idiote as to bee imposed upon by them'.[4] It was because Shrewsbury wanted his duchess to be a lady-of-the-bedchamber, said Sarah, that he blocked a reconciliation between herself and Anne. He denied that he had ever spoken to Abigail, but this in Sarah's opinion was 'very foolish because everybody saw that the Duchess of Shrewsbury was continually with her and made a most low & nausious court to her, which the Duchess of Somerset was too proud to do publickly'.[5] ''Tis certain', she concludes, 'that the Queen never had a thought of taking away my employments . . . till the Duke of Shrewsbury thought it convenient for his own scheme to assist the Duke of Somerset in that matter'.[6]

Eight days after Sarah's last interview with the Queen the Marquis of Kent, a simpleton nicknamed the Bug, was dismissed as Lord Chamberlain and consoled with a dukedom, so that the Duke of Shrewsbury might be given his office. This caused astonishment, partly because Shrewsbury was known to have voted against the Government at the trial of Sacheverell, and partly because Lord Treasurer Godolphin was not consulted but was told at Newmarket of the *fait accompli*. With candour he wrote to the Queen, 'Your Majesty is suffering yourself to be guided to your own Ruin and Destruction as fast as it is possible for them to compass it, to whom you seem so much to hearken'.[7] It was literally true. For whatever might be said against the Marlboroughs and Godolphin—the avarice of the Duke, the tantrums of the Duchess, the treasurer's lack of resolution—they had made Anne's reign glorious and only when they had been dispensed with would she as a queen cease to shine. Added to this, a glance at the opposition—Harley, St John, Abigail and the rest—was more than enough to convince the impartial that, for the most part, they were out for themselves and had the Devil devotedly on their side. They flourished in the dark. Their plots had been hatched in the stuffy closets of Windsor and Kensington, but now they must come out into the open so that the heads they had blacklisted might begin to roll.

Sarah meanwhile had not been idle. Soon after the Kensington interview she wrote to the Queen and enclosed two other letters: Anne's own congratulations to Marlborough on the victory at Blenheim, and a letter of the Duke of Somerset's to Sarah, to show on what friendly terms they used to be. Not only was all this ignored but Sarah was shocked that Anne failed to return Somerset's letter.* It was only by accident that she happened to have a copy, her chambermaid 'when she writt out one [the Queen's] took the other too without being order'd & 'tis very exact even in the speeling & the nonsense which I have marked'.[8]

Maynwaring urged her to assure the Queen that, in the crisis over Jack Hill, she had not advocated an address against Abigail. She did so and received a cold answer, the Queen at the same time charging her with having broken her promise never to mention Abigail again. This in turn called for another long letter, dated June 13th, in which Sarah explained that her promise had been conditional on Anne's assuring her she had read and pondered her narrative-sermon on *The Whole Duty of Man*, which she never had. It was the sort of profitless bickering that can go on forever. This however was cut short two days later when Lord Sunderland, Secretary of State and Sarah's son-in-law, was dismissed, to be succeeded by Lord Dart-

---

* 'Yr Majesty refusing to send mee back yr letter as I humbly desired obliges mee to take a little better care of the rest, but I can't imagine why you are not pleased to lett mee have the Duke of Somersetts letter again; tho' his carriage to lord M: & me, so very different from that letter, makes no impression upon yr Majesty I am perswaded I can make other people ashamed for him when I shew it them.' Sarah to Anne 13 June, 1710 (Blen. G-1-7)

mouth, a Tory dubbed by Sarah 'a Jester himself and a jest to all others'.

Anne, as we know, had never liked Sunderland and had strongly resisted his appointment. He was, she now said, 'obnoxious to all but a few', a phrase which, said Sarah, was not only untrue but uncharacteristic of the Queen and must therefore have been inserted by someone else. As for Sarah she would not, as her friends kept imploring, see the Queen, but she could and would keep on writing until domesday. Marlborough implored her not to. '39 [himself] begs of 240 [Sarah] that they will not on any account be prevaill'd upon to write any more to 239 [the Queen]'; and in another letter, 'For God's sake lett me begg 240 to be carefull of her behavior for she is in a country amongst Tygers & Wolves'.[9] But Sarah's mood was reckless. 'I am resolved I will write once more to her', she said, 'whatever resolution Lord Marl: takes, tho' I doe solemnly protest I would not have more to doe with her then other ladys for all the treasure upon earth, but I will vex her soe much as to convince even her own stupid understanding that she has used me ill & then lett her shutt herself up with Mrs Masham . . .'[10]

The Queen, after giving assurances that no further changes in her ministry were contemplated, dismissed Godolphin. The manner of his dismissal was particularly shabby. On the evening of August 7th he asked her directly, 'Is it the will of your Majesty that I should go on?' Unhesitatingly she answered, 'Yes'; yet her letter of dismissal, sent by a servant, bore the date August 7; and this for the man who, on her accession, had saved her from her own ignorance and had since devoted his life and health to her service. But there were other signs of deterioration in the Queen. She did not, as is popularly supposed, drink,* but unquestionably she had fallen into ill hands. It was what she herself had dreaded and what Sarah had prophesied in 1706 when she wrote of the uneasiness and grief it would mean to Godolphin if he then had to leave the Queen's service. She 'seemed so desirous he should continue in it, but I see as well as he', she had added, 'the Impossibility of his being able to support it or

---

* 'I know that in some libels she hath been reproached as one who indulged herself in drinking strong liquors, but I believe this was utterly groundless & that she never went beyond such a quantity of strong wines as her physicians judged to be necessary for her'. Sarah, of Anne. (Blen. G-I-9. Undated).

himself or my Lord Marlborough, for it all hangs upon one Thread; and when they are forced to leave your Service you will then indeed find yourself in the Hands of a violent Party who, I am sure, will have very little Mercy or even Humanity for you'.[11]

Godolphin was not rich. (He had, it was said, proved a better treasurer to his country than to himself.) The Queen, in her letter of dismissal, offered him a pension of £4000 a year, but it never materialised. Indeed, had it not been for a timely legacy from his brother he would have been very wretchedly off. He lived for two more years and spent much of that time at Holywell, St Albans. His leaving the Treasury, which was put into commission, meant lack of support for Marlborough and the allies. At home, Marlborough knew, it signalled every sort of misfortune from the dismissal of his duchess to the abandonment of Blenheim,* perhaps even to his own dismissal and disgrace. In August he warned Sarah that her dismissal had, so he was assured, been settled and that she must 'expect very quickly every thing that can be disagreeable personally'. He was, he said, much more concerned for what might vex her than for anything that might happen to himself.[12]

Maynwaring, known to his enemies as Sarah's spy, kept her informed. Harley, he reported, was saying of her, 'Ah, that is the rock all will break upon if care be not taken to avoid it'.[13] He had caught a glimpse of Abigail: '. . . in all the days of my life I never saw so odious a creature, and she was so extream hot that her Fan work'd like a windmill . . . Hopkins told me he did not see one body bow to her . . . I do really believe the creature is rotten & shou'd be removed as Card: Wolsey was design'd to be for his stinking breath least sacred majesty shou'd be infected'.[14] But Mrs Still in herself remained cool and, as Sarah had so often done before her, studied the face of the Queen. 'My Aunt', she tells Harley, 'is not very well . . . She has flying pains about her . . . a fitt of the gout . . . Say nothing of it to anybody, for without she is laid up with it she does not care to have it known till it is soe bad she cannot hide it . . . Whenever I said anything relating to business she answer'd pray goe for if you begin to talk you will make it soe late I shall not gett to bed in any time. Tho I think she is in good humour & had not a disponding countenance as sometimes she has'.[15]

* The Duchess stopped the works at Blenheim in October, 1710.

It would be easy to say that if it had not been for Abigail or if it had not been for Sarah, all would have been well and Marlborough would have continued to triumph; but of course there were other factors both negative and positive. Negatively, everyone in England and in France was sick to death of the war. Positively, there was the new-found power of the Press. Opposed as he was to Marlborough, Harley needed to be lucky. He had been lucky with Abigail; and he was now to be luckier still with Jonathan Swift.

Swift, who had come to England to gain Queen Anne's bounty (the first fruits) for the clergy of Ireland (a most unlikely assignment), had not found favour with Godolphin but was soon being made much of by the Harley–St John set. Sarah, though she afterwards fell for Gulliver,* was particularly scathing about him. Writing of Harley's hacks, as they were then regarded, she says, 'The Reverend Mr Swift & Mr Prior quickly offered themselves to sale (besides a number of more ordinary scribblers), both men of wit & parts, ready to prostitute all they had in the service of well rewarded scandal, being both of a composition past the weakness of blushing or of stumbling at any thing for the interest of their new masters. The former of these had long ago turned all religion into a Tale of a Tub & sold it for a jest'.[16]

The Examiner had been launched in the summer of 1710, but it was not till Swift's famous satire on the comparative cost of British and Roman gratitude, which it published in November, that it shook the world he was aiming at, partly with mirth, partly with anger. In the cost of the Roman triumph Swift remembered to include a chaplet of laurel (twopence); and in the British triumph Blenheim, which he rather modestly estimated at £200,000.† It was a good idea amusingly projected and not grossly unfair until the

---

* 'The Duchess Dowager of Marlborough is in raptures at it. She says she can dream of nothing else since she read it. She declares that she has now found out that her whole life had been lost in caressing the worst part of mankind & treating the best as her foes & that if she knew Gulliver, tho' he had been the worst enemy she ever had, she would give up her present acquaintance for his friendship'. Gay and Pope to Swift, Nov., 1726, on the publication of *Gulliver's Travels*. (Swift's *Prose Works* VIII, xviii).

† When completed, the cost of Blenheim was at least £300,000, but of that some £60,000 was contributed by the Marlborough estate.

reader reached the end of it, where he found a thinly disguised
Duchess of Marlborough accused of peculation on a colossal scale.
That the charge was groundless made it none the less infuriating for
the victim. Without knowing who had written the libel (she
suspected everyone from Prior to Vanbrugh) she drew up a self-
vindication of twenty-two and a half pages that read like a balance-
sheet and sent it to the Queen who said, 'Everybody knows cheating
is not the Duchess of Marlborough's fault'—a remark depending
much for its significance on where, when Anne spoke it, the accent
fell.

'Swift's business', says the author of *The Pen and the Sword*, 'was
to change history, not to record it . . . He saw that the grounds of
the quarrel must be enlarged, that the war must be stripped of its
nobility and exposed as the senseless thing he had always suspected it
to be . . . Marlborough must be destroyed!'[17] And as for the duplicity
of Swift's master, Henry St John, who pretended still to be Marlborough's admirer, 'Deceit on such a scale', observes Mr Foot, 'has
the quality of grandeur'. 'I have very good reason to believe', wrote
Sarah to Sir David Hamilton, 'that Mr St John's is the chief instruction of the person that writes it [*The Examiner*], who has not one
single qualification of any merit & is notorious for being of a
scandalous & profligate life & conversation. Now I beg of you to
tell me upon this occasion whether you do not think it is pritty
difficult to be silent under such provocations and . . . very hard &
unjust in Mrs Morley to suffer such things'.[18]

Maynwaring with *The Medley* did his best to meet the challenge,
but as antidote to Swift's acid the alkali was too weak. Perhaps
Sarah herself might have done better. 'I have read your Grace's
account', Maynwaring told her, 'of what passed between 42 [the
Queen] and 240 [herself] which, notwithstanding your great
modesty, I do think is better put together than anyone else could
have done it, & had two very different effects upon me in reading
it; for all the time I read what 240 said it affected me extreamly, as
'tis natural when one sees one's best friend ill used to be moved at it
& to hate those that do it; & yet when I came to the delicious replys
of 42, to hear the same senseless words repeated over & over, & a
statue lined with earth & stone speaking like the groaning Board &
saying so often that it would say nothing was so very ridiculous that

it really made me laugh several times. If you had not said the account was exact I should have known it to be so, 'tis so natural, & I wonder you could remember it so exactly, to put it together in so lively a manner, though I need not say now what opinion I have of your good parts for doing anything you have a mind to. I have a great desire to know the particular reason that made 42 so much more brutal now than ever'.[19]

It was Maynwaring, people said, who was begging Sarah not to resign, and to such purpose that her gold key of office came to be called Maynwaring's key. However, he had lost none of what he called his frolick fancy and, reminding Sarah of Tiberius's retreat to Capri with his favourite, Sejanus, remarked, à propos of Anne and Abigail, 'Tis pity this kingdom has no such delicious retreat near it. What think you of the island of Silly?'[20]

In the summer of 1710 Maynwaring was approached by one of the Queen's physicians Sir David Hamilton* with the earnest request that Sarah be dissuaded from her project of publishing the Queen's letters. Before this, says the Duchess in one of her many accounts, it had not occurred to her to do so. It was an idea. After all, the very threat of publication might be enough to postpone her dismissal until Marlborough was ready for it, which would be at the end of the campaign. She had been stung by *The Examiner* and warned that she lived among tigers and wolves. Cautiously therefore, for she never trusted him, she wrote letters to Hamilton, which he promised to read aloud to the Queen. She was satisfied that he did so, but annoyed when he told her that the Queen had made no comment. All she could get was negative, as in December when Hamilton was told to 'hinder' her from helping with Anne's new outfit; nor was she on any account to be encouraged to nominate (as she had suggested) 'any clergyman of good reputation' to referee their quarrel. On the question of the letters, except that she refused to return them, Sarah held her hand. Coxe believed that at this point Hamilton 'represented to the Queen the danger of provoking to extremity a woman of the most imperious character';[21] while to Sarah he (treacherously as she afterwards supposed) gave the impression that an abject apology might now be accepted. 'I am of

---

* Sir David Hamilton (1663-1721), physician to Queen Anne and to Queen Caroline. Said to have lost £80,000 in the South Sea Bubble.

Arthur Maynwaring. Kneller

Sir John Vanbrugh. Attributed to Thomas Murray

opinion', he advised her, 'today is most fitting. There seemed to be great tenderness'.[22]

Accordingly, on January 17th, 1711 Marlborough carried his wife's letter to the Queen. It read:

> Though I never thought of troubling your Majesty in this manner again, yet the circumstances I see my Lord Marlborough in and the apprehension I have that he cannot live six months if there is not some end put to his sufferings on my account makes it impossible for me to resist doing every thing in my power to ease him; and if I am still so unlucky as not to make use of any expressions in this letter that may move your Majesty, it is purely for want of understanding; for I really am very sorry that ever I did any thing that was uneasy to your Majesty. I am ready to promise any thing that you can think reasonable; and as I do not yet know but two things in my whole life that ever I did that were disagreeable to your Majesty, I do solemnly protest that as long as I have the honour to continue your servant, I will never mention either of those subjects to you or do any one thing that can give you the least disturbance or uneasiness. And these assurances I am desirous to give your Majesty under my hand because I would not omit any thing possible for me to do that might save my Lord Marlborough from the greatest mortification he is capable of and avoid the greatest mischief in consequence of it to your Majesty and my country.
>
> I am with all the submission and respect imaginable your Majesty's most dutiful and most obedient subject and servant
>
> _S. Marlborough_[23]

The Queen at first declined to open the letter and then, having yielded to Marlborough's persuasion and read it, she said, 'I cannot change my resolution'.

'Having delivered this letter', one of Sarah's accounts continues, 'he represented to her Majesty by all the most reasonable arguments and in the most moving manner imaginable how necessary it would be to her service as well as to his own satisfaction not to remove the Duchess of Marlborough till she [the Queen] had no more use of him, which in all probability would be in less than nine months, and then he beg'd that he and she might retire both together, which he could not but think better even for her Majesty than to part with one of them in so extraordinary a manner as would oblige her to be always upon her vindication.

'Then he endeavoured to shew that her Majesty's own character was a little concerned in this matter, since he believed there was no precedent for proceeding in such a manner against a woman to whom she had been pleased to make declarations of her friendship both publick and private for so many years, and who was sorry for any mistake she had ever committed and ready to give all possible assurances of never doing the least thing to make her Majesty uneasy for the future; and since an honourable retreat was all he beg'd for, he hoped that would appear so just and reasonable in all respects that any faithful servant she had must wish it.

'For the Queen's sake, as well as for his and the Duchess of Marlborough's, he added that as no Prince ever used any servant so very hardly that had been guilty of great faults, if pardon was asked and firm promise of amendments were made, so in this case there was something yet more cruel not only because nothing had been ever ill meant and what was desired was so small a favour that it would be barbarous to deny it even to one that had never been capable of doing the least service, but also because her Majesty had never laid any thing to the Duchess of Marlborough's charge, nor given any reason for proceeding so harshly against her, to him or to any other person.

'Only once she said to him, when he pressed her extremely upon that subject, that it was *for her honour* to remove the Duchess of Marl: but what that meant he could never learn, any more than what faults she had committed.

'And now if I may be allowed to speak in this case', interposes the Duchess, 'I cannot help saying it was indeed much for her honour to part in that manner, after a friendship of near 30 years, and give no other account but that wise reason for it, which I neither understand nor comprehend; and I do solemnly protest that I never writ or said any thing to Her Majesty in my whole life that I did not think for her service or that I should have been sorry to have all the world witnesses of'.[24]

As Marlborough himself had said, 'All truths are not to be spoke';

and again, some things—a look, a manner, an attitude—no matter how offensive, are not to be tied down and argued about. There are hints that at this time Anne found the very demeanour of the Duchess frightening and resented her hauteur. 'The word disdaine she makes use of', Sarah scornfully comments, 'to discribe my looks is an expression as if it came from a man & mighty rediculous, for I never looked upon her att all but talked allways to other people when I waited upon her in publick places, which I can't but think a very naturall way & nothing indecent in it considering my cercomstances & the manner she treated me'.[25]

However it was and whatever was uppermost in the Queen's mind, her only response to Marlborough's pleading was to demand Sarah's gold key. It must be handed to her within three days. The Duke, on his knees, pleaded for ten.* The Queen countered by making it two days. 'Let us make haste', writes Sir Winston, 'to draw the curtain upon an unnatural spectacle which reduces the stature of a soldier without raising the majesty of a queen'.[26]

When Marlborough, if only perhaps to change the subject, began to protest against the dismissal of three excellent officers merely for drinking his health (and damnation maybe to his enemies), the Queen cut him short and refused to discuss it or anything else till she had the key. 'As soon as I heard this', says Sarah, 'I begged of Lord Marlborough the very same night to carry this key that was so much longed for. Tho he was undressed I got him to put his cloaths on again;† & the true reason why I was in so much hast to have it given was because I hoped hee might have been allowd to have quited upon the Affront in the affair of the officers & I had a mind to have the key given before this came out, that people might not say hee quited upon the account of my places, which many thought

* 'He never had petition'd her before for any thing in his whole life with so much submission & earnestness, which only gave her an occation of shewing him in how inhuman a manner she could now treat him'. (Blen G-I-16. Undated fragment in the Duchess's hand).

† Marlborough would of course have been wearing court dress. 'The manner of her Grace's surrender, as I was told by one who was very intimate in the family was that when the Duke of Marlborough told her the Queen expected the gold key, she took it from her side & threw it into the middle of the room & bid him take it up & carry it to whom he pleased'. Lord Dartmouth (Burnet, op. cit. VI, 33).

was wrong, tho I confess I thought using his wife so ill was as great an affront as any, but could not be sure I was not too partial in that matter . . . I must not forget that when Lord Marl: delivered the key I desired to know what her Ma: was pleased to say upon it, but hee could give me no other account then that she mumbled something which hee could not understand nor make any thing of, by which I concluded that speech was her own; & indeed after they had got the key it was needless for them to make any more speeches for her upon that subject, which would have been so much labour lost, besides the pains of geting them by heart, & she has an easy way that I have often known her practice with great success upon many occasions when she has not known what to say which is to move only her lips & make as if she had said something when in truth no words were uttered'.[27]

Sarah remained, so she tells us, puzzled. The Queen 'lookd as if she wishd she could give some reason' for her dismissal, but still gave none. It was a quite extraordinary dilemma. To be faced with the world's most winning diplomat—her personal friend and the nation's hero—and deny him even one good reason for his wife's dismissal, one needed to be made of stone. Again, what tipped the scale? Loathing, we may be sure, plus embarrassment, plus something she would keep forever to herself. 'I must again desire you would excuse my not answering some things in your letters', she told Sarah in an undated letter of 1708 or 1709, 'not for ye reason you give for that is a strange unkind one, but because I know it is better not to do it for both our sakes'.[28] And if she would not tell it to Sarah, how much less likely was she to unbosom herself to a man. Whatever Abigail may have told her of Sarah's prattling, that will not have been enough to harden Anne's heart. There must, one feels, have been confirmation from others which, added to Sarah's letters and tantrums—her long absences, her 'saying shocking things', her ill humour and disdain—succeeded in locking the Queen's heart against her forever. But the last clue or straw is missing—'There are yet many things untold', adds the Duchess darkly, 'for which there wants a name'[29]—and we are left to wonder and at the same time to admire the reserve of a queen.

Now was the moment for Sarah to send in her accounts, and at the same time to claim with arrears the £2000-a-year offered by the

Queen in 1702. 'I am persuaded your Lordship* must have observed', she writes in the introduction to her *Conduct*, 'that all those who declare themselves careless about what the World [may] say of them when they are dead are quite as unconcerned to deserve a good Character while they live . . . My chief Aim has been both in publick & private Life to *deserve* Approbation; but I have never been without an earnest Desire to *have* it from the wise and virtuous'.

What, then, are the wise and virtuous to make of this claim for back pay to the tune of £16,000? 'I did not much like doing this', she admits, 'but I was advised to do it and I did do it'. And the Queen? She 'blushed and appeared to be very uneasy . . . looked out of countinance & as if she had much rather not have allowed it'.[30] But she did allow it and, as with Griffith's winnings from Prince George, when Sarah considered how many of her 'dear hours' had been spent in Anne's tedious company, she was not sure if the Queen might not still be her debtor; for the cost of boredom is not to be measured.

As Keeper of the Privy Purse the Duchess was succeeded by Abigail, and as Groom of the Stole by the Duchess of Somerset. For the latter, as for all his acquaintance, Godolphin had a nickname—Troule-it-away—for which there seems no obvious explanation, unless it may have been a phonetic transliteration of 'truly to weigh',† a phrase she could have used to a half-attentive treasurer or queen. Sarah, who disliked red hair and rivalry, calls her obsequious, insinuating, intriguing and absolutely the greatest liar in the world. She may have been all or none of these things. Swift, who so rashly offended her in his *Windsor Prophecy*, said she 'openly professed the utmost aversions from the persons, the principles & measures of those who were then in power and . . . quickly grew into higher credit than all her (Queen Anne's) ministers together'.[31]

In a period with mistrust as its keynote humour is rare enough to be prized when chanced on; for Sarah's humour is almost always sarcasm. Here then, when the two rival duchesses met at the Meredith‡ christening and a tolerably good joke was cracked, the scene might have been cheering. After deliberation it had been decided

---

* Lord Cholmondeley, to whom the *Conduct* is dedicated.

† I am grateful to Mr R. S. Green for this suggestion.

‡ Meredith was one of the officers cashiered for drinking Marlborough's health.

to give the child the Queen's name, and when this had been settled, says Sarah, 'I turnd to the Duchess of Somerset & said to her in a smiling way that the Duke Hamilton had made a boy a girl & christened it Ann & why should not we make this girl a boy & call it George. This was then understood to be meant no otherwise then as a jest upon Duke Hamilton, as it plainly was, & the Duchess of Somerset laughed at it, as the Queen herself I dare say would have done if she had happened to be present. But this as I had it afterwards from very good hands was represented to the Queen in as different & false a way as was possible, who was told that I said, Don't let the name of the child be Ann for there never was one good of that name. I leave you to judge who was most likely to give this story this rediculous turn & who was to find their account in it'.[32]

In March, 1711 luck for the third time came to Harley, melodramatically disguised as a French assassin. The attempt of de Guiscard is at least outlined in every history book: the spy arraigned before the council; his attack on Harley; the pen-knife stabs which St John claimed were meant for himself. But it is as always the detail that fascinates. 'I believe you remember the waistcoat', Harley's sister writes chattily to another sister, 'it was blue & silver ground with rich gold brocade flowers. Sister had kept it up & that waistcoat served for the birthday & this occasion (only a silver fringe put round it & looked very well) . . . The knife struck first in the turning up of the right sleeve of his coat, which the surgeon says broke the force of the blow . . . It struck thro' his coat, which was open at the breast (and they now so far as the buttonholes put a buckram between the cloth & silk lining); through these three it went & into his waistcoat just in one of the gold flowers, which also must have broken the force of the blow . . . The Queen did not believe they had told her truth, but that he was dead'.[33]

As a contemporary ballad-monger sublimely put it:

> Meantime thy Pain is gracious Anna's Care;
> Our Queen, our Saint with sacrificing Breath
> Softens thy Anguish: In Her Pow'rful Pra'r
> She pleads thy Service and forbids thy Death.

The wound, though not deep, took weeks to heal, and in that

Harley was less fortunate because in his absence St John gained ground with Abigail and secretly promised that Honest Jack Hill should lead his expedition to Quebec, an adventure which ended in August in complete fiasco. In his thanks to the Commons for his recovery from the 'barbarous & vilainous attempt' Harley said, 'Whenever I look upon my breast it will put me in mind of the thanks due to God, my duty to the Queen & that Debt of Gratitude & Service I must always owe to this Honourable House'.[34] In May, for his pains, he was made Earl of Oxford and Mortimer.

Sarah now retired, says Lediard, in 'uncommon splendour', to St Albans. There was plenty to do. For one thing she was beginning to plan a 'history' which would run from the Revolution of '88 to Queen Anne. Maynwaring, encouraging her as usual, praised her style. 'You allways write so clearly & properly', he told her, 'and with such natural expressions in which you excel everybody . . . In your letter that lyes now before me, one part is written exactly after Montaigne's manner, so much has your Grace profited by those few Books* which you say you have read!'[35]

In his efforts to please her he confers with her architects and potters about the works at Marlborough House. 'I wish you were well in your own house by St James's', he writes to her, 'for that I dare swear is built strong enough to stand till the General Conflagration & I hope & believe too that you will yet be very happy there & like it better than any of your other houses, because as you observe in the country you are generally quite alone or in too much company, either of which extreams you may avoid here'.[36]

But Marlborough House, rushed though it was, could not be ready until the autumn. Wren (the 'poor old man', she suspected, was imposed upon by his workmen) she had had to part with, but she enjoyed finishing it herself; and even if it had cost £50,000, it had been but two years in the making and was, in her view, the

---

* A list of the Duchess's books at Blenheim, dated Sept., 1719 and now at Althorp, includes *The Anatomy of Melancholy*, *The Whole Duty of Man*, Burnet, Clarendon, Milton, Dryden, Spenser etc. Her books at St Albans in 1721 included Shakespeare, Ben Jonson, *Don Quixote* (a great favourite), Montaigne, Cowley, Waller, St Evremont, Plutarch and Epictetus in translation and several volumes on medicine, architecture and theology. Swift and Addison are represented as are Congreve and Nathaniel Hooke. There is also Young's Spelling Book.

strongest and best house that ever was built.* 'I always disliked Blenheim', she writes in one of her jottings, 'and laughed at Sir John as often as I could, saying that the Duke of Marlborough should be always welcome to see me at my houses, that I would visit him sometimes at Blenheim & that I would fade his furniture in my houses before Sir John had half finished his'.[37]

It would be strange to be home-making next door to a queen—living almost in her garden, one might say—with whom one was no longer on speaking terms; and in the meantime there was this ridiculous affair of the St James's lodgings, which Sarah (moving out) was accused of stripping even to the chimneypieces and the brass locks. Marlborough, in his letter to her of May 25th, after chiding her for writing again so freely of 199 [Harley] when he had begged her not to, referred to the lodgings and said, 'I beg you will not remove any of the marble chimneypieces'.†[38] Sarah owned she had taken the locks, which were hers. The chimneypieces, she insisted, she had not taken, and she had the housekeeper sign a statement to prove it. The Queen, they said, was furious. Whether or not the lodgings were intended for Abigail, the Duchess had no right to leave them as she had. '42 is so angry', Sarah was told, 'that she says she will build no house for 39 [Marlborough] when 240 [Sarah] has pull'd hers to pieces'.[39] If Sarah chose to wreck the Queen's lodgings, no further supplies would be voted for the building of Blenheim.

In his estimate of Marlborough and of his reactions Harley was astute. Sarah's dismissal, he believed, would very nearly but not quite compel him to resign; whatever his agony, Marlborough would not desert Prince Eugene and the allies. Blenheim, on the other hand, was a trump to be played with discretion. Everyone knew that Marlborough had set his heart on it. Nothing then could be plainer but that it must be used as a carrot to tempt him on until peace had been made without him; on which happy day he could be dropped.

* Marlborough House, since much altered (a storey has been added), was built of brick with stone dressings, in Wren's no-nonsense style; a well-mannered building which nevertheless showed how dull Blenheim might have been in other hands.

† The probability is that Sarah's letter in which the possibility of removing chimneypieces was mentioned, was intercepted by a spy, and read before being forwarded to Marlborough.

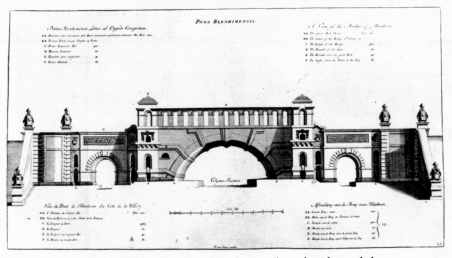

Blenheim: Vanbrugh's Grand Bridge, as planned with arcaded
superstructure and eighty-foot towers

Blenheim: the canal-and-pool scheme west of Vanbrugh's truncated
bridge. The project supervised by the Duchess in the seventeen-twenties

Blenheim: The Kent-Rysbrack monument in the chapel. The first
Marquis of Blandford stands next to his father, John first Duke
of Marlborough

When in the autumn of 1710 Sarah stopped the works at Blenheim, the building was reckoned to have cost rather more than £130,000, £10,500 of which was owed to the Edward Strongs, the chief masons who had supplied much Cotswold stone from their quarries near Burford. The sudden stoppage caused distress among the workmen and a dilemma for Marlborough, who realised that if he anticipated a Treasury grant and relieved them he might saddle himself with the cost of completing the half-finished castle. Rioting was prevented by Samuel Travers, the paymaster, who paid the most necessitous out of his own pocket.

Now in 1711 Harley made the seemingly magnanimous gesture of another £10,000 grant so that the works might be resumed. In Marlborough's letter to Harley to congratulate him on his recovery from Guiscard's attempt he says, 'I am extremely obliged to you for the assurance you give me that the building of Blenheim shall not be neglected. I cannot dissemble the desire I have to see that monument of her Majesty's goodness and the nation's acceptance of my service brought to some degree of perfection. I hope I shall give no just reason for posterity to reproach you for having been the finisher of it, and if I have the good fortune to spend any part of my life there I shall always have in my view a remembrance of the obligations I owe you on this account. I am with much truth, sir, your most obedient humble servant'.[40]

This was a little different from his instruction to Sarah four years before: 'I must beg the favour of the Queen that she will allow Sr Godfrey [Kneller] to come three or four times to draw Hers & the Princes pictor for Bleinhem. If I am ever to enjoye quietness it must be there, so that I wou'd have nothing in my sight but my friends'.[41]

Sarah, while congratulating herself on Marlborough House, where she proposed elegant assemblies for the autumn, had begun to call Blenheim 'this unfortunate present', 'a monument of ingratitude' (a phrase of Vanbrugh's); or she simply adopted Godolphin's sour disclaimer: 'Let them keep their heap of stones'. Marlborough might in his optimism be planning to move in 'next summer'—or the one after—but she told him that since Vanbrugh was busy with bridges and grottoes miles from the main building, the house would never be finished. At the beginning of the works Godolphin, after viewing them with Sarah, had written to Marlborough: 'My Lady Marlb: is extremely prying-into and has really found a great many errors but very well mended such of them as could not stay for your decision. I am apt to think she has made Mr Vanbrugh a little cross, but you will find both ease and comfort from it'.[42]*

It was not a trait to endear her to a spirited architect who, as his biographer says, liked masculinity in life as much as in art,[43] and was unlikely to take kindly to the interference of women. In time he hoped to humour her, but from the first it must have been plain that she lacked imagination and could never be brought to see that, to perpetuate the epic the place was named after called for architecture and landscape on the heroic scale. At one early stage, in her folly, she transferred all the skilled masons to the garden walls, telling them His Grace wanted the gardens finished, and since all the walls must one day meet, it could not matter where they began.

Along the sanded paths and pleached lime-alleys of Wise's un-finished 'military' garden Maynwaring dutifully wandered, to be able to report his impressions to the owner, as he had at Marlborough House. 'The garden was very pleasant and sweet', he tells her, 'with that one fine day after the rain, and I walk'd in it as long as it was light to try if I could find any of the satisfaction which 240 so well describes in being alone in a sweet place: and 'tis certain there is something very pleasing in it but it is of the melancholy kind'.[44]

Marlborough, Sir Winston reminds us, had set his heart upon Blenheim in a strange manner. Broken in health, he knew he could not live long there but still yearned for it as a monument to stand, if only as a ruin, for thousands of years. 'About his achievements he preserved a complete silence, offering neither explanations nor excuses for any of his deeds. His answer was to be this great house. This mood has characterized dynasts in all ages, and philosophers in none. Remembrance may be preserved to remote posterity by piling great stones on one another and engraving deep inscriptions upon them. But fame is not to be so easily captured'.[45]

Writing to Sarah after Bouchain, perhaps the most brilliant action of his career, Marlborough sounds anything but triumphant. His health he despairs of but—'if I cou'd in quietness & without great

* Godolphin himself was responsible for condemning the ruins of Woodstock Manor and for changing the position of the chapel, which now has its altar at the west.

inconveniency of old age injoye two or three Yeares of Yours & my children's Company I shou'd blesse God & think my selfe happy ... I know the intentions of those that now govern is that I am to have nothing to do in the peace. This is what I am extream glad of, but they must not know it, so that I beg you will in your letters by the post never mention the peace, ministers nor the Queen, for your letters are constantly read before they come from England ... I shall take my measures for living a retier'd life; if it may be in England I shall be glad of it. If not, my businesse shall be to seek a good climate, for my constitution is extreamly spoilt'.[46]

For one of the greatest generals known to history, for the hero of Blenheim, Ramillies and Oudenarde the knives were now being sharpened. 'While his friends were engaged in the most spectacular piece of treachery in English history', writes Mr Foot of Jonathan Swift, 'and in defiance of the reputation and policy of the most successful of English soldiers, Swift so turned the tables that the Tory case now appeared in the guise of a more discriminating patriotism pitted against all the forces of avarice and pride'.[47] Swift's friends were of course Harley, now Lord Oxford, and St John, soon to be Viscount Bolingbroke; and Swift's pamphlet—perhaps the most effective ever written—*The Conduct of the Allies.**

It was a direct attack on the Marlboroughs for prolonging the war and exploiting it at the country's expense and to their own advantage. As for the bullied Queen, all but edged off her throne, she had, Swift averred, been driven from Windsor Castle to a cottage, 'pursuant to the advice of Solomon who tells us it is better to dwell in a corner of the housetop than with a brawling woman in a wide house'.[48] From not very promising material—a little truth, a few half-truths—but with much skill and malice a weapon had been forged which, if it did not of itself change history, at least accelerated it. In the humour of the hour—war-weary, sour, splenetic—it struck a harsh yet welcome clang: the knell of Marlborough. Returning in time for Christmas, he was dismissed on the last day of the year. Again out of next to nothing a frivolous charge of peculation was trumped up. The Queen's letter of dismissal is missing, since Marlborough, for the only time in his life, gave way to rage and flung it in the fire. Sarah says it was written 'in a very odd & low manner,

* Published 27 Nov. 1711.

as if all respect & common civility were now become a crime towards a man to whom she owed the security of her life as well as the glory of it; there was something so surprisingly shocking & hard in ye manner of expressing her self'.[49] Marlborough's reply was polished till it gleamed like a rapier.[50] One can only hope that it found its mark.

Few pens could do justice to such a crisis and the strange thing is that Sarah having, with or without assistance, done just that, decided to discard from her printed *Conduct* one of the most telling passages she had ever written. Here it is:

When I reflect upon all this I sometimes think that when Posterity shall come to read the annals of our times: a scene of glory, conquest, victory without intermission, at last ending in this manner, were there not authentick records to the contrary, they must certainly conclude that just in the most unhappy crisis of time Queen Anne the wise, the good, the just, the honourable, unfortunately died & that she was succeeded by another of the same name but of a temper & principles directly opposite, one who loved only those whom her predecessor hated & hated those whom she loved, one glorying in breaking the contracts & unravelling* the scheme in which her predecessor had triumphed, one taking a pride in raising those up whom she had cast down as public enemies & in casting those to the earth whom she had seated on thrones, one in a word untouched with a sense of ye miseries of her country & posterity, unmoved with the unhappiness of the world about her, giving back as it were in sport the glories & victories purchased with her subjects' blood & treasure & abusing them to their own unhappiness & misery; one uncapable of understanding or of following the good counsels which had made her predecessor so great; but selfish, passionate, headstrong, preferring the satisfaction of her own private humour or resentments before the safety of her own people & of all Europe.

But when they shall be assured by all the monuments & records of history that this was one & the same Queen Anne who filled this whole period of time, the same who, after having

* 'Undoing' would be more in context.

fought so long & so successfully against France, raised it to a greater pitch of power than it ever enjoyed before, the same who, after having made Charles King of Spain presently dethroned him, the same who, after having entered into the most solemn alliances & contracts, broke through them with so much resolution & ease, the same who, after having owed the quiet & security of her life to her great General & other faithful ministers, afterwards rewarded them with all the ignominy & disgrace she could heap upon them, who . . . but I am weary of recounting these unpleasing things. When posterity comes to be assured of this, will it not shake & surprise them? And will not many be apt to ask what part her justice had in this procedure? what her pity, what her gratitude, what her honour, what her faith & what her constancy? I will give no further answer . . . Facts speak too plainly to be denied.[51]

CHAPTER IX

A Sort of Pilgrimage

1712-1714

———————◆———————

'If the fault was mostly Sarah's', writes Trevelyan, 'the tragedy was mostly Anne's. For Sarah was left less forlorn. She had more resources in herself; and she had the unchanging love of her husband, of which she was far more proud than she had ever been of the royal friendship even in its palmiest days'.[1]

For Anne the world had, by a series of mischances with the Devil driving, become second-rate; and where before it had been peopled with giants and heroes, now, wherever she looked—the army (Ormonde), the treasury (Oxford), the privy purse (Abigail)—there seemed to be shuffling dwarfs and puppets.* Where among all these little people was greatness? She was friendless, gout-ridden, insecure. Well may she have envied Marlborough pitching his campaigning-tent in the gardens at Holywell or Sarah who, as she had heard with misgiving, was about to begin her self-vindication.

'The Calumnies against me were so gross', Sarah explained, 'and yet so greedily devoured by the Credulity of Party Rage, that I thought it became me to write and publish something in my own Justification . . . a sort of Memorial which . . . I drew up in 1712'.[2] Two years before she had been urged by Maynwaring to write 'a

---

* 'Of all the nonsense that ever I knew in my life nothing ever surprised me so much as that any Prince that knows hee must ask advise of somebody should not think it more for his honour as well as safty to take it from the best of his country [men] & his great councell that hee appears to adviss with who have generally great stakes than to have it from little od people that come in the dark & that are not own'd.' (Sarah to Lady Cairns Undated. Blen. G-I-16).

true history of the present time . . . There is nobody that I know but
240', he told her, 'that is capable to write one or that has so great a
love of Truth as to be able to follow a thing so despised & forlorn
& to quit all other considerations for the sake of it: honours, profits,
courts, and even 42'.[3]

It was tempting. For Mrs Burnet, who had 'such a violent passion
for Queen Mary', she had long since set down her account of that
queen and the 'Monster' she had reigned with. And now, in her
Brown Book, Sarah had all the letters of Queen Anne . . . But it was
not until *The Examiner* had goaded her to fury that she decided she
must publish no matter who smarted or, as she put it, 'whoever's
ears may tingle'.

'I have been a kind of Author', she said later. She had indeed; and
there had been a succession of more or less talented and more or less
helpful collaborators, beginning with Bishop Burnet ('not well
done'), continuing with Maynwaring, St Priest and Hutchinson and
concluding with Nathaniel Hooke. There were those too—a distinguished trio—privileged to comment before publication: Pope,
Voltaire and Robert Walpole, the last perhaps, in view of her
subsequent loathing, the most surprising of all. But in 1712, 'thinking
him extremely her friend', as he had been Marlborough's, Sarah sent
Walpole her manuscript in the Tower where, in Marlborough
tradition, he had been immured on a false charge. He read it and
'persuaded her by no means to do [publish] it, saying that the
Ministers would employ all their pens by the most scurrilous people
whom they had in pay to write against her & that she had better
defer her vindication, tho' 'twas a very good one, to some other
time;* & he prevailed upon her much against her inclination; & his
argument was rediculous, because at that very time they had printed
all the falsities against her that even Malice could invent'.[4]

Maynwaring, who had taken great pains with it and, on Sarah's
behalf, clamoured for vengeance, must have been disappointed. He
was not to know that the *Conduct* for which he had laid a foundation
would not appear until thirty years after his death. All he could do
was to predict, 'Whoever shall read it a hundred years hence will
think and say, the Lady that writ this had the most honesty & the

* In another version this reads: 'to defer the doing it tell people were less madd'.
(Blen. G-1-10).

rightest principles & notions of things in the world'.[5] In the meantime as the lady herself admitted, 'I have a great deal of pleasure in thinking every day what sad wretches I shall make all these people appear to the whole world a little sooner or later, so much that I doe protest I would not part with it [her manuscript] to have Blenheim finish'd & every thing added to it that is in the power of this infamous foolish Court to give'.[6]

There were times, she said, when she heartily wished Blenheim burned.* She sent Maynwaring and Godolphin down there to try out the wing Vanbrugh had added to High Lodge, the ranger's house on Blenheim's western axis, remote and romantic, where Burnet had heard the deathbed confession of John Wilmot Earl of Rochester. Godolphin reported, 'I never lay in so good a bed'. Everything was perfect, even to a dessert of peaches, nectarines, figs and green plums. The company too, except of course for the owners' absence, could not have been better, since they had with them the architect of Blenheim and author of *The Relapse*: 'allways', as Maynwaring said, 'the best company when his Whym is at its highest, tho' perhaps not the best architect.' Good food, good wine, good company in a lodge set high among oaks above the Evenlode, what could be jollier? Yet even in that Arcady there were shadows. Dr Garth shook his head over the decline of Maynwaring while Maynwaring drank deep and tried to ignore it. He moved on to St Albans. 'Several of the best authors, even Plutarch', he reminded his absent hostess, 'have written the praises of illustrious Ladies, & if I shou'd ever turn author I shou'd say so much upon the subject of one of them that I shou'd deserve to be buried in the same manner that a German writer was . . . The women pour'd so much wine upon his grave that it overflow'd the whole church. Something like this I hope you will live to do over my poor Remains, for I am confident your friendship will extend beyond my life . . . a wearisome life which without it would be a real punishment'.[7]

Maynwaring longed to write but was past writing; and indeed on all fronts the enemy looked to have the field to themselves.† Swift in his own chosen company read *The St Albans Ghost* to Abigail and

* The works at Blenheim were stopped officially on June 1, 1712.

† On May 10, 1712 St John sent secret restraining orders to Ormonde (Marlborough's successor as commander-in-chief), forbidding him to engage the enemy.

her husband, now ennobled as Lord and Lady Masham.* 'I went to Lord Masham's tonight', he records with relish, 'and Lady Masham made me read to her a pretty two penny Pamphlet calld The St Albans Ghost. I thought I had writt it myself, so did they, but I did not. Lord Treasurer [Oxford] came down to us from the Queen & we stayed till 2 a Clock. That is the best night place I have. The usual company are Lord & Lady Masham, Lord Treasurer, Dr Arbuthnot & I; sometimes the Secretary [St John]† & sometimes Mrs Hill of the bedchamber, Lady Masham's sister'.[8]

It was the set Maynwaring had so often jeered at. The ghost in the pamphlet, crudely drawn, was the late Mrs Jennings; but at St Albans itself this was indeed a time for ghosts. Godolphin, visited there on his deathbed by Robert Walpole, is credited with having turned to Sarah and said, 'Madam, if there is such a thing as a possibility of spirits returning from the other world I shall certainly appear to you if you should ever abandon this young man'.[9] When on September 15th he died, Sarah wrote in her bible: 'The best man I ever knew'.

Maynwaring is said to have caught a chill on an evening stroll in the grounds of Holywell but, when he died on November 13th, the post-mortem named tuberculosis. In *The Life & Posthumous Works of Arthur Maynwaring*, published in 1715 and dedicated to Robert Walpole, the anonymous author says:

> It is to his Glory that the greatest Lady in England wept often by the side of his Death Bed, which he water'd as often with his Tears, being sensible how much he ow'd to such an Illustrious Mourner, when he was sensible of little or nothing else. He had not Words to express the Transport of his Soul when he was almost in the Agony to see him self so far in the good Graces of a Lady of such high Rank & Merit as that his Danger should strike her Dumb & leave it to her Eyes to express the Sorrow of her Soul. It was suppos'd that he would have endeavoured

* Though Abigail's soul might be fitted for grandeur, it was with great reluctance that Queen Anne turned so useful a servant into a Lady, at the risk, as she put it, of 'having a peeress lie upon the floor'. However she did so and for good measure made her two-year-old daughter Ranger of St James's Park.

† In July, 1712 St John was to his fury created Viscount Bolingbroke. He had, like Harley, expected an earldom and blamed him for the disappointment.

to have broke thro' the Excess of his Grief & form'd some Utterance for it but his Sister remain'd in the Room. This Emotion of his was the more extraordinary on account of a slight Misunderstanding at that Time between this Great Lady and him. He had given her some Occasion of Offence but was not conscious to him self in what, and it is thought that his Perplexity about it contributed somewhat to the encrease of his Distemper. He would fain have come to an *Eclaircissement* in that matter but he was too near Death and in a few hours after she left him expir'd in the Arms of his Faithful Servant.

Maynwaring, offering to follow the Marlboroughs into exile, had jokingly suggested Mindelheim or America; but that was not to be. There was little enough now however to keep them in England, and Marlborough, a pall-bearer at Godolphin's funeral, turned his thoughts to living abroad. After one has lived a great many years in a hurry, he had once written to the Queen, it was very natural and very desirable to enjoy some quiet; and that quiet he could no longer count upon in England where, as Burnet observed, he was pursued with malice. There was even talk of prosecution for the cost of Blenheim; and there may have been other reasons.

> When vice prevails and impious men bear sway,
> The post of honour is a private station.

On December 1st he left. Sarah was expected to join him almost at once, but there was much to see to and there were difficulties too about boats and passports. 'I did not know', she wrote afterwards, 'whether I should ever see my own country again'. She had long since remarked to Maynwaring, 'Perhaps travelling and a bottle of Spaw watter every morning may have as good an effect upon the passion of hatred as upon love. I am satisfied they are both very uneasy companions & the first is the worse of the two but I fear I am not clear from it . . . At the same time I am sensible that 'tis a great weaknesse & I can say nothing in my excuse but that I think I doe not hate Mrs Morley for loving another but for being so brutall to me after such professions to me & such very faithfull service . . . but as the great author says that lyes before me, one must not bee angry with thistles that they don't produce apples'.[10] She still found it hard to shake off the shock, the outrage, the unbelievable betrayal of Abigail. 'Surely', she exclaimed, 'there never was any time since Adham that such a woman as Ab: gave so many great & good men so much trouble'.[11]

But now there were other things to think of: keepsakes for friends, luggage, servants . . . 'The Duchess of Marlborough hath given great presents at her taking leave of her friends', Lord Berkeley noted, 'severall fine diamond rings & other jewells of great value, to Dr Garth for one'.[12] Her grandchildren too came in for diamonds —'a lottery of all my fine things', as she put it, 'which I made them raffle for'.[13] It was, as Bishop Hare said, to be a sort of pilgrimage; yet even for a pilgrimage it can be surprising how much one needs. There were all the obvious things like wig-boxes and candlesticks, but in uncivilised countries almost anything might be useful. She took forty mantos [*manteaux*] and petticoats and a vast quantity of linen. She took a tea-kettle to hold five pints, a chocolate-pot, 'a blew bagg lined with fox skins', a powder-puff and seven leopard-skin muffs. When all had been packed she found she had a hundred and twenty large parcels weighing a hundredweight. She hoped nothing had been left out.

And then just as she was due to leave, two vexing things happened. Mary King the laundrymaid refused to join the pilgrimage and had to be paid off with two months' wages (£1); and even more tire-some, while sifting last-minute oddments Sarah chanced on Queen Anne's miniature set in diamonds . . . Swift gives the sequel:

April, 1713. I dined at Lord Treasurer's . . . who shewed us a small Picture, enamelld work & sett in gold, worth about 20 ls, a Picture I mean of the Queen which she gave to Dutchess Marlborough sett in Diamonds. When the dutchess was leaving England she took off all the Diamonds & gave the Picture to one Mrs Higgins (an old intriguing Woman whom everybody knows), bidding her to make the best of it she could. Lord Treasurer sent to Mrs Higgins for this Picture & gave her a hundred Pounds for it. Was ever such an ungratefull Beast as that Dutchess? or did you ever hear such a Story. I suppose the Whigs will not believe it, pray try them: takes off the Diamonds & gives away the Picture to an insignificant Woman as a thing of no consequence & gives it her to sell like a piece of old fashioned plate. Is she not a detestable Slut?[14]

Writing later from Frankfurt Sarah sent her own explanation:

I have heard lately that there has been a heavy outcry against me & that my Lady Burl:* was very angry with me that I gave her a picture of the queen to give to Mrs Higgins† who has nothing to eat but by a pention of the queen which I got her & even in this ungreatfull age she acknowledged it more then it deserved & I really thought it would doe her some little good & that some flattering fool would buy it; tho I did not forsee that she would have it in her power to oblige Cato,‡ nor that a lady should bee angry that I had lived so long freely with & that parted with me very kindly; & much less did it enter my head that any body should think it reasonable for me to keep a thing that could put me in mind of one that had used the D: of M: & my self so barbarously after such long & faithfull service, but this it seems was a great crime, but I own to you I don't care what such people say or think of me, nor did I ever pretend to bee so good a christian as to love my persecutors; tho' to you I will bee so religious as to make a thorow confession: I did in one of my letters or more say something of the Rt Reverend *The Examiner*, after hee had writt the last infamous one I saw concerning the D: of M: & my self, & every body knowing that the author of that Libell is the new Dean who writt the Tale of

---

* Lady Burlington. 'I carry'd her my Bird to take care of & desired . . . she would give Mrs Higons from me a little picture of the queens'. (Sarah to Mrs Clayton. Blen. G-1-16. Undated).

† The ever grateful and obsequious Mrs Higgins later became an embarrassment. A letter in which she offers to throw herself at the Duchess's feet is endorsed in Sarah's hand: 'I have don her a great deal more good then she mentions in her letter, with no other design then to assist her because I believed her very poor, but I never cared for her nor could not tast her witt & was so weary of her that when I sent her mony & cloaths I would have put away my porter if he had let her in to me'. (Blen. E 46).

‡ On the first night of Addison's *Cato*, in April 1713, Bolingbroke rose and congratulated Booth (in the name part) for his oration against a dictator: a hit against Marlborough. Here however the Duchess seems to be referring to Harley (Lord Oxford), then Lord Treasurer.

the Tub, a book not only against all religion but against all morality. I writt some thing to this purpose, that I was surprised (I could not say that I was sorry) to see the Rt Reverend Do: Swift so highly preferred in the church just after it had been so piously recommended to punish all men that writt libells & against Religion. Now if this reflects upon the ministers, I am ready to come over & stand my tryall; & you may be sure I will never write any thing that I care who sees as to my own perticular; & as wicked as my enemys are, I think my self very safe because it is not possible for them or any body to counterfeit my hand.[15]

Before she had joined him Marlborough had written, 'I am extremely sensible of the obligation I have to you for the resolution you have taken of leaving your friends & country for my sake'.[16] They met at Maestricht in February, a place full for him of campaigning memories, and from there with a cavalcade of horses and servants they made stately progress to Aix, to Frankfurt, to Antwerp.

At first everything was wonderful. It was soothing to be away from a carping court and among friendly, admiring people who would stop their coaches and take them to see their gardens. Wherever they went they were made much of. Banquets were arranged, regiments turned out, cannons fired; even Mindelheim went en fête to pay its prince and princess respectful if diminutive honours.* Sarah liked it better than she had expected, 'but not so as to think of living there'. And then of course the gradual disillusion: too cold, too hot—'Their manner is Stoves which is intolerable & makes my head so uneasy that I can't bear it'—until after a winter of it Sarah finds herself longing for her friends in a clean sweet house and declares roundly, 'Tis much better to be dead then to live out of England'.[17] What that old campaigner Dr Hare had said was true: 'The elegance & ornaments of life which your Grace has always enjoyed without any interruption have made a thousand things

---

* 'At Mindelheim they have entertainments too & I think the whole world is but a sort of a popit shew, but sure in noe place there ever was such a farse as in England where men seem to bee giving up with joy & thanks what they preserved at soe much expense for soe many years'. (Sarah to Craggs, 7 June, 1713. BM Stowe 751, f 61).

disagreeable to you which to persons less polite would be tolerable enough, especially considering how much you are a stranger to the language, as well as faces, of the persons you must converse with'.[18]

The sort of pilgrimage was fast becoming a sort of exile, but the Duchess was never starved of news from home. 'What now seems to possess everybody's mind', wrote the lately widowed Lady Mohun, in April, 'is a new tragedy called *Cato* . . . The cause is liberty, the character the Duke of Marlborough, as near as one great, wise & virtuous man can be compared to another . . . Heaven forever preserve our dear Cato, or publick ruin will make every private person's case as precarious as mine'.[19]

Sarah sent for Addison's play and read it. 'It pleased me extreamly', she wrote, 'but it was a melancholly sort of a pleasure that made me drop a great many teares & I fancy'd I saw my children doing the same at many expressions, perticularly when tis said that Cato was allways mild, compassionate & gentle to his friends, fill'd with domestic tendernesse, the best, the kindest father . . .' Had she been at the first performance, she adds, she (like Bolingbroke) would have risen and 'poynted at my Lord Mortimer* whenever a perfidious villian was named that ruind his country to sett up himself. I suppose before this', she concludes, 'you will have seen the conditions of the Peace for it is here in French'.[20] This of course was the Treaty of Utrecht (March 31, 1713), Bolingbroke's triumph, to be later condemned by Pitt as an indelible reproach. Marlborough was, as he had said, thankful not to be concerned in it. He was taking his own measures for the future and had come to an understanding with Hanover upon which not all the wiles of Oxford and Bolingbroke would be able to make the least impression.

Marlborough, his wife tells friends in England, was too lazy to write, (so 'intolerable lazy' he had not even written to his daughters); but that of course by no means applied to herself. She wrote to Robert Jennings, cousin and lawyer (he had seen her off at Dover) about business and politics; to Mrs Clayton, wife of William Clayton the Duke's agent, and to her business-manager James Craggs, whom she called Craggs the Father to distinguish him from James Craggs the Son, who had deeply offended her.† Often, to fox spies, her

---

* Robert Harley Earl of Oxford and Mortimer.

† James Craggs junior the Duchess suspected as the writer of an anonymous

correspondents are unnamed. Often she uses cypher, which she tends to find confusing. 'My last letter was full of heavy complaints from the inconvenience of this place & the cold I suffered, but now it is warmer', she writes from Frankfurt in May, 1713 to an unnamed friend. 'However, I begin to build a chimney which will be finishd today, & that looks as if we were to stay here a long time . . . My strange hand so much in cypher which I am very likely to mistake puts me in mind of a thing a friend of mine writt me upon the receipt of one of my letters: Is it to try the Eyes, wits & patience of the readers, Madam, that you write in such a manner? Which was a very just repremand & upon the thought of it I will end your trouble'.[21]

It amused her that her handwriting was, as she said herself, ridiculous. It was spiky and characterful and could not be forged. She often apologised for it,* only to be assured by the obsequious that it could easily be read from the other side of the room. 'I am so hurryd & interrupted', she explains, 'that I fear I make many mistakes, & I write so fast that my hand is very rediculous'. And to Craggs: 'If you are peevish at my long leters I can only say that I am sure at first sight they seem to bee much longer then they really are & that there are not more words in this notum then might have been put into two sides of this paper if it were writt in your hand'.[22]

The notum, lengthy indeed, contained as usual 'oridgenal speelings'. In an age that had yet to make up its mind about a number of words, Sarah's spelling was no worse than her friends' and in old age showed improvement, but she was apt to come down heavily upon the 'ill English' and bad spelling of others including Vanbrugh, the Dukes of Somerset and Newcastle and Queen Anne. She herself spelt 'guess' 'ghesse', 'citizen' 'cittyson', 'stratagem' 'strataghem' and 'Adam' 'Adham' or even 'Addham'. Sometimes her spelling gives a hint of her pronunciation, as when she sends for 'pattrons of selver & yellew satin & blew tafaty. I think all selver', she adds, 'will make

---

letter she received in November, 1712; but the evidence on which she based her suspicion (a seal) is unconvincing.

* 'Pray let me know freely & plainly if you can read what I writt, because I could make it much plainer by writing slow if it is necessary to bee understood.' Sarah to Craggs, undated. (BM Stowe 751, ƒ 217).

most shew upon yellow by candle light'. Marlborough calls a bird a
bord, says the battaile of Rammillie has worsened his head-eake and
sends for ruborb and lickerish. Four years after the battle of Blenheim
he is still spelling it Bleinhiem; but there could be no better instance
of Sarah's self-assurance than when she alters his 'forenur' to
'foruner', when what both were groping for was 'forerunner'. Lady
Bathurst bemoans her life, finding 'ye pleasures but very unserting,
ye troubles sarting'; while Lady Dorchester confides, 'My Neece is
preety & Yong enough to wate for preferment some years, being
not foreteen'. Proper names of course were always a stumbling-
block: Malbarow, Vanbrook or Vanbrugg, Draydon, St Talbons...*

In the meantime Craggs the Father dutifully wrote by every post
and Sarah as unfailingly replied. At Frankfurt in the summer of 1713
she found that neither travel nor the waters of Aix had cured her
bitterness. With her vindication in mind she sent for copies of all her
papers—'7 or 8 parcells of them so writt with my own fine hand'—
and for good measure three ballads to be sent with them, 'that which
was first made upon the Credit that wee sang at St Albans so often
to poor Mr Escourt's tune; that of giving up Spain; and that of the
History of Abigal & the back stairs, to the tune of fair Rosimonde'.[23]†

When in August they moved to Antwerp she continued to brood
morosely upon past and future, upon death and exile. 'That which I
dread most', she wrote, 'is the power of France'. She was convinced
that at Anne's death Oxford and Bolingbroke meant to bring in the
Pretender, and then (quoting Steele): 'Farewell Liberty, all Europe
will soon be French'. Again: 'I know one must dye some Time or
other, & I really think the Matter is not very great where it happens
or when; but if I could have my wish it should bee in England, in a
clean hous where I might converse with my Children & Friends
while I am in the World; but if that must not bee I submitt, & I will
own to you that I am not so much to be pittyd as some People,
having never seen any Condition yet that was near so happy as
'twas thought. When I was a great Favourite, I was raild at &
flatterd from Morning to Night, neither of which was agreeable to
me; & when there were but few Women that would not have

---

* A number of words used by the Duchess have since changed their meaning,
e.g. 'aggravation' for 'exaggeration', 'clutter' for 'clatter'.

† See appendix IV.

poysond me for the Happynesse they thought I enjoyd, I kept the worst Company of any Body upon Earth and had Reason to be much more weary then of any [thing] that can happen. Still wee are like a sort of banishd People in a strang Country; and I could say Something to every Part of my Life that would convince you that 'tis only a new sceen of Trouble which few are free from'.[24]

When her papers arrived at Antwerp Sarah called in two writers, St Priest and Hutchinson, to help her with her *Conduct*; but without Queen Anne's letters (too precious to be sent or even copied) she could not hope to complete it. It must still wait for another day.

She did a modicum of sightseeing—churches, convents, processions—and wished 'our wise Cittysons & country Gentlemen could travell & see with their own Eyes the sad effects of Popary & arbitrary Power'.*[25] In all her travels, she told Jennings, she had seen nothing worth telling him about, unless it was the castle belonging to the Elector of Trèves, where the Rhine meets the Moselle. 'There was an air of Greatnesse in every Thing about him'; and as for the Schloss itself, she sent a lyrical description to Kneller, then keeping an eye on Laguerre's fresco-painting at Marlborough House. 'It was a place for Jove himself to live in', she told him, 'my friend Mr Vanbrugh would lay out all the King of France's revenue with the addition of the Indies upon it, without ever finishing of it'.[26]

For the first time since her brief childhood, time was on Sarah's hands. She put on weight.† There were no friends to talk or gamble with; nor could one always be writing ('I doe think tis great goodnesse in me', she told Craggs, 'to consider my friends soe much as not to write to them when I have nothing else to doe'). And this of course resulted on the one hand in introspection—'Living abroad makes one very indifferent whether one's life be long or short'[27]—and on the other in making the utmost of such incidents as the loss of a diamond; an event which afforded scope for Sarah's powers of narration.

Writing from Antwerp she tells Craggs:

* '. . . all the history of our Saviour represented by the trades people of the town twice a week . . . the whole thing more impious then tis possible for any body to imagin that had not seen it'. (Sarah to Mrs Clayton. Undated. Blen G-1-16).

† Of the Elector of Mainz the Duchess wrote: 'His shape is, like my own, a little of the fatest'. (Madresfield, p. 32).

It is the fashion in these countries to wear bracelets of dyamonds & pictures about their rists, buckld on in a manner that they cannot come off without undoing. And I came out of a room one evening, immediatly after it had been seen on my rist, into my dressing room, took it off & layd it down upon the dressing table: and I was thinking to undress me, but while I was setting there alone, Ned the black footman that you have seen came thro my bed chamber by the Duke of Marlboroughs order to let me know that the tea stayd for me. And I call'd him in & bad him stoop down to put on my shoe, which I had just pulld off because it hurt me, by which means he had a full oppertunity of seeing the dyamond, for I satt so close to the table that it was just in his Eyes.

After my shoe was on I rose up & hee lighted me into the other room where the tea was to bee made & where it was very naturall for him to have stayd to have assisted in serving the tea, but hee went out immediatly. And upon my missing my Bracelet, which I ded in a very little time, and examining into the matter, the Gentleman of the house, who has all the appearance of a very honest and sensible man . . . said that he was coming down a pair of stairs by chance out of his lodge that looks upon a back door that opens into my dressing room & hee saw a lacky of Madam's open the door & goe into it in the dark.

This is the fact and I think it a plain demonsteration that Ned must have the dyamond, which is [not?] of a great value, but it was the most agreeable & pritty fine thing that ever I saw in my life & I think I would give the full value of it to have it again.

There needs no more than I have [said?] & did to convince any body that this man must take [have taken] the dyamond, who certainly saw it, & hee knew no body was in the room where I left it & that hee could goe round to the back door in a minute & take it up; and no footman ever went into that room without being call'd. Besides, most of my other servants were abroad; and in the examination of Ned there appeard severall marks of guilt; and the Duke of Marlborough was so sure by these demonsterations which I have repeated that hee sent for the magistrates of this town & told them what could bee given upon oath against this man, upon which they sent him to prison; and the laws of this country are soe severe in these cases that a less evedence would hang one of their own people; but the manner & custome is to wrack them till they confess, which is soe dreadfull a thing that I rather chose to give up my dyamond than suffer it in my owne concerne.

And Ned is soe very obstanate a rogue that while hee had any hope of escaping the torments of this world hee would not confess; soe wee have sent to the magistrats to discharge him, & I fancy hee will come for England, which is the chief reason of my troubling you with this long account, that you may think if by any surprise you can have him searched there & by that means find the dyamond about him, where hee thinks him self secure, for I can't imagine that hee will soe much as aim at selling this dyamond in a country where hee knows no body & where it has made such a noise. But I reckon hee has hid it some where & if hee can't get it from the place him self hee will press some person to assist him; and in soe great a family [household] tis to bee feared there may bee one not unlike him self, for hee had companions that used to drink with him; and since I was abroad I have observd upon some occasions a more then ordinary greedynesse to get mony.

Pray do me the favour to consult with Hodges in this matter & desire him to goe to my hous & to give the servants warning to have noe correspondence with him nor suffer him upon any account to come there; and to look if all doors & windowes are all securd for hee knows the hous soe well that there is no doubt but hee will rob it if hee can . . . .

The Duke of Marlborough lost a ring of about 150 ls at Aix; but that being a thing that came off easy & always pulld off when hee washd his hands, hee did not remember enough of it to charge any body with it; so it passed off so easy that I believe it might be some incouragement to Ned in this villiany that hee has don . . . Twas a great temptation to make his fortune . . .[28]

Alas for intuition! 'I have lately sent for near four hundred Pounds', Sarah tells Jennings a month later, 'part of which was to get a Jewell I have lost and to recompense an innocent Servant that had been put into Prison about it and that was soe innocent that it gave me a great deal of Trouble when I saw hee had been wronged'.[29] It is only when one sees the account Sarah sent to Mrs Clayton that one realises that the lost diamond must have been the Marlborough portrait ring, given by Chandos and since made into a bracelet, in which form Sarah bequeathes it in her will. 'Tho I had fancyd when this diamond picture was lost', she tells Mrs Clayton, 'that I would give twice the value of it again, yet when they brought it to me, instead of being pleased I could not help bursting out into a great passion of crying to think how much I had wronged a very inosent man and as soon as I had recovered my self I sent for the footman & gave him 50 pistoles to make amends for his ill lodging in prison, assuring him at the same time that if hee would leave a great fault hee has of drinking that I would bee very kind to him'. 'I am glad your diamond is found & no body guilty', writes Lady Sunderland to her mother, 'I dare say the man thinks you have very well made him amends'.[30] It would be pleasing to think it had taught the Duchess a lesson.

But there was no doubt about it, England was the only place to live. 'I should be very well content', she wrote now, 'with the worst of my country hous's'.[31] If need be, she would live disguised in a cottage; though she would much prefer Windsor Lodge, 'of all the Places that ever I was in the most agreeable'. Marlborough too was impatient to return, 'which', said his wife, 'I beleive you can't blame him for. There was only one good reason for his leaving it that ever I could see & that seems to bee very remote at present'.[32]

And then in March, 1714, as hopes were turning homeward, they had tragic news. Their third daughter, Elizabeth Countess of Bridgwater, had died of smallpox. On hearing the news of his favourite daughter's death Marlborough fainted. Sarah wrote to Jennings:

> The Loss of my poor dear Child is indeed very terrible to me ... That she is happyer I don't doubt then in such a World as this where time generally passes away in trifling, in things that are tedious & in many frights for what may happen, which is yet worse ... but all the Arguments that I can possibly think of cant hinder me from lamenting as long as I live the loss of what

I had soe much reason to love as I did my dear Child, who had a perfect good mind & every thing I could have wish'd in her ...[33]

'My grief & my loss are inexpressible', wrote the widower, 'your Grace's concern for my poor children* is a great comfort to me ... having no other thoughts but to tend my children & teach them to imitate their dear Mother in her love & dutifulness to your Grace & the Duke ... I know but little of the Publick', he added, 'but I flatter myself that ye Monsters will so fall out amongst themselves that we shall have ye comfort to have your Grace & the Duke of Marlborough return more belov'd than ever'.[34]

Bridgwater's prediction of dissension among the Tory 'monsters' of course came true, and their house of cards collapsed at the first clap of misfortune. Gone were the days when Anne could turn to a Freeman or a Montgomery. There was only Abigail, who had fallen out with her Treasurer, Oxford,† who in turn had fallen out with her Secretary of State, Bolingbroke. They raged even in the royal presence, even as the distraught Queen approached her death.

But long before she died Anne appeared to be in an advanced stage of decomposition, like some unfortunate host to a parasite which grows beneath the skin; as though God had 'sent a worm to madden his handiwork', or rather, that she were helplessly in the power of some evil spirit. Mrs Danvers, coming to call her one morning, found her with her back towards her, gazing fixedly at a clock. When questioned,—'What is it with the clock, Ma'am?'—she turned slowly about with 'so woeful and ghastly a regard' that Mrs Danvers 'saw death in the look' and, frightened, summoned assistance.[35] 'She appeared to be the most despicable mortal I had ever seen in any station', a shocked visitor reported, 'The poor lady ... was again under a severe fit of gout, ill-dressed, blotted in her countenance & surrounded with plaisters, cataplaisma, & dirty-like

* The Bridgwater children were John Viscount Brackley (born 3rd Feb., 1704, died 30 Jan., 1719), a son who died in infancy and Lady Anne Egerton, who was taken into the Marlborough household and married (i) the Duke of Bedford and (ii) the Earl of Jersey.

† In March, 1714 Abigail refused to carry Lord Oxford's offer of resignation to the Queen. 'She had credit enough to hurt Lord Oxford, by which she destroyed her own foundation'. (Lord Dartmouth in Burnet, op. cit., VI, 33.)

rags'.[36] It was Abigail who told Swift, 'This good lady deserves pity'.

The Queen had been desperately ill at Christmas and now in July, as the Marlboroughs prepared for their journey home, began to succumb to what Sarah called a complication of diseases. It was an age ago that she had written, 'I realy beleive one kind word from deare Mrs Freeman would save me if I were Gasping'; and Mrs Freeman was no longer within call. During her last days Oxford and Bolingbroke 'played the double game of intrigue with the courts of St Germains and Hanover less expertly than the Duke of Marlborough* . . . and the quarrel between the two Tory leaders, despite all Swift's efforts at reconciliation, ended in a furious clash',[37] that clash in fact in the Queen's presence, which she truthfully said she should never survive.

Oxford resigned that same day (July 27th). On the 29th Anne sank into a coma from which she recovered only enough to let her hand be guided with the Treasurer's white staff, which was given with the Council's approval to the Duke of Shrewsbury. She died on August 1st. 'She had lived long enough', writes Sir Winston, 'to strip the name of Britain of most of the glories with which it had shone . . . She sank into her mortal collapse with her country in the jaws of measureless tribulation. But luckily she expired while there was still time to save it'.[38]

For the second time Somerset had taken the lead in a crisis by suddenly appearing, with Argyll, at the Council on July 30th, to thwart the Jacobite machinations of Bolingbroke. To the end Anne kept her people guessing (and we are guessing still) as to her own intentions for the succession; for although she appeared to favour Hanover, her personal loathing for that family was to the last evidenced by her cold letters, which were said to have speeded the death of the Electress Sophia. There was also that sealed packet which Anne 'always carried about her and put every evening under her bolster. She changed the envelope when it got worn or dirty. It was suspected to be a will concerning the Pretender'. It may have been; yet she must have known James III could not have succeeded without changing his religion, which he commendably refused to do. The packet was burned unread.

* Marlborough sought a pardon from St Germains in February, 1714.

In the event the vigorous measures provided for by the Act of Settlement and now taken to protect the Hanoverian succession were successful; although, in Sir Winston's view, if the Queen had lived six weeks longer, Bolingbroke would probably have plunged the country into civil war. He was soon to show his colours by joining the Pretender as his Secretary of State; while Oxford, who in Sir Keith Feiling's opinion never seriously intended a Stuart restoration, remained to be impeached and to languish in the Tower.

From contemporary accounts it would seem that Abigail behaved disappointingly. After coaxing some of the proceeds from the Asiento slave-trade out of Bolingbroke she is said to have ransacked St James's for something better than brass locks, two days before the Queen's death;[39] but since Anne's will remained unsigned, there could be no provision for her favourite beyond that which she had made for herself. 'Can she', Swift was asked, 'hereafter make any figure in the drama but a *persona muta*?' The answer was no. With her lord she retired in quiet state to Langley in Buckinghamshire.*

And Queen Anne? If greatness lies in the conquest of matter by mind and of weakness by will power, then Anne was a great queen and what befell her great tragedy.

On August 2nd, the day after the Queen's death, the Marlboroughs landed at Dover.

---

* Writing from Langley in 1724 to Swift ('one whose goodness to me has always been abundantly more than I could deserve'), Lady Masham says, 'I do assure you from the bottom of my heart there is not a person living I have a greater friendship for than yourself and shall have to the end of my life . . . I long to see you at my retired habitation, where you will meet with a most hearty welcome and faithful friends'. (Swift Corresp. III, 190). She died in 1734. Langley was bought from the widower by Charles Third Duke of Marlborough and rebuilt.

CHAPTER X

No Armour

1714-1717

———————◆———————

For Hanover and the Protestant Succession long wars had been fought, fortresses taken, villages burned, friends betrayed, conquerors exiled . . . So that now, with Anne dead, it was felt that the scene called for a prince indeed, for some Olympian Phoebus Apollo, but all benevolence, all virtue, to justify the blood and the anguish and with godlike serenity to land on his sceptred isle and claim his own.

A little late on cue at Greenwich there landed, on September 18th, an elderly German gentleman, to be acclaimed as George I of England. There was it seemed no queen (she had been put away for adultery), but there were mistresses—Frau Schulenburg and Frau Kielmannsegge—one fat, one thin. There was also a son George whom his father disliked. The King spoke German and a little French, no English. England, said Lord Chesterfield, was too big for him. But he was not a Stuart. Turning to Marlborough whom he had, against Sarah's wishes, restored to his post of Captain-General he said, 'My lord Duke, I hope your troubles are now all over'.

In their glass coach the exiles had returned amid cheers and flowers. All was sunshine again. Sarah of course would accept no office, but she saw to it that those of her family who wanted appointments had them: this for Mary Montagu and that for Francis Godolphin . . . though she was sorry that the widower Bridgwater was such a manifest fool that she could get him nothing better than Chamberlain to the Prince of Wales. Vanbrugh was knighted and so was Dr Garth, the fat doctor dubbed, at his request, with Marlborough's sword. Even Mrs Clayton, whom Horace Walpole called a pompous simpleton, was squeezed in as lady-in-waiting to Caroline, Princess of Wales.

For a time they were restless. 'Since my last to you from Windsor', Sarah wrote from St Albans to Jennings on August 23rd, 'I have been at the Bath and at Woodstock, and when I came to this Place I was more tird then [on] any of my Travels'. She praised Holywell ('however ordinary I would not part with it') and seemed happy to stay there for the rest of her life; but that was not to be. For one thing, and to her a most vexatious one, there was Blenheim.

Before going abroad in 1712 Marlborough had left the shell of Blenheim in the care of a young man called Henry Joynes, a skilled draughtsman (he later became an architect) regarded by Vanbrugh as his clerk of the works. Hawksmoor called him Honest Harry. He was twenty-one. According to Joynes, the Duke took leave of him on cordial terms, hand on shoulder, and entrusted the building to him; a gardener, Tilleman Bobart, being left in charge of the grounds. In practice two men responsible for three acres of building and two thousand acres of park and garden must either kill themselves in a frenzy of futile labour or do nothing. Sensibly enough Joynes and Bobart plumped for the latter course, except that they would make hay, occasionally show the house to the curious, and fish in the lake; while Vanbrugh, doubtless blessing his luck, moved into the ruins of Woodstock Manor. It would be safe to say that never in the history of Blenheim has life come nearer to Arcady. 'I was fishing last week', Joynes tells a friend at the Treasury, 'and I can't avoid telling you what I catch't, a Brace of good Trouts about 14 ins, a Chub about the same length and eight Dace ten inches each . . . and since, a brace of Chubs one 17 ins, a brave fish to Catcht tho' course to Eat . . .'[1]

It was good going; too good indeed to last. When the Marlboroughs returned they were angry about the haymaking (the gardens had run to ruin) and still angrier that Vanbrugh, instead of demolishing Woodstock Manor, had gone to live in it. The Duchess alleged that on the roof he had built himself a closet, 'as if he had been to study the planets'; though from that point he was far more likely to be studying the perspective of his own masterpiece, 'the cast and turn of the House' that meant so much to him.

However, Vanbrugh was not, like Wren, easy to be got rid of. He had powerful friends at the Kit-Cat: Carlisle, Newcastle, Manchester, and of course Marlborough himself. 'I have just now been with Lord Carlisle', Vanbrugh tells the club's founder, Jacob Tonson, 'who has named Friday for the Barns Expedition. I have seen Lady Marlborough since & she agrees to it & will order a Bardge at Whitehall. The Company she names are Two Ladies besides her Self, Ld Carlisle, Ld Clare, Horace Walpole, Dr Garth and Mr Benson'.[2] How discharge a man with whom one was on such terms? Besides, he might still be useful, if not as an architect (and she might yet manage him in that), then as a matchmaker.

For her Godolphin granddaughter Harriet, a disappointingly plain girl of fifteen, she had her eye on the young Duke of Newcastle, a rich and foolish young man known to fellow-members of the Kit-Cat as Permis, from the phrase he was fond of using: *Est-il permis?* In this delicate project Vanbrugh, who knew him well and was to build for him, offered his help. Sarah gratefully accepted; but the thing went sluggishly. The Duke, Vanbrugh told Sarah, seemed convinced of the fine attributes he had mentioned but voiced 'a sort of wish (express'd in a very gentle manner) that her bodily perfections had been up to those I describ'd of her mind & understanding'. Vanbrugh had been honest about her face and yet was gallant enough to bet that in two years' time no woman in town would be better liked. While the match hung fire, the Duchess put out a feeler in the direction of Wentworth Woodhouse—'vast woods, a great seat in Yorkshire and a mighty rich family'—but Harriet, after meeting the heir, burst into tears; whereupon her grandmother wept too, hugged her and said she need not marry the emperor of the world unless she liked him.[3]

For Blenheim Marlborough sent for estimates with a view to finishing it himself; but there were disputes as to what was owing, and building was not resumed until the summer of 1716; by which time many of those who had worked on it had died or for one reason or another declined to return. These last included Grinling Gibbons, who had been responsible for all the enrichment in stone and marble; Edward Strong, the chief mason; and Henry Joynes, who was about to succeed Hawksmoor as clerk of the works at Kensington Palace.

It was six years since Marlborough had written to his duchess, 'After the many troubles & dependencies wee have labord thro during almost all our lifetime for the good of our children I think it very reasonable, tho we had met with no ungratefull disapointements, that wee shou'd before wee dye be masters of some litle time for our own ease & quiet'.[4] And it was now, in quiet retirement, that they should have reaped that modest reward.

On April 15th, 1716 their second daughter Anne Countess of Sunderland died of what was then called a pleuritic fever. She was, said Sarah, everything that was good and everything that was charming. To her parents her death brought profound grief and shock. She had inherited Sarah's beauty without her bitterness and had been the toast of the Kit-Cat as the Little Whig. There was a tenderness about her which was said to have a softening influence upon her mother. As a child she could never bear to be in her bad books—'What have I done that you think so ill of poor me that loves you so passionately?'—and on one such occasion tells her she had not been to bed for a fortnight without weeping.*

Her own children—Robert, Charles, John, Anne and Diana—she loved dearly and, with a seeming premonition of death, wrote movingly about them to her husband. 'As to the children, pray get my mother, the Duchess of Marlborough, to take care of the girls, & if I leave my boys too little to go to school—to be left to servants is very bad for children, and a man can't take the care of little children as a woman can—for the love that she has for me & the duty I have ever show'd her I hope she will do it, & be ever kind to you, who was dearer to me than my life . . . Pray let Mr Flournoys get some good-natur'd man for Lord Spencer's governor, who may be fit to go abroad with him . . . and don't be as careless of the dear children as when you relied upon me to take care of them. But let them be your care, though you should marry, for your wife may

---

* At Blenheim an undated letter from Anne Sunderland to her mother reads: '. . . I have one of my dear Mama's Colds with very great pleasure, for it was a great uneasyness to me to hear you say you thought it a sign your constitution was broak, but I hope it looks more now like being naturall. I am sure whatever it is I shall like being as you are & indeed I should have more ease in indureing anything then I can express if it could take off any pain from my dearest Mama that I adore more then I can ever show'. (Blen E 6)

wrong them when you don't mind it. We must all die, but 'tis hard to part with one so much belov'd and in whom there was so much happiness as you, my dearest, ever were to me . . .'[5]

With a great many tears Sarah read the letter and wrote to the widower, 'You may be very sure that to my life's end I shall observe very religiously all that my poor dear child desired. I was pleased to find that my own inclinations had led me to resolve upon doing every thing that she mentions before I knew it was her request, except taking Lady Anne, which I did not offer, thinking that since you take Lady Frances* home, who is 18 years old, she would be better with you than me, as long as you live, with the servants that her dear mother chose to put about her . . . But I will be of all the use that I can be to her in every thing that she wants me; and if I should happen to live longer than you, though so much older, I will then take as much care of her as if she were my own child. I have resolved to take poor Lady Anne Egerton,† who I believe is very ill looked after. She went yesterday to Ashridge, but I will send for her to St Albans as soon as you will let me have dear Lady Di;‡ and while the weather is hot I will keep them two and Lady Harriet with a little family of servants to look after them and be there as much as I can; but the Duke of Marlborough will be running up and down to several places this summer, where one can't carry children; and I don't think his health so good as to trust him by himself'.[6]

On May 28th Marlborough had his first stroke, which resulted in partial paralysis and loss of speech. By the summer, speech had returned and, with Garth in attendance, he was well enough to be moved to Bath. On the subject of Bath Sarah was in agreement with Queen Anne who had called it stinking. 'Of all the places upon earth', wrote the Duchess, 'tis the most disagreeable'. Nor did she believe in the efficacy of its waters; but when the doctor not only recommended them but insisted on staying there with his patient, what else was she to do?

'I think Sr S: Garth is the most honest & compassionate', she told

* Lady Frances Spencer, his daughter by his first wife Lady Arabella Cavendish. She married Henry Howard Earl of Carlisle.

† Lady Anne Egerton, daughter of Elizabeth Countess of Bridgwater, deceased.

‡ Lady Diana Spencer, Anne Sunderland's second daughter and Sarah's favourite granddaughter.

Craggs, 'but after the minuets which I have seen him dance and his late tour into Italy, I can't help thinking that hee may some times bee in the wrong'.[7] Marlborough's health, she added, was of more consequence to her than all the money in the world. Would he please consult his 'club of physicians' in London and let her know what they thought? The symptoms, some of which frightened her, she observed and, in letter after letter, described minutely:

Hee is vastly better in his head & in his speech, there is not the least doubt of that, but tis certain that his limbs are weaker a good deal then they were even at St Albans. Hee can't come upstairs without uneasiness, & some times hee has some thing that I don't know very well how to express of grunting & bemoaning of him self that looks like sicknesse or want of spirits, but when I ask him if hee is sick hee says no, but hee is uneasy & won't or can't discrib what it is. Hee says his belly is harder then it used to bee & tis certain that his cote does not butten easy that was too big when wee came here . . .[8]

Perhaps it was too much to hope that, with a leading doctor in residence, doctoring by post could produce the remedy; but at one stage it did succeed in making the patient laugh. This was when one of Craggs's club of physicians conjured him to 'keep up the dignity of his stomack'. On a good day he could still be 'pritty chairfull' and take a hand at ombre. Sarah tried him again with ass's milk, which 'hee took two days & left it off, fancying it did not agree with him; but that, I believe', added Sarah, 'could bee nothing but fancy'. It was hard to prescribe for one more used to giving orders than taking them; but since the symptoms were alarming, could it be that the remedies should be also?

'I have been told today', writes Sarah, 'that vipors boyl'd in the Duke of Marlboroughs broath is an Admerable thing & will mend his blood & take off the lownesse of his spirits . . . An apothecary here told me hee had known severall take it with good success but the Dutches of Shrewsbury says there is non good in England & that I must send into France & they have the best in the world that comes from Mumpillio [Montpelier]. She talks of having them come alive in boxes with holes fill'd with bran, but I fancy they have a more easy way of sending them'. Craggs hastens to tell his son in Paris to order vipers, only to be informed next post, 'I have a leter from one I think an oracle who . . . has seen that Broath used by severall a considerable time. They that took it complained that the loathing of the Vipors made their other food less usefull to them & that jelly of heartshorn & calves feet was much better'.[9] It was unfortunate that in Paris Craggs the Son had already popped the vipers into the post.

In Sarah's enormously long letters to Craggs from Bath three themes recur: Marlborough's health, Cadogan and Blenheim. William Cadogan,* formerly Marlborough's companion-in-arms, was his closest friend. When in 1706 he had been reported killed or captured Marlborough wrote, 'He lov'd me and I cou'd rely upon him';[10] and three years later, when he was wounded, 'I hope in God hee will do well for I can intierly depend upon him'.[11] When in 1712 Marlborough went into exile, he asked for Cadogan, who met him at Ostende and went with him to Holland, a gesture which cost him his job. As insurance against the worst that might happen in England, Marlborough then asked him to invest £40,000 for him in Dutch government funds. This he did, later switching the investment to Austria in the hope of better interest there. As things turned out, the rate of interest in Austria fell; and when Sarah got wind of it she wrote to Craggs:

> I must tell you a secret great as the world & I conjure you by all that you value upon earth never to breath the least word of it to any man or woman upon earth, for I would not say what I am going to write even to you if I did not find it was a thing absolutely necessary to have your help in in order to save a vast loss that may very probably happen to the Duke of Marlborough or to his family . . . Lord Cadogan has a great many usefull & good qualities, but hee has a passion for mony that is beyond any thing that ever I knew . . .[12]

And so it all came out, the long sad story which exposed Marlborough's jolly, fat, Irish quartermaster-general as a 'vile creature' and a common thief. Whatever happened, said the Duchess, Marlborough need not know. 'The letters come three hours before hee reads or sees any thing, so that I can easyly take any thing out that

---

* William Cadogan (1675–1726), M.P. for Woodstock, created first Earl Cadogan in 1718.

hee would bee peevish to see'.[13] In the end, Cadogan paid in full; but the cost in fret and friendship was incalculable.

As for Blenheim, even to think of it, said Sarah, was enough to turn one's brain. It was a chaos which only God Almighty could finish. Nevertheless she would have a try. If while she lived she might hope 'to compass a habitation at Woodstock', she might even attempt to sell her crown lease of Windsor Lodge. Craggs, Vanbrugh's friend who had introduced him, must somehow manage him now and keep him sweet, he seemed so easily offended. 'For I really love the man', she admitted, 'and I never saw any thing that I did not like in him but these high flights in building which I can never tast, especially tell I have a habitation to live in, which [it] is high time at our age to have'.[14]

There was something in that; for there was no denying that, owing to a chain of mischances, though building had begun in 1705 now, in 1716, the Marlboroughs' private apartments were still not habitable;* whereas Marlborough House, inside and out, had been completed in two years. On the other hand they had, in addition to that London house (much smaller than Blenheim but still commodious), two good country houses; and Marlborough, though keen to move into Blenheim, seems to have cared less about his own short time and where he spent it than about posterity and a fitting monument to his armies' achievements. His attitude was impersonal; Sarah's was personal; and as they moved from Bath to Blenheim and put up at High Lodge, she decided it was time to take matters into her own hands. 'I don't tell him the tenth part of the maddnesse of it', she wrote to Craggs, 'for fear of vexing him, which must bee avoided as much as possible upon all occasions'.[15]

All she saw at Blenheim then appalled her and the most daunting thing of all was the bridge with which Vanbrugh had begun to span the valley. Wren had suggested a far more modest approach but had been outvoted. The bridge, Vanbrugh decided, must be worthy of a Roman conqueror and that was what, with enormous courage and brilliance, he prescribed. No matter if, with its rooms and towers and arched superstructure, it was entirely unorthodox and looked more

---

* Then as now the private apartments are self-contained in the east wing which, following common practice, Vanbrugh completed first. Working westwards, his team was completing the first stateroom west of the Saloon when in 1716 he left.

like a Roman aqueduct than anything normally met with in the English landscape. It proclaimed no local hero but a world figure who had marched across Europe to save it and had frustrated the pretensions of France.

All this Marlborough could see and rise to and Sarah could not. When well enough to ride he rode to the bridge head and asked if Vanbrugh was sure there was enough earth for Wise to link the bridge to the valley. He was assured that there was. But in the meantime Sarah mocked at it as Vanbrugh's 'bridge in the air'— unconnected, isolated, leading from nowhere to nowhere and with next to no water beneath it—and fumed that a skilled mason* and countless workmen must waste their time on it when they might have been finishing rooms one could live in. It was unreasonable. It was madness: 'a prodigious expence to no manner of purpose'. Patience was wearing thin.

The Duchess wrote again to Craggs:

I will say as little as I can upon Sir Johns subject since I see plainly you are partial to him, & I beleive in that affair of the Building to a great degree, but whatever one says one can't help thinking as one thinks & I am allways of the opinion that I have great difficulties to strugle with in that building. I have no mind to fall out with Sr John & much less so vex the D: of Marl: at a time when his health is so bad. At the same time I think I owe it to him & to my family to prevent if I can having a great estate thrown away in levilling of hills, filling up pricipices & making bridges in the air for no reason that I or any body else can see but to have it said hereafter that Sr John Vanbrugh did that thing which never was don before.

You seem to think that hee & Mr Hawkesmore are the only people to bee consulted with. The last I have spoken to this morning & hee has promised to get a fair computation made of what the charge will bee to finish this unnecessary & rediculous thing. How far hee will be able to perform it I don't know, for hee is but one & not the head, but hee appears reasonable &

Bartholomew Peisley (c.1654–1715), the Oxford mason who, with his son of the same name worked on the Grand Bridge and was 'very proud & overjoyd' when the main arch was keyed, 'it being a great & nice piece of Work'.

allows me that I am in the right to see whether what is intended is more to bee liked then the mony that it will cost, but for Sr John I can't imagine what I can say to him . . .[16]

The cost of Blenheim to date she reckoned at £260,000. 'Tis time', she wrote, 'to put a stop to such a maddnesse'.

In one of many subsequent lawsuits Sarah referred to Vanbrugh as a fish of great size, hard to net. So now at Blenheim, the bridge though gargantuan was not in itself monstrous enough, even in Sarah's opinion, to cause his downfall. There needed to be a number of things—Woodstock Manor, where he had staged a pantomime of demolition while buttressing the parts he most cared for; the pretentious kitchen-court ('covered ways for servants'); the blocked views (Sarah vetoed the western orangery but sadly agreed with Wren that the water would still be visible only from the Gallery);* and for good measure, the muddle over the Newcastle match with Harriet Godolphin, which the Duchess without warning had put into the hands of a professional matchmaker. This last, which had embarrassed Vanbrugh with Newcastle, coupled with Sarah's notum of Blenheim grievances, sent to Craggs's brother-in-law, resulted in Vanbrugh's blunt letter of resignation:

Whitehall, November 8th, 1716

Madam

When I writ to your Grace on Tuesday last I was much at a loss what cou'd be the ground of your having dropt me in the service I had been endeavouring to do you and your family with the Duke of Newcastle, upon your own sole motion and desire. But having since been shewn by Mr Richards a large packet of building papers sent him by your Grace, I find the reason was that you had resolv'd to use me so ill in respect of Blenheim as must make it impracticable to employ me in any other Branch of your Service.

---

* The Gallery, now called the Long Library, runs the whole length of the west front. On August 31, 1705 Marlborough wrote from Tirlemont: 'What Sr Chri: Rhen says as to the watter not being seen in the two apartments [Hall and Saloon] is very trew for that prospect is from the Gallerie'. (Blen E 3) But Vanbrugh reminded the Duchess: 'You cannot see all things from all places'.

These Papers, Madam, are so full of far-fetch'd, labour'd Accusations, mistaken Facts, wrong Inferences, groundless Jealousies and strain'd Constructions that I shou'd put a very great affront upon your understanding if I suppos'd it possible you cou'd mean any thing in earnest by them. But to put a Stop to my troubling you any more, you have your end, Madam, for I will never trouble you more unless the Duke of Marlborough recovers so far [as] to shelter me from such intolerable Treatment.

I shall in the mean time have only this Concern on his account (for whom I shall ever retain the greatest Veneration), that your Grace having like the Queen thought fit to get rid of a faithfull servant, the Torys will have the pleasure to see your Glassmaker, Moor, make just such an end of the Dukes Building as her Minister Harley did of his Victories for which it was erected.

I am
Your Graces most obedient Servant

To which the postscript read:

If your Grace will give me leave to print your paper I'll do it very exactly; and without any answer or remark but this short letter tack'd to the tail of them, that the world may know I desir'd they might be published.[17]

In many ways, notably medicine, the age had its drawbacks, but for writing what it meant, for those few who could write a letter, it was glorious. Not many had acquired such finesse, but in his leave-taking of the Duchess Vanbrugh showed how to combine candour with dignity and at the same time work in a thrust at the new favourite, James Moore the cabinetmaker,* referred to by Sarah as her oracle and cynically watched by Vanbrugh in his versatile acrobatics.

At High Lodge two days later, while the Duchess was still smouldering over Vanbrugh's letter, (resilient herself, she had meant him, she said, to laugh at her notum over a bottle of wine), came Marlborough's second stroke. She summoned three doctors and her

---

* 'I think him very honest & understanding in many Trades besides his own'. Sarah to Jennings, 2 July, 1714. (Madresfield, p. 107).

two daughters, Henrietta Godolphin and Mary Montagu. The last, being ill, could not come; which was as well because the house—'a very little lodge where there were but three rooms to lye in & garrets'—was 'prodigious full'.

Before setting out, Henrietta, in her bold scrawl, had written to her father ('I am extream tenderly as well as most dutifully yours') as she vainly hoped in secret. When she arrived she brushed past her mother to go to his bedside. 'She took no more notice of me', wrote Sarah afterwards, 'then if I had been the nurse to snuff the candles'. Next morning, although barely on speaking terms Sarah, for Marlborough's benefit, took Henrietta in her arms, 'whether she would or no, for he could see nothing of her shy look; and afterwards', she continues, 'when we were alone again I asked her if I had not dissembled very well & begged of her that she would do the same, for in this case I thought it as great a virtue as truth. She would not say anything but looked as if she would kill me, and as soon as her lord came I told him how she had used me. He looked uneasy . . . The Duke of Marl: mended and they soon went away with all the doctors but one; and the morning she took her leave I went thro the rooms with my arm in hers to hide this matter even from the servants; and when she came into her own chamber, as I was talking to her without disguise, she seem'd mighty easy & indifferent & looked in the glass, upon which I said, "You're extream pretty", and so left her . . . When we returned to London we went on in the usual manner—dogged rudeness, and I trying to hide it'.[18]

When most needed Sarah had had too little time for her family; though perhaps too she had strange notions of upbringing. 'A horse not broken becometh headstrong,' she copied from Ecclesiasticus, 'and a child left to himself will be wilful'. Now she had too much time for all of them, and especially, in 1717, for her son-in-law Charles Earl of Sunderland, who decided to remarry.

It was a curious thing that almost always when the Duchess heard of an impending marriage in her family, unless she herself had arranged it, it meant bad news; and this of Sunderland was deplorable. He was of the type that works hard (he was now again Secretary of State), plays hard (a gamble, as for most of the Spencers, was irresistible), and falls repeatedly and passionately in love. His letter to Sarah in the fourth year of Anne's reign (a letter in which he assured her, 'Every honest Englishman will acknowledge that whatever good has been done is entirely owing to 201' [Sarah]) is sealed with a device that shows Cupid shooting at three hearts on an altar; and it was this third involvement which Sarah called a ridiculous match.

It was not of course for her to say that the bride, Judith Tichborne, was unsuitable, but of course she did say so. She was, Sarah found, 'a woman unknown, without a shilling and without a name'. Sunderland told his mother-in-law in what he probably thought her language that he needed 'a companion and one to manage the concerns of his family in order to lessen his expenses'. And so, adds Sarah bitterly, 'he chooses one of about fifteen. Upon this I took the liberty to tell my Lord Sunderland that no body could imagine that those ends could be answerd by one of Mrs Tichborne's age and that I should think the conversation of such a one could not be agreeable to him; that it was marrying a kitten; and really I do think it is very odd for a wise man at forty-five* to come out of his library to play with puss'.

But her main objection—and here Sarah had a duty—was in the terms of the marriage-settlement, which appeared to prejudice the interests of Anne Sunderland's five children. With alarm their grandmother envisaged 'another brood of children†—beggars with the titles of lords & ladies—that can have nothing but what he almost robs his former children of'. As for Sarah's own grandchildren, she might yet live to see them 'come to London behind coaches, as the Duke of Bolton's children did, to get shoos & stockings from their Aunts'.[19] The more she thought about it, the more indignant she grew. How could he 'so soon forget the passionate expressions in his last dear wife's dying letter to be good and tender to her children?'[20]

Almost invariably with these marriage-settlements, she had found, one had but to scratch the surface to find a bishop; and in this one, sure enough, the abettor turned out to have been the Bishop of Norwich, 'a little mean churchman with a poor understanding'. And indeed, now that Sarah called him to mind she wryly realised that

---

* Sunderland in 1717 was 42. At his death his famous library went to Blenheim, in discharge of a debt. It was sold in the late nineteenth century.

† By his third wife, Judith Tichborne, Sunderland had two more sons and a daughter.

Marlborough House: South elevation overlooking St. James's Park

Blenheim: the Column of Victory

had it not been for her own influence with Queen Anne 'hee had not been a bishop god forgive me for it'.[21] In her letters to him she wastes no time beating about the bush. 'One thing is very sure', he is told, 'that she will be a kind of a Beauty at thirty yeares old when my Lord Sunderland is three score . . . I wish', she added, 'you had said more at first to discourage him from so wild a thought'.[22]

The settlement was amended and they married; and as with Cadogan so now with Sunderland, Sarah wrote off another friend. She searched for the tribute she had paid him years ago—'a man of the most open, undisguised, honest zeal for the interest of his country that could possibly be found'—and crossed it through;[23]* for now he was 'a furious madman without any principle',[24] and 'there was nothing base or foolish that hee ded not do'.[25] For his part Sunderland remained, on the surface, friendly; but his was a complex character, staunch in friendship but, as Swift had found, 'implacable towards those to whom he hath given greatest cause to complain'.[26] To fall foul of him was unwise.

The Duchess now began to discover that to a conscientious grand-mother a large family can be a blessing or it can become a kind of hydra, so that no sooner has one member been dealt with but another springs up to threaten crisis or calamity. Now, to almost everyone's surprise, Permis Newcastle married Harriet Godolphin. In this case the settlement asked was £20,000,† and although Marlborough at first demurred and said he never gave more than ten, Sarah coaxed him to agree to it. The reception was at Marlborough House. Laughingly Sarah begged a favour of the bride, that the first day her lord did not go out with her, she would call for her in her fine, gold chariot to drive to Hyde Park. But nothing came of it, and when she did call it was only to sit in a dead way and be pumped for questions. The most she would volunteer was, 'How does my grandpapa?' She was a sad disappointment and had no child. As for her husband, he sided with the wrong people, 'being under a great enchantment by Sir John Vanbrugh' and a friend of Sunderland's. However, he had taken Harriet off her hands, though they were still more than full enough, for there was always her ailing lord, and there was Blenheim.

* At Blenheim. In the version at Althorp the same passage has not been deleted.

† The Duchess maintained that the original demand, via Vanbrugh, was for £40,000, and protested that her granddaughter was 'neither citizen nor monster'.

Marlborough was the better for the waters of Tunbridge, she had told Sunderland at the start of the settlement trouble, 'and hee is always the better for travelling and is so strong that yesterday, after having been at the building in the morning, hee went to see one of Sir John Vanbrugh's last follys, the old mannor hous, where hee went up a vast number of steps while I was glad to take my ease in a chair at the bottom of it. It is impossible for me to bee at this place', she adds, 'without being very melancholly, which has already cost £315,000* without one room in a condition to put a bed in; but the vast bridge in the air, without so much as a possibility to have watter, and the prodigious cavitys, as the workmen call them, which all the hills in the park cannot fill up,† is such a picture of maddnesse & folly as no person can discribe; & I am confydent that if Sr John had been continued in these works hee would have confounded as much mony as any tyrant ever wrackd from his subjects, without a possibility of finishing of it, as hee proposed, even at the expense of £70,000; for all the mony upon earth can't make watter stand in the summer in this sort of ground but in durty little spitts which would poyson the air'.[27]

It is unworthy of her, this defeatist pose; yet what visitor would guess, looking today from the triumphal arch she erected, across the serene lake to the bridge, that it was in spite of rather than because of her that the scene etched for Marlborough by his architect was allowed to become something more substantial and more lasting than a dream? Marlborough was never to see it as we see it, but he was big enough to imagine it and to make it possible.

People said that at Tunbridge he had not known them. At Blenheim he rode a little, talked a little, but the unconquerable Freeman Queen Anne had known had already, as it were, withdrawn into another world. In Kneller's portrait that still hangs at Blenheim he saw the armoured figure he dimly remembered he once was. He studied it sadly and was heard to murmur, 'This was once a man'. They told him the Earl of Oxford and Mortimer was about to stand

---

* This figure shows an unexplained increase of £55,000 on her last estimate, since when little had been done.

† The hill upon which Woodstock Manor had stood was levelled and the earth used for the causeway joining the bridge to the sides of the valley. Medieval masonry from the manor house was used for rubble filling inside the bridge.

his trial. They meant Harley, Robin the Trickster, the arrant tricking knave who had tricked him into exile. For more than two years he had been in the Tower and now, with Marlborough's help, might be sent to Hell. But what was the use of one invalid's tripping another? In agony from the gravel Harley made his last public speech:

> For my own part, as I always acted by the immediate direc-
> tions and commands of the late Queen and never offended
> against any known law, I am justified in my own conscience and
> unconcerned for the life of an insignificant old man; but I
> cannot without the highest ingratitude be unconcerned for the
> best of queens: a queen who heaped on me honours and prefer-
> ments, though I never asked for them, and therefore I think
> myself under an obligation to vindicate her memory and the
> measures she pursued, to my dying breath . . . I shall lay down
> my life with pleasure in a cause favoured by my late dear royal
> mistress.[28]

It was a speech that 'fetched tears either of rage or compassion from the greatest of his enemies; the Duke of Marlborough himself saying that he could not but envy him that under such circumstances he could talk with so much resolution'.[29] But Harley was not to be executed. A fortuitous muddle in procedure led to his release, and he outlived Marlborough by two years. 'Lady Marlborough', Swift was told by Erasmus Lewis, 'is almost distracted that she could not obtain her revenge'.[30]

CHAPTER XI

The Crooked Scythe

1718-1722

Sarah Duchess of Marlborough was of those who are sufficiently literal-minded to believe that genius amounts to no more than an infinite capacity for taking pains. Everything, she was convinced, from a lintel to a lawsuit could and must be rationalised and reduced to plain terms of sensible men and money; and this she would demonstrate to the world in law, in medicine and in architecture. The only mystery in architecture was what architects chose to invent. Now that she was rid of Wren, Vanbrugh and Hawksmoor (though the last would be recalled later),* she could, for the finishing of Blenheim, turn to her oracle James Moore; while a couple of gardeners—Charles Bridgman and John Hughes—could attend to the gardens.

Luckily for Blenheim, two of the master masons had left worthy successors—William Townsend and Bartholomew Peisley junior—and these, directed in the middle twenties by Hawksmoor, would make of the Long Library the noble apartment it is. Moore was a first-rate London cabinetmaker (his pierglasses and consoles still grace the Bow Window Room), who might have done better to stick to his trade. As clerk of the works John Desborough made a

---

* On April 17, 1722 Hawksmoor wrote to the Duchess: 'Your Grace, I am inform'd, is finishing the Bridge and other affairs ... The Gallery will be a room of distinguished Beauty if rightly managed and on the other hand it may suffer much if it is not finished with Skill'. (BM add. ms 9123, f 158). Evidently, when her amateurs reached the Gallery (Long Library) the Duchess found it essential for a professional to be recalled.

poor substitute for Henry Joynes. Except, then, for two good masons and a gardener (Bridgman was excellent), the works, like Anne's ministry in the Great Change, had become second-rate, and full of conundrums.

Among the discreeter withdrawals of front rank craftsmen had been that of Henry Wise, the 'royal' gardener. Like Wren, he was next to impossible to fall out with; so the Duchess wrote to him and he replied:

> I received your Graces letter last night and should have been very glad to have given your Grace the Draught or Lines of the Court and Causeway which your Grace requires, but those works being Sr John Vanbrugh's and Mr Hawksmoor's design, I never had any perfect Draught of them; and expecting for some time to have received your Graces Commands to wait on you at Blenheim I have forbore coming there, so that I have not been there since the Late Works began and therefore cannot say exactly what part is Sunk or Raised, Sr John himself having given the directions; but as to what your Grace fears of not having a free passage from and through the East and West Courts to the Great Court, I never understood but that Sr John always intended it should be so, and is I believe the present design.[1]

She supposed he meant to be helpful, but she was no clearer than she had been before. She had put a stop to the arcades intended for the bridge, demolished Woodstock Manor and called in an engineer, Armstrong,* to see to the canals and cascades beneath it. They must all work it out between themselves. For her part, in the intervals of stitching bed-curtains, she would come out to superintend. She could do no more. In the meantime of course the lampoonists had been busy and Sarah found this written on the back of a Thornhill sketch:

> "See, sir, here's the grand approach,
> This way is for his Grace's coach;

* Probably Colonel John Armstrong, who served with Marlborough and is painted with him in the double portrait which hangs in the third stateroom at Blenheim.

There lies the bridge and here's the clock,
Observe the lion and the cock,
The spacious court, the colonnade,
And mark how wide the hall is made!
The chimneys are so well design'd
They never smoke in any wind.
This gallery's contrived for walking,
The window's to retire and talk in;
The council chamber for debate,
And all the rest are rooms of state."

"Thanks, sir," cried I, "tis very fine,
But where d'ye sleep, or where d'ye dine?
I find by all you have been telling
That 'tis a house, but not a dwelling." [2]

It was not the kind of wit that Sarah appreciated; nor did she smile
at jests about the bridge—

The minnows, as through this vast arch they pass,
Cry, "How like whales we look, thanks to your Grace!" [3]

'The best thing I have heard since I came to this place', she told
Craggs, 'is that the bridge in the air is decaying and I hope it will fall,
for one may goe under it but never upon it, no more than one can
goe into the moon'. She went on to tell him that Sir James Thornhill* was still offering to paint frescoes in the Saloon, although she
had crossed swords with him over his charges for the Hall ceiling.
'I told Mr Thornhill', she added, 'that I was very sure that there never
was a piece of painting of the size of that in the Hall even of Rubins
or the greatest master that cost so much as this had don at the time
that they were painted, tho they were of more value when they were
dead. This hee would by no means agree to, and if I should have told
him what I believe that there is no great value in his painting which
is seen at such a distance from the eye as 78† feet hee would have
thought me very ignorant and therefore I keept that to my self &

* Sir James Thornhill (1675–1734). His charge for the Hall ceiling at Blenheim
was £987. For painting the ceiling of the Banqueting House, Whitehall, Rubens
was paid the agreed sum of £3000.
† The actual height is 67 feet.

wee parted very civilly & I am to give him the Duke of Marlborough's resolutions in this affair in the winter. I am in some doubt
as to his great skill in painting, but I never saw any great man more
imposing then hee is in all that concerns his trade'.[4]

In the midst of all this the Duchess was suddenly summoned to
another Vanbrugh house, Claremont near Esher, where her granddaughter Harriet Newcastle was said to be critically ill. Arriving
before ten in the morning Sarah found Permis 'weeping very much
and really in so much sorrow that I believed there was no hopes of
her life, which made me', she owns, 'forget all my ill usage and I sat
down and wept with him'. The young Duchess of Newcastle, said
to be suffering from a malignant fever and attended by three doctors,
had in fact, according to her grandmother, nothing worse than 'a
sore throat taken in coming over the water at four a clock in the
morning from Hampton Court'.[5] Sarah was not allowed to see her
and was not even properly thanked. Driving back in her chaise she
felt rejected and desolate. What had been the use of rushing to the
rescue? Why expose oneself to indifference and ingratitude? She
retreated within herself and found little comfort. Long ago Maynwaring had written:

> One that enjoys so much health & that has nothing to ask of
> Fortune cannot fail of being tolerably happy any where with
> the blessing of so good a mind, and yours does really resemble
> the pleasant place you are in [Woodstock], where there are
> nothing but agreeable objects and plain natural Beauties, so that
> wherever you look into yourself you must allways be pleas'd &
> satisfy'd. This is the true reason why you can better bear to be
> alone than any one that I ever yet knew.[6]

If only it were so! And now, alone, as she had planned the
pilgrimage, so she must begin to make inventories and every kind
of provision for the move to Blenheim. Hitherto they had put up at
High Lodge, but now at last they were to take possession of the
house itself. She listed the plate, heading it: *To go to Woodstock 17
May, 1719.* But even that was anything but straightforward. The big
things—the cistern (1944 ounces), the lesser cistern (467 ounces), the
ice-pails, the large gold ewers, the fountain (420 ounces)—all these
were on the Blenheim scale and could be dumped there; but how

many dishes ought one to take, how many candlesticks, how many silver chamberpots? Though she meant to fill the attic storey with her friends it would be silly to overstock Blenheim and denude Marlborough House. She made a few quick notes: 'When I received the plate that belonged to the commander-in-chief from Mr Cadogan's servants, it was found that there was but 44 dishes, which by the indentures ought to have been 48 dishes . . . Candlesticks to be brought up to see . . . One chamber pot the French fashion & another of the same sort reckon'd in the Groom of the Stole's plate . . . A Tea Kettle & lamp bought at Lord Cadogan's auction'.

And that of course was only the beginning. The pictures and tapestries alone called for several secretaries to list them and a corps of carpenters to hang them: Madonnas by Raphael, Rubens, Van Dyck; Queen Anne's full-length portrait for the dining-room; the vast Van Dyck of Charles I on horseback, for the northern end of the Gallery; and two more women by Rubens, 'one taken in Adultry, the other in a Ruff'. Of the countless pieces of furniture she knew every stick and stitch, from the blue Indian-damask bed 'imbroider'd' for her own bedchamber to the 'Bedstead for a servant of Walnut-tree that looks like a Cabinet'. There were 'an Omber Table, 3 corner'd' and several black lacquer tables made by James Moore, who had his own room and closet with yellow serge hangings; and everywhere, even in the postilion heights, the beds* must be stuffed with 'good & sweet feathers, even for the servants'. For herself she kept an 'extream fine quilt stitched in all manner of colours, all work'd by Mrs Jennings's own Hands'.[7]

For Lady Anne Spencer's apartment Sarah had chosen hangings of 'sprigg'd Indian Callicoe with a border of strip'd green, red & white; the window curtains of white Birds Eye Dimetty'. She hoped she would like them, but in any case that would be of small consequence since she would soon be marrying Mr Bateman. It was vexing that, unlike her own children, Sarah's granddaughters, with one or possibly two exceptions, were unattractive if not downright plain.

* In the course of a lawsuit against Joynes in 1738 the Duchess refers to 'the great allowance he charged for the rent of his own house in Woodstock, tho there was a great room for keeping papers in the house [Blenheim] and 300 Beds at least'.

It had cost her £20,000 to marry Harriet; and now Anne, with her big nose and no-nonsense manner, looked like being just as awkward and costly. This Bateman the child had taken to (she had cried mightily when he was ill—a good sign) was not as rich as Sarah had been led to suppose. In fact he was worth only £200,000 or £9000 a year. 'I find his fortune is not so great as the town reported', she wrote to a go-between, but 'though there must bee mony to make a family easy, I shall allways prefer sence & vertue before the greatest estate or tittles'. As for her granddaughter, 'I have had so much experience', she added, 'of Lady Anne that I am perswaded that she has all the qualities of her dear mother'.[8] It was an opinion that was not to last.

However, the match was made and, with the wedding imminent, the family, in the summer of 1719, moved into Blenheim and did their utmost to enliven what Sarah had begun to call that wild, unmerciful house. By the autumn the grandchildren and their friends had mastered Dryden's *All For Love* sufficiently to perform it before Marlborough in Sarah's Bow Window Room. Lady Anne Spencer took the part of Octavia, her sister Di and cousin Anne Egerton playing Antony's children. Mark Antony, wearing Marlborough's sword, was Sarah's page, Humphrey Fish. Cleopatra was Lady Charlotte McCarthy. Sarah herself censored the love scenes and made it clear that there were to be no embraces. Bishop Hoadly* wrote a prologue. The players were much bejewelled and draped with the Genoese velvets and damasks not yet cut for curtains and covers. Marlborough was so delighted, there had to be three performances.

'I am mighty glad to hear the Duke of Marlborough has been so well all this summer at Blenheim', wrote Sunderland, now head of the Treasury, from Hanover, 'and that he has had so much satisfaction in seeing it made habitable. I pray God he may live long to enjoy it . . . I am glad the dear children are all well. I hope they will ever deserve your goodness & kindness . . . I wish I had had the happiness of being with you at Blenheim to have seen the play acted & to have heard that prologue spoke . . . I love you and your family beyond

---

* Benjamin Hoadly (1676–1761), successively Bishop of Bangor, Hereford, Salisbury and Winchester. An extreme latitudinarian. Never visited Bangor and probably not Hereford. (*D.N.B.*)

everything in this world. If you saw my heart you would believe me'.[9]

It was the kind of 'profession' Sarah had seen much of and in her long experience it meant nothing at all; 'having', as she said, 'had millions of professions under the hands of people I had obliged and some in very great places about court, all which I would sell for sixpence a piece'. In this case her cynicism was to be abundantly justified the following year.

1720 was the year of the South Sea Bubble, wildest of all speculations yet one from which, before it burst, Sarah with what Sir Winston calls her almost repellent common sense creamed something to the tune of £100,000. She was right of course in prophesying disaster,* and when it came, Sunderland, Craggs, Vanbrugh, Chandos and thousands more including the royal mistresses were more or less alarmingly involved.

Sarah was not sympathetic. On the contrary, she cried for vengeance, 'being', as she put it, 'always mighty averse to that scheme and wishing to have the directors punished'.[10] But while men are in power, as Dr Hare ventured to remind her, nothing is got by provoking them. On this occasion, as he happened to know, Sunderland had been driven to fury by 'continued provocations which he could no longer bear'; while 'as for Lord Cadogan, what your Grace says is very natural & pretty, but with submission I would not tell everybody I was robbed on the highway & describe the man if I thought that it would expose me to be robb'd again & perhaps murder'd by him'.[10]

No one gave more sensible advice, but it came too late. Sunderland and Cadogan had put their bludgeoned heads together and decided that their best defence was an attack on the Marlboroughs as Jacobites, the most farfetched charge that could be thought of, but at least it would be certain to enrage the Duchess. When the rumour first reached her she laughed at it. 'It appear'd so extreamly ridiculous', she wrote later, 'that I could not believe it, notwithstanding that at that time I had no opinion of my lord Sunderland's sincerity'. But the charge was more serious than she had supposed.

* When James Craggs senior suggested Marlborough should buy South Sea stock the Duchess told him, 'I had persuaded him to sell out of the South Sea and I would do all that I could to oppose his buying again'. (Blen. G-1-16. undated).

Looking back on the crisis the Duchess remembered 'the great struggle concerning the South Sea affairs and the punishing the Directors, upon which subject I used to talk very freely, thinking there was no way of recovering the credit of the nation but for the parliament to do as much justice as they could. My lord Sunderland hearing of this was in a great passion against me and in a very mad fit (for I don't know what else to call it) sent to the Duke of Marl-borough to come to his house where, after he had made great professions to him, he fell upon me most bitterly, quite left out the Duke of Marl: in this plot, and told him that I carried on a treason-able correspondence abroad and that I had remitted a great sum of mony when the last fright of a Scotch invasion was I think from the Spaniards, and at that part of the discourse he held up his hand in a great fury and added that the King could prove it.

'When the Duke of Marlborough came home to me he gave me this whole account.* 'tis easy to believe that in his distemper any-thing of trouble has a great effect upon him. He was half dead when he came into the room, but before I knew what was the occasion of it I revived him with a great glass of strong wine and toast, upon which he had spirits to make this relation, but he was so ill when he went to bed that I sat up with him two or three hours and recovered him by a double dose of Sr Walter Rawleigh's cordial.†

'There is something so foolish & so barbarous in this proceeding that I know of no words that can express it . . . Knowing that there was no possibility of the King's knowing the truth but from myself, I went to the Duchess of Kendal‡ & desired she would do me the favour to obtain for me a very short audience of His Majesty, not letting her know what my business was'.

When the audience had been granted, Sarah took with her a letter

---

* When Marlborough returned from Lord Sunderland's Sarah was, according to Lady Blayney, playing ombre with the Duke of Buckingham and Lady Burlington. Next day Sarah asked Lady Blayney's mother to accompany her to the royal drawing-room and to observe the King's face closely, since she herself was shortsighted. (Blen E. 49).

† Sarah's favourite remedy for everything and especially for smallpox. Its 31 ingredients included ambergris, to be ground by a strong man. The prescription is at Blenheim (Blen G-I-17).

‡ Née Schulenberg. George I's favourite mistress at this time.

and gave it to the King, who was gracious and 'looked very good-natured . . . And as I was going away', her account continues, 'the Duchess open'd the door and in a mighty obliging manner took me by the hand and desired me to go in to the King, which I excused saying that by no means I would not trouble His Majesty anymore at that time. This I think was the simplest [stupidest] thing that I ever did in my life or that any body could do, for had I gone in then I dare say the King would have told me that he had never heard of any accusation against me, but I was delighted to think that I had done my business effectually in giving my letter into his own hand, not reflecting that my lord Sunderland & others could make him in a minute do what they pleased, & it being an awkward thing to me to talk by an interpreter to two persons that I had never had any conversation with, I indulged my self in the ease of going away. How wrong that was, the King's letter will show . . . after he was advised what he should answer. By what I have heard of this matter', she concludes, 'I believe they did not even then tell him that I was in this terrible plot, but that I was a madwoman & that I did him a great deal of mischief'.[11]

George I's note, in answer to hers, was brief:

17 December, 1720

Whatever I may have been told upon your account, I think I have shown on all occasions the value I have for the services of the Duke your husband; and I am always disposed to judge of him and you by the behaviour of each of you in regard to my service. Upon which I pray God, my Lady Marlborough, to preserve you in all happiness.[12]

It was far from satisfactory. 'I think His Majesty seems to be satisfied with the Duke of Marlborough's and my past services', Sarah comments, 'and to desire the continuance of them; but the middle part of the letter is very haughty & what I know to be my Lord Sunderland's style, and therefore I thought it best not to write any more to the King'.

She might do better, she thought, to write to the mistress and so she did, at the same time apologising to anyone who might after-wards read it for its sycophantic tone: expressions which went much against her inclination, 'but those', she explains, 'are things of form, and they say one must thank kings even when they injure one, and tell them that one is mortified to the last degree upon things that are so preposterous that they can only make one laugh . . . You will observe', she points out, 'that I don't name my Lord Sunderland in either of my letters, but I thought it not amiss to name Secretary Craggs, having heard that the King was of a humour not to believe anything to the prejudice of another if it came from their enemy, and I knew Craggs was in all my Lord Sunderland's councils and was wicked enough to do anything'.[13]

As she had implored Queen Anne so now she begged her successor for a chance to vindicate herself and as before she was to be denied. To the King she described herself as 'the most unhappy of all your Majesty's faithful subjects', and to the Duchess of Kendal she offered to defy the whole world; throwing in for good measure the information that she had not allowed Craggs [junior] to speak to her for nine years. To her dismay she found that neither King nor Duchess would show a glimmer of interest. She was left with silence, which in itself might have taught her not to lay herself open to dusty answers.

She found little satisfaction in Blenheim, 'so vast a place that it tires one allmost to death to look after it and to keep it in order'; and the very year they moved in, the Barons of the Exchequer gave their verdict in favour of the workmen: the debt was the Duke's and not the crown's. For this verdict the Duchess blamed Vanbrugh and his friend 'Old Craggs', once her only true friend with understanding but now as ill a man as ever she knew. She appealed of course, but before the appeal had been heard and lost, both Craggs, father and son, had died. The handsome son, praised by Pope, was thirty-four when he died of smallpox in February, 1721. A month later his father, who had been so faithful to the Marlboroughs in their exile, died from an overdose of laudanum.

The Duchess wrote to the Earl of Carlisle:

> The counsel on Sr John's side laid great weight upon my Lord Treasurer Godolphin's warrant to Sir John Vanbrugh, and the Judges ran into that very willingly, for to my certain knowledge two of them were gained by old Craggs' interest & artifices. I thank God he is now no more able to do any mischief, and the Parliament seem to be dissatisfied with his

illgotten estate & have a mind to recover what they can of it for the use of the unfortunate South Sea people. I know it was very difficult to get the better of Mr C when he was living, but perhaps his ghost may not have so much influence upon the members of Parliament.[14]

At the appeal, as at the first hearing, everything turned upon the warrant Vanbrugh had been granted by Godolphin at the beginning of the works. The Marlboroughs denied all knowledge of it, but Vanbrugh, in a long document referred to by the Duchess as his libel, wrote:

Will any one believe that in so many quiet, fireside, evening Conferences as happen'd between those two great Lords and her Grace, the manner and method of receiving in & laying out those Hundreds of Thousands of Pounds should never be part of the Amusement? Sure there's some great forgetfullness in this matter.[15]

At the cost of much chaff from fellow-members of the Kit-Cat Vanbrugh had, at fifty-five, married Henrietta Yarburgh, a great-niece of Margaret Blagge and second cousin to Harriet Newcastle. 'I find all his works are large', writes Lady Lechmere,* of Vanbrugh, to Sarah, 'for I hear his Child is ye biggest that ever was seen of its age. I think you may ye easier forgive him his vast designs at Bleinheim since it appears to be so much ye tendency of his Nature'.[16] And in the following month she returned to the same theme:

I hear you are about finishing ye Bridge. I hope it pleases as well as employs you, for I believe you don't proceed in ye manner Sr John did, but calculate an end of your labours, which is an agreeable thought in ye progress of them. For by what I have heard you say, some parts of Bleinheim were so vast in ye designs that tho' they were form'd by a man, they ought to have

---

* Daughter of the Earl of Carlisle. Married (i) Lord Lechmere, whom Sarah called 'the worst man that ever I knew in my life'; (ii) Sir Thomas Robinson, who completed Vanbrugh's Castle Howard asymmetrically so that the west wing is out of keeping with the rest. 'It is impossible to hear and see him', wrote Sarah of Sir Thomas, 'without thinking she must have been mad'. She [Lady Lechmere] gambled, borrowed from Sarah, and died in 1739.

been executed by ye Gods, if one could hope to have seen them finished; and since Jupiter has forgot to come down among us, as one has heard he has sometimes done, Sr John is not quite so proper a builder for this Age as he might have been when ye Gods were in better humour & made nothing of a jant from Heaven to Erth, as I have been told.[17]

Any disparagement of Sir John was welcome, Sarah's own attitude towards Blenheim now hovering between the cynical and the sardonic. That a man should have to pay for a building to compliment himself was the most bizarre thing she had ever heard of; although, as she added, she could never 'enter into ye flattery of having the publick finish it. I was always contented', she told her counsel, Pengelley, 'that that misfortune should fall upon ye Duke of Marlborough as a punishment for having consented that Sr John should have ye management of it'. She reminded him of all she had gone through with Vanbrugh; and even now she was faced with the labours of Hercules to finish a building in which she never had nor ever could have any pleasure.[18]

This her friends found hard to understand. 'Tho' I know Dear Lady Dutchess is not fond of being at Blenheim', wrote Mrs Clayton, 'yet I must own I cannot help admiring of it extremely & wondering you don't like it more; but maybe that may be from my never having had any of those uneasinesses that I believe always attend great Grandure'.[19] The woman was a fool and Sarah had her to thank too for having introduced their 'sacred domestick', the obsequious chaplain Dean Jones, at this moment at whist with Marlborough, who found him witty. Laguerre had caricatured the fellow on a wall of the Saloon . . . The Duchess was watching him. But Marlborough was failing. It was worth much to be able to keep him entertained.

'I hope My Dear Grandfather finds Blenheim air agree with Him as well as this does with me', Henrietta's son Willigo, now twenty, wrote to Sarah from Amsterdam, where he was enjoying the pictures and the canals with Sunderland's heir, Lord Spencer, 'extremely kind and good-natured, which you know he has by inheritance from his mother'. Their governor or tutor, Mann, had, it seemed, to be apologised for. 'There is not an honester man breathes upon the earth', Willigo assured his grandmother, 'and I am sure what faults there were in his behaviour were owing purely & unavoidably to a Scholar's education which hindered him from knowing enough the rules of politeness & behaviour'. Mann never missed an opportunity 'to speak with all the most passionate tenderness & fondness imaginable for the memory of one Dear Person that he formerly belong'd to, Whom You will guess but too well without naming him'.*[20] Yes indeed, the loss of a son is a wound that can never heal. And now Willigo's companion, Robert Spencer, was hurriedly sent for; his father, Lord Sunderland, had suddenly died.

Sarah acted promptly but, it seemed, not promptly enough. Sunderland's study was sealed and everything locked until the heir should return; but to her consternation court officials marched in, broke seals, demanded keys and, in the King's name, helped themselves to whatever they pleased. If she had at the time any inkling of what was behind it, she kept it to herself. She suspected them, she says, of conniving in the South Sea swindle in which Sunderland had been involved, and was even prepared to believe that they stole cash; but she says nothing of Atterbury,† whose Jacobite plot was in fact the chief cause of the excitement. Sunderland died on April 19th and it was not till May 8th that the plot became public and arrests were made. 'There can be little doubt', says Professor Plumb, 'that Sunderland had been in close negotiation with Atterbury before his death'.[21]

The Duchess had her own notions. To explain why Robert Spencer had inherited at his father's death nothing but debts she says this was by no means Sunderland's intention, but 'upon a terrible struggle there was at the South Sea time in the House of Lords, the Court & he [Sunderland] were very much frighted & to prevent sad things being discovered he parted with his own mony to bribe the Parliament that it might be done with more secrecy & quicker than

* Nicholas Mann had been tutor to the Marlboroughs' son Jack, 1st Marquis of Blandford, who died in 1703.

† Francis Atterbury, Bishop of Rochester (1662–1732) and Dean of Westminster. Succeeded Aldrich as Dean of Christ Church. Friend of Pope, Swift and Addison who called him one of the greatest geniuses of his day. Convicted of treason and banished, he left England in 1723 and died abroad.

Lady Henrietta Churchill
(afterwards second Duchess of Marlborough). Kneller

Francis second Earl of Godolphin. Kneller

from the Treasury from whence he was paid again, but he died before that was done'.[22]

Whatever the truth of it, this was a tragic time at Althorp. Sunderland had loved his son and yet now, Robert at his homecoming must set to and reckon his father's debts. The list in his handwriting is at Blenheim: 'Debts for building the Library, and booksellers—£3000 . . . South Sea Bonds—£20,000 . . .' and so on. He made the total £101,000. For himself, as his grandmother put it, he could not have a silver spoon without paying for it; and the Sunderland Library, which he could not bear to sell,* was packed off to Blenheim to compensate Marlborough for what Sunderland had owed him.

But Marlborough himself was now on his deathbed at Windsor Lodge. Garth was dead and so other doctors attended while Sarah, in Sir Winston's unforgettable phrase, prowled around his couch like a she-bear guarding its slowly dying mate, and tearing all, friend or foe, who approached.[23] And what could be more fitting, what more redolent of predestination, than that a great man's great descendant should, though centuries later, write of his life and of his death? Shadows fall upon shadows, so that even as one reads Sir Winston's words, thoughts inevitably dwell upon his own going, however timewasting and futile such thoughts may be:

The span of mortals is short, the end universal; and the tinge of melancholy which accompanies decline and retirement is in itself an anodyne. It is foolish to waste lamentations upon the closing phase of human life. Noble spirits yield themselves willingly to the successively falling shades which carry them to a better world or to oblivion.[24]

Writing of Marlborough's death, in her Green Book,† Sarah says she thought her soul was tearing from her body. She had never

---

* 'I hope his father's estate will come out . . . considerable enough to prevent his books from being sold, for if they are worth what is said, near £30,000, I must own I think that too much to part with for a curiosity when his own estate is small & so many younger children that I am desirous to make easy'. (Sarah to Mrs. Clayton, 1722. Blen G-1-16).

† The Duchess of Marlborough's account of the shortcomings of her children and grandchildren. It was originally bound in green vellum. (Blen G-1-9).

needed comfort more, and yet those who might have given it—her daughters Henrietta and Mary—though present, were estranged from her and 'like enemies that would report to others whatever I did in a wrong way . . . I desired Mrs Kingdon to go to them', Sarah continues, 'and tell them that I did not know what disorder it might give their father to go to him now . . . but I begged of them that they would not stay long in the room because I could not come in while they were there, being in so much affliction.* Mrs Kingdon† delivered this message & she told me that the Duchess of Montagu answered that she did not understand her, but that if she meant that they were not to see their mother, they were very well used to that.

'They stayed a great while, as I thought, and not being able to be out of the room longer from him, I went in though they were there & kneel'd down by him. They rose up when I came in & made curtseys but did not speak to me; & after some time I called for prayers. When they were over I asked the Duke of Marlborough if he heard them well & he answered yes & he had joined in them'. After which he was carried to the bed in his own room where, adds Sarah, to her great surprise, both daughters followed with young Harriet Newcastle, so that the small room, containing a duke, four duchesses, five grandchildren, surgeons, doctors, apothecaries and servants, was pretty full. Sarah dismissed the children, but neither that, nor her message by Mrs Kingdon, could make the others stir. 'Upon which', says the Duchess, 'I desired Grace‡ to go to the Duchess of Montagu & tell her that for many days I had been mightily harass'd & I must lie down, & I desired her to go into another room with the other two. She answered, "Will our being here hinder her from lying down?" Then I sent Grace to her again to ask her if she had such an affliction & was in my condition whether she would like to have me with her. She said no, but did not go out till I sent to her a third time, & then they all three went out of the

* In another version Sarah writes: 'I could have said a great deal to him had not such cruel people been by'. (Blen G-1-17).

† Mrs Kingdon, the Duchess of Marlborough's companion. She afterwards lived with Sarah's granddaughter Diana Duchess of Bedfod.

‡ Grace Ridley, Sarah's favourite servant. She was the daughter of an Oxfordshire vicar.

room & the Duchess of Newcastle went quite away but the others stayed in the drawingroom & hall till four in the morning'.[25]

For some hours Marlborough lay in a coma and died with the dawn of June 16th, in his seventy-third year. For his duchess there was to be no comfort, as she said there had been for Queen Anne, in the funeral arrangements; and her distress was increased by rumours from London, where the town talk was that she had illtreated her daughters at Windsor Lodge, while their father was dying; and that Dean Jones had written to Walpole to ask if the King would pay for Marlborough's funeral. The daughters she would deal with later. Jones she would dismiss; and the funeral of course she would pay for herself.

Dean Jones she was glad to be rid of, she had never liked him. Even Mrs Clayton who had recommended him now owned he had abundance of intolerable great faults; and Lady Lechmere was delighted that he had given himself away. 'I allways believed his being poor & sometimes making the Duke of Marlborough laugh (for he would now & then say a comical thing) was ye reason you bore with him, but I must repeat it again that I am heartily glad accident has shown you what he is, that your compassion to him may cease, & if there are any other people in ye world that are false to you I am earnest & zealous in my wishes that they may be discovered . . . & if we were to stand up for ye honour of our nation in looking for true Englishmen, we must find them in ye silent Tombs. This is a mellancholly prospect for posterity'.[26]

It would have been a melancholy prospect for Dean Jones had it not been for the curious practice in the Marlborough family of taking in each other's dismissed servants. By this system Henrietta had only to have a dishonest footman jailed for her mother to fly to the prison and bail him out; and by the same token, although the household of the new young Duchess of Marlborough (as Henrietta Godolphin now was) was too unorthodox even for Dean Jones to find sanctuary there, she sent him £100, which maddened the dowager and sent the dean into transports. Her noble bounty, as he called it, had reached him by the hand of 'Sr John Van Brugg' and had wellnigh stunned him. As for the note that had accompanied it, 'I find myself', he assured her, 'altogether unable in the least to express ye very transporting sense I have of it; in my whole life I never read anything so transcendently Benigne and Good, for every line breathes the most condescending sweetnesse, ye most emphaticall Goodnesse . . . And I shall constantly & earnestly beseech The Infinite Goodnesse', he concluded, 'which only could Inspire so Divine a likenesse in your Grace's breast, to give & continue to Your Grace all the Blessings of this Life, that you may long enjoy the most comfortable Reflection of your owne Good Actions here & the certaine Reward of them in a Blissfull Eternity'.[27]

In the opinion of the new Duchess's mother, to whom the letter was mistakenly delivered, this amounted to 'something like blasphemy in comparing her to God'. Luckily she did not see the Dean's other letter to her page, Humphrey Fish, asking for the return of a book she had borrowed—Pliny's *Panegyric of Trajan*. The note ended: 'I pray God to give her a Better Temper'.[28]

The lying-in-state was to be at Marlborough House and the temporary burial in Westminster Abbey, since the chapel at Blenheim, Marlborough's ultimate destination, was far from finished. 'Here is a pompous funeral preparing', wrote Vanbrugh to Lord Carlisle, 'but curb'd & crippl'd by her Grace, who will govern it by her fancys . . . I don't know whether it won't cost her Ten Thousand pounds. What a Noble monument wou'd that have made, whereas this Idle Show will be gone in half an hour & forgot in two days. The other wou'd have been a Show & a Noble one to many future Ages. I shew'd the Young Dutchess what your Lordship writ about so great a Fortune falling into such generous hands; which she took mighty well. She says Covetousness has happen'd to appear to her so very odious in some other people that she is sometimes frightened lest she shou'd have seeds in her blood that may spring up one time or other . . . This Will was made but in March last & hurts nobody but her. I don't find however that either she or my Lord Godolphin have the least disposition to dispute it, and I hope nobody else will . . . Her Grace has by this Will (for to be sure that was her doings) made my Lord Blandford independent of his Father & Mother, depriv'd her Daughter of the Jewells & cater'd bravely for herself . . . The whole amounts to a great deal above two millions . . . 'tis a great pitty, as your Lordship observes, that the Duke made no disposition to publick uses, the want of which reflects cruelly upon him . . .' And to his old friend Tonson of the Kit-Cat Vanbrugh wrote: 'He has given his Widdow (may a Scotch Ensign get her) £10,000 a Year to Spoil Blenheim her own way, and £12,000 a Year to keep her Self clean, and go to Law'.[29]

'They say', wrote Dean Jones naughtily to a friend, 'that the Duke has left a letter seald, with the Lord Cadogan, not to bee opend till after his funerall, commissioning his Lordship to dispose of 60,000 l which hee had in the bank of Holland, towards the relief of soldiers' widows that were killed under his Grace's command; but I have some reason to look upon this as satyrical banter'.[30]

It was not etiquette for the widow to attend the funeral. Sarah sent her black coach* containing the Duke of Montagu as chief mourner, to be followed by eight other dukes and a long procession of soldiers and horses, not forgetting the 'Horse of Honour, richly caparisoned, led with a silken Rein by Captain Fish in his Military Mourning, walking on foot'.[31]

'I cannot help touching upon the Melancholy Ceremony that was perform'd yesterday', an eyewitness reported to the Duchess, 'nothing could be finer nor better executed, no disorder whatever, nor one Stop from the beginning to the End; and Everybody agreed that the Musick that Bononcini made was the finest & the most proper for the occasion that could be immagined. A more Generall concern was never seen. Even the Mobb were touch'd for the loss of the Glorious Assertor of their Liberties. Notwithstanding my Lady Scarborough died so lately, Lord Scarborough attended and march'd all the way with his Regiment . . .'[32]

Other observers sent other accounts. One had noticed that, contrasting with his glossier brethren, the Dean of Winchester was wearing an old black coat grown grey with years. Sarah, taking her cue it might be from Henrietta, sent him £100, 'at which, astonisht', she was told, 'he repeated the words "a hundred pounds?" Then vail'd his Reverend Hatt and slowly raising it up to his melting Eyes he with true Devotion ask't God's Blessing on your Bounty'.[33]

A third informant had been invaluable in checking everything and, doubtless in the privacy of a black coach, noting it down. It was thus that the bill for the funeral (£5265 if household-mourning was

* The Duchess found herself charged for 48 yards of black cloth to line and cover the mourning coach and 6 for harness, 'which', she said 'is enough to cover my Garden'. (Madresfield, p. 149).

included) came by its endorsements showing that no fewer than seven trumpeters and two chaplains charged for had simply not been there; while 'ffeathers for the horses' had been invoiced twice over.[34] Everyone said Bononcini, in the anthem, had been good, but he was expensive. For a similar engagement the Duchess of Buckingham had paid him £100 and so, Francis Godolphin advised his mother-in-law, they had better do the same, 'tho had there not been that precedent for it, perhaps half the sum would have been very thankfully accepted'.[35]

The Duchess, after sending for Bishop Hopkins' *Death Disarmed of Its Sting*, turned her attention to her recalcitrant daughters. It had been more than unkind of Providence to take her favourites, Anne Sunderland and Elizabeth Bridgwater, and leave her with two duchesses, Henrietta Marlborough and Mary Montagu, both of them self-willed and intolerant and impossible to live amicably with. Henrietta at this moment was at Bath with Congreve; but Sarah had long since desisted from warning both daughters against low company. Mary was almost as bad. From her youth she had been immodest, followed by a train of fops as she walked of an evening in St James's Park, or sitting at an assembly 'with many fine ladys in a row as if it were a market for sail', a habit that invited sniggers. Sarah herself, at basset, had overheard a beau say, 'Here will bee fine doings ere it bee long I'le warrant you', or to that purpose.[36] She was scandalised. What had she done to deserve such children? 'I chalenge all the world', she wrote sadly, 'to shew a woman that has don what I have don for all my children from their birth, & loved them so many yeares notwithstanding their terrible usage of me, all which time I loved them enough to have dyed to have saved their lives & to have made them hapy.'[37]

It was a tragic situation if, in an extreme form, a familiar one; for it was not in the big things that Sarah had failed her children but in the small ones, as their tearstained scrawls at Blenheim still show. Mary, when a child, for example, was forever mislaying her clogs. 'I can't help thinking my case very hard', she writes to her mother (and why should she have to write?) 'that you will give me over for so small a thing & which is not my fault, for if I should buy a pair every day I should never have any, for the moment I take them off they are lost. So I don't know what to say since it is not in my power to say what I would, that you should never see me without them any more; but since you won't have me ask you to go out, I am sure I shall have very little ocasion for clogs. I believe you could not be so angery with me for this but that you are angery for so many other things that if I should begin to speak of now I should never have don, so I will say no more but that since you have been so angery with me I have been so misarable that I have wish'd & pray'd for nothing so much as to dy that I might be no trouble to my dear mama & I hope much happier my self'.[38]

And later, 'I am so unfortunate that you take so many things ill of me without saying what . . . I think I always make a chursy or a bow when I see you, and that I ought not to be taken out of Bedlam if I could think it not reasonable to doe so'.[39]

And her sister Henrietta: 'I was the gladdest in the world to receive a letter from my Dear Mama, little thinking upon my word it would bee such a one as I found it, and ever since I have read it I have allmost wished myself dead . . . Dear Mama reproaches mee so much about the company I keep. I really know but of one that you yourself can dislike and hee is one that the people you think best off are very often with . . .'[40] And later, 'Anything that I can do as long as I live I shall never think too much if my dear Mama were but satisfied, which I can't but think she would easily bee if she did but remember she was once of my age her self'.[41]

It surprised only Sarah when her 'poppets' grew into wilful, eccentric, unmanageable women. 'Go tell the fool', Henrietta is reported to have said, 'that I have got him an heir'.[42] And the wilder she became, the tamer and steadier seemed her husband Francis, the worthy offspring of 'Patricio' Godolphin and the saintly Margaret Blagge.

When Sarah's friends reported to her the account London had had of the deathbed scene at Windsor she pronounced it a monstrous distortion. As the gossip ran, Henrietta and Mary, with young Harriet in tow, had been offered nothing to eat or drink, had been treated throughout abominably and all but turned out of doors before their father's death. Sarah wrote and re-wrote her account *in extenso*; she went further. With the help of grandchildren and servants she reconstructed the scene in a full-scale post mortem, though without of course Marlborough and the three duchesses;

and there was close interrogation as to the part they had all played. Thus—'Mr ffyshe was the first person they saw & that helped them out of the coach. They asked him how their father did . . . Little Di said that she ran to meet them & went with them to the diningroom where she asked if they would have any wine and bread . . . Mrs Kingdon said she sat in the window . . . about two in the morning & that I came down to fetch a cordial & begged of her that if she would do anything for me as long as she lived that she would go out & go to bed . . .'[43] and so on for many long pages.

There had of course to be a scapegoat and the Duchess decided it must be Mrs Kingdon. Either she had muddled her message to the duchesses, when Sarah begged them not to stay, or else—worse and more probable—she had softened it, for she was far too much inclined to take their part. She was even suspected of having shrugged. 'All that malice can invent', protested Mrs Kingdon, 'is only that I made some motion that they interpret their own way. I know of no such motion I made* . . . There is nothing I would not do to obtain your pardon . . . I thought I had found in your Grace every thing that was desirable in a freind & I had no aprehensions of loseing you unless by my own fault. I had for a long time treated you with all the respect & distance that was your due & it was by your own repeated commands I had laid it quite aside & lived with you as with the kindest freind . . .'[44] As for Sarah's daughters, Mrs Kingdon could not think it wrong to wish that they might yet all live in amity with each other, nor that Sarah would object to its being said that the two duchesses, particularly Henrietta, whom Mrs Kingdon loved and who had done a thousand obliging things for her, had a great many virtues and might one day see and mend their faults.

'With this way of thinking', Mrs Kingdon concluded, 'it was natural to say I wished that what faults they had could have been concealed even from you, & if that was not possible, at least from all the rest of the world, for when once things of this nature are made publick a reconcilement is almost impossible . . . nor could I believe it necessary for your vindication'.[45]

This was disloyal thinking and she must go; but it was Mrs King-

* A version in Sarah's hand reads: 'She ded not know what interpretation could bee made of a motion in her shoulders . . . I do think that a shrugg upon this occation is more malicious then any thing that can bee said'. (Blen G-I-17).

don herself who insisted on the last candid interview, when Sarah calmly told her that she had not the same pleasure in her she had once had, 'for tho I beleivd she could never do anything that she thought wrong, & was more agreeable then most people, I thought she could not bee so good a friend as I could bee'. And so, for that and other reasons, the friendship had to end. Sorrowfully Sarah told her, 'since friends were so hard to bee found I must content my self in doing what I knew my self was right without minding what people said'.[46] The woman had even found nerve enough to say that if the poor Duke of Marlborough were still living he would have been on her side! That certainly made it easier to write her off with a light heart.

Directly their last interview had ended, as in the more celebrated case of Queen Anne, of which in this there were echoes, the Duchess sat down and wrote it all out, 'having been so often represented as a very cholerick & angery person; Mrs Kingdon has the good luck to have an other charecter of being all goddnesse & sence'. Come to think of it, she had only tolerated her for her conversation, and that one could always cull from books. As for the dropping of her, it was so gentle and Mrs Kingdon 'had softened her self so much at parting that when I waited upon her to the door she desired to take leave of me with a kiss'.[47]

There was only one thing that still rankled a little with the Duchess and that was the suggestion that she had made her family quarrels public. 'It is not my fault', she protested, 'I was not the aggressor, & am the mother, & by the long patience which I have had I have shewn that nothing but what human nature neither can nor ought to bear could have made me complain of children to any body but a friend in private. There are not many people yet that know this story, but as many as do, weep and tell me that I ought not to trouble my self, having done what I could to prevent these misfortunes, and every body that is good I believe wishes that my children may see their errors and repent'.[48]

The Duchess reached for her Green Book.

CHAPTER XII

Provocations and Proposals

1722-1727

———◆———

The Duchess of Marlborough's Green Book was a book that could not easily be put down; and this applied to the writer as well as to the reader. In spite of gout—'I have no strength in my hands but my heart is as good as any body's'[1]—she wrote rapidly, yet so thickly did events crowd upon her widowhood, incident upon incident, outrage upon outrage, that she could not close the green covers without hearing and having to note yet more distressing news of her family.

The full title of the book—*An Account of the Cruell Usage of my Children*—barely did it justice, since several sons-in-law and grand-children played prominent parts. It was written, she explained, with reluctance and only for particular friends, to vindicate herself and to make them judge of her patience and sufferings; and let it be said at once that almost without exception the reactions of those carefully chosen friends were all she had hoped for. They were, so they told her, appalled; though whether in fact her family squabbles could mean more to them than the bickerings of sparrows or something to smile at, was not her concern. What she wanted was their shocked sympathy and that they readily gave.

Sarah is seldom dull. When her theme is humdrum, the detail is still likely to sparkle. When things seem at their worst she will suddenly rally and mend her mood; as when Henrietta Godolphin calls for her in her chariot and they drive to Hyde Park. 'She did not call me till it was almost dark and I remember we met the company coming out of the Ring. However I never reproached her, loving

234

her and seeing her of a careless temper, and we sang all the way'.[2]

This is poignant; and indeed it was sad that her sufferings, no matter how well earned nor how trifling to others, were real. 'Tis not to be expressed', she writes in old age, 'how much I suffered before I could overcome the tenderness I had in my heart for them; but thank God I am now at ease as to that matter, and if I have done any thing wrong I am sorry for it . . . and if there is any mother that has had more patience I wish I could see her, for I have yet met with no such person'.[3]

The Green Book, then, is something more than a venting of spleen; it is a Domesday, a book of judgment from which nothing has been omitted, from the youngest daughter's childhood—'She would often snap me up'—to the death of Marlborough, not forgetting a postscript to include 'that very great hypocrite' Dean Jones. *En route* we attend assemblies, go to the opera or stay at home while the masquerade comes to us.* We meet the sons-in-law: Francis Godolphin in tears for his wife's shortcomings; Montagu stout and loyal ('If I liked not to see his wife, he liked it better'); and Sunderland the sorrowing widower who soon married again and came out of his library to play with puss.

There is Henrietta as a child with smallpox (Sarah nursed her through it); Henrietta as a young wife living with her husband and babies at Sarah's lodgings in St James's; and Henrietta with Congreve and Gay, 'the worst company a young lady could keep'.† There is Mary Montagu offending Lady Hervey in 1711 (Sarah took Mary's part; the rift lasted for years); and Mary inviting her father to meet

---

* The masquerade when one of the mummers disguised as a monk warned Sarah that she might be harbouring her own estranged daughters in disguise. Although he denied it, Sarah was convinced that the monk was Craggs junior and never spoke to him again.

† 'I am setting just now before her picture when a child', Sarah writes to Mrs Clayton in 1722, of Henrietta, 'which has a gentle good natur'd look as ever I saw & it amazes me to think that such a face, with such kindnesses as I have express'd to her, could bee made by ill company such a creature as she is now. This shews that the saying does not allways hold that put nature out with a pitch forke it will come in again, for I am sure there can never bee any alteration in her for the better after so many yeares'. (9 Oct., 1722. Blen G-I-16).

her friends, including Vanbrugh (or so Sarah guessed) in 1721. There are storms and absurdities and a great many tears and hysterics of the kind known to have been cured at one stage or another by a good spanking.

In the farce over Harriet's mourning for Lady Waldegrave (Arabella's daughter by James II) we learn of Marlborough's disapproval (and of course Sarah's) of mourning for all royal bastards and their connections: 'And if the Duchess of Cleveland and the Duchess of St Albans don't mourn for such sort of relations, they have very few to mourn for'. And in the still more trivial incident of the cup of tea we get an insight into children's upbringing in the reign of Anne.

This was when Sarah, on the verge of exile in 1712, made her grandchildren raffle for diamonds and afterwards gave them tea. 'I called for some tea and milk to please the children', she remembers, 'and at the second cup they told me that Mama [Henrietta] had said they should drink but one cup, upon which I made the second half milk and said they might drink it, for I would take it upon me that it should do them no hurt . . . The next day when I was melting in tears at the thought of parting from my children & to go in a packet-boat to Flanders I received a letter from Lady Godolphin:

> Dear mama you have bid mee allways when I took any thing ille to tell you, and I can not help for severall reasons beeing concerned that after the children said I had told em not to drink two cups of tea, that you made em, for I remember wee was allways brought up to know what you said to us was law, as I think it was very fitt it should bee to all children, and that they should bee brought up to think so, and since it cant bee of any use to their health, and may make em venture, and sertinly will, to do other things that I forbid, I hope you will grant this request from your most Dutyfull Daughter.

A tactless note, one might think, to tear up or even to smile at, but humourlessness on both sides did nothing to help; nor did, many years later, Henrietta's cold note to her mother, within a month of Marlborough's death, crudely signed 'Marlborough'. Towards the end of Marlborough's life both sides had appealed to him. Sarah, in her role of kindest of mothers, knew how to make her case and to shape his answers, herself dashing off a letter to which in a shaky hand he might add one sorrowful line. 'I am sure it is my duty not to complain of her', Mary wrote to him, 'but I believe she will tell you herself some things she has done to me that were never done before by a mother kind or unkind'.[4]

After Marlborough's death there was of course even less hope of a lasting reconciliation, so that mother and daughters settled into a chronic state of mutual disgust which did no good to anyone. 'I have seen such behaviour from them to her', wrote Lady Blayney, 'that, young as I was, it shocked me ... but the Duchess used to say she had made them all such great Ladies that it turned their heads'.[5]

Other loyal friends held similar views. 'In Bed we began to read ye Account* you were pleased to send', wrote Robert Jennings. 'Ye extraordinariness of it prevented our rising till we had made an end of it ... so much ffolly & undutyfullness ... I conclude there can be no reconciliation at present, since he is removed that indeavourd it & cou'd not'.[6]

Mrs Boscawen, a Godolphin connection, was appalled, as indeed nobody that, as she put it, had either children or bowels could fail to be. 'Ye Behaviour is certainly most monstrous and, if I may have ye liberty to say it, not only despicable but detestable too in a person of Quallity with a grain of sence'.[7] Without question it was a book to set old heads wagging. 'I can't tell what reigns in this age', wrote Lady Portland, 'for respect & regard for parants seem extinguisht & people have a pleasure to do what they can to make children fly in their face'.[8]

Notes like these were to be treasured, and none more perhaps than poor Lady Bristol's, for she herself with a house full of in-laws which she called her Kennell of Vermin, knew what such suffering meant. Lady Bristol, then, having read Sarah's notes of 'monsterus behaveour', handed them to her husband and—'My lord', she tells Sarah, 'all the while he was reading them often cry'd out O Monsterus! O vile wretches!'[9] A *cri du coeur* so spontaneous and so soothing that it made it all seem worthwhile, all the writing and re-writing, and all the trouble Sarah had long since gone to in getting him his title.

* Sarah's Green Book.

It was a pity books needed to be bound within covers, there was already so much more to add, some of it perhaps even more startling than what had been recorded. This of Bridgwater,* for example. Could anything be more barbarous than the way he had snatched his daughter from under her grandmother's nose? For years Sarah had cared for the motherless child, Anne Egerton, as her own daughter and would have married her to Chandos† if her rich father had agreed to the settlement, but he would not. Now, soon after Marlborough's death Bridgwater, who was dissatisfied with the will and had pointedly absented himself from the funeral, married‡ Lady Rachel Russell and commanded his daughter to come to Ashridge to wish him joy. Sarah saw through his scheme at once. He wanted Anne to marry the Duke of Bedford, a match which should make the Bridgwater coffers still heavier. But she would nip it in the bud. The child should not go. After some thought she dictated what she herself called a very dutiful and good letter:

> My Grandmama hopes you will excuse her for not sending me now, I have had so great a cold & pain in my ear that my head is now wrapt up in Flanel . . .

As soon as she is well she will go to him. In the meantime, 'My lady Dutches is in a melancholly condition which makes her unwilling to part with me'.[10] It sounded reasonable enough. And so what did the Duke do? Without warning and at eleven o'clock at night he strode into the forecourt of Marlborough House, 'with a candle & lanthorn before him, a footman's coat upon him for fear of catching cold, and the air of being quite mad'. He demanded his daughter. Sarah's account continues:

> The first person that saw him was Lady Anne's woman, who made as much haste as she could to come & tell the Dutchess of Marl: that she might not be surprised. My Lord ran after her & bid her say to the Dutchess that he desir'd she would not make his child undutiful to him. The Dutchess of Marl: was appre-

* Scroop Egerton, Duke of Bridgwater, widower of the Marlboroughs' third daughter Elizabeth.
† James Brydges, 1st Duke of Chandos (1673–1744).
‡ On August 4th, 1722.

hensive that he would have come in to her, which would have been extream disagreeable, & therefore . . . sent the woman out with this answer, that she would obey him.

It is a scene from Hogarth: the alarm of a sick child, head swathed in flannel, reflected in the face of her grandmother, herself a bundle of black nightclothes and nightcap, with wobbling candle-sticks. Bridgwater left but returned next morning before anyone was up. More scurrying, more pleas for postponement; but the furious Duke 'made the servant come in to the Dutchess of Marl: who was in bed, to tell her that if Lady Anne was sick, it was she that had made her so & that he would have her away; upon which she said, For God's sake let him take her. He would not go into any room, tho' he was desired to do it, but walk'd about in the Hall like a madman with the most ill natur'd Countenance that ever was seen in any humane Creature. As soon as Lady Anne was dress'd she came down, but being half dead with grief, the servants gave her some water & drops, & after that he took her away in his coach'.[11]

In the life of every woman of robust common sense there must inevitably be times when, except for herself and a few close friends, the whole world seems to have gone mad; when, as Sarah put it, there is some tincture more or less of madness in almost everybody that one knows. The curious thing was that this latest epidemic, in the first months of her widowhood, seemed confined to the aristocracy, since it had begun with the Duke of Bridgwater before, in various forms, infecting the Duke of Chandos, the Earl of Coningsby and the Duke of Somerset.

Chandos, the same who as James Brydges had sent Sarah the diamond portrait-ring mislaid at Antwerp and had supported Marlborough in the Lords, was now the fully-fledged Timon, his villa at Cannons, near Edgware, the wonder of England. In the South Sea calamity of 1720 he had lost heavily and had borrowed from Sarah; 'after which', she remarks, 'he was so mean as to refuse to let me have a Statue of the Duke of Marls tho I offerd to pay . . . His Grace had got it by a trick'.[12]

This was not quite true. Chandos, finding in 1721 that two marble statues commissioned in 1710 of Baratta by Vanbrugh for Blenheim were still languishing at Genoa and still not completely paid for, wrote to Sarah: 'They represent Fame & Glory* . . . there being no personall resemblance in either to his Grace† . . . I'l entret your Grace will honnour Cannons so far as to come & see them & if you like Either or Both they shall be at your service on no other Terms than that you'l have ye Goodness to leave them to my Family at your decease'.[13] Sarah, who in 1716 had told Craggs, 'Tho I would give 73 pounds for a dead fly as soon as for these statues I think the Duke of Marl: is oblidged to pay for them since they are don',[14] now turned them down; only, two years later, to change her mind and send for them. In his reply Chandos sadly tells her that they are now heirlooms entailed upon his title. 'Mean and ungratefull', was Sarah's comment, 'full of compliments & prodigious professions but of no reall worth & ment nothing but his own interest'.[15] And so another old friend is shown the door and regretfully walks out of her life.

Earl Coningsby's‡ madness was of quite another kind. This seventeenth-century lord, who had moved the impeachment of Harley, had been twice married, having divorced his first wife and buried his second. Of his ten children, five daughters were living but there was no male heir. One of his sons had died from choking on a cherrystone, in 1708. In 1722, within five months of Marlborough's death, Coningsby proposed to the Duchess.

'I live in hopes', he declared, 'that the Great & Glorious Creator of ye World whoe dos & must direct all things will direct you to make mee ye happyest man upon ye face of the Earth and Enable mee to make my dearest dearest Lady Marlborough as she is ye wisest & ye Best, ye happyest of all Wemen. I am Yr Grace knows I am with ye Truest, ye Sincerest & ye most faithfull hart Yr Graces most dutifull, most obedient humble servant'. And to this he added the postscript: 'There is no such Cattle as Sheep as yr Grace desires to be had tell July next'.[16]

For his proposal Coningsby could not have chosen a worse time nor a worse approach. He and the Duchess had but one thing in

* One of these statues is now in the Fitzwilliam Museum at Cambridge. (See also Webb, op. cit., pp. 38–40).

† Marlborough.

‡ Thomas Earl Coningsby (1656–1729).

common and that was love of litigation, a hobby she had only now begun to enjoy. Otherwise there was nothing at all to tempt her to throw in her lot with the sad and irritable father of five new recruits for her Green Book. Her reply is not extant; but it would be surprising if any such offer made to the world's richest widow, as she was now said to be, was not viewed with suspicion. Their correspondence ceased.

Her second suitor was more surprising, more important, more decorous, more persistent and altogether more difficult to shake off. Even in an age when pride was a virtue and snobbery something to be proud of, Charles Seymour sixth Duke of Somerset was, says Sir Keith Feiling, one of the most arrogant oligarchs even of the eighteenth century. Nicknamed the Sovereign, the legend of his vanity is well known: how a daughter was disinherited for sitting in his presence, how servants were instructed by signs, and the roads scoured by outriders before his progresses, to protect him from the gaze of the vulgar. Yet there was another side to the man and it was surprising. He was Chancellor of the University of Cambridge and a great patron of the arts (witness Gibbons' carvings at Petworth and in the library of Trinity College, Cambridge); and he had a sense of humour.

Sarah's early dislike of him was twofold. She had found him a fool and a trimmer who, having failed to impress Marlborough had, temporarily at least, gone over to Harley, in the vain hope of power. She suspected too that Troule-it-away, his redhaired duchess, had for years had her eye on her gold key of office as Groom of the Stole and Mistress of the Robes, posts in which she did in fact succeed her; and that neither of them had done her anything but harm with Queen Anne.

If, then, Sarah's invective had lighted upon the Sovereign—'false', 'malicious', 'insolent', and 'working to doe me all the mischief hee could'—it had played like summer lightning about his duchess who was, she said, plotting and insinuating, mean of soul and the greatest liar in the world; yet—and perhaps that was her greatest shortcoming of all—Queen Anne liked her and was prepared to defend her as she had defended Mrs Freeman and, afterwards, Abigail. Sarah remembered her conduct at the trial of Sacheverell . . . such venomous rivalry, such intensity of hatred; and now death had made nonsense of it all, for Marlborough and the Duchess of Somerset had both died in the same year.*

In the following summer the outriders sped from Petworth to clear the lanes for the glorious equipage emblazoned with bull and unicorn, heading for Blenheim. And what a sight that must have been for those bold enough to gaze at it! The gleaming coach-and-six jingling between the green hedgerows, the horn calling and winding in the clear air over the unpoisoned fields; and within the coach Lord Foppington in full splendour, the periwigged beau, the ardent impatient lover, heaving huge sighs, at sixty-five, for the woman he already called his *souveraine*, now sixty-three.

Sarah was still beautiful. Though gout and gravel attacked her (Coningsby was shocked at how ill he had found her at Blenheim), her hair kept its colour and, except for plumpness, her looks were unchanged. 'If I durst show youer pictors', Frances Tyrconnel wrote from France, 'I wish I had youer one in litle by some sure hand, just as you are, which I heare is mighty well for a grandmother'.[17] We have nothing of Sarah however to compare with Kneller's portrait of Mrs Jennings; and even in the Kneller at Petworth (p. 272) we find her still wearing her gold key.

In the eyes of Somerset she was flawless. His proposal, a dignified document not at all like Coningsby's, speaks of unalterable love and affection, deep rooted and of long standing. 'I will not have a thought', he vows, 'but what shall bee to make you Happy & Easy in all things whatever. Your Grace shall command & make your Tearmes & Conditions. Give mee but your most charming Person, I neither covett nor desire more nor greater riches, for that is the onely & most valuable Treasure to mee . . . Apoynt mee an hour when I may lay my selfe at your ffeett, never to rise till my Pardon is sealed'.[18]

Sarah's answer was less harsh and histrionic than Horace Walpole and his followers supposed. She did not say, 'If I were young and handsome as I was, instead of old and faded as I am, and you could lay the empire of the world at my feet, you should never share the heart and hand that once belonged to John Duke of Marlborough.' What she wrote to him was firm but gentle:

* Marlborough died in June, the Duchess of Somerset in November, 1722.

My lord,

I am at a great loss to know how to express my self upon the subject of your Grace's letter of yesterday. There cannot possibly bee a greater mark given of your esteem then in the offers which you have been pleased to make to me and I am confydent that there is very few wemen (if any) that would not bee extreamly pleased with what your Grace proposes to me; but I am resolved never to change my condition and if I know any thing of my self I would not marry the Emperor of the world tho I were but thirty yeares old.

I hope your Grace will not dislike my truth in this declaration and that you will reward it by giveing me the honour of your friendship, which I am extreamly desirous of, and I asure you that I will never do the least thing to forfeit it as long as I live, but I will endeavour upon all occasion to deserve it as much as I can by shewing that I am with all the respect imaginable

Your Grace's most faithfull and
most humble servant[19]

Had the Sovereign been of the kind that readily takes no for an answer he might perhaps have admitted defeat, but he was of different mettle. Living up to his supporters of bull and unicorn he took it as a challenge and pursued Sarah with all the ardour of a fullblooded man passionately in love.

Surprisingly though slowly, Sarah softened. Had she not lectured Queen Anne on his disloyalty and sent her his illiterate letter? And had he not secretly visited the Sorcerer, Robin the Trickster,* in a chair with the curtains drawn? There was a great deal to pardon, and that on both sides. There were talks and explanations. She lent him her Brown Book of Queen Anne's letters, to which his response was unexceptionable. 'It is most notoriousely plain', he declared, 'that the latte Queen's treatment of your Grace was the very reverse of the expressions in most of Her letters to you, for Her expressions were generally kind & tender but her treatment was hard & very unjust to you the most faithfull of servants & best of women. Such are your perfections in Body & in mind that I am every day in a

* Robert Harley Earl of Oxford.

continuall admiration how the Queen could bee soe prevayled with to treat you in soe ungrattefull & soe Barbarouse a manner'.[20]

This was encouraging. She decided to try him with the Green Book, and again the reaction was gratifying. 'Your Grace', he assured her, 'dosse show throughout the wholle a more than ordinary tenderness for all your children, but your children in return doe seem to affect a most unnaturall & most Barbarouse part to the best of mothers & very best of women'.[21]

In everything, she was to find, she could count on him, whether savouring her broth of vipers or, in milder mood, taking a hand at ombre with her favourite granddaughter Di.* There is, again in contrast with Coningsby, some pleasing chaff about a prayer. Somerset tells Sarah, 'I never was in more need of a good prayer than now . . . My words may ffly up to Heaven but my thoughts will forever remain with you Below, and words without thoughts, Shakespeare sayes, will ne'er to Heaven goe'. And so he steals a prayer of Di's and owns to it—'that I may not lye under your Ladyship's youthfull censure that an old man is a heathen & doe want a Prayer & all other good things, when I stole yours the other night off from your Mama Dutchesses Table. I confess I did want that very Prayer, I doe admit it'. Di copies it out for him and, at his bidding, ends with 'Diana' instead of 'Amen'.†[22]

It is a playful duke, and then again, a too serious one. 'Madame', he exclaims, 'you declare to have the courage of a Roman & I doe joyn in opinion with the wholle world to declare that you have likewise the wisedome of a Minerva, & that Divine Providence did at your birth very liberally bestow all Perfections of Nature in forming your body & mind and your Grace dosse mee now the Honour to confess that I doe love & adore you with an inviolable passion. Madame, my life, my heart & my soul now are & must bee forever with you, they are noe more mine . . . Give mee your most charming Person as the reward'.[23]

Something had to be done. For a time it had amused Sarah to toy

---

* Lady Diana Spencer.

† This prayer is missing, but on another occasion Sarah copies out a prayer she likes for Mrs Clayton: Great God, give us the good things that are necessary for us and keep evil things from us, even when we ask them of thee. (Blen G-I-16 Undated).

with him in light flirtation, but Somerset was too obviously in earnest and determined enough to sweep her off her feet if not deflected. To save all faces and feelings there was but one way out and that was to find him another wife. This she did in the person of Lady Charlotte Finch, daughter of the Earl of Nottingham, with whom Somerset appears to have been delighted. They married and had two daughters.

Replying to Sarah's letter of congratulation Somerset begged for the continuance of their friendship. 'Noe change in the way of life or of ffortune', he insisted, 'shall ever change mee from beeing the same man I have many years professed to bee'. It would not have been the moment to remind him that he had not long since assured her, 'You are the woman, the very woman, the only woman I doe love, I doe value, I doe adore the most & that I doe & will forever seek for all occasions to give Prooffes & Demonstrations of it to you & to the wholle world, my most Dear Dear Dear charming Souveraine'.[24]

It says much for his charm that he succeeded in changing Sarah's mind as to his character, a revolution borne out by her frequent deletions of disparaging references to him at Althorp and at Blenheim. 'I think the historian has been a little too severe in this part', she writes after one such passage, 'for which reason I have blotted it out, the Duke of Somerset having acted a very handsome part to the Duke of Marlborough after the queen's death & likewise done me a great deal of service after the Duke of Marlborough's death'.[25]

For both of them it must have been a heartening interlude and now that minds had grown tranquil Somerset, as the builder of Petworth, could still be helpful with Blenheim. 'You have very right thoughts', he told her, 'to make Blenheim Beautifull & worthy to perpetuate the memorys of the Duke & of the Dutchesse of Marlborough'. They exchanged long letters about it, he consulting Hawksmoor and Pope, while she with James Moore, John Armstrong the engineer and the masons struggled to tame not only the wild house but the landscape. He approved of her plan to channel the Glyme into a canal and to give it three waterfalls as it passed under the middle arch of Vanbrugh's bridge and into a large oval pool on the western side (see p. 172).

Because these waterworks were not Vanbrugh's but Armstrong's under her supervision she found something approaching enthusiasm for them. 'I beleive', she told Somerset, 'it will bee very beautyfull, the Canal & Bason (which is allready don) look very fine. There is to bee a lake & a cascade on the side of the Bridge next Woodstock, which I think will bee no inconvenience & bee a great addition to the place. Sr John never thought of this cascade which will bee the finest & largest that ever was made & the watter constantly fall from it without any trouble. The fine green meadow between the hous & the wood is to remain as it is, & I beleive your Grace will think in that, nature can not bee mended, tho Sr John formerly sett his heart upon turning that into a lake as I will do it on the other side & I will have swans & all such sort of things in it. All the marble Pillasters except three are put up in the Gallary . . . Upon the whole I believe everybody will allow that there is a great deal very fine in this house, as well as many great faults which I can bee very well contented with since they were not by my derection . . . I have reduced the stables to one third of what was intended by Sir John and yet I have room for about fourty fine horses . . . but what I value myself most upon is the fourniture which I have don at home & have made very little use of upholsterers, which has made it cost less by a vast summ & is ten times more agreeable & hansome then if it had been done by them . . .'[26] *

It would have been too much to expect the Duchess and her friends to realise how far Vanbrugh the visionary was in advance of his time, with his love of ruins and of lakes; and it was an ill chance that snatched Blenheim from its creator and gave the credit for its lake to Brown, who did little more than cut through a causeway-dam in the seventeen-sixties. Sarah, as she said, laboured like a packhorse, but it was a packhorse in blinkers, at times almost totally

* 'All the hills that you see from under the great Arch of the Bridge will bee in a deep sloop of green like those at Windsor Castle. There will bee a canal of sixty foot wide which watter will run thro the great Arch of the Bridge & on each side of this watter under the Arch there will bee a fine grass walk of twenty foot broad & there will bee a room paved that comes into this Arch which will bee very pleasant by the watter to sett in in a very hot day & the sight of the woods from that place beyond the watter that will run thro that beautyfull green meadow will certainly bee very uncommon & a very pleasing prospect allways. At Rosamonds Bower I will have something like those temples which they talk of that are at my Lord Burlingtons country house'. (Sarah to Lady Cairns. Undated. Blen G-I-16).

blind; for on the one hand she thought it her duty, with the world's deepest coffers and best craftsmen to draw on, to save money, and on the other to raise to the glory of Marlborough monuments which were more personal than he would have wished.

There was Hawksmoor's triumphal arch at the Woodstock entrance, erected soon after Marlborough's death. The obvious place for it would have been on the east to west axis at what is now called the Hensington Gate, but tradition insists that a gardener whose cottage occupied that site defied the Duchess with 'Go round the other way!'[27] The Roman arch as built Sarah thought too narrow and she was told that its inscription read better in Latin than in English. However, there it was. It kept the secret of the prospect till one had passed through it and it served as pointer to the great obelisk or Column of Victory, with its all-important inscriptions, which had yet to be determined and built.

A book could be written and not a dull one on the trouble that was taken and the people that were consulted for that monument; and indeed there is at Blenheim a portfolio entitled *Explanation of the Obelisk*, though by no means all of the project has been explained. For the monument itself, whether obelisk or column, Hawksmoor drew a dozen or so sketches, some based on the Column of Trajan, others on Bernini's river-gods fountain, only to find at the eleventh hour the commission snatched from him and given to Lord Herbert and his protégé Roger Morris.*

But the problem of the panegyric was far more formidable. Three sides of the dado were for the Acts of Parliament† which had bestowed the estate upon Marlborough and ensured the succession through the female line; the fourth, facing Blenheim, being for the panegyric itself. And who should write it? Who was big enough to extol the greatest of all heroes? Somebody (Marlborough himself?) had suggested Pope ('except that his inclinations are so different from ours as to Liberty'), but that was long ago, before Vanbrugh had lost

---

* Roger Morris (1695–1749), employed by Sarah at Blenheim and at Wimbledon and by Charles 3rd Duke of Marlborough at Althorp. His most celebrated work was the Palladian Bridge at Wilton (1736–7).

† 'The Acts of Parliament inscribed on this Pillar shall stand as long as the British name and language last, illustrious monuments of Marlborough's glory and of Britain's gratitude'. (Part of the inscription on the Column of Victory at Blenheim).

favour and when the obelisk might have commemorated Woodstock Manor and the amours of Henry II. It was not in the least what Sarah now had in mind; for if, as she had written above that proposal, obelisks were to be raised to 'all our kings have don of that sort, the countrey would bee stuffed with very odd things'.[28]

But now in 1723 Somerset was asked to approach Pope and did so. 'Mr Pope is mighty well pleased with the Honour your Grace designs him', Sarah was told, 'and promises to doe his utmost to please you, thô hee sayes hee never did doe any thing of this kind before . . . Hee alsoe hasse one condition to make. Hee prays that if hee should bee so fortunatte as to please your Grace, it may not bee known hee is the auther. This last condition supports your Grace's first apprehension of him, but yet lett that bee my care, hee shall very strongly exert all your thoughts & directions'.[29]

The Duchess thought, consulted others and thought again. 'I believe', wrote Lady Lechmere, 'you could engrave some mighty sentences, but the times are dangerous & 'tis not worth going to the Tower for it, or else one might—cut deep'.[30] Sarah strongly agreed. 'If I should have a mind', she mused, 'to expose the ingratitude even of those that reaped the advantages of these successes, the whole park & gardens would not hold pillars sufficient to contain the infamy of that relation'.[31] Yet tempting as it was, it could not have been called typical of Marlborough. She resisted it.

We hear no more of Pope's attempt at the panegyric; nor was Bishop Hare's effort any more successful. As the months and the years went by in the vain quest for a worthy writer Sarah saw only too plainly, with the great column rising and no fit inscription ready for it, the makings of a desperate if not a ludicrous situation. And nothing short of desperation, surely, could have persuaded her ultimately to accept, for Marlborough's panegyric, an inscription written by one of his greatest enemies and betrayers, Henry St John Viscount Bolingbroke.

On the death of Anne and the collapse of the Tories Bolingbroke, it was said on Marlborough's prompting, fled to the Pretender, to help plan the Jacobite rising of 1715, which Marlborough helped to quell. In 1716 he was dismissed by James and it was not until 1723 that, partly by bribing the Duchess of Kendal, he was granted a pardon by George I and, in 1725, allowed to return to England. His one possible claim to Sarah's favour and that a strong one was his opposition, with William Pulteney and Sir William Wyndham (Somerset's son-in-law), to Sir Robert Walpole, and in that, though excluded from the House of Lords, Bolingbroke was influential and sincere.

Sarah's attitude was equivocal and interesting. Of Bolingbroke she had written, 'I have no notion of my lord Bullingbrooks honour, after all the mischeifs which hee did his country & the publick professions which hee made every day in a most solemn manner, which the whole earth knows since to have been all false . . . hee has forfeited all pretentions to any one single vertue'.[32] But on the other hand she had written too: 'I am grown to bee wonderfull fond of usefull knaves, which some people would push into the pond as soon as they had lent their hand to help the person out . . . but that is not my humour at all, for if I thought it fitt & necessary to make use of an ill man or to bee reconciled to my enemy in appearance I would certainly never fail him in any thing that hee could expect from me'.[33]

On July 25, 1728 Pulteney wrote to the Duchess:

I have enclosed sent your Grace the Draught of the Inscription which I received a few days ago from Lord Bolingbroke, and also those other Draughts which I formerly had from you. I have taken the liberty likewise to send you his letter to me, because as it may be of service to those who are to engrave the Inscription (who should take the utmost care to be extreamly exact in the manner of performing it), so will it also convince your Grace with how just and sincere a Regard for the memory of the Duke of Marlborough my Lord undertook it . . .

It was formed, Pulteney added, on classical models and 'not writ by an Able Hand only but done with a good Heart'.[34] Sarah, blind to the merits of heroic architecture, instantly recognised this as the heroic prose she had for years been seeking. The writer's heart was no matter. His sentences, crisp as words of command, were indeed from an able hand:

The Battle was Bloody: the Event decisive. The Woods were pierced: the Fortifications trampled down. The Enemy fled. The Town was taken . . .

Whenever she read it, she said, she wet the paper. Bolingbroke's hero-worship of Marlborough, begun in youth, had run full circle and now his long panegyric was published in full in *The Craftsman*, the paper he ran with Pulteney. If, as he had said, he really wished to remain anonymous, that was a mistake because it gave the *Gentlemans Magazine* the chance to observe that 'as no monumental Marble or Inscriptions could add to Marlborough's Glory, so no Recitals of those Inscriptions in *The Craftsman* could take away from B-l-ke's Ingratitude'.[35]

And even then, Sarah found, her difficulties with the column were not over. There was frost. There was delay. Boards with black lettering were raised to the dado so that she, half crippled with gout, might be carried to see them. The lines were too long; the marble was uneven. In 1730 she tells Townsend the mason she is very much disappointed and troubled to find that after all her pains the inscription is still not finished. 'But I am tired out', she adds, 'and I must now make an end of it as well as I can . . . It will be cruel if I should be disappointed in every thing'; and later, 'I hope you will take effectual care that there is no more Blunders made; for it will be a most terrible thing if there is, to me who have so long set my heart upon this Pillar's being well performed'.[36]

So there it is, the 'lasting monument of his glory and her affection to him'.* Hawksmoor, passing through Woodstock the following year found, as he told Lord Carlisle, no great matter added 'either of good or any more mischief don' since his last visit. 'The Historicall Pillar is set up in the park (conducted by my Lord Herbert).† It is . . . above a hundred feet high. Ye inscription is very long but very legible . . . The Lake is beautifull but ye Cascade does not play, all ye Rivers are almost dry. I forgot to tell your Lordship', he ended, 'that her Grace at Blenheim was not so Gratious as to see me, and I did not ask her only to try what she wou'd doe. I don't know whether I did right in it or not'.[37]

It was six years since Vanbrugh, with perhaps even greater curiosity, had tried to see his own masterpiece and had been turned

* From the inscription on Hawksmoor's triumphal arch at the Woodstock entrance.

† Henry Herbert, 9th Earl of Pembroke (1693–1751), succeeded to the earldom in 1733. Owner of Wilton. Known as the architect earl.

away. Arriving with Carlisle's party he had found 'an order to the Servants, under her Graces own hand, not to let me enter any where. And lest that shou'd not mortify me enough, She having some how learn'd that my Wife was of the Company, sent an Express the Night before we came there with orders, if she came with the Castle Howard Ladys, the Servants shou'd not Suffer her to see either House, Gardens or even to enter the Park, which was obey'd accordingly, and She was forc'd to Sit all day and keep me Company at the Inn'.[38]

Closely watched, Vanbrugh, the Duchess was told, 'went up by the Cock Pitt, expecting to get in at the litle gate that used to be there & when he found he could not get in he walked back again down to Old Woodstock & looked over the wall to see the watter'.[39] However, it would be surprising if a man of Vanbrugh's resource let himself be thwarted by toadying servants, even if it meant scaling the wall by moonlight, which very possibly it did.

That was in August, 1725. Two months later Vanbrugh wrote to Jacob Tonson:

> Being forc'd into Chancery by that B.B.B.B. Old B. the Dutchess of Marlb: & her getting an Injunction upon me by her Friend the late Good Chancelr. who declar'd I never was employ'd by the Duke of Marlbh: and therefore had no demand upon his Estate for my Services at Blenheim, I say since my hands were tyed up from trying by Law to recover my Arrear, I have prevail'd with Sir Rob. Walpole to help me in a Scheme I propos'd to him by which I have got my money in Spight of the Huzzys teeth, and that out of a Sum She expected to receive into her hands towards the discharge of the Blenheim Debts, and of which She resolv'd I shou'd never have a farthing. My carrying this point enrages her much, and the more because it is of considerable weight in my Small Fortune, which She has heartily endeavour'd so to destroy as to throw me into an English Bastile to finish my days as I began them in a French one.[40]

He was not to enjoy his triumph long, dying as he did of a quinsy on the 26th of March, 1726 at the age of 62. Like Wren, who had died three years earlier, he had raised his own monuments; and though the Duchess might bar him from Blenheim she could not keep out his name and fame which for all time must be linked with it. If his gay spirit dwells there, its lodging is surely the bridge, where a vast V is incised over a sealed-off window.

The Chancellor Vanbrugh referred to was Lord Macclesfield who, in the case against the Blenheim workmen (four hundred and one 'confederates') had worked himself into a righteous passion against them and had forbidden Vanbrugh ever to sue for the £1660 he was owed. Indeed, had it not been for a letter of Marlborough's which showed that he had had 'a kindness for Sir John', Vanbrugh would have been ordered to pay back even that which he had had. 'It is to be hoped,' comments Dr Coxe, 'no undue share of the immense wealth of the Duchess influenced the judgment of this impeached Lord Chancellor. It appears that he was shortly afterwards fined £30,000 for bribery and embezzlement in the discharge of his official duties'.[41] Sarah, delighted with his decree, in due course rescued him from prison.* His grateful letters to her are from the heart.[42]

In her sixties, then, we watch the machine that is the Duchess of Marlborough, well fuelled with time and money and without the brake once applied by Marlborough, running to dangerous extremes. Semi-invalid though she is, she still has courage and zest enough to challenge the world, if the world will only give her a hearing. As always she enjoys a fight. Disappointed in George I she turns to his son, only to find him and his wife Caroline ('I really love her') committed to Sir Robert Walpole, with whom she must always be at war. She talks, writes, dictates, buys land, hurls herself into elections and lawsuits and into endless family quarrels. From friends all she asks is sympathy and confidence. They must tell and keep telling her she is right and has always been right and this very nearly all of them do. The courageous exception is Marlborough's ex-chaplain Francis Hare, Bishop of Chichester. His long letters to

* 'I own I love him [Mecklesfeild, as she spells him] for the justice which hee ded in so hansome a way to the Dear Duke of Marlboroughs memory & for exposing the knaves as hee ded in the Blenheim cause, but nothing can ever make me do injustice & I think the suiters mony should bee every shilling made good to them . . . I beleive nothing wants reformation more then the courts of law.' (Sarah to Lady Cairns, 25 Feb., 1724. Blen G-1-16).

her glint with the gold of sense. And so from a welter of broken friendships, recorded at Blenheim, the heart lifts as he tells her:

> You say you can't think you are obliged upon any account not to say the truth or to deny yourself the pleasure of speaking your mind upon any occasion, which opinion is the Foundation of all I think wrong in your Grace's conduct. You seem to think nothing ought to be censured as evil speaking if it be speaking truth, but your Grace will find every writer of morality against you and with great reason, for if people were at liberty to vent in all places all the ill they thought true of others, it would destroy Society and there would be no living in the world . . .

If only she could even now be taught to hold her tongue! He cites Godolphin and Marlborough who, provoked to distraction, yet said nothing. 'Where Lord G: said ten words at table before servants or in mixt company your Grace will give me leave to believe you say 10,000. But . . . his silence was very particular and . . . perhaps would not become your Grace; it would take too much off from ye life of conversation & destroy the pleasure you give your friends by saying perpetually things which are extremely diverting & agreeable.* But your Grace will have no exception to make to the example of the Duke of Marlborough, who was always agreeable in conversation & yet always inoffensive & whatever resentments he had, suppressed them to that degree as made him universally beloved & the idol of all who had the honour to be near him. There was in his whole Behaviour an inimitable sweetness which was not only easy to himself & delightful to others, but what he abundantly found his account in . . . If your Grace would in any measure imitate either of those examples, 'tis impossible but that you should have the most friends & the greatest interest of any subject in the nation'.[43]

But of course she would do nothing of the kind. Her friends, to remain friends, must accept her as she was. Why, should the Duchess of Marlborough cease from speaking her mind of everybody to everybody she would no longer be herself, she would be unrecognis-

---

* On another occasion Dr Hare tells the Duchess: 'It is as impossible for your Grace to converse without warmth & force as it is for you to be dull or ugly, to whom God has given so fine an understanding & so much beauty'. (Blen E 38).

able. The man was a fool and a grossly impertinent one. He even had the effrontery to censure her for forbidding her daughters to enter Blenheim.* 'I am so far from defending them', he had said, 'that I am persuaded they are extremely to blame, but yet I must own I always thought this was carrying things to too great an extremity . . . One must wink hard and connive at many faults to preserve peace & love in familys . . .'[44]

The advice came too late.

---

* 'I don't know what your friends mean by the difficulty in their seeing this house', Sarah writes to Lady Cairns from Blenheim, 'for no one mortal is ever refused it'. (Blen G-1-16. Dated Sept. 29—no year given but in Marlborough's lifetime).

CHAPTER XIII

The Fruitful Vine

1727-1735

———◆———

There could be no denying that under the Hanoverians family quarrels were the fashion. Not that everyone chose to follow the royal lead, but for those that did the standard was very high or very low according to how one viewed it. In the reigns of the early Georges fathers and sons were at loggerheads; and there were subsidiary squabbles and rivalries among seconds and mistresses, which made for diversion in distant and otherwise stodgy courts.

Sarah, with so small an opinion of the whole pack that she had all but forgiven Queen Anne, would have scoffed at the notion of apeing them in anything. Yet her large family now rivalled if it did not outdistance theirs in what seemed to her outrageous and unforgivable behaviour.

By an understandable law of nature the most scandalous thing of all, as the world thought, she wrote least about, going no further than passing references to her eldest daughter as Congreve's moll. After her father's death in June, 1722 Henrietta Godolphin Duchess of Marlborough went to Bath, where most of her time was spent with Congreve who, at fifty-two, suffered cruelly from gout and cataract. Henrietta, who was forty-one, had had four children two of whom, Willigo Blandford and Harriet Newcastle, survived. In November, 1723, having ceased bearing for nearly twenty years, she gave birth to a daughter, Mary. If when Congreve died in 1729 any doubt remained about paternity it was dispelled by his bequest to the immensely rich duchess of £10,000, leaving only £200 for his former mistress Mrs Bracegirdle.

The strange fancies of Henrietta's monument to Congreve in Westminster Abbey, where she herself was to be buried,* and her wax-effigy of him at her dinner-table are too well known for repetition.[1] Her eccentricity bordering on madness, delightful at a distance, must certainly have been hard to live with, and there can be no doubt but that her dull husband's patience, inherited from both father and mother, was stretched to the uttermost.

Less than two months after the birth of Mary Godolphin (a charming girl nicknamed Minos, who became Duchess of Leeds and died at forty) Sarah, writing to Mary's brother Willigo—'My letters are the longer from tumbling out every thing that I think without study'—said, 'Concerning your mother living with me as she has don for many years,† I am her mother & never yet was the agressor, but she is in so ill hands that she finds new ways every day of surprising the world with her behaviour or rage against me, which is much increas'd since the death of her father'.[2] A sad situation which would drag on till the younger duchess's death in 1733.

Early in the seventeen-twenties Sarah, battling with ill health and litigation, had decided to write her two daughters off. Godolphin's assurance long ago that she (Sarah) had been the best mother in all respects made Henrietta's behaviour the more monstrous. 'But no more of that', she wrote in 1730, 'it is now all over & I shall never have no more to do with her'.[3]

Henrietta's sister, Mary Montagu, Pope's Angel Duchess, was as bad or worse. A fancied slight over the eve-of-exile diamond-raffle of 1712, from which Mary's children had been excluded ('because I knew', explained Sarah, 'you had at your marriage diamonds enough to cover a table'), had led to a lasting coldness which reconciliation-attempts by go-betweens (a Mrs Hammond was the latest) did little or nothing to thaw. Nor did it cheer Sarah to find the quarrels

---

* '. . . and it is my desire & express will that my Body be not at any time here-after or on any pretence whatsoever carried to Blenham . . . I also give to my said daughter Mary all Mr Congreves Personal Estate that he left me & all my own money or which I enjoyed as such'. Excerpt from the will of Henrietta Duchess of Marlborough dated 11 July, 1732 (BM add ms 28071 ff 34–9).

† The two duchesses, Sarah and Henrietta, did not of course live in the same house. The reference here is to the bad terms on which for many years they were to each other.

Mary Church
Daughter to
Duke of Marl
l, & Wife to
uke of Mont,
agu.

Lady Mary Churchill (afterwards Duchess of Montagu). Kneller

Diana Duchess of Bedford. Attributed to Thomas Hudson

carried to the next generation: Willigo on bad terms with his mother, and Bella Montagu, who in 1723 married the Duke of Manchester, likewise out of favour with hers. 'I have been told by several', wrote Sarah, 'that she longed to be rid of her. The Duke of Manchester had a very small estate and in half an hour's conversation with him the Duchess of Montagu must know that a woman that had sense must be very miserable with him . . . Most mothers would have been touch'd to have reflected upon her being married to such a man . . . but when she was like a bird out of a cage & knew nothing of the world, the Duchess of Montagu never minded her . . . How cruel must a heart be not to be reconciled to a child that had made such submissions !'[4]

However, there was always for a Marlborough grandchild the consolation that to be out of favour with mother meant being in grandmother's good graces; and in this case Sarah set to work, furnishing Bella's house as she did many another. 'I think myself,' she wrote gaily, 'the best upholsterer in England. You may do what you please', she added, 'with the old soldier's verses,* for I have got them by heart and after my fashion can sing the Ballad'.[5]

With Bella's mother Mary, Sarah's only child to survive her, there could be no lasting reconciliation; for now, to top all her former misconduct, she had behaved most extraordinarily in of all places the workshop of Rysbrack the sculptor. 'She went to see the Tomb for Blenheim (p. 173) at Mr Rysbrack's', Sarah explains, 'they always make a Model in Clay to make that in stone by & what is done first in Clay is often more like than that in marble. She lik'd that extream-ly of Lord Blandford & got Mr R: to tell her she should have it, which I suppose he was not unwilling to gratify her in as she would pay him for it . . . But when I saw that of my Son it was so extream like that I was fond of it & desir'd him to bake it & send it to me, which he did. And liking that model so well I ask'd Mr R: for that of the Duke of Marls Statue . . . but he excus'd giving it me, saying that some accident had happen'd to it. I beleive he had let the Duch-ess of Montagu have it, but that I am not sure of as I am that she was in a most violent rage when she heard I had got Lord Blandford's model & said it was only out of Crossness to her that I had taken it,

* The verses, to the tune of *To All You Fair Ladies*, were sent to Sarah by an ex-ADC of Marlborough's. See also appendix IV.

tho' I never had heard the least word of her having a mind to it till some time after I had it . . .'⁶ The Green Book began to burst its covers as Sarah scoured her vocabulary. Such conduct wanted a name.

'I married her', Sarah patiently told Mrs Hammond, of Mary Montagu, 'to the chief match of England . . . and if it had not been for my favour she must have been married to some country gentleman of 1500 or 2000 pounds a year, which for ought I know might have been better both for her & for me; at least 'tis probable it would have made her behave better . . . But now I have taken my resolution unalterable that I never will have any thing more to say to her. My life is very near run out & I am sure she can now never give me any Pain or Pleasure, & therefore I desire that you would never name her more to your most faithfull humble servant'.⁷ And again later: 'I am what is called Bedridden & Dying & tho' I beleive her Wit entertaining I can read that out of any Book & am content with the very few friends I keep company with when I am out of Pain & at my age 'tis impossible to love any body with passion as I did her a great while, but I own that has been long burnt out & I have now nothing to do but to be as quiet as I can'.⁸

There could be no question but that it had been the more lovable and dutiful of her daughters, Anne and Elizabeth, who had died; yet even they had left daughters who, to the kindest of grandmothers, could and did give infinite trouble. It was not enough, Sarah found, to take them into her home, teach them, tend them, dress them and make matches for them. Ingratitude on a more or less monstrous scale was almost always the reward. No one could have been kinder than she had been to Elizabeth's daughter Anne Egerton, the same who had been snatched by an infuriated father intent on her marrying the sixteen-year-old Duke of Bedford. But her behaviour since had proved disappointing, and on Christmas Day, 1724, her grandmother wrote to tell her so:

I can't help saying that I should have taken the message you sent me very kindly had it been sincere, that you were very sorry that you did not stay long enough in town to come to me, but as I know you had been with several people to whom you never had the least obligation . . . and that you did protest to me that your father never restrained you from expressing your affection to me by letter, so long ago when you were taken away in so very strange a manner, I can impute this last neglect of me to no body but your self, and certainly it would have been better in you not to have sent me any message at all than one that was plainly so insincere to one who, you must be sensible, has been so good a friend to you as well as a parent.

When you left me I had reason to believe that you felt a great deal by the tears which you shed and the expressions which you made to me, and tho' I could not like that you took no manner of notice of me in so many months when you writ to others, I was very easy to you when you came to me in town the following winter, and what has occation'd this last behaviour I can't imagine; but I am sure that you could not possibly apprehend that I should not be very well pleased that you were to marry the Duke of Bedford, so that I must impute it to your want of Nature to me and add what the world calls it, indecent.

You will remember that allways from a child I endeavoured to convince you that you must never depart from the truth upon any account whatsoever and that no fault that you could commit was so bad as any sort of falseness. I am sure you will never have better advice or instructions given you than that and according to that principle I can assure you with the greatest sincerity that I was, as long as it was possible, your most affectionate grandmother.[9]

The account continues:

In answer to this letter the Duke of Bridgwater sent for the servant that carried it to Lady Anne and then called for one of his own servants into the room, saying that he was to be a witness to what he said to the Duchess of Marlborough, which was as follows: 'Tell her that I have commanded my daughter never to go to her, nor to write or to send her any message, nor to receive any from her; and I desire that she never will send any servant to my house; and tell her that I understand the duty to a mother better than she does her duty to her children'. The servant that brought this message said that he observed that his Grace was in a great agony and tho' he pronounced all this he seemed to be very much out of breath.[10]

The truth was the Duke was as near combustion as a man is ever likely to get. Silence ensued, and it would be pleasant to suppose that afterwards Anne Egerton settled happily with the Duke of Bedford, whom she married in 1725. Her grandmother was delighted with him, and dubbed him her secretary; but he gambled astronomically, fell out with his wife and died young, leaving his title to his brother who, in 1731, married Sarah's favourite granddaughter Lady Diana Spencer. The widow, Anne Duchess of Bedford, married the Earl of Jersey.

Manifestly, to be a Marlborough grandchild and remain on good terms with the dowager was not simple. To love and cherish one's grandmother was one thing, to hate her enemies quite another, particularly when those enemies happened to be one's brothers and sisters. Sarah was fond of Di Spencer, adopted as 'a pritty talking child' of six when her mother died in 1716, but she made it clear to her from the first that there could be no half-measures about loyalty; it must be all or nothing. Her brothers, Robert, Charles and John, drifted in and out of their grandmother's favour while they were at Eton and later while they were abroad. Her unremitting displeasure was reserved for the other sister Anne, married to Mr Bateman in 1720 and now a viscountess.

Though Sarah had never liked Anne Bateman and accused her of 'a thousand mean tricks, even from 14', there may until 1732 have been some possibility of a reconciliation. After that there was none, because Sarah was convinced that she had 'sold' her brother Charles in marriage to Elizabeth Trevor, of whose grandfather she strongly disapproved. If there was matchmaking of that order to be done (and Charles was by then the Marlborough heir), Sarah would do it. For Di she had chosen Frederick Prince of Wales, a project thwarted at the eleventh hour, it was said, by Sir Robert Walpole; and though other more or less unworthy suitors followed—Lord Middleton, the Earl of Chesterfield*—she kept her Cordelia, as she fondly called her, for Lord John Russell, who soon afterwards became fourth Duke of Bedford.

Behind her, in her early training of Di, Sarah had had the benefit of the mistakes she had made in the upbringing of her own children.

---

* In his proposal from the Hague, dated 14 Aug. 1731, Chesterfield writes: 'The honour I should have of being so nearly related to you is not one of my least temptations'. (Blen E 37).

She taught her history and obedience and nursed her through small-pox; and at the age of twelve Di was writing to her French gover-ness, at Sarah's dictation, 'My Mama Dutchess is resolved to let every fool & every wicked person say what they will without giving herself the least trouble'; and later, to Sarah herself, 'The study of my life shall be to deserve the kindness you shew me & to acknowledge my gratitude'.

Thus, when the harsh test of loyalties came—loyalty to her sister Anne or loyalty to her grandmother—Sarah knew she could count upon her. In a typically long letter, sent a week after the burial of Di's son who lived only a day, a letter in which she refers to 'the monstrous treatment I have met with from the rest of your family, which I do believe you have been sorry for, tho I have often observed that you have been very partial to them', Sarah explains, 'I don't mean that you should not see your brothers, but she [Lady Bateman] is a Disgrace to any body's sister. It has been the custom of all times to put a mark upon the person that has been the contriver of any great mischief, & as to my two grandsons, they can't help their weakness . . . But for lady Bateman I must declare that I can never have any satisfaction in the conversation of any body that has any commerce with her . . . I desire, my dear, you will consider very well before you take your resolution . . . You must be very plain with lady Bateman in letting her know that you can have no commerce with her, that you are very sorry that she did not reflect upon the ill consequences of what she has done before it was too late; that all people that are either good or reasonable are & must be sensible that there is no precedent of such a treatment to a grandmother that for thirty years has been labouring to assist & serve a whole family & that has done it with great success; & that you could not live with any ease if you did any thing that was grievous to me. I think I am not in my Nature at all partial . . . There is no acting by halves or trimming in such an affair as this, but I do again protest to you that I would have you do in it as you like best. I only desire to be as easy as I can make my self & whatever you do I shall allways be most affectionately yours'.[11]

Though Di's answer is missing, Sarah vouches for it herself that she was not disappointed. 'I could not bear the thoughts', she says, 'of her coming to me in the same manner she us'd to do, when I knew she came from such a viper . . . I press'd her extreamly to do what would make her most easy and she chose to take leave of her sister and to come to me with the same friendship & openness she us'd to do'.[12] From the age of six Di had been learning her lesson, so that later she could assure her grandmother, as it would seem almost mechanically: 'Anybody must have a very bad heart indeed that does not endeavour to make all possible returns to anybody who has shewn a perpetual kindness to them their whole lives as my dear Grandmama has done to me & which I shall ever study to deserve'.[13]

After marriage, as *Letters of a Grandmother*[14] show, the correspondence increased. Sarah wrote fast and often, sometimes twice a day. 'Pray tell me sincerely', she begged, 'if you can read all I write, for I beleive no body ever before writt so long a letter without stoping & so fast that the letters are worse shaped I think then usual'. From court gossip to architecture, from music to medicine, there is hardly a subject left untouched. It is the one delight left to the ill and ageing Duchess, to pour out her thoughts and troubles to the one person she loves, her dear Cordelia, and to build and furnish a house at Wimbledon for her to live in.

In the summer of 1732 the dowager took Woburn on her way to Scarborough and for Di wrote down her impressions of both. She was carried round Woburn, she told her, in a chair with short poles and noticed that, in the picture-gallery especially, the young Duke of Bedford, who had married Anne Egerton, kept sitting down. 'If I had time & spirits', she added, 'I could tell you a thousand pretty things he said & there is nothing so amazing to me as to see a man that seems to have so much sense & yet to have made such a havoc of his constitution & of his estate'.[15] When someone remarked that part of the house was in danger of falling, he said it would outlast its owner, and he was right.

At York Sarah made time to see and disapprove of Lord Burlington's Assembly Rooms before taking coach to Scarborough which, like Bath, she found noisy and dirty. She had gone there (she was seventy-two) to see if the waters could help to make her 'tolerably easy . . . but whether life is long or short, I think 'tis a very indifferent thing to me.'[16] The lavatories shocked her. Lord Chesterfield pleased her . . . and so on. She had observed at York 'a vast deal of what they call architecture', and she was to see more of it, by Vanbrugh and

Hawksmoor, at Castle Howard. 'My Lord Carlisle', she reported to Di, 'is laying out a mint of money in making an extraordinary place to bury his own family in a finer manner than I have ever heard of & for a great number of them which are yet to be born'.*[17]

While she looked at the plans and buildings of others, Sarah had in mind her own projects at Wimbledon, where in 1723 she had bought an estate from Sir Theodore Jansen, a bankrupt South Seas director; and at St Albans, where she was planning almshouses for 'forty miserable old Creatures' who had never known happiness. Blenheim and Marlborough House had had to be finished without help from their architects; but now surely, at Wimbledon where she had a free hand, a reliable architect might be expected to stay the course. Lord Herbert's success with the Column of Victory naturally led her to consult him; whereupon she found herself landed with his protégé Roger Morris, whom she soon came to dislike.

Long long ago, at the start of the Blenheim works, it may be remembered, Godolphin had told Marlborough that his wife, as she viewed them, was proving extremely prying-into. She had not changed. 'For tho I am not an architect', as she explained to Lady Cowper, 'I find one can't bee long from any building without the danger of having a window or a door or somthing or other that one does not like, & yet I think I am in the best hands we have, but their rules does not allways agree with my fancy, & I am forced to bee perpetually on the watch'. For some reason she suspected that Morris meant to crown Wimbledon with a turret, a thing she could not abide. Asked for a drawing of it Morris, so Sarah told Lord Herbert, refused to leave it with her and this gave offence for though, as she said, her taste might be faulty, she was certainly at seventy-two old enough to know what she liked. When she dismissed him he had the impudence to ask £300 for plans Wren would, he said, have charged £2000 for. This was asking for trouble, for Sarah happened to know that 'for the whole direction & management of St Paul's' Wren had had only £200 a year, 'and was pull'd up in a basket twice a week to the top'.[18]

In one of her twenty-six draft-wills at Althorp Sarah directs that Wimbledon be finished without carving, gilding or foolish ornaments, 'nor a Turret upon the top of the house . . . I desire', she adds,

* Hawksmoor's masterpiece, the mausoleum, now in need of restoration.

'that Mr Bridgman may finish the ground & gardens . . . and I positively direct that nothing be done by the direction of my Lord Herbert or Mr Morris & I desire that Mr Smith of Warwickshire the builder may be employed to make Contracts and . . . complete the work as far as the distance he is at will give him leave'.[19]

It was bad enough that Morris had embarked on works at Wimbledon without her direction. Only later did she discover that Di's brother Charles had allowed him to lead him into huge expense at Althorp, with a replica of an Inigo Jones church for stables, an elaborate dwelling for a gardener and a great deal of work in the house itself, leaving it, in her opinion, much the worse, when all it needed was sash windows and a plain, useful stable for thirty or forty horses. Morris, who had in fact done work of distinction still to be seen at Althorp, was referred to as infamous, his name added to the black list; so that we find Di's younger brother John promising not only to have no truck with the Batemans but none, too, with Morris. For just as she had long since seen through almost all doctors and lawyers so now, Sarah decided, she had seen through all architects. For her almshouses* she would manage without them.[20]

It could be that that excellent builder Smith of Warwick, whom she may not have regarded as an architect, helped her. The almshouses, as they stand today, look pleasing enough and may be comfortable. All, with one exception, is modesty; and that a central pediment worthy of Blenheim, bearing on its tympanum the arms and supporters of Churchill and Mindelheim, embosomed by a two-headed eagle on the heroic scale.

In Sarah's letters now there is much about illness: gout not only in hands but in knees, which she remembers Garth calling incurable; and scurvy which drives her mad with itching; and there is much too about death. Her own, come when it may, Sarah views with indifference, but the death of a young man is always shocking and, though she had expected it, she was shocked to hear of the death at Corunna, on October 23rd, 1732, of the young Duke of Bedford.† From their first meeting she had been charmed with his behaviour—

---

* The St Albans almshouses were begun in February, 1733. A fine cedar, said to have been planted by the Duchess, in the forecourt, was recently felled.

† Wriothesley 3rd Duke of Bedford, not to be confused with his brother John 4th Duke of Bedford who married Lady Diana Spencer. (See pedigree at p. 312).

'just as I should have wishd had hee been my own son'—so that she was prepared to believe Providence must have sent him to make up for those others who had been 'like wild creatures without sense or nature'. Now that Providence had taken him she sorrowed more than the widow who had not found the marriage a happy one. She thought, to Sarah's alarm, of marrying John Spencer but, luckily, thought again.

In the following October came the death of Henrietta Duchess of Marlborough. 'I am sure', wrote Di to Sarah, 'you feel more upon this subject than you thought you should yourself'.[21] Sarah owned that she did. She had, she added, vainly attempted reconciliation. Henrietta in youth had been so goodnatured, 'the modestest young creature', till 'flattered & practised upon by the most vile people upon earth'.[22] How often had she herself warned her against that rabble—Lady Oxford and her daughters, Lady Sandwich, yes and Lady Fitzharding, 'for though she had a great deal of wit & humour that was diverting, her house was a dangerous place for young people'.[23] But all to no purpose, 'and I think the consequences of conversing with such ill people', she wrote sadly, 'has sufficiently justified me . . .'[24]

There were rumours that at the last she had turned Roman Catholic. Sarah refuted them. 'What was don about the peice of wood', she assured Di, 'was only folly, for as to religion she had none. It is better to be a Roman Catholick or any thing then to have [no] religion at all, but 'tis certain the company she had long keept, both men & women, had corrupted all her morals & she shewd at last that she had no principle of any sort & was vastly ill natur'd to every body but la: Ma:* . . . but familys seldome agree to live easyly together'.

This was the gloomy side and there would be more of it: yet if gout abated, the dowager could still rally and cry, 'Nobody upon earth ever governed me nor ever shall!' It was the same spirit that she admired in her grandson Charles Spencer, now third Duke of Marlborough,† when he refused to vote the way he was bidden.

* Lady Mary Godolphin, aged ten, went to live with her sister Harriet, Duchess of Newcastle at Claremont near Esher in Surrey.

† Charles Spencer, 5th Earl of Sunderland (1706–1758), became in 1733, on the death of his aunt Henrietta 2nd Duchess of Marlborough, 3rd Duke of Marl-

Charles was large and ponderous and not brilliantly clever, but this show of resistance, said his grandmother, 'was so much after my own heart that I believe it would have animated me enough to have given me strength to have lifted him up from the ground and kissed him'.

At times she sounds positively gay as when, for Di's benefit, she recalls the marriage of Dutch William. 'I saw both the weddings of the two last queens', she writes to her, 'which was all private as yours, but I remember one thing that deverted the young people: the Prince of Orange came to bed in a blew sattin wascoat which was the Dutch fashion'.

She goes on to tell Di about her Jacobite house-guests, the Ladies Dillon* and Muskerry,† 'neither of them entertaining', whom she will see only at mealtimes. The devout Lady Muskerry,—'so extreme simple'—has been teased about the thirty-nine articles. 'I made Mr Stephens read them', Sarah writes, 'but after she had said she would defend them all by Scripture, upon consideration I found she was afraid of the debate for she would not own that they were in her Bible, when upon producing it we found them'.

The Duchess seldom descends to bawdy, but when she does the anecdote is worth telling: 'I was told another very foolish thing last night, which I believe is true', she confides, 'that a woman is taken up for having wished the wind was in the King's arse. I must own it was not a very polite expression, but the poor woman has explained it very well, for every body wishes him in England, & he can't be here till the wind is in his back. If the magistrate happens to be a very simple man there may possibly be another subject for a Ballad, but I have not yet heard what they have done with the woman'.

Evidently there were other ways of getting even with the Georges besides plotting with the Jacobites. Sarah scoffed at them and at their

---

borough. He left Althorp in 1734 and lived mainly at Langley, Bucks. In 1817 the 5th Duke of Marlborough was authorised to add the name of Churchill to that of Spencer, 'to perpetuate in his Grace's family a surname to which his illustrious ancestor John first Duke of Marlborough added such imperishable lustre'.

* Lady Dillon, one of the three viscountess-daughters of Sarah's sister Frances Tyrconnel who died in 1730.

† Lady Muskerry was the daughter-in-law of the Earl of Clancarty.

supporters, her arch-enemy being Sir Robert Walpole. It was many years since, as a friend, she had sent him the manuscript of her *Conduct*, though his rejection or postponement of publication may have sown the first seed of animosity. It was to be followed by many more: the dismissal of Marlborough's secretary Cardonnel (for which Sarah held him responsible); the taxing of the £5000-a-year Marlborough grant; his refusal to extend Sarah's lease of Windsor Lodge or to bar the Duke of St Albans from driving through Windsor Park. . . Even her grant of £500-a-year as Ranger of Windsor had been withdrawn; and there had been a rumpus too over Wimbledon, where Queen Caroline, needing a short cut to Richmond, demanded rights Sarah was not prepared to concede. When the Queen threatened to sue, Walpole, as always, supported her. Sarah had not forgotten that when Walpole was responsible for the post-office (or its equivalent), in Henrietta's lifetime, letters for the two Duchesses of Marlborough were constantly delivered at the wrong address. She was certain it was deliberate.*

If in Sarah's view Walpole was the successor of Harley, then Permis Newcastle was the equivalent of St John, with Mrs Clayton (the same of whom she had written, 'God Almighty bless my dear dear Mrs Clayton and all that she loves') an unconvincing yet nevertheless noxious Abigail. And indeed, to one of her many accounts of Abigail's shortcomings Sarah adds: '. . . but I think the mischeifs that have been don since by Q: Car: assisted in all vile things by Mrs Clayton are much greater and seems impossible to be recover'd'.[25]

Newcastle she felt competent to jeer at for his spelling. 'I know', she writes, 'his Grace affects to be a great scholar, which for ought I know may be the reason of his writing Honour out of the common way [Honor] & likewise for writing At with a duble t, but as I am ignorant I may not be right in my remark'.

As for Mrs Clayton, it was disappointing indeed that after all Sarah had done for her (had she not recommended her to Caroline as 'of a perfect good understanding, a reputation without the least blemish, good principles of all kinds and of an extream good family'?),[26] she should toady to royalty as she now so blatantly did. In order that the two ladies (Queen Caroline and Mrs Clayton)

---

* For Walpole's teasing of the Duchess over the approach to Marlborough House etc. see Hugh Phillips: *Mid-Georgian London*, pp. 49–51.

might play at cards together, or so Sarah alleged, it had been found necessary to confer upon Mr Clayton an Irish title. In her description, for Di, of the pretentious portrait of the newly created Lord and Lady Sundon, as the Claytons now were, Sarah enjoyed herself to the utmost:

> It is drawn in the manner of Hogarth's conversation pieces, but not by him, nor with a design to ridicule; but seriously directed to be done by my Lord and Lady Sundon, who are sitting at a table in their supposed library. My Lord has a book in one hand, a paper in the other . . . There are some books lying on the table besides . . . There stands by Mr Clayton a bookcase with the doors thrown open; and a servant, who I suppose is a page, with a book taken out of the bookcase, which my Lady Sundon holds out her hand to take . . . My Lady's picture I should not have known. Her dress is a fine pink colour with diamond buckles and a great deal of ruffled lace upon her head, and a bunch of pink coloured ribbons on the top of it, and a white apron. For you are to suppose she is undressed early at her studies. And in short I think nothing can be added to make these two figures better if I were to draw them myself, but to put two crowns on their chairs and to dress them in Irish robes.'[27]

At less frivolous times, when gout tortured her as it had tortured Queen Anne, her secretary and doctor, Stephens, would write to Di, 'I think her in no manner of danger, but she is not only in too much Pain to write but so low spirited that she cannot dictate'. On a good day Sarah would write in her own hand, 'I thank God I am never weary of being alone'; and on a bad one, 'It is dismal to be always alone, and the generality of company one meets with is yet worse. Most people are disagreeable for one thing or another, and I think if I could walk out of life without the pain one suffers in dying I would do it tomorrow. For go I must, a little sooner or later, and when pleasures are very small & troubles many there is no reason to be solicitous for the continuation of such a life'.

But she could not be tranquil, she could never relax. It was her duty, she told Di, to save her brother Charles from the cheats; and that meant, among other things, lawsuit after lawsuit against everyone who had been concerned in the building of Blenheim; or if, like

Vanbrugh and Travers, they happened to be dead, then with their executors or assigns. 'You know', she told Lady Cowper, 'I pretend to be a great lawyer' and so, in a sense and by much practice, she had become. For one slight reason or another she had worked herself into a lasting passion against Honest Harry (Henry Joynes), who at twenty-one had been recruited as clerk of the works some thirty years ago and was now an architect of some standing. One might have thought Lord Macclesfield's decree against Vanbrugh and the workmen inviolable, but since he had so sententiously pronounced it, things had taken a different turn. Vanbrugh by a trick had snatched his earnings, Macclesfield had been clapped in the Tower; and now in 1734 another Chancellor, Talbot, had had the effrontery to over-rule Macclesfield's decree. How could this have happened? 'All the reason that appears to me for my lord Chancellor's extraordinary Proceeding', Sarah wrote to Di, 'is that Mr Joyns who has been the vilain in all this affair of Blenheim building has been his architect and built his house for him in Lincolns Inn Fields'.* All the Chancellor had said and done was 'extream indecent', but then what was to be expected of the son of a weak father who, because he happened to be a Whig, Sarah had persuaded Queen Anne to advance from 'a small Bishoprick of Oxford' to the glittering glories of Salisbury?

She prattles on ... Does Di approve of the tomb Kent has designed and Rysbrack sculpted for Marlborough in Blenheim chapel?† She does. (Not for her to remark that no daughter is mentioned nor depicted). And will she help translate the Latin inscription for Marlborough's bust in the Great Hall? She will. Oh and one last thing: she must see and approve the Blenheim statue (and its inscription) to Queen Anne. 'I am going to Rysbrack to make a bargain with him for a fine statue of Queen Anne', she tells her, 'which I will put up in the bow window room at Blenheim with a proper inscription.‡ It will be a very fine thing & though but one figure will cost

---

* Joynes built what are now numbers 57 and 58 Lincolns Inn Fields for Lord Chancellor Talbot in 1730. (See Colvin: *Biog. Dic. Eng. Architects*, p. 329.)

† The chapel was consecrated in 1728. The tomb, bearing the date 1733, shows Marlborough in Roman dress, the Duchess in robe and coronet, and their two infant sons. Fame and History are prominent. Envy is crushed by the sarcophagus which bears a relief of Tallard's surrender at Blenheim. (p. 173)

‡ In 1738 the statue is recorded as standing not in the eastern bow but in the

me £300. I have a satisfaction in showing this respect to her, because her kindness to me was real, and what happened afterwards was compassed by the contrivance of such as are in power now'.[28]

It was typical of Sarah, in her long inscription, to score a left and a right by making her forgiveness of Anne the excuse for a reflection upon George II's queen Caroline who, by backing Walpole and Mrs Clayton and in other matters such as Wimbledon, the veto on Sarah's driving through St James's Park, Sarah's four-hour wait in her ante-room and a libel on Marlborough spoken in the Queen's drawing-room,[29] had proved herself worthless and without manners or breeding. True, as Sarah said, she had never flattered anyone living and she could not be accused of flattering Anne when she was dead. In private she made it clear to her friends that she might have said very much more of Anne's shortcomings; yet even so, she pointed out, they still made her a goddess in comparison with the reigning Queen. 'As I had great obligations to the Queen [Anne]', she explained, 'I thought it unbecoming in me to relate anything to her disadvantage'.

For the public at large, then, Queen Anne's blemishes were to be hidden; but for the more private record squeamishness might be flung aside: 'She certainly, as is said on the inscription, meant well & was not a fool; but nobody can maintain that she was wise, nor entertaining in conversation. She was in everything what I described her; ignorant in everything but what the parsons had taught her when a child . . .'[30] And so on. Once—nay twice—and for all, the Duchess had spoken. Queen Anne had not after all been succeeded by another of the same name. In her public image and in her private image Queen Anne of immortal memory was one.

So much for the castle of Blenheim, which Queen Anne never saw and where the Duchess, on her visits, used but one of its hundreds of rooms. And what of the grounds? 'You say nothing', she wrote to Di, 'of the garden and court being so ill kept, though it has cost me a great deal every year; and I will take another method of doing it, which will make it better & with a great deal less charge'.[31]

---

western one of the Gallery or Long Library, in which position it would be seen immediately one entered the Great Hall. It now stands at the south end of the Long Library, without the original inscription.

The charge was then £250 a year and for that John Hughes the head gardener had undertaken

to keep the Gardens & Courts at all Times so neat that at all times of the Year they may look hansome if that any Company comes to see them & with the greatest Nice'ty when My Lady Dutchess is at Blenheim. And I likewise promise to cutt any Weeds that looks ugly . . . all round the Courts . . . If any great Tree falls downe or is taken up in the Garden, that is for my Lady Dutchess's use . . . and I am to raise whatever she Directs & to keep the Walls allways full of good fruit . . . all sorts of Roots for the Kitchin, Sparragrass etc. . . . all sorts of Sallad-tings & usefull herbs & a great deal of Lavender & Roses & Borders of Pinks, Jessamin, Lilly of the Valley, Clove gilly-flowers, Rosemary, Honey-Succles, White Lillys & in Short any thing that my Lady Dutchess shall think proper to Order & in the places which she shall direct . . .[32]

When, smarting under 'the Disgust of my Lady Dutchess', Hughes left, visitors were shocked. 'My wife was much Surpris'd at the Story of Hughes', wrote one of them. 'She says if she could envy anyone it would be Mr Hughes, he had soe quiet & soe plentifull a Situation that she thought he had nothing to wish & therefore nothing to doe but to be honest & thankfull'.[33]

It had been Sarah's boast that in the finishing of Blenheim she had saved the Marlborough trust £20,000; but now she felt less sure. 'I would leave nothing there', she told Di, 'to be done by Mr Morris. Nor do I think it of any use to save money now as I have formerly done for the trust estate, which I am sure no good use will ever be made of '.[34] After all her struggles she found herself in the mood of the psalmist:

For man walketh in a vain shadow and disquieteth himself in vain: he heapeth up riches and cannot tell who shall gather them.[35]

Di attempted to cheer her by offering to take her to the opera. 'It would please me', Sarah replied, 'a thousand times more then any musick that can ever be perform'd, but I fear I shall never be able to go . . . because I can't get out of my chair without two people to help me & when I am got out I can't stand nor goe one steep without two chair men to hold me up'. She would content herself with her chamber-organ which played eight tunes and had cost less than many a bishopric.

In spite of music and pet dogs and of all Di could do for her, however, Sarah lapsed into gloom, wished she could have predeceased Marlborough and, with all her vast possessions and wretched health, compared her lot to Job's. 'I can't say I am quite living, nor am I dead, which perhaps is the best state that one can be in. But I can say with Job that my eyes are dim with sorrow & my nerves are as shadows, & indeed I think my circumstances is more like his than anybody's that I have heard of or read of'.[36] Addressing Di as she did as Cordelia, it was surprising that she never saw herself in the role of Lear.

Throughout 1734 the letters continue, the gloom deepens. Over Di's 'very kind expressions' she weeps: 'Perhaps too I may feel it the more from the dreadful usage I have met with from others'. In December there are hints of friction, not with Di but with her husband the Duke of Bedford, who has differed with Sarah over the parliamentary election of John Spencer. Something—an explosion?* —happens and, after letters-by-every-post year in year out, suddenly, for five months, there is nothing at all; and when in June, 1735, we are again allowed an insight, the shadow of anxiety falls across every line. Sarah has found 'full employment in furnishing Wimbledon for dear Cordelia', while growing more and more concerned about her health. Di is said to be pregnant, but is she? The symptoms Sarah hears of bring nothing but worry.

Oh for a charm to ward off evil, some spell or philtre, some consoling thought, some sanctuary for what was left of happiness, to keep it safe. 'I wish', writes Sarah, 'you could send me a receip to think upon all occasions what will make one most happy, that would be a charming thing'. With an effort she rallies for Di's birthday, 'keept in my family [household]', she tells her, 'with great splender, all my servants had joyful faces & all the wemen made a much better figure, in my mind, then any of her Majesty's maids of honour upon the great days at court. As for my self I need not say

* In her letter dated March 16, 1737 to the Duke of Bedford Sarah refers to it as a storm which blew over. (Scott-Thomson, op. cit., p. 177)

Sarah Duchess of Marlborough. Kneller. The Petworth portrait

Charles Seymour sixth Duke of Somerset. Kneller

how much I wish you may live as long as 'tis possible to do . . . but I must own I am extreamly uneasy at the account you give me of the way you are in'.

She wrote to Di's doctor and sent Marlborough's campaigning tent for Di to lie in. At the end of August she insisted on her coming to London, but nothing could be done. On September 27th, in her twenty-sixth year, Diana Duchess of Bedford died of tuberculosis.*

From what Sarah wrote to the widower eighteen months later one suspects that, at the last, she desperately tried to act the doctor and was prevented. 'Your Grace knew very well', she says, 'that I must have [had] more experience than any body about her. It would be too much to repeat the monstrous usage which I received . . . But I sat silently in outward rooms, bathed in tears; and I own I flattered you . . . which was out of fear that if I did not take that way, you would order the porter not to let me in . . .'[37]

It was a most miserable end to Sarah's last, deep friendship. 'I need say nothing of my heart', she had once told Di, 'for you know that has allways been yours and will be so till I dye and after to all Eternity, if that can bee . . .'

Wimbledon, finished and furnished, was now meaningless. There was nothing to do but burn bundles of Di's letters and this she did, having most of them by heart.

Long ago, in the year of Marlborough's death and in the lifetime of her two daughters Henrietta and Mary, Sarah had written to her kinswoman Mrs Ann Jennens:

> You have stated my misfortunes kindly in hopes to make me feel them the less, but you ded not consider that I have no children, for tho I love these poor grandchildren & will take care of them for their Mothers' sakes, yet that is nothing like having good children of one's own, & I beleive that Dear Mrs Jennens will allow that whoever has been once so happy as I have been & have nothing left but mony, which from my humour I don't want much of, deserves to bee pittyd.[38]

* Several references to a swelling in the neck suggest that Lady Diana Spencer may have suffered from tubercular glands. Although today with proper treatment she would almost certainly have been cured, in 1735 her case was hopeless.

But without counting on pity Sarah had long since become fatalistic. Even as long ago as in the reign of Anne, when peace was imminent, she had told Lady Cowper, 'I pray heartily for it, and whenever that is [comes], I think I shall live without hope or fear, which I really beleive is the best condition'.

CHAPTER XIV

The Grandsons

1720-1740

◆

It has often been observed to what a striking extent the regular features of Marlborough, 'handsome as an angel', have been transmitted to his descendants, even to the tenth, to the eleventh, to the twelfth generation. All his grandsons had charm and some were handsome, though none showed more brilliance than most of his Eton contemporaries, nor did any display that ineffable sweetness discerned by Dr Hare in their grandfather.

Charles and John, Di's younger brothers, followed Robert, the Spencer heir, to Eton, after a brief stay at a school in Hampstead. 'I have heard Hampstead school found fault with', wrote Sarah to their father, Lord Sunderland, in 1720, 'and Eaton commended, but I don't know which is best. If they are at Eaton I shall have opertunitys of seeing them oftener then at any school, for as I have alterd Windsor lodge 'tis a thousand times more agreeable then Blenheim & I shall pass the greatest part of my life there, but I fear Eaton is not a wholesome place. One of the children* has got over that terrible destemper the smallpox. Poor little John has not had it. I hope you will leave such orders that hee may not bee murderd as poor dear Ld Barkely was, beeing blooded & removed after the smallpox was on & had not the least cordial to support nature in such an extremity. If hee has it when I am at Windsor hee may as easyly bee brought to me as his brother was to London, and Mr Gerney has more sense & more experience then most of the doctors at this time'.[1]

No school was ideal, but in handiness and cheapness Eton manifestly scored over others, ('Children can be put there for about

* Charles Spencer.

threescore pounds a year'); and so without further argument the motherless brothers were packed off to it. At such times a stout-hearted and unsentimental grandmother can be, on the surface at least, a greater asset than an emotional mother, no matter how beloved. How embarrassing, for example, to have a mother like Lady Scarborough! She had written to the Duchess:

> I will goe to Windsore to pay my duty to the Princess, which I designed doing ye day I settled my children at Eaton . . . but play'd ye foole soe much when I parted with them that I was ashamed to make my Court, but I think truly I should have overcome that if you had bin there.[2]

Charles, who was ten when his mother died and was little marked by the smallpox, inherited from his grandmother a forthrightness and a stoutness of spirit which, with lack of imagination, made ideal material for the soldier he was to be. John, far more sensitive, was a typical Spencer, a lover of cards, a lover of music; one could not be sure that his heart would be ruled by his head. Though occasionally out of favour, as when he declined to have 'no commerce' with Charles, he won, in spite of herself, his grandmother's heart and became her *Torrismond* and chief heir; while his brother lost favour, regained it and then lost it forever.

In Sarah's experience it was almost always the most lovable that were snatched from her. Her sons, her favourite daughters, her favourite granddaughter, and now her favourite grandson Robert Spencer, Lord Sunderland, who at twenty-eight died in Paris, unmarried, in 1729. It was true, she admitted, that he had gambled excessively, but to her he had been kind and goodnatured and, in sharp contrast with others, had done 'very little mischief to the estate'. As to his premature death of a 'fever', that was scandalous. 'There is no such thing', she declared, 'as a good physician in France, or medecine . . . What they did was directly contrary to the methods of our physicians here in the same destemper. I lament extremely', she added, 'that at the beginning of his illness I was not acquainted with it, because as he had strength to hold out for so many days, notwithstanding so much Bleeding & Purging, always thought prejudicial in a fever . . . I cannot but think there was time for me to have sent medecines & a physician from England that might in all probability have saved him. But it is now too late to make these reflections & all the comfort I have at present is that his brother who succeeds him [Charles] is perfectly honest, goodnatured & has as many vertues as I could wish. But still I have lost one that I passionately lov'd of a Branch who have all very good sense'.[3]

It only remained to 'do him all the honour with Decency without Follies even to his Grave'; and it was astonishing how costly, in Paris, such modest honour could be. Without quibble Sarah settled the account of £8430, which included £650 for embalming, an apothecary's bill for £1379, 'un nécessaire de porcelaine' £144, a £200 coffin and a further £600 for bringing it home.[4]

The Duchess was now left with two daughters, seven granddaughters and only three grandsons: Charles and John Spencer and their cousin Willigo Blandford; the Bridgwater heir Viscount Brackley having died at Eton in 1719 at the age of fifteen.

After Eton, in the usual course of things, every young nobleman not at a university needed to be sent abroad. It was a pattern—the Grand Tour—first laid down in the sixteenth century and now, though scoffed at by Pope and others, considered *de rigueur*.

'Most of our travelling youth neither improve themselves nor credit their country', complained Lady Hartford, writing from Florence in 1740. 'This I believe is often owing to the strange creatures that are made their governors, but as often to the strange creatures that are to be governed. Travelling is certainly carried a great deal too far among the English . . . and the fortune which should be increasing . . . is often decreasing in dress, equipage and sometimes in worse things. Could you see the inundation of poor creatures from all the three kingdoms that at the regular seasons overrun the different parts of France and Italy you would with me lament the approaching month of July in which I am destined to receive them here'.[5]

Charles was eighteen months senior to his brother John, and Willigo seven years older than his cousin Charles; so Willigo, with Mann his governor, went ahead to Holland and Switzerland, meeting Charles in Geneva in 1723. When Willigo returned to Utrecht, Charles remained boarded with a Swiss tutor, Gallatin, to be joined there by John with Sarah's ex-page, Captain Humphrey Fish, in 1725.

In their grandmother's opinion all three grandsons were poor correspondents, and Willigo, though he blamed the mailboats, hardly ever wrote at all unless for funds. Then his rare scrawls, in an alarmingly unbalanced hand, would reach the dowager from Utrecht, from Antwerp, from Rome . . . 'Lord Blandford', Sarah learns from Mrs Boscawen,* 'is not for hurrying and especially [not] out of Italy, which country he prefers to all ye world besides & I find intends to visit all ye little courts & states of it . . . They are very busie in viewing all ye paintings of ye greatest masters, but . . . musick is ye thing in ye world in which he expresses ye most delight'.[6]

But the Duchess, like Marlborough before her, had spies throughout Europe, and the reports she was now receiving from them were not reassuring. Concerned, she compared notes with Mrs Boscawen, who replied:

> I really hope & believe those common malicious reports of many are alltogether groundless . . . His delight is in seeing antiquities & curiosities of all sorts & that place [Rome] abounds with them; & consequently does not spend his time as most other young men doe . . . Lord Blandford was gone into ye mountains to visit some old convents . . . Whatever becomes of their letters & how they manage them, there must be a great many lost . . . God send him well home in his owne good time with ye same good principles of honour, vertue & piety that I'm sure he carried out with him & all will doe well.[7]

When Sarah did at last hear from him she remained unconvinced. He wrote from Rome of church music, adding, 'I believe there is no town in the world that is better fitted to give one an abhorrence of the tricks & nonsense of popery'.[8] She hoped he meant it. She had heard he had leanings in that very direction. On the back of his letter (for she is finishing the chapel at Blenheim) she scribbles: 'The panel of wanscoat for the cloath at the Alter 3 yards high wanting 3

---

* Mrs Boscawen, related to the Godolphins and at this time nearly 80, refers to herself as 'very simple' and 'a worn out insignificant old creature'. As the Blenheim records show, she had the courage to take the Duchess gently to task for having appointed herself Queen Anne's mother-confessor and for having sent her *The Whole Duty of Man*.

inches, broad 2 yards 2 inches . . . 2 black steeps of marble up to the Alter'. From Antwerp Mann, himself frowned upon for not writing more often, writes of Willigo, 'His chief business is usually to view everything that is rare and remarkable, but not to engage much in the conversation of the natives'. Even so, he was not allowed to be solitary. 'I was entertained very civilly and handsomely', wrote Willigo, 'by some English officers who . . . enquired much after Lady Tyrconnel and drank her health often'. He had admired the 'extremely pretty & handsome house' in which the Marlboroughs had made their 'long and melancholy stay', a sight which had led him to reflect on 'the great vicissitudes that attend all human affairs'; but otherwise Antwerp and its society held small appeal. 'I cannot say', he ended, 'that there was anything to recommend it to any person that desired to live as he should do & at the same time not lock himself quite up from company. For all the gentlemen there are the heartiest drinkers & the most entirely given up to it that ever I saw in my life'.[9]

The tone was just a shade too shocked to deceive a sharpwitted grandmother. Sarah suspected that Willigo was himself becoming a hearty drinker. While he stayed abroad there was little she could do but hope that he would come to his senses. In the meantime, though opposed by his mother, she squeezed from the trust a separate settlement which would make him, if he lived, one of England's richest men. It was asking for trouble and sure enough, as the years went by, the reports of Willigo became more and more disturbing.

'I have been told from a very good hand', Sarah writes from Bath in 1727 to her ex-page who signs himself Hum: ffyshe, 'that Mr Montgomery's relation has a very great inclination to a lady who I doubt is a sad tawdry creature & that the journey into Holland was chiefly to see her . . . Pray let me know if you think young Mr M is in danger of being drawn into any thing mischievous of that sort'.[10]

It was only too true. Willigo, now referred to even by his sister Harriet as Lord Worthless, had taken up with a burgomaster's daughter at Utrecht. Sarah, who had had her eye on a daughter of the Duke of Bedford's, wrote desperately by every post. Surely he could not be such an ungrateful fool? Surely he would at least return to England first and consult his father? 'I do protest', she writes on thick, gilt-edged paper, 'that I never was so much affected at any thing that has ever happened to me as I am at what you have written except the death of the Duke of Marlborough and my only son. Since that I have had no sort of pleasure but in doing every thing in my power to perpetuate the glorious actions of the first & before his death I took more pains than you can easely beleive . . . to establish you in the place of a son . . . and when I am dead, which I beleive is not far off, you will have a better estate than most people have in England . . . I hope you will not return this by breaking my heart, which it will certainly do to see the Duke of Marlborough's heir marryd to a burgomaster's daughter. As to what you say that she is as good a Gentlewoman as any in Holland, which I think is not saying much . . . I have heard several say that she is neither hansome nor so much as agreeable & therefore I must conclude that there has been many artifices used to bring you to such lengths as you seem to bee in so disadvantages & impudent a match without so much as consulting your father . . .'[11] and so on for eight pages. That Marlborough's heir should think of marrying 'a woman unknown to all the world but low people' was unthinkable. It was 'as if a daughter were run away with and had lost her reputation'. It wanted a name.

In his replies Willigo, now twenty-nine, sounds collected and dignified. His girl is the sister of the Countess of Denbigh, very beautiful and altogether one of the finest women of her time. But Sarah remains sceptical. Most people in English society, she says, are too shocked even to mention it to her. Indeed, it was by the merest chance that she had heard the rumour of his engagement to this 'very low and odd woman'. And as to beauty, 'I must say', she wrote frankly, 'that in all the time that I was in Holland I never saw but one woman that looked like a human creature & that was the dowager Lady Albemarle. If this person is no more tempting than Lady Denbigh, you must allow that people will wonder at your choice, who might have had any person undisposed of . . . and as for her birth . . . if you had said wee were all Adhams children & twas no matter for birth, it had been better'.[12]

Sarah consulted Willigo's father, Francis Godolphin—'the most worthy man in the world'—and Sir John Evelyn. Nothing could be done. On the 25th of July, 1729, in Utrecht, Willigo married Maria de Yonge.

Surprisingly, when the worst or what she considered the worst had happened, Sarah simmered to calmness; so much so that in 1730 we find Willigo thanking her for a very kind and affectionate letter. To her pleas to return he says he would like to, 'but as my Mother's long ill conduct towards my Father & Me had obliged me to take a resolution never to see Her, I was Willing to have my Father's Consent to return upon that condition & applied myself lately to the Duchess of Newcastle* to intercede with him for that purpose, which with much Reluctancy she has at last done but without any effect, for instead of consenting to what I thought & shall ever think I most reasonably desired, he only upbraids me for what he calls Indecent Omissions towards my Mother & has told my Sister 'tis a Proposal he can never come into . . . When you reflect', he reminds his grandmother, 'how Good a Daughter she has made to You, a Wife to my Father & a Mother to Me, you will see what reason she can have to complain of my want of duty'.[13]

Francis Godolphin, writing to his mother-in-law of his son's 'weak, improper, ill-judged step' (the kind of folly he himself would never have dreamed of), adds, 'As he has baked, so he must brew'.[14] Neither he nor his wife would take any hand in the brewing.

But Willigo was not to brew for long. Two years after his rash marriage, while drinking heartily at of all things a Tory meeting at of all places Balliol, he suddenly collapsed and died. Sarah, arriving too late with Di, is reported to have said, 'Ay, I suppose he's dead. I would have given half my estate to have saved him. I hope the Devil is picking that man's bones who taught him to drink'. And then, turning to Di, 'Where is my basket, Di? Did I not charge you to bring it?' Di ran to the coach for a heavy basket which may have held money. For two hours Sarah then discussed the case with the doctors and sympathised with the widow, who had since arrived. Which done she left for Blenheim, murmuring as she did so that she would take some other opportunity of satisfying the woman of the house.[15]

The widowed Lady Blandford complained of poverty, but it seems that her jointure provided her with £3000 a year, mainly drawn from the rentals of Holdenby, a large estate Sarah had bought within sight of Althorp. She soon married en deuxième noces Bolingbroke's friend and Somerset's son-in-law (then a widower) Sir

* His sister Harriet.

William Wyndham,* who took up her cudgels and sued the Marlborough trust for a better settlement. Her father-in-law refused to see her, while her mother-in-law, Henrietta, directed in her will that on no account was her daughter Mary to give her anything.[16]

Sarah wrote: 'I am told the Duke of Somerset did all he could to hinder Sir William Wyndham from beginning this suit & that when he first saw my Lady Blandford he looked as if he was amazed that such a woman should be married for beauty, but that was not Sir William's case. And poor Lord Blandford was always drunk & in the hands of robbers & people brought out of gaol to make a prey of him'.

In 1734, on hearing that Lady Blandford was pregnant, though in fact she was not, Sarah told Di, 'If it be true, I think your brothers have had as great an escape as another Duke [Bedford] you love very well, for if she had brought a son to my Lord Blandford it would have been a sort of Regency for the use of a Dutch family, & your brothers are got very well off by only paying a great jointure. Who will be heir to your grandfather's great estate at last God only knows. I can only say that I have taken a great deal of pains both in getting & preserving it from abuses, tho' in the last I have not been very successful'.

What Sarah kept asking herself was, were the grandsons worth it? Abroad, Charles and John had been so reckless with time and money —with clothes, for example: 'As rediculous', commented their grandmother, 'as if I should go into Wales & lay out a great deal of money to dress my self up on King George's birthday'—she often wished she had never sent them. 'Dancing gives men a good Air', she wrote to Fish in Geneva, 'and fencing should be learnt . . . Drawing may be useful and is a pretty entertainment, but as to architecture I think it will be of no use to Charles or John, no more then Musick,† which are all things proper for people that have time upon their hands & like passing it in idleness rather then in what will

---

* Sir William Wyndham (1687–1740), baronet, Secretary at War (1712). Chancellor of the Exchequer (1713). Jacobite, implicated in the 1715 rising and sent to the Tower but never brought to trial. Sarah, meeting him in 1734, was surprised to find him 'extream agreeable & of much good sense'.

† 'Wee have as good mussick as there is any where, & some people think as good conversation'. Sarah to Gallatin, 18 Sept. 1726. (Blen E 31).

be profitable'.[17] She was cross when she heard that Johnny, as she called him, had been playing the flute. This he knew was forbidden, for fear it distorted his face.

The boys were stoutly stuck up for by their governor, Fish, who unlike Mann wrote sympathetically and often. Time, he admits, was wasted in Switzerland (a country, in Sarah's opinion, to be passed through on the way to somewhere else), 'because it was very natural for men so young & so full of fire to have a much stronger bent for pleasures than labour . . . However, they understand French very well & speak it & write it very fluently & intelligably but there is room for improvement . . . They have read & understood the best part of Horace,* which is an author your Grace has heard of more than once . . . Mr Charles has very little curiosity & looks upon all travelling as a very insipid entertainment & thinks of Italy with great dread . . . but Mr John is far from being in the same case'. Both have readily and he believes steadily resolved to dedicate all their mornings to useful improvements. 'Mr Charles', he concludes, 'gave his voice strongly for Paris'.[18]

'I cannot with a good conscience blame Charles's want of curiosity', replies his grandmother, 'because I have none my self for such things as you mention . . . You tell me that the expence at Paris will scarce be less than £200 a month. That is more than the Duke of Marlborough and I spent when we were abroad with more than twenty horses & a house full of servants . . . I have been told lately by a great traveller that there is fixed prices for seeing the greatest curiosities & that six people may see them for eighteenpence & an opera for three halfpence'. She suspects that they gamble and if they do, she warns Fish, either abroad or in England, 'unless it be in my company, I will never give them a shilling, either living or dying, tho' I am tenderly theirs'.[19] And again, 'All the French wemen are cheats & they will bee much ceviller if you don't play with them'.

---

* In March Fish, writing to Sarah, had referred to Horace as 'an Author mightily esteemed by all people of good taste & famous for writing good sense agreeably & genteely'. In April Sarah wrote to him: 'Talking lately to men of very good understanding they named an Author to me which if I don't mistake was Horris & I think in one of your letters lately you said that you were all to bee employ'd in that study . . . I am told that when young people begin it, if they have any good tast they cannot leave it off'. (Blen E 31).

From Paris the brothers send Sarah and Di two *mantilles* (Sarah: 'We don't know what it means'), with instructions how to wear them, for which Sarah returns thanks. The 'directions how to dress my self' were 'very particular . . . and yet I doubt we have not yet attain'd to putting them on in the best air'. But Charles is disappointed in Paris and makes for home, while John moves on with Fish to Dijon.

At Windsor Lodge Sarah looked forward to welcoming Charles warmly and to hearing him prattle away in French to Di; but once again she was expecting too much. To begin with, he looked 'not near so well as he did when he went out of England'; and what was worse, he was inarticulate in all languages not excluding his own. She was disgusted. 'He speaks', she complained to Fish, 'without opening his mouth, thro' his teeth,* & it is difficult to know even whether he says yes or no, without a great attention, which few things are worth . . . There are several wemen in this country who don't articulate & who think it pritty to make a noise like a bird, & this has troubled me so much to find in Charles that I am very desirous to know whether Johnny has got into the same manner of speaking. If he has, I think it is very indifferent what language he talks in'.[20]

Why, even an old Frenchman could put them both to shame! 'Here is a Frenchman', she tells Fish, 'that I believe is about three-score, who has learned in a year's time to read all the English authors & both to write & speak English: his name is Voltaire'.[21]

The more she sees of Charles the more her affection warms towards distant Johnny, and again she confides in Fish. 'I ever liked him', she owns, 'from a little child & tho' there used to be many complaints against him, I must own that I never saw any thing my self that I could bee really angrey with him for, tho' I affected to be so often. I allways thought hee had a great deal of spirit & quickness & has much good nature, which are charming qualities . . . I will not restrain him in the pleasure which hee takes in playing upon the flute.

* To preserve their teeth Sarah recommends the brothers to chew tobacco for 'half an hour or thereabouts' before spitting it out. 'If it be from the scurvy which most people have more or less there is nothing in the world that will preserve them so much as chewing tobacco. Tis what most people do now in this country & if I had known this sooner I should have lost none of my teeth'. (Blen E 31).

The reasons you give for his doing it have convinced me, since you say it does not hurt his face'.[22] But how unselfish she had been to send him abroad, 'not to see him perhaps [again] while I live; but as the gout does not always kill in a few years I will still hope to live to see him, & so well accomplished as to answer all my wishes'.[23]

Certainly when a few months later crisis came and Humphrey Fish died of a fever in Paris, John Spencer, at twenty, proved remarkably competent. 'I have had his body embalmed', he tells his grandmother, 'till such time as I know whether his father would have it sent into England. If he has no mind for that, I can get him buried here. Sir John Dolbin . . . read the burial service over him yesterday & I have sent his body to Dijon till I know his father's resolutions. I am at present at Plombières with the Duke of Kingston. I dare not venture to Dijon as yet upon account of a malignant fever, very common there at present, of which no one has as yet recovered. Mr ffish had this fever, but I believe he could not have lived otherwise, for when he was opened they found several ulcers in his lungs & his heart full of polypuses'.[24]

Sarah was shocked—'He had all things that I could wish for'—and told Johnny, 'I have sent the dismall account of poor ffyshe to his father and . . . will let you know . . . I hope in God you will come to England as soon as you receive this letter, for I am so terrify'd with what has happen'd that I shall not sleep one night in quiet till I see you here . . . No words can express how dear you are to me & I shall be in torture till I see you . . . who am with all the tenderness that ever was in any heart my Dear Dear Johnny yours . . . And for the gold watch, you will bring it in your pocket, which I will pay his father for & you'll wear it for his sake'.[25]

It was one thing to cock a snook at death oneself and quite another to sit by while he snatched these young men, one after another, from under one's very nose: today Humphrey Fish, tomorrow Willigo Blandford, and the day after—? It was intolerable. By 1730 death had taken all male heirs (Sarah made it 'about a dozen') except the two grandsons Charles and John, who kicked over the traces as only rich young Spencers could. They had vowed, it was said, never to soil their fingers with silver, and they unloaded the guineas hoarded by Marlborough, as though they were tiddlywinks. 'What he has spent', Sarah told Di, of her brother Charles, 'is a great deal more than his Grandfather Marl: & I spent when he was at the head of the Army & allmost in the place of a King'. He gambled wildly. Sarah, watching him play at Tunbridge, was wounded at his incompetence. 'It was impossible for him to win', she groaned, 'and if he loses but one hundred pounds in a week . . . it comes to £5000 a year & 200, but alass that summ is nothing in such company . . .' What nonsense it made of all her lawsuits and estate-buying. She kept him as short of cash as she could; but there is no armour against folly.

With Charles for pattern Johnny, to whom Sarah had given the pet name *Torrismond*,* was not to be outrivalled in scandalous escapade and managed to 'make the town ring with some wild frolic every day';[26] although it must be owned that when the frolics are particularised they make tame reading. By a singular law of history the slightest of incidents involving male nudity has almost always been exaggerated and immortalised. Rochester's frisk in the meadow below High Lodge, after swimming in the Evenlode; Bolingbroke's nude scamper through St James's Park; the race between two naked footmen in Woodstock Park ('ye Height of Impudence & ye greatest Affront to the Ladies');[27] these trifles and many like them have for no good reason been perpetuated; while Queen Anne's sealed packet goes into the fire. And so it was that for even less cause one still senses Society's *frisson* when John Spencer, surprised in his bath, 'out of a sprightly & frolicsome humour leaped out of it naked as he was & waited on his visitor down to the very street door.' In a court starved of wit it was considered sensational enough to be told to the Queen at her levée; whereupon Lord Peterborough, on the top of his form, remarked that Mr Spencer was a man of extraordinary breeding to acknowledge the favour of a common visit in his birthday clothes,[28] a quip that must surely have all but brought down the palace.

It was no effort for the Duchess to treat all such nonsense with the contempt it deserved; but the frailer she became, the shorter seemed the intervals between major crises; and that of Charles's bride, Elizabeth Trevor, seemed quite the most shattering of all. Of the girl herself she knew nothing, though she gathered from friends that she had bad teeth, a very indifferent person, was ill bred and obviously not used to the best company. It was her background to which she

* From Dryden's *The Spanish Friar*.

violently objected. 'As to the woman', she told Charles's brother, 'I
don't know what she is nor I don't care, but I do beleive, as bad as
the world is, there are men that have honour enough not to have
lik'd to have marryd the granddaughter of a remarkable Prosecutor
of their own Grandfather who gave him such a title and such an
estate'.[29] It was not one of her plainer statements. The girl's grandfather happened to have been one of the twelve Tory peers created
by Queen Anne to ensure the safe passage of the treaty of Utrecht.
And on top of that, said Sarah, the whole family of Trevors were
'sad people'. It was worse than the case of Willigo. Why, Charles
might have married anyone on earth, yet here he was, ready to link
himself with a family, 'every one of which are so mean & rediculous
that no man of sense but must be ashamed to have any of them seen
in the house'. One of their connections, she had heard, was Sir
Richard Steele—'a most illustrious alliance!'

At the bottom of it all, Sarah felt certain, was Lady Bateman, that
falsest of granddaughters, that Iago who plotted in the dark and sent
her grandmother abusive, anonymous letters. She who was capable
of anything had now, for her own purposes, sold her brother to a
nobody. Sarah had long since ceased to have commerce with Anne
Bateman, but her own duty was clear. She must attack Charles and
she must certainly investigate the marriage-settlement. Charles was
obdurate, defiant, indignant. From his grandmother's letter he
learned that he could not possibly be in love with Elizabeth Trevor,
'for they say she is not at all handsome & has a mean, ordinary
look. I beleive her Grandfather was not a Gentleman . . .' Charles
replied:

> Madam, I receiv'd Your Grace's extraordinary Letter last Night
> & I own my Discerning won't let me see any Reason in what
> Your Grace is pleas'd to say against my Marrying; unless
> Invectives are to be look'd upon as Arguments. I shan't
> endeavour to convince Your Grace that it is a Match of my own
> seeking & not of my overbearing sister's (as you are pleas'd to
> call her) because in the Passion Your Grace must be when you
> wrote such a Letter all Arguments would be of very little use.
> As for your putting me out of your Will, it is some Time since I
> neither expected or desir'd to be in it. I have nothing more to

add but to assure Your Grace that this is the last time I shall ever Trouble You by Letter or Conversation.[30]

How extremely brutal and rude; yes and muddled too, for Charles, as Sarah commented, clearly misunderstood the meaning of 'invective'—'for I take Invectives to be Falsities; but my letter was nothing but plain Facts which every body knows to be true'.[31] She could not prevent the wedding. It happened on May 23rd, 1732. But she sent for the marriage-settlement, read it, scratched it and found 'one of the greatest Rogues of any Coat', the Bishop of St Davids.* At her interview with the Bishop Sarah, having nothing to lose, set out to tease him and, as her narrative shows, thoroughly enjoyed it:

Saturday morning the good Bishop came to me to give me an account of his negotiation with my Lord Trevor. He began my Lord's answer, which I interrupted saying, My Lord, I desire to see his letter. He answered he could not do that.

Duchess: Why, my Lord?

Bishop: I have left his letter at home.

Duchess: Then you may show it me another time.

He put his hand in his pocket & took out a paper which he had writ & call'd the minutes of my Lord Trevor's letter.

Duchess: Pray, my Lord, give it me. I'll read it myself.

Bishop: No, Madam, I can't do that.

The Bishop read the minutes: The match not his seeking but the Duke's desire . . . Her Grace's threatening had not been a right way etc.

Duchess: Pray, my Lord, give me that paper.

Bishop: No, I can't possibly do that.

Duchess: Then, my Lord, let a servant of mine write it out.

He was extremely averse, but I rang the bell and with great difficulty persuaded him to let it be copied & at last he did permit Loft to do it, but kept it in his hand as if he had been with pirates that would force it from him. And it being so tedious & awkward to have Loft reach over to look upon every line he was to write, I said:

* Nicholas Clagett, Bishop of St Davids from 1732 to 1742 when he was translated to Exeter. Ob. 1746.

Elizabeth third Duchess of Marlborough (née Trevor). Artist unknown

Charles Spencer (afterwards third Duke of Marlborough)
as a Roman consul. Stephen Slaughter

Duchess: Pray, my Lord, let it lie before him, it will be done much sooner. What are you afraid of? You are able to get the better of us two if we should offer to force it from you.

Bishop: Is this talking to me like a bishop?

After it was done he went away and said he was my Grace's humble servant, to which I answered I could not say I was his or that I ever would be so.[32]

All this and more was written down for John Spencer's benefit, although as his grandmother said, 'I know you don't love writing, nor perhaps to receive letters, & I don't wonder that you should love the company of those little hounds, for I think them much more agreeable than the greatest part of those whom I am obliged to converse with here.' In a classically characteristic sentence she explains (sic): 'There is no possibility of any body's loving three persons that mortally hate one another and especially when two of them have done such things to one of them as no person that knows what a principle is but must abhorr'. By which she tries to convey her disappointment in Johnny, who has attended the wedding and is still on good terms with brother Charles and sister Anne Bateman.

The most Johnny would do at this stage was to promise to renounce the Batemans; nor would he marry without his grandmother's consent; but to Charles he would remain loyal, no matter what the cost. This was in 1732. In the following year, on his accession to the dukedom,* Charles was advised to make his peace with the dowager and did so in a tearful scene which saw not only her acceptance of his apology but, still more surprisingly, her apology to him. She was even gracious to his wife Elizabeth. 'I really love them both', she told Di, 'and am convinced that the Duke of Marl: has many vertues'. She was glad she had agreed to see them, she so nearly had not. To Charles's request for the interview, which had found her in low spirits, she had replied:

I am as much pleased as I can be with any thing to read such a letter as I have received from you, but it is for your own sake,

---

* In 1729, on the death of his brother Robert, Charles Spencer became 5th Earl of Sunderland. In 1733, on the death of his aunt Henrietta Duchess of Marlborough, he became 3rd Duke of Marlborough and, by agreement, surrendered Althorp to his younger brother John, ancestor of the Earls Spencer.

for as to my self I am so humbled & worn out with continual afflections & desappointments that I can never more be sensible of any great joy, and as I expect non I grow fond of entertaining my self with my own melancholy & nothing is so desagreeable to me as what go's about to devert my mind from it. This is a sort of nonsence that one must feel before one can understand, but I grow so well acquainted with this desmal kind of ease that I shall not goe to London till somthing calls me that I cannot avoid, having noe tast for any thing that is there; but when I must go I shall be glad to see you, who was allways your affectionate grandmother

S: *Marlborough*[33]

It would have been a good moment for the Duchess to die, and it was no fault of hers that she had to go on witnessing and chafing at Charles's extravagance: at Althorp (the stables etc.), at Langley (the Mashams' 'retired habitation' rebuilt),† at Bray (Monkey Island),[34] at Windsor (mounts and a serpentine river for Little Lodge)‡ ... On all sides he spent wildly, and gambled like a maniac. The Spencer estate was Johnny's and in the meantime, while Sarah lived, Charles could not touch his ducal inheritance. His large allowance went nowhere and he soon found himself begging loans on the expectation of the dowager's death. 'This contented the lenders', Sarah, who had been dangerously ill, commented, 'but I unluckily recovered'. Their friendship deteriorated.

When an heir was born to Charles and Elizabeth, Charles 'came in his chair to Marlborough House, call'd for my porter', notes the Duchess, 'and desir'd him to tell the Dowager Dutchess of Marlborough that his wife was brought to bed of a son, & went away the same moment without asking to see me. This was extreme rediculous

† Abigail Masham died in 1734. Charles Duke of Marlborough bought Langley of Lord Masham in 1738.

‡ Sarah accused Charles of providing Little Lodge in Windsor Park with 'serpentine rivers deep enough to hold his ship, & two mountains, one very high which was to have a large room on the top of it; the other lower, only for a tea-room'. Charles protested that he had done nothing more ambitious than 'cut a narrow ditch a little broader to hinder it from stinking'. A plan for his ship survives at Blenheim.

& stupid, to call me Dowager Dutchess to my own Servant, which look'd as if he apprehended otherwise that my Porter might go to the other Dutchess to tell her she was brought to bed'.[35]

In his efforts to handle his grandmother Charles, bluff and straightforward, certainly lacked finesse. He was, as Sarah said, wonderfully unbusinesslike, useless at cards, hopeless at money. His wife adored him, and he her. When in 1740 Sarah heard that he had kissed the King's hand and set a cockade in his hat to lead a regiment, she could not believe it. This indeed was folly. In her will she had stipulated that on pain of forfeit none of them was to take office nor 'put on a fool's coat & take posts from soldiers of experience & service, who never did any thing but kill pheasants & partridges'.[36] It was too late.

'Your Brother', Sarah told Johnny, 'has done a thing lately that I am sure must be purely his own, without the assistance of any counsel. Whood the painter* has drawn his Picture in the figure of an old Roman Consul with a truncheon in one hand & one arm drawn quite naked, I suppose going to do some great execution. A gentleman that saw it found fault with the arm, saying that it seemed to him to be drawn too large. "Pardon me", replied Mr Whood, "it is as it should be, for my Lord Duke sate himself naked to have it done exactly by the life". This makes several people merry & I must own I think it would have been as well if he had deferred the drawing this graceful figure till he had been in some battle'.[37]

In contrast to Sarah's rift with Charles, which ended in the law-courts, it is pleasant to turn to Althorp and find his brother Johnny happily married, and with not only a wife (Lady Georgina Carteret, chosen by Sarah) but with children of whom his grandmother could approve.

I saw Mrs Spencer and your children last night', Sarah writes from Windsor Lodge in 1742, 'They are both of 'em charming & they talk enough & I find they are mighty fond of coming to me, for I play at drafts with 'em & they both beat me shamefully. I beleive really they like to come to me extreamly, tho' I

* Lord Spencer assures me that the portrait, which hangs above the main staircase at Althorp, is not by Whood but by Stephen Slaughter. With the owner's kind permission it is reproduced here facing p. 273. D.B.G.

heard they had been told I intended to give them a present; upon which they press'd Grace mightily to know what it was, and after she had acquainted me with their curiosity, I asked 'em if they would have a kiss or gold & they both cried out very eagerly mony.

I am always yours,

S: Marlborough[38]

CHAPTER XV

Without Hope or Fear

1740-1744

———◆———

Although Sarah, with but little reserve, was prepared to welcome it, there seemed no time for death. With three cases still pending ('Sure there is nothing so horrid as the Law') she was sick to death of litigation; sick to death of suffering; sick to death of buying estates and of managing them and the Marlborough trust, this last an onerous chore of which Francis Godolphin refused to relieve her. And yet . . . 'You express so much goodness', she had written to the Bishop of Exeter, 'in wishing the continuance of my wretched life, which I assure you I am very weary off, and yet perhaps I should start at death, tho' tis not reasonable because it must come sooner or later . . .'[1]

And to Willigo, six years since:

I have two terrible distempers, the Gout & the Gravell, but I thank God my pain is almost gone & nothing remains now but weakness, so that I beleive (for this time) the danger is over, but I must expect returns, & to die a little sooner or later, as one's friends will have it by the assistance of doctors. When I am well enough to reason I think it very indifferent when this happens, and yet there is somthing in nature that contradicts reason & makes one start at pain, & then one takes nautious medecines in hopes they may keep one longer in a world I have been a long time very weary off, and if I could have walked out of it I am confident I should have been gone many yeares ago, for I can have no notion that any place can be worse then this, as the

Generallity of the world is made. This will appear strange nonsence to so young a man as you are, but I tell you very sincerely my thoughts.[2]

Since then Willigo had died* and she herself had been dangerously ill. 'She must be blistered or she must die', whispered a doctor in 1742; whereupon she sat up and declared, 'I won't be blistered and I won't die!'[3] And she lived for another two years.

Prognostications of her death were frequent and not always kind. 'Since this last winter I find people think she won't last long', Lady Vanbrugh wrote to Henrietta in the late seventeen-twenties, 'and they say here, whenever she goes 'tis impossible any body can be sorry and all the Spencers must rejoice'.† And yet in very old age—and to live to eighty was then phenomenal—she was, at the back of the nation's mind, an institution to be preserved with amused tolerance. At the coronation of George II, when she was sixty-seven, she had raised a cheer by walking in the procession in her robes until, exhausted, she had subsided upon a drum. Death was now overdue but, as with our treasured antiques today—a building it may be or a magazine or a politician—the machinery for despatch is missing or seems too crude to use. As Pope put it:

> Old politicians chew on wisdom past
> And totter on in business to the last.[4]

For the grandsons, at Woodstock and at St Albans, Sarah had, sometimes without even bothering to tell them, fought election after election, if only to keep a Walpole candidate off home ground. Woodstock, she maintained, was the Marlborough birthright; and after some trouble, when he was declared by a rival to be under age, Johnny was returned for that borough and continued to sit for it for some years.

As for litigation, experience had shown that the Law was slow and

---

* William (Willigo) 2nd Marquis of Blandford (1699–1731) is buried at Blenheim. In the chapel vault his coffin closely neighbours those, covered in red leather stamped with coronet brasses, of John and Sarah first Duke and Duchess of Marlborough.

† An undated and unclassified letter at Blenheim addressed to the younger Duchess but probably delivered to the dowager.

corrupt and she was disgusted with it. At one time she had thought of reforming it herself but from that she had been discouraged. 'If your Grace will please only to reflect', Francis Godolphin had written in 1730, 'that no less a Man than Oliver Cromwell, when in the height of his Grandeur & Authority, was seriously bent upon redressing not only the delay but many other grievances & abuses that by degrees had crept into the practice of the Law, & had made some steps in Parliament towards it, yet was soon obliged to quit the design as finding it attended with more difficulty & opposition than either his great abilities or unbounded power could get the better of, I believe you will easily give up any sudden thought or hope you might have entertained of success from any attempt of that kind'.[5]

As a business manager Sarah—more capable of business, as Maynwaring had said, than any man—had met with incompetence and (or so she maintained) dishonesty; for the two men of business she had trusted most—Craggs and Guidott—had (again in her view) proved the greatest rogues. Investment had been just as troublesome. True, she had creamed her £100,000 from the South Sea Bubble, but she had been much shocked by the whole enterprise and said so. For years, in the trust's interest and with Charles Spencer's approval, she had bolstered Government funds until rifts with Walpole and with her grandson ruled out all such investment.* The only alternative was to buy land and so she bought it and went on buying until she had, in various counties, thirty estates† which brought with them the oddest and most tiresome responsibilities. Here for example was the vicar of Willington writing to tell her:

* The well-known anecdote of the Duchess of Marlborough's 'rescue' of Childs Bank, by writing that bank a cheque for £700,000 on the Bank of England, said to be threatening foreclosure, appears from *An Old Legend Examined* by S. W. Shelton, archivist of Glyn, Mills & Co., to be, like many another tale of the Duchess, apocryphal. The Blenheim records make no mention of it; although in an undated fragment (G-1-16) she writes, 'If by giving £100,000 immediately I could save my country, I should think it better laid out then in any other way'.

† In addition to Blenheim, Wimbledon, Holywell, Marlborough House and Windsor Lodge (the last two crown-leases), the Duchess died possessed of estates in Bedford., Berks., Bucks., Herts., Huntingdon., Kent., Leics., Middlesex., Norfolk, Oxon, Staffs. and Surrey. John Spencer, her chief heir, already owned Althorp and Northants. His brother Charles was to have Blenheim but he was forbidden in Sarah's will, to take goods or furniture from Althorp.

Next July it will be sixteen years since you was pleased to put me into the vicarage of Willington with thirty pounds a year & no more . . . My wife is now ready to lye in of her tenth child . . . Sr Will: Gostwick's family has a Vault under the Chancel, part of which is fallen in & all ye Coffins lie open to all Spectators, which is a very dismal & melancholy sight.[6]

Would her Grace be pleased to order Mr Rudd to make it decent? 'I think Land is the troublesomest thing in the world to have to do with', she writes to John Spencer in 1742, 'and I believe when we are undone 'twill be all alike whatever one's fortune is in. Therefore when I have any money I had rather avoid the troubles of land & have it where I can easily get at it that I may give it away when I see the storm near & disappoint any Government from taking it away from me'.[7]

Infirm as she was, it was simply not worth the struggle. Posterity was a spendthrift and herself a fool to fight for it. 'I am quite tired out', she wrote, 'with struggling against knaves that 'tis impossible to get the better of, without any help or any hope of return from those that I have taken so much pains for . . . I have nobody or but few to take care of when I am dead, [so] I will venture to play [at ombre] with Mr Neville & my Lord Cardigan all the time I am at Woodstock if I can keep them so long with me'.[8]

At one time not only had she looked forward to filling Blenheim's attic storey with her friends, she had even gone to the lengths of inviting royalty.* 'I beleive you will see her Royal Highnesse [Queen Caroline] before me', she had written to Mrs Clayton, 'and if you do I desire you will tell her with my humble duty that I am now come to the end of my leabours of near 22 yeares which I shall think quit thrown away unless she & his Royal Highnesse will bee prevaild upon to doe me the honour, which I flatter my self that they will not refuse, because this place was Erected to bee Built in memory of the servises which the Duke of Marl: ded to the Publick & of

---

* 'There is 20 apartments with all sort of convenience fit to lodge any body, but upon the principal floor there is three that are really so fine that they are too good for any body to make use of except their R: Highness's & the Dear Prince William'. (The Duchess, writing of Blenheim to Mrs Clayton. Undated. Blen G-I-16).

which I hope they & their posterity will allways have the advantage'.[9] But that visit was never paid and now she felt differently. People had died or she had fallen out with them; and she blamed Blenheim too for gout. 'I never design to see Blenheim again', she wrote in 1736, 'In a lodge I have every thing convenient & without trouble'. She had always loved Windsor Lodge. Without the Duke of St Albans, who constantly baited her by careering through Windsor Park, that place would have been perfect.

She had even tried harbouring poor relations; but sooner or later, she had found, they only increased one's spleen. She often wondered, rich and independent as she was, whether it was worth bothering with people at all. 'The kindness & good opinion of one's general acquaintance', she noted, 'are so far from being absolutely necessary to one's happynesse that they are somthing like fair weather which makes one's days pass a little more pleasantly but is of no reall importance to one's satisfaction'.[10] When all was said and done there was still much to be said for good servants, and of course for dogs. As Lady Howard had so sensibly written:

> As to the generality of friendships, those are commonly sincerest & most to be depended upon which are bottom'd upon interest . . . My own relations are all of them as good people as any are in the world, but my notion is that people often find more comfort in their old age from a goodnatured servant that they give good wages to than from all the relations they have.[11]

In the goodnatured Grace Ridley Sarah was certainly lucky and would show herself grateful; and for amanuenses she had the excellent if sometimes peevish Stephens, Loft, and her porter, Walter Jones. She found plenty for them to do. There were letters. There were inscriptions. There were narratives: An Account of the Duke of Bridgwater's Proceedings; An Account of the Present Duke of Marlborough . . . and so on, running to a great many pages. There was the Green Book to be kept up to date. There was the Duchess's will—in need of constant revision—and its codicils. There was, until 1742 when it was published, her own vindication; and there was the groundwork for the biography of John Duke of Marlborough.

For this last Sarah had chosen two recommended historians, Mallet* and Glover,† but she was not prepared to hand them the documents until she had read and endorsed every one, and there were thousands. At Blenheim, to come upon a letter bearing five separate endorsements, all in Sarah's hand, is not uncommon; and at Althorp her Instructions to the Historians for Beginning the Duke of Marlborough's History[12] are as original as everything else she undertook. The biography was to begin: 'I write the History of the Duke of Marlborough', and it was to continue in that same flat manner, for it would require 'no Flourishes to set it off, but short plain Facts'. They must remember to say how cheaply Marlborough had managed the war, and how generous she knew him to have been with pensions. He had, she could honestly say, left King James 'with the greatest Regret imaginable', though doubtless he would have won still greater renown had he helped him establish popery. But 'No King', she added, 'is to be trusted'.

The biographers would be rewarded with £500 each, their work being supervised and approved by Lord Chesterfield and her executors. 'And I desire', she concluded, 'that no Part of the said History may be in Verse, and that it may not begin in the usual Forms of writing Histories but only from the Revolution'. About the latter end of the reign of Charles II too much had been written already; and she had had more than enough too of lampoonists and balladmongers. Besides, as in mock-modesty she had told Charles Spencer, 'You know that I am so very stupid as to have very little taste for poetry'.

The wretched Lyttelton‡ had been gauche enough to show her his poem on liberty, in which she could find no reference to Marlborough at all. Luckily, catching her glance, he had instantly realised his mistake. 'He looked a little out', she noticed, 'took his verses away and later returned them'. But then as she herself remarked, 'Painters, poets and builders have very high flights, but they must be kept down'.[13] And the same went for historians and biographers.

* David Mallet (1705?–1765). Literary executor of Lord Bolingbroke.

† Richard Glover (1712–1785). M.P. for Weymouth and opponent of Walpole. Published much blank verse.

‡ George Lyttelton, 1st Baron (1709–1773). Opponent of Walpole. Friend of Pope.

Mallet, recommended by the Duke of Montrose and dubbed by Dr Johnson 'the prettiest drest puppet about town', told the Duchess a month before she died:

> As I am thoroughly sensible both of the dignity & difficulty of the undertaking your Grace has honoured me with, I will throw all other business aside, even the work I have been so long engaged in, that I may enter upon this with my whole attention & application. This I dare promise because it is in my power. Could I add with equal certainty that my abilities are in some degree equal to the task, your Grace might then hope to see a history of the Duke of Marlborough not inferior perhaps to any history that ever yet appeared in the world.[14]

For that biography, as we know, the world had in fact to wait very nearly two hundred years. 'Mallet, I believe', said Dr Johnson, 'never wrote a single line of his projected life of the Duke of Marlborough, but groped for material and thought of it till he had exhausted his mind'. Glover too made no beginning and is said to have returned his £500.

With Nathaniel Hooke, the last of the collaborators in her *Conduct*, Sarah was luckier. Introduced by Pope he proved competent and industrious, which was as well since Sarah, directly she saw him, though bedridden, dictated without stopping for six hours. Without the aid of notes, says a contemporary, she delivered her narrative in a lively and connected manner, and gave Hooke £5000 for which, having lost his all in the South Sea Bubble, he was thankful.

'I shall leave this place with true regret', Pope wrote to Sarah from Twickenham, 'but as you said you liked it so well as to call here in my absence, I have deputed one to be ready to receive you whose company you own you like and who I know likes yours to such a degree that I doubt whether he can be impartial enough to be your Historian. Mr Hook & his daughter (I hope) will use my house while your Grace is at Wimbledon. You see what artifices I use to be remember'd by you'.[15]

All went well until Hooke, a man of courage, attempted to convert the Duchess to Roman Catholicism; after which of course he was *persona non grata*. The *Conduct* however was out and, as

Johnson said, showed an unaffected dignity of style and an artful simplicity of narration. He was shocked at Hooke's 'inserting so profligate a maxim as that to tell another's secret to one's friend is no breach of confidence',* but that, he supposed, was at the Duchess's dictation. Of the Duchess herself Johnson had formed a poor opinion: she 'had not superior parts but was a bold, frontless† woman who knew how to make the most of her opportunities'; and in his brilliant review of her *Conduct* he gently cautions the reader of the possibility that this suppliant for esteem may have indulged to some extent in disguise and suppression. 'Every man that is solicitous about the esteem of others', he points out, 'is in a great degree desirous of his own and makes by consequence his first apology for his conduct to himself; and when he has once deceived his own heart, which is for the greatest part too easy a task, he propagates the deceit in the world without reluctance or consciousness of false-hood'. The successful salesman sells to himself first and squares his conscience before beginning on the customer.

Johnson's judgment on Queen Anne, as he reads her in the letters published by Sarah, is interesting. He finds in those letters 'un-common clearness of understanding, tenderness of affection and rectitude of intention', but discerns too 'a temper timorous, anxious and impatient of misfortune, a tendency to burst into complaints, helpless dependancy on the affection of others and a weak desire of moving compassion . . . She seems', he concludes, 'born for friend-ship, not for Government'.

Horace Walpole, as might be expected, is more frivolous and less polite. 'Old Marlborough', he writes, 'has at last published her *Memoirs*. They are digested by one Hooke . . . but from her materials, which are so womanish that I am sure the man might sooner have made a gown and petticoat with them'.[16]

But the *Conduct* is better than that. Indeed, had it been published in 1712, when Robert Walpole advised against it, it must have burst like a bombshell. In 1742 it could be no more than a squib. The

---

* Referring to Sarah's remonstrating with Queen Anne for not having told her of Abigail Masham's wedding: 'putting her in mind of what she often used to say to me out of Montaigne, that it was no breach of promise of secrecy to tell such a friend anything, because it was no more than telling it to oneself'. (*Conduct*).

† Frontless: unblushing, shameless, audacious. (O.E.D.)

Press as a whole was not reverential. *The Other Side of the Question* (not very good) was countered by Fielding at his most fulsome: 'Why, if this be true', he hopefully quotes a *Conduct* reader as saying, 'the Duchess of Marlborough is one of the best as well as greatest Women ever born'. What a glorious woman! No name should be so dear as hers to the people of England. And as for her pride, that too was a virtue. Fielding himself was prepared to vouch for it that 'no such Pride hath ever been shewn to those who have acknowledged themselves to be her Inferiours, to whom none can equal her in Affability and Condescension'.[17]

After which, one might think, there was nothing left to be said. Horace Walpole however continued to be scathing:

> From her Grace of Marlborough we may collect that Queen Anne was driven to change her ministry and in consequence the fate of Europe because she dared to affect one bedchamber-woman as she had another. The duchess could not comprehend how the cousins Sarah Jennings and Abigail Hill could ever enter into competition, though the one did but kneel to gather up the clue of favour which the other had haughtily tossed away and which she could not recover by putting *The Whole Duty of Man* into the Queen's hands to teach her friendship.

The Duchess's *Conduct*, for the most part 'the annals of a wardrobe rather than of a reign', did contain, he owned, 'a few of those sallies of wit which four score years of arrogance could not fail to produce in so fantastic an understanding'. But it was a pity it had been so much altered and edited and withal was so petty. However, 'Little circumstances indeed convey the most characteristic ideas, but the choice of them may as often paint the genius of the writer as of the person represented'.[18]

Sarah's contempt for the critics was of course Olympian. 'Some', she observed, 'have writ a foolish book to find fault with the *Conduct* and the same person has writ another to answer himself . . . I have done what I had great pleasure in, vindicated myself by incontestable proofs from the vile aspersions that had been thrown upon me by the rage of parties . . . This I have done very clearly and I do not care what fools or mad people say of me, which will always be a great majority'.[19] She admitted that, in an earlier draft at least, she had suppressed much; but what she had written she had written 'with a sincerity that had not so much as the least mixture of art or dissimulation in it'.[20]

Like Blenheim's Column of Victory, the *Conduct* was for posterity. Of her contemporaries Sarah at eighty-two expected nothing. Tiffs of former reigns, no matter how volcanic, had long since been buried beneath the huge mounds of dead leaves which were the squabbles of the royal Georges. The self-vindication of an old duchess, a relic of the reign before last, could be of no consequence.

Towards the end few saw her, but those that did testified to her beauty. 'She had still at a great age considerable remains of beauty', wrote Lady Mary Wortley Montagu,* 'most expressive eyes and the finest hair imaginable, the colour of which she said she had preserved unchanged by the constant use of honey-water'.[21] Again it is tantalising to have no portrait. One of the last things she did was to send one to Pelham's secretary,[22] though whether it showed a lined face or a smooth one ('like a white candle in a holy place') or even the radiant bloom of that unageing Groom of the Stole, we are left to guess. Lady Lechmere, in the steps of Frances Tyrconnel, begged for a portrait 'as you are now . . . Ye knowing you now', she explained, 'makes me wish to have you what you now are, since I find in you what is so agreeable to me that I am unwilling to give it up for a younger face'.[23] Kindly meant no doubt, but perhaps it was just as well she had not complied with it; for she had since fallen out with Lady Lechmere and had no more to do with her.

Just as Sarah believed that ingratitude was the deadliest of all sins, so she esteemed friendship the greatest of all blessings and virtues; and yet, through no fault of hers, the firmest of friendships, if not broken by death, disintegrated. From exile she had written, 'I long to embrace my dear Mrs Clayton and I hope I shall never part from her again for any long time . . . I would fain end my

---

* It was Lady Mary Wortley Montagu who first told the since much told story of the shorn locks. (How in a rage Sarah had once, to spite Marlborough, cut off her hair; how at the time he had ignored it; and how after his death she had found the hair carefully kept in his private drawer). The connection however between this anecdote and Kneller's 'shorn locks' portrait of the Duchess at Althorp has not been substantiated.

life in England with my friends if I can . . .'[24] But then Mrs Clayton (now Lady Sundon) had changed and proved unworthy of her friendship, as had so many more. 'I think the generallity of people in England are rediculous', Sarah decided, 'and I had reather bee shut up between four walls then converse with them, and I have seen people of very good sence that came out of Ireland . . .',[25] though there again, Lady Muskerry had proved a fool. Perhaps she herself just happened to be unlucky, for there could be no doubt, as she wrote, that 'some people are born to receive all the back strocks of fortune'.[26]

With Di gone and Johnny married, Sarah could no longer say she was devoted to anyone; although of course there were more or less loyal servants and more or less entertaining callers and friends. There had been Voltaire, who had asked to see her memoirs before her *Conduct* was published. 'Wait a little', she had told him, 'I am altering my account of Queen Anne's character. I have begun to love her again since the present lot have become our governors'. After which, according to Goldsmith, she asked Voltaire to collaborate and he, reading the manuscript, not only declined but went so far as to remonstrate with her for her bitterness and indiscretion. 'I thought the man had sense', she is quoted as having then said, 'but I find him at bottom either a fool or a philosopher';[27] a remark that hardly rings true.*

Only one of her friends could be as outspoken as Sarah herself without wrecking friendship and that was Lady Mary Wortley Montagu. She was, or so she boldly boasted, out of the Duchess's hurricane-latitude, and eccentric enough to be excused anything and everything. 'I had this day', Sarah told Di, 'a very great dispute with a woman that has more wit than any body I ever knew, my Lady Mary Wortley, and tho' she said a great many pretty things, I stood to my point as most people (you know) do & would not seem to be convinced. She talked mighty prettily, but it is too much for a letter . . .' What a pity! No topic, it seems, was barred, though of Queen Anne Sarah spoke guardedly and far less readily than of the Hanoverians, of whose arrival in England she enjoyed making an *opera bouffe*. None knew better than Lady Mary, however, just how

---

* Nor would Sarah have used the expression 'the present lot'. Both phrases suggest mistranslation, but the sense is probably correct.

thin the ice was. 'The most vindictive Highland chief', she wrote later, 'never had so many feuds, but her deadliest were in the bosom of her own clan'.

Who else ventured near her? Lord Chesterfield ('civiller', she found, 'than any body in the present age'), the pious Lady Hunting-don ('all goodness & kindness'. See appendix v), Lord Marchmont (her executor),* James Stephens (now styled 'Doctor in Physick'. He too was to be an executor and to vet Marlborough's biography); and at the last, of all people, Alexander Pope. For both poet and Duchess, one suspects, this was a playing-at-friendship, a tongue-in-cheek diversion to enliven old age; for what had they else in common (certainly not poetry) but sense and bitterness and an un-dying distrust of Walpole? But Pope chose to pretend otherwise. 'What can I say to your Grace?' he writes to her, 'You think the same things, read the same books, like the same people that I do . . . Be but so good as to like me a little and be assur'd I shall love you extremely'. And again, 'You are directly kind to me and I shall love you. This is very ill bred but it is true and I cannot help it'.[28]

His failure with Marlborough's panegyric has been forgotten and all is lighthearted banter. She sends him the Green Book. He reads it or says he has read it three times and cautiously comments, 'I wish everybody you love may love you, and am sorry for everyone that does not'. He invites her to Twickenham to spend 'a few hours' in his grotto (that obsession of which Dr Johnson said 'His vanity produced a grotto where necessity enforced a passage'). Amazingly, she accepts.

'The Duchess of Marlborough makes great court to me', Pope told Swift, 'but I am too old for her mind and body'.[29] (He was by twenty-eight years her junior). Sarah, while distrusting his malice (had he not turned against Sappho,† his former friend?), was yet sufficiently fascinated to try to humour him; though whether she bribed him on the understanding that Atossa was not to be published has never been proved. Pope is supposed to have told the Duchess of Buckingham that Atossa in his Moral Essays was Sarah; and then to have assured Sarah that it was intended for the Duchess of Bucking-

* Alexander Earl of Marchmont died in 1740 and was succeeded (in the earldom and as Sarah's executor) by his son.

† Lady Mary Wortley Montagu.

Lady Anne Bateman. Enoch Seeman

The Honourable John Spencer with his son, the first Earl
Spencer, and their negro servant Caesar Shaw. Knapton

ham. It is easy to believe that the trick proved irresistible, for

> Whether the charmer sinner it or saint it,
> If folly grow romantic I must paint it.

For better for worse, *Atossa* was too good to scrap. Posterity must decide for itself who it was meant for:

> But what are these to great Atossa's mind?
> Scarce once herself, by turns all womankind!
> Who, with herself or others, from her birth
> Finds all her life one warfare upon earth:
> Shines in exposing knaves and painting fools,
> Yet is whate'er she hates and ridicules.
> No thought advances but her eddy brain
> Whisks it about and down it goes again.
> Full sixty years the world has been her trade,
> The wisest fool much time has ever made.
> From loveless youth to unrespected age,
> No passion gratified except her rage;
> So much the fury still outran the wit,
> The pleasure miss'd her and the scandal hit.
> Who breaks with her provokes revenge from hell,
> But he's a bolder man who dares be well.
> Her every turn with violence pursued,
> No more a storm her hate than gratitude:
> To that each passion turns, or soon or late;
> Love, if it makes her yield, must make her hate.
> Superiors? Death! and equals? What a curse!
> But an inferior not dependent? Worse.
> Offend her and she knows not to forgive;
> Oblige her and she'll hate you while you live;
> But die and she'll adore you—then the bust
> And temple rise, then fall again to dust.*
> Last night her lord was all that's good and great;
> A knave this morning, and his will a cheat.

* Said to allude to a bust of Queen Anne, within a temple, erected by Sarah (site unspecified), which by 1740 had crumbled to dust.

Strange! By the means defeated of the ends,
By spirit robbed of power, by warmth of friends,
By wealth of followers! Without one distress
Sick of herself through very selfishness!
Atossa, cursed with every granted prayer,
Childless with all her children, wants an heir.
To heirs unknown descends the unguarded store,
Or wanders, heaven-directed, to the poor.[30]

Not every line fitted, but those that did, and they were many, were too close to be doubted. No wonder Sarah showed anxiety.† 'I am not arrived at so much philosophy', she wrote to Lord Marchmont, 'as not to think torturing pain an evil; that is the only thing I now dread, for death is unavoidable and I cannot find that anybody has yet demonstrated whether it is a good thing or a bad one. Pray do not think me wicked in saying this, and if you talk to Mr Pope of me, endeavour to keep him my friend: for I do firmly believe the immortality of the soul as much as he does, though I am not learned enough to have found out what it is'. And later: 'I have a great mind to believe that kings' and first ministers' souls, when they die, go into chimney-sweeps'. This last because, while bedridden at Marlborough House, she had had the sweep and 'One of the chimney-sweepers', she found, 'was a little boy, a most miserable creature without shoes, stockings, breeches or shirt. When it was over', she remembered, 'I sent a servant of mine to Windsor with him, to equip this poor creature with what he wanted, which cost very little, not being so well dressed as the late Privy Seal [Lord Hervey]. And as I could not be sure the souls of these chimney-sweepers had [not] come from great men, I could not repent of their being so much overpaid as they were'.[31]

'I hear you live', Pope wrote to her in the summer of 1743, 'and I hope with all that spirit with which you make life supportable both to yourself and those about you'.[32] And early in the following year, 'What a Girl you are! . . . I sincerely wish your health better than my own and you younger than I that the Tables may be turn'd and I leave you a Legacy at my death'.[33] In a sprightly joint-letter with

† According to the D.N.B., Nathaniel Hooke was authorised by Sarah to offer Pope £3000 for *Atossa*'s suppression.

Marchmont Pope assures Sarah that her soul is certainly immortal and, judging by her last letter, her mind unaffected by her body and her body in tenantable repair.[34]

But she knew she was dying—'No physicians can be of any use to me'—and as Abigail said, in like case, of Queen Anne, 'This good lady deserves pity'. 'I am going soon out of the world', she told Johnny Spencer, 'and am packing up'[35] (for eternity one needed so little); and again, within two months of her death, to Francis Godolphin, 'I am packing up to be gone'.[36] To her own way of thinking she was more than ready. Among the scores of maxims, proverbs and aphorisms copied into her commonplace-book she had noted: 'Not to grow weary of oneself'. She had now reached that stage.

Of her death almost nothing is known except date and place: October 18th, 1744 at Marlborough House. Smollet baldly records: 'Mr Pope, the celebrated poet, died in the month of June. In October the old Duchess of Marlborough resigned her breath in the 85th year of her age, immensely rich and very little regretted either by her own family or by the world in general'.[37] Having seen six reigns, or part of them, most of those who had known her in her prime and might have regretted her going were themselves long since dead.

On the death of Marlborough Princess Caroline, in Hanoverian French, had tried to console his widow with the assurance: 'Il y aura un tems ou vous le rejoindrais et ou vous melleres vos louanges pour ce grand Dieu plain de misericorde avec le mari qui a fait la sattis-faction de votre vie'.[38] Had she known her better she would have realised that the Duchess was less fond of hymns than of ballads; but there it was, for better for worse the day she wrote of had arrived.

Every detail of funeral and will had of course been thought of: the interment 'only decent and without Plumes or Escutcheons'; the will itself to be on paper, not parchment, and to be written (the last of the twenty-six versions) by someone that would not tattle. After years of cogitation and vacillation she had finally decided, with certain safeguards, to leave as much as possible to John Spencer, who survived her by only two years, and as little as she decently could to his brother Charles Duke of Marlborough, then in debt, as she reckoned, to the tune of half a million pounds. The chief surprises were in the codicil, where she left £20,000 and her 'best & largest brilliant Diamond Ring' to Lord Chesterfield, and £10,000 to William Pitt 'upon Account of his Merit in the noble Defence he has made for the Support of the Laws of England and to prevent the Ruin of his Country'. Substantial indeed were the rewards of opposing Walpole.*

It must too have surprised her youngest and only surviving daughter Mary Montagu to find herself mentioned and not unfavourably: 'I give to my Daughter Mary Dutchess of Montagu my Gold Snuffbox that has in it two Pictures of her Father the Duke of Marlborough when he was a Youth. Also a Picture of her Father covered with a large Diamond & hung to a String of small Pearls for a Bracelet. And two enamelled Pictures for a Bracelet of her Sister Sunderland and her Sister Bridgwater'. The diamond-covered miniature was of course Chandos's present to Sarah, lost at Antwerp, found again, and spitefully labelled by Lord Dartmouth (quoting Harley) as the gift of Queen Anne.[39]

It was pleasing to find that from Dr Stephens to the chairmen ('the best that I ever knew') and the porter ('I employ him to copy my papers') all her staff had been remembered and recommended to John Spencer;[40] while to her favourite servant Grace Ridley she left a fortune (£16,000), her striking watch, a miniature of Marlborough 'and my own Picture drawn by Sir Godfrey Kneller, which is only a Head'.† Three hundred pounds was to be distributed among the poor of Woodstock.

Marlborough's diamond-studded sword was to go with the title, though she feared it would not stay bejewelled for long. 'What makes me the more uneasy about the diamond sword', she had written, 'is that I do think Lady Bateman is capable of getting it to make buckles for stays'.[41]

John Spencer, Lady Bolingbroke told Lady Denbigh, might count upon a lump sum of £94,000 plus an income of £27,000 a year. 'Vangeons nous de la fortune', she urged, 'par la mépriser et par en médire, comme dit Montagne de la grandeur'.[42] These were sour grapes indeed, and it was disappointing to find that when the Duchess had boasted, 'I think I am lucky in having so much that

---

* Sir Robert Walpole died the following year.

† Now in the Gallery at Althorp. (p. 48)

every knave may have a bit of me' she had not meant it literally.

On October 30th Marlborough's body was brought from Westminster Abbey to lie with Sarah's in the chapel vault at Blenheim. The journey was by no means as costly as the funeral had been twenty-two years before; but even so there was a coach-and-six to be paid for, bearers, cloaks, a room hung with mourning, sconces, fourteen crêpe hatbands and fourteen pairs of men's black-topped gloves;[43] but none of that was now his widow's concern. Of her own journey we hear nothing; nor was there need for inscription, since over and over again in various forms she had written it herself. Her chief aim, she had often declared, was to deserve approbation and to have it: 'Of all human creatures upon the earth I would not bee the person that no body speaks well of'.[44] And she wished posterity to speak well of her too.

At Blenheim there is a small, undated scrap of paper bearing on both sides writing in the Duchess's hand. On one side it has this:

I forsee the world will interpret whatever I do that may look descontented & perticular to my having lost the queens favour & my great Employments. That may vex me a little, to be soe much mistaken, but I hope you will never think my misfortunes can be one graine heavier upon that account, for as long as I can live in quiet & safty with the Dear Duke of Marlborough I shall have very little more to wish for.

And on the other:

As one is the worst judge of one's own simplicity, one is the best of one's sencerity, I will therefore say nothing of the first.[45]

'There is nobody like her', Arthur Maynwaring had long ago written, 'nor ever will be'.[46]

Appendices
Bibliography
References
Index

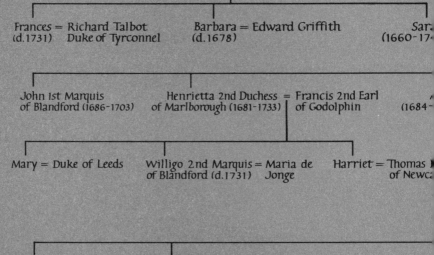

1643

Richard Jennings = Frances Thornhurst

Frances = Richard Talbot   Barbara = Edward Griffith   Sar
(d.1731)   Duke of Tyrconnel   (d.1678)   (1660-17-

John 1st Marquis   Henrietta 2nd Duchess = Francis 2nd Earl
of Blandford (1686-1703)   of Marlborough (1681-1733) │ of Godolphin   (1684-

Mary = Duke of Leeds   Willigo 2nd Marquis = Maria de   Harriet = Thomas
                          of Blandford (d.1731) Jonge   of Newc

Robert 4th Earl   Charles 5th Earl of Sunderland = Elizabeth Trevor
of Sunderland (d.1729)   3rd Duke of Marlborough (d.1758)

N.B. The two other children born to the first Duke and Di
died in infancy, as did two boys and a girl born to
✱ Hon. John Spencer (1708-1746), ancestor of the Ea

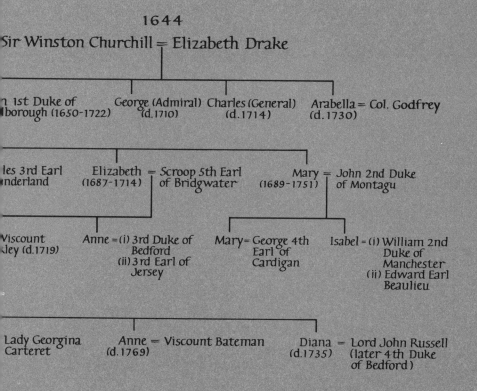

1644

Sir Winston Churchill = Elizabeth Drake

n 1st Duke of | George (Admiral) | Charles (General) | Arabella = Col. Godfrey
borough (1650-1722) | (d.1710) | (d.1714) | (d.1730)

les 3rd Earl | Elizabeth = Scroop 5th Earl | Mary = John 2nd Duke
nderland | (1687-1714) | of Bridgwater | (1689-1751) | of Montagu

Viscount | Anne = (i) 3rd Duke of | Mary = George 4th | Isabel = (i) William 2nd
ley (d.1719) | Bedford | Earl of | Duke of
| (ii) 3rd Earl of | Cardigan | Manchester
| Jersey | | (ii) Edward Earl
| | | Beaulieu

Lady Georgina | Anne = Viscount Bateman | Diana = Lord John Russell
Carteret | (d.1769) | (d.1735) | (later 4th Duke
| | | of Bedford)

borough (Harriet born 1679 and Charles born 1690)
ke and Duchess of Montagu.

APPENDIX I

Sarah Duchess of Marlborough to Queen Anne

(Undated)

Tis so natural a thing for one that has served you so many years (not to mention anything else) to say what was possible might bee of use to you that I have noe reproaches to make my self upon anything in my last letter, which was express'd with so much tenderness & respect that I might reasonably have hoped that it could not give your Majesty any offence tho it had come from any of your subjects that has not had the happiness of knowing you soe long as I have don, but I see it put your Majesty into soe much passion that you quit mistook the whole meaning of the letter, which you will find if you will please to look upon it again.

I ded not take a copy of it because I could not dream of what has happen'd, but I am sure I can repeat the meaning of it and I believe the very words without any materiall alteration, which was upon my lord Marlboroughs letter in which hee thanked God for his goodness in making him the instrument of soe much good to the queen and the nation if she would be pleased to make use of it, and I added that it made me melancholly when I reflected that after three such battles wone for your servisses hee aprehended that hee had not much credit with you or that the influence of some ill meaning people might disappoint whatever your most faithfull servants could doe; that I knew your Majesty's answer to this would bee that there were noe such people, but everybody knows that impressions must be given by somebody, that the object of the Princes favour† had so sad a charecter in the world that it could not bee supposed to take informations from him; and since you would not indure to have one think you suffered your own faverit to talk to you upon anything of businesse, what account could bee given of your Majestys doing contrary to the advise of soe many of your most considerable subjects and old experienced friends?

* (Blen G-1-7.) Marlborough's letter, sent to the Queen and here quoted by Sarah, was dated July 12, 1708.

† Admiral George Churchill, Marlborough's brother (ob. 1710).

This was the part of my letter which you disliked & I find by yours that your Majesty thought when I spoke of my brothers* sad charecter & the credit hee has with the Prince that I ment another person who it seems your Majesty thinks is uncapable of any error, & yet I am sure everybody else will allways think she has committed a great many to me, which I could forgive very easyly if she had not been the occation of soe many reflections upon your Majesty; and tho you are pleased to say you will never change the good impressions that I once gave you of her, I hope you will remember that my commendations went noe farther then being handy & a faithfull servant & I ded think she had more sence & honour then 'tis possible for anybody to beleive she has now; but I never thought her Edducation was such as to make her fitt company for a great queen. Many people have liked the humour of their chamber maids & have been very kind to them, but 'tis very uncommon to hold a private correspond-ence with them & put them upon the foot of a friend & support them in all things right or wrong to the mortifycation of one you had honoured soe long with your kindnesse & who never ded nor never will doe any-thing to deserve the change.

Your Majesty now sees plainly who was ment by the sad charecter, but I beg of you not to think I am making my court to Abigail, who must never expect to have one good word from me, tho her being a woman & her being so low & inconsiderable in all things (after people have said she has had an ungreatfull behaviour to me) will [would] hender her from ever beeing named or soe much [as] thought of if it were not for her friendship with the enemys to the Government & your Majestys unaccountable aversnesse to soe many reasonable things. . . .

[The Duchess concludes by urging the Queen to dismiss Admiral George Churchill.]

* 'my brothers' means here 'my brother-in-law's.

An Anonymous Letter (undated) to Abigail Masham*

(Written in the hand of Sarah Duchess of Marlborough and endorsed by her, 'A copy of a leter by an unknown hand to Abigal'; and further endorsed—in another hand—'Penny post leter to Mrs Masham when she was in the height of her insolence'. For the composition the Duchess is known to have had the assistance of Arthur Maynwaring).

I am very sensible that the letter which I now take the liberty of writing to you is not likely to have all the effect that is intended and desired. There are such powerful charms in greatnesse that one can hardly hope to perswade you not to like it or to convince you of the danger that it will bring upon you. Tis like telling a lover what ill consiquences will attend a present passion, and to think that any arguments of mine will bring you to reason or moderation would bee to have a better opinion both of you and of my self then I am afraid either of us deserve.

But yet there are some things which I am resolved to represent to you, if not to inform your mind, att least to discharge my own. It is not my design to shew you what a hopeless project you are engaged in whilst you think of carrying on this government by the torrys. The queen tried the use & power of that party att the beginning of her reign & whenever you bring her Majesty back into their measures she will soon bee convinced that the weight of the nation & the force of truth will again prevail & that those lords & gentlemen who have already stood the shock of a stronger ministry will never bee brooken in peices by you & that wretched dabbler in politicks Mr H,† for all the scheemes that you & hee can lay will bee only like soe many plots which can never bear the light. But I only give you this hint which you may think of at your leisure, since I intend not soe much to shew the folly of your present undertaking as your maddnesse in pretending to meddle at all.

Tho you seem to have forgot your obligations of all kinds you must needs remember your origenal & your first enterance into the court. You must allsoe remember where you lived before & what was your employment, which I neither care nor need to mention, it beeing so fresh in

* (Blen G-1-9).   † Harley.

315

everyones memory. You must have heard too that Britain is naturally averse to faverites, let them have deserved ever soe well, and do you think that this nation, which sometimes murmur'd att the power even of the Duke & Duchess of Marlborough, the greatest generall & the best servant that ever any queen had, will patiently indure one Mrs Abigal & squire H? Will people who repined att the greatnesse of those who contributed so much to settle our present government set still to see your power which they know will bee employed to overturn it? What maddnesse, what witchcraft has possessed you? If you had really some of those good quailitys which you want, yet don't you know that your crying sin of ingratitude would bee alone enough to sink you, the most odious of all crimes & you of all persons the most guilty of it; but you are soe far from having any of the vertues which are necessary to support a faverite that you have not soe much as the generous vices which made some which went before you less intolarable in other reigns. And yet dare you pretend to bee att the head of our affairs & to dispose of employments & in short to give up our government into the hands of its enemys in oppossicion to all those great & noble persons who compassed [composed?] her Majesty's councell & who joyn'd with her att the time of our hapy revolution!

Bee asured the kingdom will not long bear this. Our libertys which have been settled with soe much wisdome & defended with soe much blood & treasure must not bee all given away by your management, nor the fruit of all our pains & hazard blasted by such an influence. When the Parliament meets there will bee a sad account required from you of all the uneasinesse that has happen'd in her Majesty's affairs, of all the difficulties which her ministers have undergone & of all the dangers to which the nation has been exposed.

All these things will certainly bee laid att your door because it is universally known that nobody else has any interest att this time and that you are indeed the only faverite & therefore if you doe not make as much hast to disclaim that tittle as you ded to get it & convince the world that you will never more meddle with any businesse but that of your low station, you may certainly expect before christmas to hear your self declared a common enemy to the state & a firebrand which all men will join to extinguish who have honesty, wisdome or courage or honour & who regard their own or their country's hapynesse & safty.

You cannot but have heard your master Harley often talk of the Greekes & Romans because hee is allways shewing his small learning out of season & [he will] tell you how those great & wise nations proceeded against persons that they thought indangerd their state. Death was allways the reward of such people & if it could not be compass'd by accusing them to the citizens, it was sure to bee brought about by some other practice & those who ded it were soe far from being counted infamous that in some places even their statues were erected, for it was a maxim of those famous nations that against a traytour to the state every man is a souldier, & if you & your oracle H are not traytours to this state 'tis certain there never were any.

However, I am not for punishing you after the example of those people I have mentioned. All I desire is that you will either please to doe noe more mischeif or else that a period may bee put to your rediculous greatnesse, in a parliamentary way & by methods more suitable to that christianity which wee profess.

Wee read in scripture of an namesake of yours one Abigal who had a great deal of sence, which has since been given very sparingly to some of her name; but this woman allsoe had a foolish husband who had heinously offended David, and when that great king was coming to distroy her family, Abigal got upon an ass to meet him & bow'd to the ground & fell on her face, beseeching him to forgive the trespass of his handmaid, upon which David hearkened to her voice & bed her goe home in peace.

This example I must humbly propose to your imitation, that when the Duke of Marl: (who is our David & deliverer) is coming against your family, you may noe longer think to oppose him & ruin his credit with the queen, but may reather get upon an ass & meet him in his way to London & fall down upon your frightfull face before him to try if by any submission you can escape that vengeance which you most justly deserve from him.*

---

* 'What your Grace is pleas'd to say about the letter to Abigail is much more than either that or I deserve. My onely reason for desiring it might not be shown was because I did not think it fit to be seen. But if you please to say that having mention'd to me the writing of such a letter, not as from a friend but from one that would vex & fright her, you receiv'd from me soon after that imperfect scrawl, I have not the least objection to any body's seeing it . . . I only design'd to give some hints which you might make use of or not as you pleas'd . . . The Duke of Marlborough himself has hardly more military courage than I have civil fortitude; nor can I ever care how much I offend those that I am sure I never will please & of whom I think every thing that is ill'. (Maynwaring to the Duchess. Undated. Blen E 26).

APPENDIX III

Sarah Duchess of Marlborough to Queen Anne*

26th July, 1708

I found plainly when I had the honour to shew your Majesty the two Ballads† that you never see any of them but from me, tho the town and country are full of them, and therefore I take the liberty to send you this, for 'tis noe more to bee expected that your Majesty's new favorit should shew you any of these things of which she herself is generally the subject then that she should inform you right of any other matter; and tho your Majesty was pleased to desire me not to speak any more of her, which I know to bee her own request & what would bee of great advantage to all her designs if she could obtain it, yet I must humbly beg pardon if I cannot obay that command the rather because I remember you said att the same time of all things in this world you valued most your reputation, which I confess surpris'd me very much, that your Majesty should so soon mention that word after having discover'd so great a passion for such a woman, for sure there can bee noe great reputation in a thing so strange & unaccountable, to say noe more of it, nor can I think the having noe inclenation for any but of one's own sex is enough to maintain such a charecter as I wish may still bee yours.

But to the preserving a great reputation severall great vertues are certainly necessary, such as justice & wisdome & constancy, and I hope your Majesty will forgive me if I cannot think it was very just to disgrace your faithfull servants for the sake of some that had betray'd you, nor very wise to disoblige all the honest part of the nation for a few inconsiderable people of ill principles & noe interest; nor if I may bee allow'd to say so was it any great proof of your Majesty's former constancy to leave Lord Marlborough & me for Mr Harley & a woman that I took out of a garrett. One of us I am sure long served your Majesty very honestly, and the other, I may venture to say, has don it successfully; nor can your Majesty say in good earnest that you have not left us or that Lord Marlborough still has the same creditt with you that hee used to

* (Blen G-I-7.)   † See appendix IV.

have, since you have not been pleased to approve of any one thing of consiquence that hee has advised in his letters this year out of Flanders, which I think is a pritty good proof how his creditt stands att present notwithstanding the many victories hee has gaind. And therefore Mr Harley may well assure his correspondents in Holland, as hee does every post, that Ld Marl: & Treas. & I are quit out of favour; and since that is our case 'tis easy to know who are in favour & who they use that obstruct what your ministers & all your councel adviss. For your Majesty does certainly not determine things wholly upon your own judgment, and tho you were pleased to say once that you consulted the Prince in your affairs, I can't but think that his R: Highnesse is too reasonable to meddle soe much as some people would have it thought hee does in things that it is impossible for one in his high station and way of living to bee perfectly informed of.

There can therefore bee no visible cause of all this disturbance in your affairs but that base woman & the creatures that govern her. It is a melancholly thing to remember that your Royall Father was in a manner sung out of his kingdomes by this very tune of lilly burlaro,* especially since your Majesty seems allso inclined to hazard them all reather then displease Abigal; but hee was under a great temptation of bringing in a religion which hee was perswaded was so meritorious a thing that it would secure him honour in this world & everlasting happynesse in the next, & mistakes of that kind, I beleive, there have been instances of, but no history, I am confident, in any age does give an account of a queen that was brought into such misfortunes as threaten your Majesty because she would beleive no body but a chambermaid, who of herself must bee alltogether ignorant of what is fitt for you to do of any kind; & whenever she does give you any advise it must bee from some of those whose charecters are so truely discribed in this Ballad.

Your Majesty would pardon my returning so often to this odious subject if you would but once reflect on the strange mortifying circumstances that there are to me in this affair. I took her from a broom, as the

* Lillibulero—'A foolish ballad was made at that time, treating the papists and chiefly the Irish in a very ridiculous manner, which had a burden lero lero lillibulero that made an impression on the army that cannot well be imagined by those who saw it not. The whole army and at last all people both in city and country were singing it perpetually. And perhaps never had so slight a thing so great an effect.' (Burnet, op. cit. III, 319). The ballad on Abigail, sent by Sarah to Queen Anne, was to be sung to the tune of Lillibulero. The words of Lillibulero were written by Lord Wharton.

ballad says very rightly, hoping the greatness of the obligation would have made her a faithfull servant to your Majesty & not unmindfull of what she ow'd to Lord Marl: & me. Yet you had no sooner a very ill man in your businesse but this wretch enterd into a strict league with him & became his creature, & so far she forgot me as even to marry without my knowledge, & at last to turn out Lord Marl:, for that was really the case, Madam, & will never be forgott; tho the necessity of your affairs & the discontents that were breaking out in both houses of Parliament obliged your Majesty to call him back to your Councill out of which Abigal & her new master had shut him & your Treasurer. But the wound that this gave some where will never bee eased, nor will the reflections cease that are still made upon it; but this is fitter for others to mention than my self, and many there are that doe it every day.

You cannot but remember, Madam, how many affronts King Charles had, that was a man, upon account of the Duchess of Portsmouth; & I think I need not say a great deal to shew how much worse it is for your Majesty, whose charecter has been so different from his, to bee put in print & brought upon the stage perpetually for one in Abigals post. And if by tiring out Ld Marl: & Ld Treas: you oblige them to quit your service, what can the consiquence of that bee but bringing all your businesse into confusion & exposing her charming person to bee pull'd to pieces; for as long as they are able to continue in their employments, tho with all the disagreeableness & drudgery imaginable to them selves, people only laugh at a queen's forsaking her old servants for such a favorit & are too apt to censure them for not doing what your Majesty makes it impossible for them to doe; but there is nothing more certain than that the moment they are forced to quit, after all the services the world knows they have don your Majesty & their country, she that will justly bee thought the occasion of it will pass her time but very ill & non will come into their places that will bee able to carry on your government two months. And therefor I earnestly desire of your Majesty not to make a second tryall of removing them, which will certainly cost you much dearer than the last. Tis dangerous to provoke the Whigs to make an invitation to the hous of Hanover, which they once hindered but have not had much thanks for it; and tho your Majesty told me very lately that you beleiv'd the people of England might lay you & the Prince aside but you ded not care, or to that purpose, I hope you will please to think better of that matter, for it will bee hard to find out another country where you can bee so well, & in this tis certain you may bee as happy as you please.

Tho I have writt so much I can't help taking notice of one thing, which is how much more easyly your Majesty talks now of this fine passion then you ded not long since; for when I first mentioned it you were pleased to tell me that in your life you had never been half an hour alone with Hill & disownd that you saw her but as a bedchamberwoman; and in six or eight months after you could tell me you thought you might love who you pleased; att which time tis certain you spoke her own words, because that is an expression that is used every day by those that see her. And indeed if she had no influence upon your affairs & did not make your ministers uselesse, there is no doubt but you might make her as dear to you as you pleased & might quietly injoy that inestimable blessing till you were tired of it; but whilst nothing is don that your councill adviss & whilst your Treasurer, who by his post is in a great measure answerable for your administration, presses the same things twenty times over without success, tis certain your people will not long bear patiently the ills that arise from such a passion, which if it bee not better governd for the future must prove fatal to your Majesty & them selves; & therefore you may depend upon it that all the mischief that happens will bee laid upon her, because it will bee impossible to conceive that such dangerous efects should proceed from any thing but so very bad a case.

I hope your Majesty will forgive the freedom of this letter, since you have so ordered matters for me that I can no longer bee of any use to you otherwise then by telling you such truths as these, which no body else will mention, tho most people think as I doe upon this subject. And I doe assure your Majesty that I have no view of any thing but your serviss in what I have written, which however disagreeable it may bee will I hope prove of real advantage to you in the end & that is all I aim att by it.

I remember I have formerly desired your Majesty to burn my letters. Now I make it my humble request that you will please to lay this in your cabinit & I wish that all the notams that I have writt to you were there in hopes some accident or other, when I am dead, might make you remember me & think better of me then you doe att this time. Att least sooner or later it would shew that your Majesty had once a very true friend & a most faithfull servant. I had allmost forgot to let your Majesty know that upon Wednesday, after my Lord Haversham* had waited upon you, his next businesse was to pay his duty to Abigal. I know your Majesty's answer to this beforehand will bee this, that who can help what a madman does & that is true in some measure; but one may help giving occasions for such redicules.

---

* Lord Haversham had warned the Queen of the Whig plan to invite the Electoral Prince to England. See Churchill, op. cit. II, 412–13.

APPENDIX IV

Ballads

On the 26th of July, 1708 the Duchess of Marlborough wrote to Queen Anne (see appendix III) and enclosed two ballads. Of the ballads about Abigail Masham, then current, the two she seems likeliest to have sent were:

(I) *Verses Upon Mr Harley Being Lord Treasurer**

... But then if you ask by what cunning or fate
This last of mankind is grown first in the state,
I answer, 'By neither. His titles and station
Are all the blind work of a strange princely passion;
And thus the whole secret of Britain's undoing
Is nothing but incomprehensible wooing.
Bright Masham's the whirlwind that turns us about,
One whiff of whose breath can bring in or put out ...

(II) *A New Ballad To the Tune of Fair Rosamond†*

When as Queen Anne of great Renown
Great Britain's Sceptre sway'd,
Besides the Church she dearly lov'd
A Dirty Chamber-Maid.

O! Abi—— that was her Name,
She stich'd and starch'd full well,
But how she pierc'd this Royal Heart
No Mortal Man can tell.

However for sweet Service done
And Causes of great Weight
Her Royal Mistress made her Oh!
A Minister of State.

* Blen G-I-4.
† Bodl. Firth b 21/94 f 91.

Her Secretary she was not
Because she could not write,
But had the Conduct and the Care
Of some dark Deeds at Night . . .

. . . And so on for thirty-five not very good verses. The Duchess, writing to Sir David Hamilton, the Queen's doctor, on December 6th, 1710, commented:

'. . . 'tis certain that the town & country are very full of prints that do Mrs Morley great hurt because she has given so much ground for such papers, and I hear there is some lately come out which they said were not fit for me to see, by which I guess they are upon a subject that you may remember I complained of to you and really it troubl'd me very much upon my own account as well as others because it was very disagreeable & what I know to be a lye by something of that disagreeable turn there was in an odious ballad to the tune of fair Rosamond, printed a good while agoe, in which the Queen gives an account of Mr Harleys & Mrs Mashams base designs against all those that had brought them to court, and ridiculed her very justly; but that which I hated was the disrespect to the Queen & the disagreeable expressions of the dark deeds of the night. Since that I saw another paper of verses, which was a great ridicule upon all Mrs Morley does, but it was more gentle . . .'*

In the same collection in the Bodleian Library (Firth b 21/94) other contemporary ballads touch upon such subjects as *Harley Wounded by Guiscard*, *The South Sea Whim* (to the tune of *To You Fair Ladies*), *On the Dutchess of Marlborough* ('. . . for Magick Arts do now surround ye Throne: Old Mother Jennings in her Grace is known . . .') and *On ye Dutchess of Marlboroughs Rooting Up a Royall Oak in St James's Park*:

Be cautious, Madam, how you thus provoke
This sturdy plant the second Royall Oak,
For should you fell it or remove it thence
When dead it may avenge the proud offence
And build a scaffold in another place
That may e'er long prove fatall to your Grace . . .†

* Blen G-1-8.
† Bodl. Firth b 21/94 f 67.

Two Letters (undated) from Sarah Duchess of Marlborough to Selina Countess of Huntingdon*

My dear Lady Huntingdon is always so very good to me & I really do feel so very sensibly all your kindness & attention that I must accept your very obliging invitation to accompany you to hear Mr Whitefield tho' I am still suffering from the effects of a severe cold. Your concern for my improvement in religious knowledge is very obliging & I do hope I shall be the better for all your excellent advice. God knows we all need mending & none more than my self. I have lived to see great changes in the world—have acted a conspicuous part my self— & now hope in my old days to obtain mercy from God, as I never expect any at the hands of my fellow-creatures. The Duchess of Ancaster, Lady Townshend & Lady Cobham were extremely pleased with many observations in Mr Whitefield's sermon at St Sepulchre's Church, which has made me lament ever since that I did not hear it, as it might have been the means of doing me some good— for good, alas, I do want, but where among the corrupt sons & daughters of Adam am I to find it? Your Ladyship must direct me. You are all goodness & kindness & I often wish I had a portion of it. Women of wit, beauty & quality cannot bear too many humiliating truths—they shock our pride. But we must die—we must converse with earth & worms. Pray do me the favour to present my humble service to your excellent spouse. A more amiable man I do not know than Lord Huntingdon. And believe me, my dear Madam, I am your most faithful & most humble servant.

S. *Marlborough*

---

* Selina Hastings, Countess of Huntingdon (1707–1791), supporter of George Whitefield, the Wesleys and the Methodist movement. These letters are reprinted from *The Life & Times of Selina Countess of Huntingdon*, published in 1839 (vol. 1, pp. 25–6).

Your letter, my dear Madam, was very acceptable. Many thanks to Lady Fanny for her good wishes. Any communications from her & my dear good Lady Huntingdon are always welcome & always in every particular to my satisfaction. I have no comfort in my own family; therefore must look for that pleasure & gratification which others can impart. I hope you will shortly come & see me & give me more of your company than I have had lately. In truth I always feel more happy & more contented after an hour's conversation with you than I do after a whole week's round of amusement. When alone my reflections & recollections almost kill me & I am forced to fly to the society of those I detest & abhor. Now there is Lady Frances Saunderson's* great rout tomorrow night—all the world will be there & I must go. I do hate that woman as much as I do hate a physician, but I must go if for no other purpose than to mortify & spite her. This is very wicked I know, but I confess all my little peccadillos to you, for I know your goodness will lead you to be mild & forgiving, & perhaps my wicked heart may gain some good from you in the end. Make my kindest respects to Lord Huntingdon. Lady Fanny has my best wishes for the success of her attack on that crooked perverse little wretch at Twickenham.† Assure yourself, my dear good Madam, that I am your most faithful & most obliged humble servant

S. Marlborough

---

* Lady Frances Saunderson, probably daughter of the Earl of Orkney and married to Thomas Lumley, later 3rd Earl of Scarbrough, who had assumed the name of Saunderson by Act of Parliament in 1723.

† Alexander Pope.

BIBLIOGRAPHY

1. MANUSCRIPT SOURCES

Althorp: The Spencer Papers (Marlborough volumes)
Blenheim Palace: The Marlborough Papers
British Museum: Stowe ms 751; Portland ms 29/38; Additional mss
Chatsworth: The Devonshire Collections
Harrowby Trust: The Ryder Papers (Stafford County Record Office)
Huntington Library, California: Chandos and Waller Papers (mss HM 16600–16635)
Panshanger Papers: Hertfordshire County Record Office
Public Record Office: State Papers (Domestic)
Rousham: The Cottrell-Dormer Papers
Stevens of Bradfield Papers: Berkshire County Record Office

2. PRINTED SOURCES

(i) Reports of the Historical Manuscripts Commission

The following were referred to: The 7th, 9th and 10th Reports. Appendices to the 3rd, 5th and 8th (Marlborough mss) Reports. Also the Reports classified as: Ailesbury, Astley, Bath, Buccleuch, Carlisle, Cottrell-Dormer, Cowper, Dartmouth, Denbigh, Dillon, Downshire, Egmont, Fortescue, Hamilton, Hodgkin, Lyttelton, Ormonde, Portland, Puleston, Rutland, Sackville, Townshend, Trevor, Verney, Verulam, Webb; and the Stuart Papers.

(ii) Biographies etc.

ANNE, QUEEN: *Letters* (ed. Beatrice Curtis Brown. 1935)
ASHLEY, MAURICE: *The Stuarts in Love* (1963)
BATHURST, BENJAMIN: *Letters of Two Queens* (1924)
BAXTER, STEPHEN: *William III* (1966)
BROOKE, IRIS: *English Costume of the 17th Century* (1958)

BIBLIOGRAPHY

BURNET, GILBERT: *History of His Own Times* (1823) and Supplement (ed. Foxcroft, 1902)

CAMPBELL, KATHLEEN: *Sarah Duchess of Marlborough* (1932)

CHANCELLOR, FRANK: *Sarah Churchill* (1932)

CHURCHILL, Sir WINSTON: *Marlborough, His Life & Times* (2 vols. 1947)*

COLVIN, HOWARD: *A Biographical Dictionary of English Architects* (1954)

COXE, Dr W. C.: *Memoirs of John Duke of Marlborough* (1820)

DELANY, Mrs: *The Autobiography & Correspondence of Mary Granville, Mrs Delany* (1861)

DOBREE, Prof. BONAMY: *Sarah Churchill* (*Three 18th Century Figures*. 1962)

FEILING, Sir KEITH: *A History of the Tory Party* (1924)

FIELDING, HENRY: *A Full Vindication of the Dowager Duchess of Marlborough* (1742)

FOOT, MICHAEL: *The Pen and the Sword* (1957)

GINSBURY, NORMAN: *Viceroy Sarah* (a play. 1935)

GRAMMONT, Comte de: *Memoirs* (late 17th century)

GREEN, DAVID: *Blenheim Palace* (1951)
Gardener to Queen Anne (1956)
Grinling Gibbons (1964)

HAILES, Lord: *The Opinions of Sarah Duchess of Marlborough* (1788)

HART, JEFFREY: *Viscount Bolingbroke* (1965)

HARTFORD-POMFRET: *Correspondence* (1806)

HENDERSON, NICHOLAS: *Prince Eugene of Savoy* (1964)

HERVEY, JOHN, Earl of Bristol: *Letter-Books* (1894)
Memoirs of the Reign of George II (1884)

HIGHAM, C. S. S.: *Wimbledon Manor House* (1962)

JOHNSON, Dr SAMUEL: *Works* (1825)

KENYON, J. P.: *Robert Spencer Earl of Sunderland* (1958)

KRONENBERGER, L.: *Marlborough's Duchess* (1958)

LEDIARD, THOMAS: *The Life of John Duke of Marlborough* (1736)

LEVER, Sir TRESHAM: *Godolphin, His Life & Times* (1952)

MACAULAY, T. B.: *History of England* (1861)

MALLET, DAVID: *Memoirs of the Life of Viscount Bolingbroke* (1752)

MANLEY, MARY DE LA RIVIÈRE: *The New Atlantis* (1709)
The Secret History of Queen Zarah (1743)

* I am most grateful to the publishers, George G. Harrap & Company, for allowing me to quote so freely from the signed copies of the two-volume edition given to me by the author in 1952. *D.B.G.*

MARLBOROUGH, SARAH Duchess of:
  Account of the Conduct of the Dowager Duchess of Marlborough from her First Coming to Court to the Year 1710 (1742)
  Letters from Madresfield Court (1875)
  Life of Sarah Duchess of Marlborough (anon. 1745)
  Life & History of Sarah Duchess of Marlborough (anon. c.1710)
  Private Correspondence of Sarah Duchess of Marlborough (2 vols. 1838)
MONTAGU, Lady MARY WORTLEY: *Letters* (ed. Wharncliffe. 1893)
OLDMIXON, JOHN: *The Life & Posthumous Works of Arthur Maynwaring* (1715)
PHILLIPS, HUGH: *Mid-Georgian London* (1964)
PLUMB, J. H.: *Sir Robert Walpole* (2 vols. 1956, 1960)
RALPH, JAMES: *The Other Side of the Question* (1742)*
REID, Dr STUART: *John and Sarah Duke & Duchess of Marlborough* (1914)
ROBB, NESCA: *William of Orange* (vol. II. 1966)
ROWSE, A. L.: *The Early Churchills* (1956)
  The Later Churchills (1958)
STRICKLAND, AGNES: *Lives of the Queens of England* (1884)
SUTHERLAND, JAMES: *Background for Queen Anne* (1939)
SWIFT, JONATHAN: *Journal to Stella* & Prose Works (ed. Williams. 1948)
THOMSON, A. T.: *Memoirs of Sarah Duchess of Marlborough* (2 vols. 1839)
  Memoirs of Viscountess Sundon (1847)
THOMSON, G. SCOTT: *Letters of a Grandmother, 1732–35* (1943)
  Life in a Noble Household, 1641–1700 (1937)
TREVELYAN, Prof. G. M.: *England Under Queen Anne* (3 vols. 1932, 1965)
WALCOTT, ROBERT: *English Politics in the Early 18th Century* (1956)
WALPOLE, HORACE: *Correspondences* (ed. Lewis) (14 vols. 1937-48)
  Memoirs of the Reign of King George II (1847)
WENTWORTH PAPERS 1705–39 (ed. Cartwright. 1882)

(III) Pamphlets

A Dialogue in the Shades between Mrs Morley and Mrs Freeman (1745)
A Full Vindication of the Dowager Duchess of Marlborough (1742)
Remarks Upon the Account of the Conduct of a Certain Dutchess (1742)
The Story of the St Albans Ghost (1712)

* James Ralph is named as the compiler of *The Other Side of the Question*. The author ('A Woman of Quality') was anonymous.

BIBLIOGRAPHY

(IV) Articles

GREEN, DAVID: *The First Mistress of Blenheim* (The Listener, 25 May,1950)
  Sarah Duchess of Marlborough (The Listener, 9 June, 1960)
  The Sovereign Proposes (Country Life Annual, 1966)
STRAKA, GERALD: *The Final Phase of Divine Right Theory in England, 1688-1702.* (The Eng. Hist. Review, October, 1962)

Works of general reference have included the *Oxford Companion to English Literature* and the *Dictionary of National Biography*.

REFERENCES TO MANUSCRIPTS
AND PRINTED BOOKS

CHAPTER I—*The Observant Child*

1 Blen E 25 (undated)
2 Corresp. II, 112*
3 Blen E 19
4 Blen E 53
5 Corresp. II, 26
6 Churchill: *Marlborough* I, 166
7 *An Account of the Duchess of Marlborough's Conduct*
8 Churchill, op. cit. I, 166
9 Johnson: *Essay on the Account of the Conduct of the Duchess of Marlborough.*
10 *Conduct†*
11 Blen G-I-10
12 Brooke: *Eng. Costume of the 17th Century*, p. 86
13 HMC Buccleuch & Queensbury I, 361
14 Bathurst: *Letters of Two Queens*, p. 247
15 Evelyn: *Life of Mrs Godolphin*
16 Panshanger (undated)
17 HMC Rutland II, 32, 34
18 Blen E 5
19 Blen G-I-9
20 Blen G-I-9
21 Bathurst: *Letters of Two Queens*, pp. 60-1
22 Bathurst, op. cit., p. 108
23 Spencer (4 Oct. 1744)
24 Churchill, op. cit. I, 92
25 Blen E 1. Churchill op. cit. I, 110–11 & 121–8
26 Blen E 28
27 Lediard: *The Life of John Duke of Marlborough*, I, 38
28 Spencer (To Mallet, 4 Oct. 1744)
29 Blen E 38 (24 Sept. 1726)
30 BM Add ms 29549, *f* 126 (16 Nov. 1725)
31 Blen F-I-30
32 Reid: *John and Sarah Duke & Duchess of Marlborough*, p. 30
33 Coxe: *Memoirs of John Duke of Marlborough* I, 9 f.n.
34 Blen E 2 (16 Jan. 1679)
35 Blen E 51
36 Blen F-I-30 (undated)
37 Blen G-I-9
38 Blen E 1
39 Blen G-I-10
40 Blen XIII (45)

CHAPTER II—*James and the Revolution*

1 Glyn Mills archives (15 June 1734)
2 Blen G-I-7 (26 July 1708)
3 Burnet: *History of His Own Times*, IV, 525
4 Evelyn: *Diary* (29 Dec. 1686)

* *Private Correspondence of Sarah Duchess of Marlborough.* (1838. 2 vols.)
† *An Account of the Conduct of the Dowager Duchess of Marlborough from her First Coming to Court to the year 1710.* (1742)

5 Lediard, op. cit. I, 57
6 Lediard, op. cit. I, 63–4
7 ibid, 73
8 Burnet, op. cit. supp. 291–2
9 *Conduct*
10 Blen (Long Library MSS)
11 Blen E 17
12 ibid
13 Blen E 18
14 Blen E 2
15 Blen G-I-10
16 Bible now at Althorp
17 Swift: Prose Works, X, 26
18 ibid
19 Green: *Grinling Gibbons*, pp. 52–3
20 Burnet, op. cit. III, 184
21 Lediard, op. cit. I, 69
22 Churchill, op. cit. I, 239
23 Blen G-I-10
24 Spencer (28 Sept. 1688)
25 Burnet, op. cit. III, 1
26 Thomson: *Memoirs of Sarah Duchess of Marlborough*, p. 572
27 Bathurst, op. cit. pp. 215–19
28 Walcott: *Eng. Politics in the Early 18th Century*, p. 77
29 Cibber: *An Apology For the Life of Mr Colley Cibber*, pp. 57–9

CHAPTER III—*William and Mary*

1 Corresp. I, 208
2 Burnet, op. cit. III, 123, 125
3 Blen G-I-10
4 *Conduct*
5 Burnet, op. cit. III, 384–5
6 *Remarks Upon the Account of the Conduct* etc., p. 26
7 *Conduct*
8–11 ibid
12 Foxcroft: *Life & Letters of Halifax*, II, 150
13 Blen E 48

14 Blen E 45
15 ibid
16 Spencer
17 Blen G-I-10
18 Blen G-I-9
19 Blen G-I-8
20 Blen E 19
21 ibid
22 Blen E 17
23 Churchill, op. cit. I, 130
24 Churchill, op. cit. I, 354
25 *Conduct*
26–29 ibid
30 Blen E 12
31 Blen E 18
32 Blen E 17
33 ibid
34 Spencer
35 Blen E 16
36 Blen E 16
37 ibid
38 Blen E 18
39 Switzer: *Nobleman, Gentleman & Gardener's Recreation*, pp. 57–8
40 Defoe: *A Tour Through England & Wales*
41 Green: *Grinling Gibbons*, plate 85
42 Burnet, op. cit. IV, 241
43 *Conduct*
44 Blen E 18
45 Blen E 17
46 Blen E 48
47 Switzer, op. cit. p. 57
48 *Conduct*
49 Blen E 17
50 Burnet, op. cit. IV, 440
51 *Conduct*

CHAPTER IV—*Hail, Glorious Anna!*

1 Goldsmith: *Works*, IV, 24
2 Hailes: *Opinions of Sarah Duchess of Marlborough*, pp. 2–7

3 Burnet, op. cit. v, 2
4 ibid, IV, 530
5 Blen G-I-8
6 Churchill, op. cit. I, 528
7 Blen G-I-8
8 Blen E 17 (undated)
9 ibid
10 Blen G-I-8
11 Blen G-I-9
12 Blen E 19
13 Conduct
14 Blen G-I-8
15 Lord Hervey's Letterbooks, no. 247
16 Trevelyan: England Under Queen Anne, I, 154
17 Blen E 19
18 Blen E 2
19 Blen E 5
20 Blen E 2
21 ibid
22 Churchill, op. cit. I, 614
23 Churchill, op. cit. I, 619
24 ibid
25 Blen E 17
26 Blen E 20
27 Blen E 6
28 Blen E 20
29-31 Blen E 2
32 HMC Coke, p. 53
33 Blen E 2
34 Coxe, op. cit. I, 132
35 Churchill, op. cit. I, 700
36 Coxe, op. cit. I, 133
37 HMC Rutland II, 179
38 Churchill, op. cit. I, 723-4
39 Blen E 39
40 Churchill, op. cit. I, 735-6
41 Reid, op. cit. Introduction
42 Blen E 45 (16 Sept. 1704)
43 Coxe, op. cit. I, 231
44 Coxe, op. cit. I, 232
45 Evelyn: Diary (7 Sept. 1704)
46 Blen F-I-53

47 Blen G-I-9

CHAPTER V—Princess of Mindelheim

1 Blen E 18
2 BM Add ms 35853 f 17
3 Blen G-I-8
4 Letters of the Duchess of Marlborough at Madresfield Court
5 Blen E 17
6 Blen E 18
7-10 Blen E 19
11 Blen E 17
12 Corresp. II, 120
13 Blen G-I-7
14 ibid
15 Blen G-I-8
16 Conduct
17 Blen E 18 (An unsigned fragment). The poem evidently derives from the well-known verses by Brooke, Lord Cobham
18 Blen (unclassified)
19 Blen E 13
20 Blen F-I-24
21 Coxe, op. cit. I, 190
22 Bodl. ms Top Oxon d 173
23 Blen E 3
24 Blen A-II-31
25 Blen A-I-20. I am obliged to Mr W. A. Speck for drawing my attention to this manuscript
26 Blen E 18
27 Blen G-I-8
28 Corresp. II, 148
29 Blen F-I-24
30 Blen E 17
31 Blen E 13
32 Churchill, op. cit. II, 33
33 Campbell: Sarah Duchess of Marlborough, p. 166
34 Blen G-I-9
35 Coxe, op. cit. I, 375
36 ibid

37-39 Blen E 3
40 Chandos Letterbooks in Huntington Library, California
41 ibid
42 Churchill, op. cit. II, 196
43 ibid, 198
44 Churchill, op. cit. II, 199
45 Churchill, op. cit. II, 200-1
46 ibid, 202
47 ibid, 203
48 ibid, 205
49 ibid
50 ibid, 209
51 Conduct

CHAPTER VI—*Cue for Vipers*

1 Trevelyan, op. cit. II (Ramillies) p. 99
2 Conduct
3 Blen E 25
4 Feiling: *A History of the Tory Party*, p. 334
5 Blen G-1-9
6 Burnet, op. cit. V, 326
7 Ralph: *The Other Side of the Question*, p. 301
8 Conduct
9 Blen G-1-8
10 Blen G-1-9
11 Swift: *Prose Works* V, 449-50
12 Burnet, op. cit. VI, 32-3
13 Churchill, op. cit. II, 286
14 Blen G-1-8
15 Conduct
16 Churchill, op. cit. II, 284
17 Blen G-1-10
18 Corresp. I, 92-3
19-21 Blen E 17
22 Churchill, op. cit. II, 420
23 Bolingbroke Memoirs, pp. 129-30
24 Cunningham: *Hist. of Gr. Britain* II, 141-2

25 Conduct
26 Churchill, op. cit. II, 288-9
27 P.R.O. 30/24/21/150. Stanhope to Sir John Copley 19.2.1708 (See Speck & Holmes: 'Fall of Harley in 1708 Reconsidered.' *Eng. Hist. Review* Oct. 1965)
28 ibid
29 Blen G-1-9
30 Reid, op. cit., pp. 275-6
31 Blen G-1-7
32 Blen G-1-8
33 Coxe, op. cit. II, 204-5
34 ibid
35 Blen E 4
36 ibid
37 ibid (29 April 1708)
38 Conduct
39 Blen E 26
40 Blen G-1-7
41 Blen G-1-9
42 Conduct
43 Blen E 4
44 Conduct
45 Blen E 18
46 Burnet, op. cit. V, 440 (Dartmouth)
47 Blen G-1-8
48 Coxe, op. cit. II, 360-1
49 Corresp. I, 412-16
50 Coxe, op. cit. II, 362

CHAPTER VII—*Favour Declines*

1 Blen E 19
2 Corresp. I, 411-12
3 Blen G-1-9
4 Blen G-1-8
5 ibid
6 Blen E 17
7 Blen G-1-9
8 BM Add ms 35853. f 14
9 Blen E 27
10 Blen G-1-4

11 Blen G-1-8
12 Blen E 26
13 Corresp. I, 231–8
14 *Conduct*
15 Churchill, op. cit. II, 548
16 Blen E 4
17 Blen G-1-8
18 Wentworth Papers, p. 98
19 Cunningham, op. cit. II, 227
20 Blen E 26
21 Blen E 27
22 Blen E 4 (7 Sept. 1709)
23 Blen G-1-7
24 Churchill op. cit. II, 640–1
25 ibid, 651
26 Blen G-1-7
27 Blen G-1-9
28 ibid
29 Blen G-1-7
30 Churchill, op. cit. II, 665
31 Blen G-1-8
32 Corresp. I, 289
33–35 Blen G-1-8
36 Corresp. II, 455
37 *Conduct*
38 Blen G-1-9

CHAPTER VIII—*The Great Change*

1 Blen G-1-9
2 Blen G-1-8
3 Blen E 26
4 Blen G-1-8
5 ibid
6 Blen G-1-7
7 *Conduct*
8 Blen G-1-8
9 Blen E 5
10 Blen G-1-8
11 *Conduct*
12 Blen E 5
13 Blen G-1-8
14 Blen E 25

15 BM Portland 29/38 (undated)
16 Blen G-1-9
17 Foot: *The Pen and the Sword*, pp. 304–6
18 Blen G-1-8 (Nov. 1710)
19 Blen E 27
20 ibid
21 Coxe, op. cit. III, 170
22 ibid, 175
23 ibid, 175–6
24 Blen G-1-8
25 ibid
26 Churchill, op. cit. II, 797
27 Blen G-1-8
28 Blen E 19
29 Blen G-1-8
30 Blen G-1-9
31 Swift: *Prose Works* V, 463
32 Blen G-1-9
33 HMC Harley II, 669–70
34 Blen E 46
35 Blen E 25
36 Blen E 27
37 Blen G-1-17
38 Blen E 5
39 Blen E 25
40 Blen F-1-48
41 Blen E 3 (4 Aug. 1707)
42 Thomson, op. cit. II, 521
43 Whistler: *Sir John Vanbrugh*, p. 33
44 Blen E 27
45 Churchill, op. cit. II, 754
46 Blen E 5
47 Foot, op. cit., p. 292
48 ibid, p. 301
49 Blen G-1-9
50 Churchill, op. cit. II, 912–13
51 Blen G-1-9

CHAPTER IX—*A Sort of Pilgrimage*

1 Trevelyan, op. cit. IV, 66
2 *Conduct*

3 Blen E 27
4 Blen G-1-10
5 Blen E 26
6 BM Stowe ms 751, *f* 3
7 Blen E 27
8 Swift: *Journal to Stella*, p. 494
9 *Horace Walpole Corresp.* XXVIII, 390
10 Blen G-1-4
11 Blen E 20
12 *Wentworth Papers*, p. 313
13 Blen G-1-9
14 Swift: *Journal to Stella*, pp. 658-9
15 BM Stowe ms 751 *f* 54 (to Craggs, 4 June 1713)
16 Churchill, op. cit. II, 978-9
17 Madresfield, p. 64
18 Blen E 38
19 Corresp. II, 92
20 BM Stowe ms 751, *f* 39
21 ibid, *f* 29
22 ibid, *f* 150
23 ibid, *ff* 58-9
24 Madresfield, p. 72
25 ibid, p. 100
26 BM Stowe ms 751, *f* 54
27 Madresfield, p. 66
28 BM Stowe ms 751, *ff* 83-7
29 Madresfield, pp. 45-6
30 Blen E 6
31 Madresfield, p. 74
32 BM Stowe ms 751, *f* 48
33 Madresfield, p. 94
34 Blen E 6
35 Strickland, op. cit. VI, 409
36 *Memoirs of Sir John Clarke*, pp. 71-2
37 Foot, op. cit., p. 361
38 Churchill, op. cit. II, 1012
39 Swift Corresp. II, 222

CHAPTER X—*No Armour*

1 BM Add ms 19,609

2 Webb: *Sir John Vanbrugh (Letters)*, p. 63
3 Blen G-1-9
4 Blen E 5
5 Coxe, op. cit. III, 395-6
6 Coxe, op. cit. III, 397
7 BM Stowe ms 751, *f* 142
8 ibid, *f* 136
9 ibid, *ff* 144 & 150
10 Blen E 3
11 Blen E 4
12 BM Stowe ms 751, *f* 129
13 ibid
14 ibid *f* 136
15 ibid *f* 144
16 ibid *f* 150
17 Webb, op. cit., pp. 84-5
18 Blen G-1-9
19 Blen F-1-31
20 Blen E 51
21 Blen F-1-31
22 Blen E 51
23 Blen G-1-9
24 Blen E 24
25 Blen E 15
26 Swift: *Prose Works* X, 27
27 Blen E 15
28 Memoirs of the Life of Viscount Bolingbroke, pp. 310-11
29 Churchill, op. cit. II, 1024
30 Swift Corresp. II, 391

CHAPTER XI—*The Crookd Scythe*

1 Green: *Blenheim Palace*, p. 147
2 Attrib. Dr Abel Evans
3 Ballard: *Chronicles of Woodstock*, p. 108
4 BM Stowe 751 *f* 205
5 HMC Morrison IX, 473
6 Blen E 26
7 Blen box XXII
8 Blen E 46

9 Blen E 15
10 Churchill, op. cit. II, 1033
11 Blen E 52
12 Churchill, op. cit. II, 1034
13 Blen E 52
14 HMC Carlisle, p. 31
15 Webb, op. cit., p. 184
16 Blen E 44
17 ibid
18 BM Add ms 38056 f 3
19 Blen E 35 (22 Aug. 1721)
20 Blen E 8
21 Plumb: *Sir Robert Walpole* II, pp. 40 & 48 *f.n.*
22 Blen F-I-34
23 Churchill, op. cit. II, 1032
24 ibid, 1036
25 Blen G-I-9
26 Blen E 44
27 Blen E 43
28 ibid
29 Webb, op. cit., p. 146
30 Blen E 43
31 Lediard, op. cit. III, 422
32 Blen E 46 (10 Aug. 1722)
33 Blen E 53
34 Blen Long Library (portf. II)
35 Blen E 21
36 Blen E 7
37 Blen (unclassified)
38 Blen E 7
39 ibid
40 & 41 Blen E 6
42 Manley: *New Atlantis*, p. 145
43 Blen G-I-9
44 & 45 Blen G-I-17
46, 47, 48 ibid

CHAPTER XII—*Provocations and Proposals*

1-4 Blen G-I-9
5 Blen E 49
6 Blen E 43

7 Blen E 35
8 Blen E 45
9 Blen E 39
10 Blen E 6 (20 Aug. 1722)
11 Blen F-I-32
12 Blen E 37
13 ibid (20 Sept. 1722)
14 BM Stowe 751 f 150
15 Blen F-I-31
16 Blen E 41
17 Blen E 16
18 Blen E 34 (17 July 1723)
19 ibid (18 July 1723)
20-24 ibid
25 Spencer (Book B)
26 Blen G-I-17 (20 Aug. 1723)
27 Bodl. d 173 (III)
28 Blen Long Library ms
29 Blen E 34 (10 Oct. 1723)
30 Blen E 44
31 Blen Long Library ms (To Pengelly, 3 Oct. 1728)
32 BM Stowe 751 f 127 (To Craggs, 1716)
33 ibid f 62 (1713)
34 Blen Long Library ms
35 Gent's Mag. May 1731
36 Bodl. Warwick c 2/4. See also Berks County R.O.: Stevens of Bradfield mss F 29-30
37 Walpole Soc. XIX, p. 127
38 Webb op. cit., pp. 166-7
39 Blen E 46
40 Webb, op. cit., pp. 170-1
41 Wade: *Brit. Hist.*, p. 375
42 Green: *Blenheim Palace*, p. 268
43 Blen E 38 (7 Oct. 1726)
44 ibid

CHAPTER XIII—*The Fruitful Vine*

1 Lever: *Sidney Godolphin*; and DNB (Congreve)

2 Blen E 8
3 ibid
4 Blen F-1-35
5 BM Add ms 35853 ʄ 16
6-8 Blen E 7
9 Blen F-1-32
10 ibid
11 Blen F-1-31
12 Blen E 13
13 Blen E 10
14 Scott-Thomson: *Letters of a Grand-mother* (1732–35)
15 ibid, p. 34
16 ibid., p. 41
17 ibid, p. 58
18 Blen G-1-20 (25 Mar. 1732)
19 Spencer (undated)
20 Scott-Thomson, op. cit., p. 52
21 Blen E 10
22 Scott-Thomson, op. cit., p. 96
23 Blen G-1-9
24 Blen E 21
25 Blen G-1-7
26 Blen G-1-16
27 Scott-Thomson, op. cit., p. 155
28 ibid, p. 152
29 Blen G-1-11
30 Corresp. II, 146
31 Scott-Thomson, op. cit., p. 118
32 Blen F-1-49
33 Blen Long Library ms
34 Scott-Thomson, op. cit., p. 62
35 Psalm 39, v. 7
36 Scott-Thomson, op. cit., p. 96
37 ibid, p. 177
38 Blen E 43

CHAPTER XIV—*The Grandsons*

1 Blen F-1-32
2 Blen E 41
3 Blen E 12
4 ibid

5 *Hartford-Pomfret Corresp.* I, 275–6
6 Blen E 35
7 ibid
8 Blen E 8
9 ibid
10 Blen E 31
11-13 Blen E 8
14 Blen E 22
15 Reid, op. cit., p. 435
16 BM Add ms 28071 ʄʄ 34–9
17 Blen E 31 (12 Oct. 1727)
18 ibid
19 ibid (21 Jan. 1727)
20 ibid (25 Mar. 1728)
21 ibid (21 Jan. 1727)
22 ibid (12 Apr. 1728)
23 ibid (1 May 1728)
24 Blen E 13 (14 Sept. 1728)
25 ibid
26 Lady Mary Wortley Montagu: *Letters*
27 Hearne: *Diary* VII (20 Sept. 1720)
28 HMC Egmont I, 279
29 Blen E 13
30 Blen (unclassified ms)
31 ibid
32 ibid (duplicated in Spencer mss at Althorp)
33 ibid (29 Oct. 1733)
34 *Hartford-Pomfret Corresp.* I, pp. 33–4
35 Blen F-1-33
36 Corresp. II, 171
37 Blen F-1-34 (8 Jan. 1738)
38 Spencer

CHAPTER XV—*Without Hope or Fear*

1 Blen F-1-35 (undated)
2 Blen E 8 (10 Jan. 1724)
3 Horace Walpole Letters (ed. Toynbee) I, 140
4 Pope: *Epistle to Lord Cobham*
5 Blen E 22 (15 Dec. 1730)

6 Blen E 47

7 Spencer (8 Sept. 1742)

8-10 Blen G-1-16

11 Blen E 44

12 Spencer (reprinted in Churchill, op. cit. I, Appen. II)

13 Scott-Thomson, op. cit., p. 134

14 Blen G-1-9 (23 Sept. 1744)

15 Blen E 42

16 Horace Walpole Letters I, 139

17 Fielding: *A Full Vindication of the Duchess of Marlborough*

18 Walpole: *Catalogue of Royal & Noble Authors* IV, 189

19 Corresp. II, 482

20 Blen G-1-10

21 *Letters of Lady Mary Wortley Montagu*, p. 101

22 Thompson, op. cit., Appendix

23 Blen E 44 (undated)

24-26 Blen G-1-16

27 Goldsmith's Works IV, 24

28 Blen E 42

29 Swift Corresp. VI, 131

30 Pope: *Moral Essays*, Epistle II (To a Lady): 'Of the Characters of Women'

31 Pope's Works I, 439-40

32 Blen E 42 (6 Aug. 1743)

33 ibid (18 Jan. 1744)

34 ibid

35 Spencer (26 Nov. 1743)

36 Blen F-1-34 (3 Aug. 1744)

37 Madresfield, p. xviii

38 HMC Bath II, 181

39 Burnet, op. cit. VI, 30

40 Spencer (To John Spencer, 18 Aug. 1744)

41 BM Add ms 29549

42 HMC Denbigh, p. 142

43 Blen F-1-52

44 Blen G-1-16

45 Blen ms (unclassified)

46 Blen E 26

INDEX

The initials M and SM denote Marlborough and Sarah Duchess of Marlborough

Act of Settlement, 75, 81*n*, 195

Addison, Joseph, 77, 141, 171*n*, 184*n*, 186, 224*n*

Albemarle, Countess of (née Gertrude van der Duijn), 280

Albert, Prince Consort, 139

Almanza, battle of, 117

Althorp, 24, 171*n*, 225, 263, 264, 281, 289*n*, 290, 291, 298

Anglesey, Elizabeth, Countess of, 39

Anne, Queen,
early life and character 26-8, friendship with Miss Cornwallis and Frances Apsley 31-3, marriage to Prince George 40-1, appoints SM Lady of Bedchamber 41, and First Lady 46, establishes special relationship with SM as between Mrs Morley and Mrs Freeman 47, flight from London in 1688 52-4, relationship with Mary II 57 *et seq*, remains loyal to M and SM in their disgrace 59 *et seq*, kindness to SM on death of her mother 70, succeeds as Queen 77, appoints SM Groom of Stole and Keeper of Privy Purse 79, attitude to party government 80 *et seq*, accepts Godolphin Ministry 84, supports the war 85 *et seq*, makes M a duke 87, letter to SM displaying special affection 92-3, congratulates M on battle of Blenheim 97-8, insists on close attendance of SM at court 100-2, 109-10, first peevish letter to SM 109, dislike of Sunderland, but under pressure accepts him as Secretary of State 113-15, first appearance of Abigail Hill at court 118 *et seq*, quarrels with SM 125 *et seq*, death of Duke of Gloucester 126, writes to M about SM's conduct 130, becomes more estranged from SM, but attempts a reconciliation 133, 135, death of Prince George 136, growing ascendancy of Abigail 137 *et seq*, constant quarrels with SM 141 *et seq*, receives reproachful letter from SM 147-8, resists demands of Whigs 149-50, present at Sacheverell's trial 150-5, SM's final interview with 152-3, dismisses Sunderland and Godolphin 159-60, receives apology from SM, dismisses SM 167-9, dismisses M, 175-6, political strife at end of reign 193-4, death of 194-5, SM's later views on 269-70, 300 *et seq*, Dr Johnson's view of 300, further references to 200, 207, 209, 210, 211, 216, 221, 227, 241, 243, 248, 255, 268, 286, 287, 305*n*, 313-14, 318-23

Apsley, Sir Alleyn, 30

Apsley, Frances (wife of Sir Benjamin Bathurst), 32-3, 40, 45, 64, 188

Arbuthnot, Dr John, 122, 124, 137, 142, 181

Argyll, John Campbell, 2nd Duke of, 194

339

Armstrong, John (chief engineer), 213, 245

Asiento Agreement, 195

Atterbury, Francis, Bishop of Rochester, 66, 150, 224

Bach, Johann Sebastian, 17

Baratta (sculptor), 239

Bateman (Lady Anne Spencer) Viscountess, 199, 200, 216, 217, 260, 264, 287, 289, 308

Bateman, William, 1st Viscount, 217

Bathurst, Colonel Benjamin, 32

Bathurst, Sir Benjamin, 33, 40, 53

Bathurst, Lady, see Apsley

Bedford (Lady Anne Egerton) Duchess of, (later Countess of Jersey), 193n, 200, 217, 238-9, 258-60, 262, 265

Bedford (Lady Diana Spencer), Duchess of, 42, 199, 200, 217, 226n, 244, 260-4, 265, 268, 270, 271-3, 275, 281, 282, 284, 285, 289, 303

Bedford, John Russell, 4th Duke of, 260, 264n, 272, 273

Bedford, Wriothesley Russell, 3rd Duke of, 238, 258, 260, 264-5

Benson, Mr, 198

Berkeley, James, 3rd Earl of, 183

Bertie, Peregrine, 37

Berwick, James Fitz-James, Duke of, 35, 61

Blagge, Margaret (Mrs Sidney Godolphin), 30, 39, 49, 75, 222, 231

Blandford, Marchioness of (Maria de Yonge), 280, 281, 282

Blandford, John Churchill, 1st Marquis of, 48, 50, 74, 88-9, 224n

Blandford, William Godolphin, 2nd Marquis of, 75, 223-4, 255, 256, 285, 278-81, 287, 293, 294

Blayney (Mary Cairns), Lady, 219n, 237

Blenheim, battle of, 86, 96-7, 98, 99, 103-4, 111, 148, 159, 175, 188

Blenheim Palace, 103-8, 128, 131, 132, 146, 172-4, 180, 197-8, 203-6, 212-17, 221-4, 228, 245-8, 250-2, 257, 269, 270, 295n, 297, 309

Bobart, Tilleman (gardener at Blenheim), 197

Bolingbroke, Henry St John, 1st Viscount
appointed Secretary of War 93, 117, resigns 129, relations with Abigail Hill and Harley 142, 159, 162, 163, 170, 175, 181, 184n, 186, 188, 195, Secretary of State 193, relations with Pretender 188, 194, 195, later career and SM's view of 248-9, 267, 286

Bolingbroke, Marie Claire, Viscountess, 308

Bolton, Duke of, 208

Bononcini, Giovanni, 229, 230

Boscawen, Mrs (née Jael Godolphin), 237, 278

Bracegirdle, Mrs Anne, 255

Brackley, John Egerton, Viscount, 193n, 277

Bridgman, Charles (gardener at Blenheim), 212, 264

Bridgwater (Lady Elizabeth Churchill), Countess of, 48, 100n, 192-3, 230, 238n, 308

Bridgwater (Lady Rachell Russell), Duchess of, 238

Bridgwater, Scroop Egerton, 1st Duke of, 100n, 193, 196, 238-9, 259-60, 297

Bristol, Elizabeth, Countess of, 237

Bristol, John Hervey, 1st Earl of, 83, 237

Brown Book (SM's collection of letters from Queen Anne), 179, 243

Brydges, James, see Chandos

Buckingham, Catherine, Duchess of, 230, 304

Buckingham, John Sheffield, 1st Duke of, 40, 82, 102

Burlington, Dorothy, Countess of, 184, 219n

Burlington, Richard Boyle, 3rd Earl of, 141, 262

Burnet, Gilbert, Bishop of Salisbury, 44, 45, 48, 50, 55, 57, 72, 73, 75, 81, 89, 97, 118, 171n, 179, 180, 182

Burnet, Mrs, 97, 179

Busby, Richard, 120

Cadogan, William, 1st Earl, 202-3, 209, 216, 218, 229

Cairns, Elizabeth, Lady (mother of Lady Blayney), 178n, 219n, 252n, 254n

Cardigan, George Brudenell, 4th Earl of, 296

Cardonnel, Adam (M's secretary), 267

Carlisle, Charles Howard, 3rd Earl of, 105, 198, 221-2, 228, 240, 250, 251, 263

Carlisle, Henry Howard, 4th Earl of, 200n

Carlisle, Countess of (Lady Frances Spencer), 200n

Caroline, Princess of Wales, later Queen, 164n, 197, 252, 267, 270, 286, 296, 307

Carteret, Lady Georgina (wife of the Hon. John Spencer), 291

Castle Howard, 105, 106, 251, 263

Cato, 184, 186

Chandos, James Brydges, 1st Duke of, 112-13, 192, 218, 219, 238, 239-40, 308

Charles, Archduke of Austria (later Emperor Charles VI), 93, 94, 177

Charles II, 28, 29, 34, 35, 40, 41, 42, 43, 68, 72, 298

Chesterfield, Philip Stanhope, 4th Earl of, 34, 196, 260, 262, 304, 308

Chetwynd, Mrs, 141

Cholmondeley, George, 3rd Earl of, 169n

Churchill—relationship to SM in brackets—

Lady Anne (daughter) see Sunderland

Arabella (sister-in-law), 34-5, 48, 61, 236

Charles (son), 48, 66

Lady Elizabeth (daughter), see Bridgwater

George, Admiral (brother-in-law), 128, 313-14

Harriet (daughter), 39, 48

Lady Henrietta (daughter), see Marlborough

John (husband), see Marlborough

John (son), see Blandford

Mary (daughter), see Montagu

Sarah, see Marlborough

Sir Winston (father-in-law), 34, 36

Churchill, Sir Winston, K.G. quoted, 17, 18, 27, 34, 35, 37, 38, 61, 64, 78, 84, 85, 87n, 88, 92, 93, 94, 96, 97, 110, 113, 123, 149, 167, 174, 194, 195, 225

Cibber, Colley, 54

Clagett, see St Davids

Clarendon, Flower, Countess of, 46

Clarendon, Edward Hyde, 1st Earl of, 171n

Clarendon, Henry Hyde, 2nd Earl of, 46

Clayton, Mrs Charlotte (later Lady Sundon), 186, 192, 197, 223, 227, 235n, 244n, 267-8, 270, 296, 300, 301, 302-3

Clayton, William (later Lord Sundon), M's agent, 186

Cleveland, Barbara Villiers, Duchess of, 34-5, 36, 42, 62n, 142, 236

Coggs (goldsmith), 108n, 112

Compton, Henry, Bishop of London, 28, 32*n*, 44, 51, 52-3

Conduct, 27, 54, 68*n*, 96, 154, 169, 176-7, 179, 189, 267, 299-302, 303

Congreve, William, 77, 171*n*, 230, 235, 255, 256

Coningsby, Thomas, Earl of, 239, 240-1, 242, 244

Cornwallis, Miss, 27, 31, 32, 46

Cowley, Abraham, 171*n*

Cowper, Mary, Countess, 263, 274

Cowper, William, 1st Earl, 109, 116

Coxe, Archdeacon William, quoted, 38-9, 93, 107, 131, 164, 252

Craggs, James (Junior), 186, 201, 202, 221

Craggs, James (Senior), M's business manager, 105, 106, 186, 187, 188, 189, 201, 202, 203, 218, 221, 240, 295

Cromwell, Lady Elizabeth, 95

Crowne, John, 30

Cunningham, Joseph Davey, quoted 127

Danvers, Bell, 145

Danvers, Mrs, 53, 145, 193

Darcy, Mrs, 152, 154

Dartmouth, William Legge, 1st Earl of, 123, 159, 308

Declaration of Indulgence, 50

Defoe, Daniel, 73, 77, 88, 107, 108

Denbigh, Elizabeth (née de Yonge), Countess of, 230, 308

Denmark, Prince George of, see George

Desborough, John, clerk of the works at Blenheim, 212

Dillon, Frances Hamilton, Viscountess (daughter of Frances Jennings), 266

Dolbin, Sir John, 285

Don Quixote, 171*n*

Dorchester, Catherine Sedley, Countess of, 36, 188

Dorset, Charles Sackville, 6th Earl of, 53

Dryden, John, 171*n*, 217

Egerton, Lady Anne, see Bedford

Egerton, John, see Brackley

Egerton, Scroop, see Bridgwater

Elizabeth I, 92, 107

Eugene, Prince of Savoy, 97, 172

Evelyn, John, 29, 39, quoted 44

Evelyn, Sir John, 280

Evelyn, Lady, 90

Examiner, The, 37*n*, 162-3, 164, 179, 184

Exeter, Bishop of, 293

Feiling, Sir Keith, quoted 116, 195, 241

Fenwick, Sir John, 3rd Baronet, conspiracy of, 74

Fielding, Henry, quoted 301

Finch, Lady Charlotte (second wife of 6th Duke of Somerset), 245

Fish, Humphrey (SM's page), 217, 228, 229, 232, 277, 279, 282, 283, 284, 285

Fitzharding, Barbara (née Villiers), Viscountess, 48, 49, 53, 54, 59, 62, 63, 64, 65, 73, 80*n*, 130, 141, 265

Flournoys, Mr, 199

Foot, Michael, quoted 163, 175

Freeman, Mrs, name used by SM in dealings with Queen Anne

Frescheville, Anna-Charlotta, Lady, 48, 141

Gallatin, E. (tutor), 277

Galway, Henri de Massue de Ruvigny, Earl of, 45

Garth, Dr (Sir Samuel), 17, 20, 180, 181, 183, 196, 198, 200, 225

Gay, John, 162*n*, 235

George I, 40, 45, 94, 102, 196, 219-20, 227, 252, 302

George II, 43, 196, 252, 282, 294, 302

George, Prince of Denmark (husband of Queen Anne), 40-1, 45, 49, 52,

60, 85-6, 88, 97*n*, 120, 122, 126, 127, 128, 135-8, 140, 169

Gibbons, Grinling, 44, 50, 73, 198, 241

Gibraltar, capture of, 77, 98

Gloucester, William, Duke of (son of Queen Anne), 58, 69, 74, 75, 88, 120, 126

Glover, Richard, 298, 299

Godfrey, Colonel Charles (husband of Arabella Churchill), 35

Godolphin, Francis, 2nd Earl of, 39, 75, 90, 196, 230, 231, 235, 280, 281, 293, 295, 307

Godolphin, Lady Harriet, see Newcastle

Godolphin, Henrietta, Countess of, see Marlborough

Godolphin, Lady Mary, see Leeds

Godolphin, Sidney, 1st Earl of, 39, 48, character 49, 54, 60, 61, 63, 67, 74-5, 77, appointed Treasurer 78, mentioned 82, 84, 89, 90, 106, 113, 114, 115, 117, 120, 125, 128, 140, 141, 143, 148, 149, dismissal of 160-1, in retirement 169, 173, death 181-2

Godolphin, Willigo, see Blandford

Goldsmith, Oliver, 303

Gramont, Philibert, Comte de, 25

Green Book, 18, 225, 233, 234 *et seq*, 241, 258, 304

Griffith, Edward (SM's brother-in-law), 23, 38, 140, 169

Guidott, William, 295

Guiscard, Antoine de, attempt on Harley's life, 170, 173

Halifax, William Savile, 1st Marquis of, *quoted* 61

Halifax, William Savile, 2nd Marquis of, 84

Hamilton, Lord Anne, 170

Hamilton, Sir David, 163, 164, 323

Hamilton, Sir George (first husband of Frances Jennings), 29

Hamilton, James, 4th Duke of, 170

Hammond, Mrs, 256, 258

Handel, George Frederick, 17

Hanover, Elector of, see George I

Hanover, Electress of, see Sophia

Harcourt, Sir Simon (later 1st Viscount), 129

Hardy, Thomas, 21

Hare, Francis, Bishop of Chichester (M's chaplain), 21, 26, 37, 152, 183, 185, 218, 248, 252-3, 275

Harley, Robert, see Oxford

Hartford, Lady, 277

Haversham, John Thompson, 1st Lord, 102, 321

Hawksmoor, Nicholas, 77, 104, 106, 197, 198, 204, 212, 213, 245, 247, 250, 263

Hedges, Sir Charles, 115

Heinsius, Anton, 85, 87

Herbert, Sir Edward, 45

Herbert, Henry, Lord (later 9th Earl of Pembroke), 247, 250, 263

Hervey, John, Lord, see Bristol

Hervey, John, Lord (Lord Privy Seal), 306

Hervey, Lady Mary, 235

Higgins, Mrs, 183, 184

Hill, Abigail, see Masham

Hill, Alice, 119, 120, 145, 181

Hill, Jack, 120, 148, 149, 159, 171

Hill, Mrs (nickname for Viscountess Fitzharding), 64-5

Hoadly, Benjamin, Bishop of Bangor, 217

Holywell House (St. Albans), 23, 26, 41, 48, 105, 161, 178, 181, 195

Hooke, Nathaniel, 171*n*, 179, 299, 300, 306*n*

Hopkins, Ezekiel, Bishop of Derry, 230

Horace, 283

Howard, Lady, 140, 297

Howe, John, 108

Howe, Mrs, 140

Hughes, John (head gardener at Blenheim), 212, 271

Huntingdon, Selina, Countess of, 304, 324-5

Hutchinson, John, 179, 189

Hyde, Anne (Duchess of York), 26, 28, 34

Hyde, Lady, 150, 151

see also Clarendon and Rochester

James II, 26, 28, 29, 30, 32, 34, 36, 39, 40, 42 *et seq*, 49, 55, 57, 61, 76, 80, 81, 236, 298

Jansen, Sir Theodore, 263

Jeffreys, George, 1st Lord ('Judge'), 42, 43, 44, 116

Jennings—relationship to SM in brackets—

Ann (kinswoman), 273-4

Barbara, Mrs Griffith (sister), 23, 38

Frances, née Thornhurst (mother), 24, 30-31, 39-40, 41, 46, 48, 69, 70-1, 181, 216, 242

Frances (sister), see Tyrconnel

Sir John (grandfather), 26, 119

Richard (father), 24, 119, 308

Robert (cousin), 186, 189, 192, 197, 237

Sarah, see Marlborough

Jersey, Barbara, Countess of, 62n, 76

Jersey, Edward Villiers, 1st Earl of, 62n, 76, 82, 93

Jersey, William Villiers, 3rd Earl of, 193n, 260

Johnson, Dr Samuel, 18, *quoted* 27, 108n, 171n, 299, 300, 304

Johnston, James, 110

Jones, Dean, 223, 227, 228, 229, 235

Jones, Walter (SM's porter), 297

Joynes, Henry (clerk of the works and architect), 197, 198, 213, 216n, 269

Kendal, Duchess of (Ehrengard Melusina von der Schulenburg), 196, 219, 221, 248

Kent, Henry Grey, Marquis (later Duke), of, 158

Kent William, 269

Kielmansegge, Sophie Charlotte, Countess of Darlington, 196

King, Mary (laundrymaid), 183

Kingdon, Mrs, 226, 232-3

Kingston, Evelyn Pierrepont, 2nd Duke of, 285

Kirk, General Percy, 43

Kit-Cat Club, 17, 37n, 133, 198, 199, 228

Kneller, Sir Godfrey, 24, 49, 64, 91, 104, 133, 173, 189, 210, 242, 308

Laguerre, Louis, 189, 223

Lechmere, Elizabeth, Lady, 222, 227, 248, 302

Lediard, Thomas, 34, 37, *quoted* 44-5, 50, 54, 171

Leeds (Lady Mary Godolphin), Duchess of, 282

Leopold I, Emperor, 99

Lewis, Erasmus, 211

Lille, siege of, 134

Lindsey, Robert Bertie, 4th Earl of (later Duke of Lancaster), 37

Louis XIV, 76, 78, 85, 114

London, George, (gardener), 53

Loughry, Mistress, 25

Lyttelton, George, 1st Lord, 298

Macaulay, Thomas Babington, Lord, 35, 74, 116

McCarthy, Lady Charlotte, 217

Macclesfield, Thomas Parker, 1st Earl of (Lord Chancellor), 252, 269

Mainz, Elector of (Lothar Franz von Schönborn), 189*n*

Mallet, David, 24*n*, 35, 298, 299

Malplaquet, battle of, 144-5, 175

Manchester, Isabella (Montagu), Duchess of, 257

Manchester, Charles Montagu, 1st Duke of, 132, 198

Manchester, William Montagu, 2nd Duke of, 257

Manley, Mrs Rivella, 40*n*, 142-3

Mann, Nicholas (tutor), 223, 224, 277, 279, 283

Marchmont, Alexander Hume, 3rd Earl of, 304, 306, 307

Marchmont, Hugh Hume, 4th Earl of, 304*n*

Marlborough, John Churchill, 1st Duke of

early life 34, affair with Duchess of Cleveland 34-6, 142, marriage 38-9, created Scottish baron 40, created English baron 44, battle of Sedgmoor 44, relations with James II 45, 50 *et seq*, 63, children of 48, created Earl 58, supposed Jacobite sympathies 61, 74, dismissal and imprisonment 61 *et seq*, 66-7, released but out of favour 67 *et seq*, appointed Captain-General 78, joins Government 84, Flanders campaign 85-7, 90, created duke 87, death of son 88-90, returns to England 93, intrigues against 94, returns to Flanders 95, battle of Blenheim 96-7, granted Woodstock 103, chooses Vanbrugh as architect 105 *et seq*, victory of Ramillies 111, attitude to political situation 113-15, 117, 128-9, view of Abigail Hill 127, attempts to reconcile SM with Queen 128 *et seq*, 144, receives letter from Queen about SM's conduct 130-1, victory of Oudenarde 132,

abortive request to be made Captain-General for life 146, resists military appointment of Abigail's brother 148-9, interview with Queen and failure to oust Abigail 148-9, attitude to dismissal of Godolphin 161, pleads with Queen to prevent SM's dismissal 165-7, relations with Harley 172-3, 211, resolves to remain to finish the war, 172, preoccupation with Blenheim Palace 172, 197, 198, victory of Bouchain 174, Tory campaign against 175, dismissed 175-6, in voluntary exile 182-95, return to England 195, first stroke 200-1, convalescence at Bath 201-2, second stroke 206-7, convalescence at Tunbridge 210, moves into Blenheim 217, death 225-7, lying-in-state and burial at Westminster Abbey 228-9, reburial at Blenheim 309

Marlborough, Charles, 3rd Duke (5th Earl of Sunderland), 199, 264, 275, 276, 277, 282-5, 289, 295, 298

Marlborough, Charles Richard (Spencer-Churchill), 9th Duke of, *quoted* 96

Marlborough, Henrietta (Godolphin), Duchess of, 39, 48, 79, 90*n*, 111*n*, 200, 205-7, 223, 226, 227-8, 230, 231, 232, 234, 236-7, 273, 282, 289*n*

Marlborough, Sarah, Duchess of

Career—birth and family 23-6, first meeting with Anne 26-7, Maid of Honour to Duchess of York 29-30, courtship of Churchill 36, proposal of Lindsey 36, marriage to Churchill 38-9, early married life 39-40, Lady of Bed Chamber to Anne 41, 45, First Lady thereof, 46, adopts name of Freeman 47, children 40, 48, affection for Godolphin 49, assists in flight of Anne, 52-4, views on

Marlborough, Sarah, Duchess of
William III 55-6, on Mary II 57 *et seq*,
helps Anne to secure allowance 59-
60, relations with Lady Fitzharding
59, 63-5, death of mother 69-70,
appointed Groom of the Stole,
Keeper of Privy Purse and Mistress
of Robes 79, influences Anne in
favour of Whigs 82 *et seq*, 93,
becomes a duchess 87, death of son
88-9, letter from Anne expressing
her devotion 92-3, finds Court life
tedious 99 *et seq*, letters from Anne
100-1, 103, attitude to Blenheim and
Vanbrugh 104-8, 111, 128, first
peevish letter from Anne 109,
beginning of deterioration of their
friendship 113-15, relations with
Chandos 112-13, 239-40, account of
rise of Abigail Hill 119-22, quarrels
with Anne over Abigail 125-7, 129
et seq, 134-5, further letters to Anne
about Abigail 141-3, 146-8, 314, 318-
21, present at Sacheverell's trial 150-
1, grows suspicious of the Somersets
150-1, 157-8, 159, last interview with
Anne 152-7, dislike of the Shrewsburys 157-8, further letters to Anne,
159-60, 165, Swift's attacks on 162-3,
dismissal 167-9, retires to St Albans
and occupies herself with her estates
171-4, shares M's exile 183-95, returns to England on Anne's death 195
Later Life—secures offices for rela-
tives 196, problems at Blenheim 197-
8, death of Anne Sunderland 199,
further problems at Blenheim 202
et seq, objections to Sunderland's re-
marriage 207-9, preparations to
occupy Blenheim 212-16, moves in
217, attitude to South Sea Bubble
218-19, 224, audience with George I
219-20, more troubles at Blenheim

221-3, death of Sunderland 224, M's
death 225-31
Final Years—relations with children
230-1, 234 *et seq*, quarrels with
Henrietta Godolphin 235-6, 255-6,
265, quarrels with Bridgwater 238-9,
and with Chandos, 239-40, rejects
marriage proposals from Coningsby
240-1, and from Somerset 241-6,
further difficulties at Blenheim 246-7,
250, views on Bolingbroke 249-50,
bars Vanbrugh from seeing Blenheim
250-2, quarrels with Mary Montagu
256-7, and with Anne Egerton 258-
60, and again with Bridgwater 259,
dislike of Anne Bateman 260-2,
builds house at Wimbledon 263-4,
special affection for Diana Spencer
260 *et seq*, dislike of Claytons 267-
8, cost of Blenheim 271, death of
Diana Spencer 273, further dealings
with grandchildren: marriage of
Willigo Blandford 279-80, and
Charles Spencer 287-91, last years
293 *et seq*, publishes *Conduct* 300-3,
Lady Mary Wortley Montagu's
impressions of 302-4, relations with
Pope 304-5, death 307, will 308,
Views on Anne—77-8, 79-80, 83,
177-8, 269-70
Miscellaneous—books 171*n*, spelling
187-8, 267
Marlborough House, 105*n*, 132, 145-6,
171-2, 174, 189, 203, 209, 216, 228,
238, 263, 290, 306, 307
Mary II, 27, 29, 30, 32, 45, 50, 51, 56,
57, 58, 59, 68, 149, 179
Mary of Modena, 28, 29, 30, 31, 38,
39, 40, 49, 50, 51, 52, 53
Masham (Abigail Hill), Lady, family
relationship with SM 64, 117-19,
SM's patronage of 117-121, appointed Belchamber-woman 75,

Masham (Abigail Hill), Lady, 119, marriage and SM's attitude towards 39, 121-3, character of 123, troubled relations with SM 123-6, dealings with Harley 118, 119, 122, 129, 135, 162, 193, M's attitude towards 127, ballads against 141, 322-3, takes SM's lodgings 141-2, personal relations with Queen 125-6, 127, 134, 136-7, 139-40, 143-4, 145, 155, letters of SM to Queen complaining of 142, 143-4, 147-8, 314, 318-21, SM's efforts to displace 148-9, Godolphin's attitude towards 149, relations with the Shrewsburys 158, Maynwaring's views of, 161, 315, appointed Keeper of Privy Purse 169, 178, attitude to Queen 123-4, 193, retirement of 195, 290, subsequent references to 241, 267, 307, death 290n

Masham, Samuel 1st Lord, 39, 119n, 120, 121, 181, 195

Maynwaring, Arthur (SM's 'secretary'), 21, 23, 37, 55, 116, 133, 134, 141, 143, 145, 148, 149, 159, 163-4, 171, 174, 179-80, 181-2, 215, 295, 309, 315

Medley, 37n, 163

Meredith (officer in M's army), 169

Methuen, Sir Paul, quoted 96-7

Middleton, Thomas Willoughby, 1st Lord, 260

Milton, John, 171n

Mindelheim, Principality of, 99-100, visited by M and SM, 185, 264

Mohun, Elizabeth, Lady, 186

Monmouth, James Scott, Duke of, 30, 43, 44

Montagu, Lady Isabella, see Manchester

Montagu, Mary (Lady Mary Churchill) Duchess of, 48, 100n, 196, 207, 226, 230-1, 232, 235, 236, 256, 257, 273, 308

Montagu, John Montagu, 2nd Duke of, 100n, 229, 235, 239

Montagu, Lady Mary Wortley, 302, 303, 304n

Montaigne, Michel Eyquem de, 121, 171, 308

Montgomery, Mr, Queen Anne's name for Sidney Godolphin

Montrose, James Graham, 1st Duke of, 299

Moore, James (cabinet maker), 206, 212, 216, 245

Morley, Mrs, name assumed by Queen Anne in her dealings with SM

Morris, Roger (architect), 247, 263, 264, 271

Mulgrave, Earl of, see Buckingham

Muskerry, Lady, 266, 303

Namur, capture of, 73

Neville, Mr, 296

New Atlantis, 142-3

Newcastle (Lady Harriet Godolphin), Duchess of, 198, 215, 226-7, 234, 255, 281

Newcastle, Thomas Pelham Holles, Duke of, 187, 198, 205, 209, 215, 267

Newton, Sir Isaac, 77

Normanby, Marquis of, see Buckingham

Northampton, Charles Compton, 4th Earl of, 53

Norwich (Charles Trunnell), Bishop of, 208-9, 215

Nottingham, Daniel Finch, 2nd Earl of, 82, 93, 245

Occasional Conformity Bill, 88, 94

Oldfield, Mrs Anne, 133

Orford, Edward Russell, Earl of, 63, 74, 75

Orkney, Elizabeth Villiers, Countess of, 48*n*, 62*n*, 63

Ormonde, James Butler, 2nd Duke of, 178, 180*n*

Ormonde, Mary, Duchess of, 95*n*

Oudenarde, battle of, 98, 132, 134, 175

Oxford and Mortimer, Robert Harley, 1st Earl of, elected Speaker 76, joins Cabinet 93, Secretary of State 115, character 116-17, connection with Abigail Hill 118-19, 122, 123, 124, 142, 193, abortive attempt to secure dismissal of Godolphin and M and consequent resignation of 129, secret correspondence with Queen Anne 129, 134-5, SM's opinion of, 135, 186, 243, relations with Somerset 157, 241, 243, relations with Swift 162, 175, 183, attempted assassination of 170, created Earl of Oxford 171, grant to Blenheim Palace 171, Lord Treasurer 178, quarrel with Bolingbroke 193-4, resignation of 194, imprisonment, trial and release of 195, 210-11, replaced by Walpole as SM's *bête noire* 267

Oxford, Countess of, 265

Parke, Colonel, 97

Peisley, Bartholomew (Senior), builder of Blenheim Bridge, 204

Peisley, Bartholomew (Junior), master mason at Blenheim, 212

Pelham, the Rt. Hon. Henry, 302

Pembroke, Henry, 9th Earl, see Herbert

Pembroke, Thomas Herbert, 8th Earl of, 129

Pepys, Samuel, *quoted* 53

Peterborough, Charles Mordaunt, 3rd Earl of, 23, 286

Philip V, King of Spain, 85, 144

Pitt, William, 186, 308

Plumb, Professor J. H., *quoted* 224

Pope, Alexander, 18, 49, 77, 113, 179, 221, 224*n*, 245, 248, 255, 256, 294, 299, 304-7, 325

Portland, Anne (née Villiers) Countess of, 62*n*

Portland, Hans Bentinck, 1st Earl of, 61, 62, 63

Portland, Jane (née Temple), Countess of, 237

Pretender, The Old (James Edward Stuart), 10-11, 75, 76, 78, 83, 102, 103, 105, 143, 188, 194, 211

Prior, Matthew, 162, 163

Pulteney, Sir William (later Earl of Bath), 249, 250

Purcell, Henry, 17

Quebec Expedition, 120, 171

Quellin, Arnold (sculptor), 44

Radcliffe, Dr John, 70, 75

Ramillies, battle of, 110-111, 175, 188

Regency Bill, 103

Reid, Dr Stuart, *quoted* 38, 140*n*

Ridley, Grace, 36*n*, 226, 297, 308

Rochester, John Wilmot, Earl of, 180, 286

Rochester, Laurence Hyde, Earl of, 69, 82

Rosamund (Clifford), 106, 322

Russell, William Lord, 42

Russell, Lord John, see Bedford

Russell, Lady Rachel, see Bridgwater see also Orford

Rysbrack, Johan Michel, 78, 257, 269

Ryswick, Treaty of, 74

Sacheverell, Dr Henry, trial of, 88, 150-1, 158, 241

St Albans, see Holywell and Sandridge

St Davids (Nicholas Clagett), Bishop of, 288-9
St John, Henry, see Bolingbroke
Saint Priest, (writer), 179, 189
Sancroft, William, Archbishop of Canterbury, 50
Sandridge, Herts., 24
Saunderson, Lady Frances, 325
Scarbrough, Countess of, 276
Scarbrough, Richard Lumley, 2nd Earl of, 229
Schulenburg, von der, see Kendal
Scotland, Union with, 77
Sedgmoor, battle of, 44
Sedley, Catherine, see Dorchester
Seymour, Sir Edward, 82, 93
Shakespeare, William, 171n, 244
Sharp, John, Archbishop of York, 44
Sheffield, John, see Buckingham
Shirley, James, 50
Shrewsbury (née Adelhida Palliotti), Duchess of, 157-8, 201
Shrewsbury, Charles Talbot, Duke of, 61, 74, 157-8, 194
Slaughter, Stephen, 291n
Smith, of Warwick (builder), 264
Smollett, Tobias, 307
Somers, John, Lord, 73, 84, 149
Somerset, Charles Seymour, 6th Duke of, 20, 68, 129, 145, 151, 157, 158, 159, 187, 194, 239, 241-3, 281, 282
Somerset (née Lady Elizabeth Percy), Duchess of, 68, 130, 145, 150, 151, 158, 169, 170, 241, 242
South Sea Bubble, 164n, 218, 219, 224, 263, 295, 299
Southwell, Sir Edward and Lady, 95
Spelling, archaic, 187-8, 267
Spencer, Lady Anne, see Bateman
Spencer, Charles, 3rd Earl of Sunderland, see Sunderland

Spencer, Charles, 5th Earl of Sunderland, see Marlborough
Spencer, Lady Diana, see Bedford
Spencer, Lady Frances, see Carlisle
Spencer, John, 199, 272, 275, 276, 277, 282-5, 291, 294, 303, 307, 308
Spencer, Robert, 4th Earl of Sunderland, see Sunderland
see also Tichborne
Spenser, Edmund, 171n
Stanhope, James, 1st Earl, 129
Steele, Sir Richard, 188, 287
Stephens, Dr James, 266, 288, 297, 304, 308
Stephens, Rev., 110
Strickland, Miss Agnes, quoted 32n, 40n
Strong, Edward, Senior and Junior (masons), 173, 198
Stuart, James Edward, see Pretender
Sunderland (Lady Anne Churchill), Countess of, 48, 75, 83, 129, 145, 192, 208, 230
Sunderland (Anne Digby), Countess of, 48, 49, 199
Sunderland, Charles, 3rd Earl of, 75, 79n
character of, 84, Queen Anne's dislike of, 86, 94, 113, 114, appointed Secretary of State, 115, 148, dismissal of 159-60, third marriage 207-9, losses in South Sea Bubble 218-19, and George I 220, 221, death of 224
Sunderland, Charles, 5th Earl of (3rd Duke of Marlborough) see Marlborough
Sunderland, Robert, 2nd Earl of, 73, 75
Sunderland, Robert, 4th Earl of, 199, 223, 224-5, 275, 276-7, 289n
Swift, Jonathan, 32, 49, 77, 105, 106, 120, 124, 142, 150, 162-3, 169, 171n,

175, 180-1, 184-5, 194, 195, 209, 211, 224*n*, 304

Switzer, Stephen, *quoted* 72

Talbot, Charles, 1st Lord (Lord Chancellor), 269

Talbot, Richard, see Tyrconnel

Talbot, William, successively Bishop of Oxford, Salisbury and Durham, 269

Tallard, Camille d'Hostun, Comte de (Marshal of France), 97, 269*n*

Taylor, Jeremy, Bishop of Down, Connor and Dromore, 39, 147

Test Act, 40, 88

Thornhill, Sir James, 214-5

Thornhurst, Frances, see Jennings

Thornhurst, Sir Gifford, Baronet, 24

Thynne, Thomas, 31*n*

Tichborne, Judith (third wife of Charles, 3rd Earl of Sunderland), 208

Tonson, Jacob, founder of Kit-Cat Club, 198, 228, 251, 254

Toulon, siege of, 117

Townsend, William, master mason at Blenheim, 212-50

Travers, Samuel, paymaster at Blenheim, 173

Trevelyan, G. M., 17, *quoted* 85, 178

Trevor, family of, 287

Trevor, Elizabeth, see Marlborough, Duchess of

Trevor, Thomas, 2nd Lord, 288-9

Tyrconnel, Frances (née Jennings), Duchess of, 23, 25, 28-9, 51, 61, 71-2, 79, 242, 279, 302

Tyrconnel, Richard Talbot, Duke of, 29, 48

Union with Scotland, 77

Utrecht, Treaty of, 186, 287

Vanbrugh, Sir John, 17, 29, 77, 103, 105, 106, 128, 132, 133, 145-6, 163, 172, 173, 174, 180, 187, 189, 196, 197, 198, 203, 204, 205-6, 209, 210, 212, 213, 218, 222-3, 236, 239

Vanbrugh, Lady (née Yarburgh), 222, 294

Verrio, Antonio, 44

Villiers, Barbara, see Cleveland

Villiers, Barbara, see Fitzharding

Villiers, Lady Betty, see Orkney

Villiers Lady Frances, 28, 46

Voltaire, François Marie Arouet de, 78, 179, 284, 303

Walcott, Professor Robert, *quoted* 53-4

Waldegrave, Henriette FitzJames, Countess, 236

Waller, Edmund, 171*n*

Walpole, Horace, 18, 197, 198, 242, 300-1

Walpole, Sir Robert, 129*n*, 179, 181, 227, 249, 251, 252, 260, 267, 270, 294, 295, 300, 304, 308

Wentworth, Peter, 119*n*, 145

Wharton, Thomas, 5th Lord and 1st Marquis of, 84

Whitefield, George, 324

Whood, Isaac, 291

William III, 29, 45, 48*n*, 49, 51 *et seq*, 55, 116, 149, 266

Willigo, SM's name for William Godolphin, see Blandford

Wimbledon, SM's house at, 20, 262, 263, 272, 299

Windsor Lodge, 105, 149, 192, 195, 227, 267, 270, 275, 291, 295*n*, 296*n*, 297, 299

Wise, Henry, (gardener), 107, 108, 174, 213

Wolseley, Garnett, Viscount, 21

Woodstock, grant of royal manor at to M, see Blenheim Palace, also 197, 210

Wren, Sir Christopher, 44, 72, 77, 105, 106, 150, 171, 175, 203, 205, 212, 213, 251, 263

Wright, Sir Nathan, 82, 108

Wyndham, Sir William, 3rd Baronet, 249, 282

Yarburgh, Henrietta, see Vanbrugh, Lady

Yonge de, see Blandford and Denbigh

Young, Robert, 66

Young's Spelling Book, 171n